Acquired Neurogenic Communication Disorders

AN INTEGRATED CLINICAL APPROACH

Acquired Neurogenic Communication Disorders

AN INTEGRATED CLINICAL APPROACH

Jerry K. Hoepner, PhD, CCC-SLP
Margaret Lehman Blake, PhD, CCC-SLP

9177 Aero Drive, Suite B
San Diego, CA 92123

email: information@pluralpublishing.com
website: https://www.pluralpublishing.com

Copyright © 2025 by Plural Publishing, Inc.

Typeset in 11/15 ITC Stone Serif by Achorn International, Inc.
Printed in the United States of America by Bradford & Bigelow, Inc.

All rights, including that of translation, reserved. No part of this publication may be reproduced, stored in a retrieval system, or transmitted in any form or by any means, electronic, mechanical, recording, or otherwise, including photocopying, recording, taping, web distribution, or information storage and retrieval systems without the prior written consent of the publisher.

For permission to use material from this text, contact us by
Telephone: (866) 758-7251
Fax: (888) 758-7255
email: permissions@pluralpublishing.com

Every attempt has been made to contact the copyright holders for material originally printed in another source. If any have been inadvertently overlooked, the publisher will gladly make the necessary arrangements at the first opportunity.

Library of Congress Cataloging-in-Publication Data

Names: Hoepner, Jerry K., author. | Blake, Margaret Lehman, author.
Title: Acquired neurogenic communication disorders : an integrated clinical approach / Jerry K. Hoepner, Margaret Lehman Blake.
Description: San Diego, CA : Plural Publishing, Inc., [2025] | Includes bibliographical references and index.
Identifiers: LCCN 2023024986 (print) | LCCN 2023024987 (ebook) | ISBN 9781635504255 (paperback) | ISBN 1635504252 (paperback) | ISBN 9781635504279 (ebook)
Subjects: MESH: Communication Disorders—physiopathology | Nervous System—pathology
Classification: LCC RC424.7 (print) | LCC RC424.7 (ebook) | NLM WL 340.2 | DDC 616.85/5—dc23/eng/20230802
LC record available at https://lccn.loc.gov/2023024986
LC ebook record available at https://lccn.loc.gov/2023024987

Contents

Preface xv
Acknowledgments xxi
Reviewers xxiii

Chapter 1. Systems-Based Clinical Approach 1
  Breaking Down the Silos 1
  Models of Communication Systems 3
    What Is the Value in Models? 6
    Speech: DIVA (Directions Into Velocities of Articulators) 6
    Language: Dual Stream Models 7
    Cognition: ACT-R (Adaptive Control of Thought-Rational) 9
    Swallowing: IFSiP (Integrated Framework for Swallowing Processes) 10
  Putting It All Together 11
  Summary 12
  Key Concepts 13
  References 13

Chapter 2. Overview of Neuroanatomy and Neurophysiology 15
  Overview 15
  Structures and Regions 18
    Frontal Lobes 23
    Parietal Lobes 23
    Temporal Lobes 25
    Occipital Lobes 26
    Insula 26
    Subcortical Regions and Structures 27
      Subcortical White Matter 27
      Subcortical Structures 29
    Brainstem 31
      Cranial Nerves 32
    Cerebellum 35
  Meninges and Ventricles 36
  Blood Supply to the Brain 38
  Neurophysiology 40
  Typical Aging 42

Summary 43
Key Concepts 44
References 44

Chapter 3. Etiologies and Pathophysiology 45
Etiologies 45
    Stroke 48
    Anoxia and Hypoxia 52
    Tumors 54
    Traumatic Brain Injury 56
    Degenerative Diseases 59
        Dementias 59
        Parkinson Disease 60
        Huntington Disease 62
        Multiple Sclerosis 62
        Amyotrophic Lateral Sclerosis 67
    Infectious Diseases 68
Prevalence Patterns 68
Brain Imaging 71
    Anatomical/Structural Imaging 71
    Functional Imaging 73
Concepts for Understanding Effects of Brain Injury 74
Summary 75
Key Concepts 75
References 76
Resources 77

Chapter 4. Communication, Cognition, and Swallowing 79
Definitions and Disorders 80
Speech 80
    Disorders of the Motor System 80
    Motor Speech Disorders 81
Language 82
    Disorders of Language 83
Is it Speech? Or Language? Or Both? 85
Cognition 87
    Attention 87
        Attention Networks 89
        Disorders of Attention 91
    Memory 91
        Disorders of Memory 93

Executive Functions... 93
    Disorders of Executive Function.. 94
Awareness... 94
    Disorders of Awareness... 95
Social Cognition 95
    Disorders of Social Cognition.. 96
Is it Language? Or Cognition? Or Both?.................................... 96
Swallowing.. 96
    Disorders of Swallowing 97
Summary... 97
Key Concepts 98
References.. 98

Chapter 5. Foundational Knowledge for Neurorehabilitation 99
Neural Plasticity 100
Historical Context 102
Framing Assessment and Intervention in Neurorehabilitation 110
Rehabilitation Treatment Specification System (RTSS) 115
Health Equity, Social Determinant of Health, Cultural/Ethnic Issues 118
    Keeping Up With Terminology.. 118
    Social Determinants of Health 120
        Access to Care and Healthy Living 120
        Education and Socialization 121
    The Coin Model... 122
Summary.. 123
Key Concepts 124
References... 124
Resources.. 127

Chapter 6. Prefrontal Lobes 129
Diseases and Disorders of the Frontal Lobes 129
    Traumatic Brain Injury.. 130
    Frontotemporal Dementia.. 130
        Assessment... 131
        Frontal Damage Treatment.. 132
Speech Disorders... 132
Language Disorders.. *133*
    Discourse 134
Cognitive Disorders.. 134
    Attention 134
        Impairments to Attention... 134

Memory ... 137
Executive Functions ... 137
Awareness ... 137
Swallowing Disorders ... 142
Summary ... 142
Key Concepts ... 142
References ... 143

Chapter 7. Left Hemisphere Perisylvian Region ... 145
Diseases and Disorders of the Left Hemisphere ... 146
Speech Disorders ... 146
Dysarthria ... 148
Apraxia of Speech (AOS) ... 148
Assessment ... 149
Treatment ... 149
Primary Progressive Apraxia of Speech (PPAOS) ... 152
Language Disorders ... 153
Aphasia ... 153
Global Aphasia ... 154
Mixed Transcortical Aphasia ... 154
Non-Fluent Aphasia ... 155
Transcortical Motor Aphasia ... 157
Fluent Aphasia ... 158
Transcortical Sensory Aphasia ... 160
Conduction Aphasia ... 160
Anomia ... 160
Disorders of Reading and Writing ... 160
Alexia and Agraphia ... 160
Gerstmann Syndrome ... 162
Surface Dyslexia/Dysgraphia ... 162
Degenerative and Progressive Aphasias ... 162
Primary Progressive Aphasia (PPA) ... 162
Assessment ... 163
PPA Specific Assessments (PPA) ... 168
Intervention ... 168
Cognitive Disorders ... 171
Attention ... 171
Memory ... 171
Executive Functions ... 172
Anosognosia ... 172

Non-Linguistic Cognitive Impairments in Post-Stroke Aphasia 172
Degenerative and Progressive Cognitive Disorders 173
Swallowing Disorders 174
Motor/Weakness Related 175
Sensory Related 175
Cognition/Attention Related 175
Summary 175
Key Concepts 176
References 176

Chapter 8. Right Hemisphere Perisylvian Region 181
Diseases and Disorders of the Right Hemisphere 183
Speech Disorders 183
Language Disorders: Apragmatism 183
Linguistic Aspects: Production 184
Linguistic Aspects: Comprehension 187
Paralinguistic Aspects: Aprosodia 188
Extralinguistic Aspects 189
Assessment of Apragmatism 189
Treatment of Apragmatism 196
Linguistic and Extralinguistic Apragmatism 197
Paralinguistic Apragmatism: Aprosodia 198
Discourse and Pragmatics 198
Cognitive Disorders 201
Attention 201
Unilateral Neglect 202
Assessment of Unilateral Neglect 206
Treatment of Unilateral Neglect 206
Memory 207
Executive Function 207
Anosognosia 208
Social Cognition 209
Swallowing Disorders 212
Motor/Weakness Related 212
Sensory Related 212
Cognition/Attention Related 212
Summary 213
Key Concepts 213
References 213

Chapter 9. Cortical Posterior Regions ... 219
   Diseases and Disorders of the Posterior Hemispheres ... 219
   Visual Pathways ... 221
      Visual Field Cuts ... 225
      Visual Processing Disorders ... 226
      Assessment and Treatment of Visual Disorders ... 227
   Speech Disorders ... 228
   Language Disorders ... 228
   Cognitive Disorders ... 228
      Visuoperception ... 228
      Visuocontruction ... 229
      Spatial Cognition ... 229
      Assessment and Treatment of Cognitive Disorders ... 230
   Posterior Damage Syndromes ... 230
   Swallowing Disorders ... 231
   Summary ... 231
   Key Concepts ... 232
   References ... 232

Chapter 10. Subcortical Structures ... 235
   Basal Ganglia ... 236
      Disorders and Diseases of the Basal Ganglia ... 241
         Parkinson Disease ... 241
         Huntington Disease ... 243
         Corticobasal Syndrome ... 244
      Speech Disorders ... 244
      Language Disorders ... 246
      Cognitive Disorders ... 246
         Executive Function and Awareness ... 246
         Memory and Attention ... 247
         Social Cognition ... 247
      Swallowing Disorders ... 247
   Thalamus ... 248
      Functions of the Thalamus ... 249
         Sensorimotor Functions ... 249
         Cognition and Emotion ... 250
         Cortical Arousal ... 250
      Disorders and Diseases of the Thalamus ... 250
      Speech Disorders ... 251
      Language Disorders ... 251

    Cognitive Disorders 251
    Swallowing Disorders 252
Summary 252
Key Concepts 252
References 252
Other Resources 254

Chapter 11. Brainstem, Cranial Nerves, and Cerebellum 255
Overview 255
Brainstem 256
    Cranial Nerves 257
    Disorders and Diseases of the Brainstem 260
    Speech Disorders 262
    Language Disorders 266
    Cognitive Disorders 266
    Swallowing Disorders 266
Cerebellum 267
    Disorders and Diseases of the Cerebellum 269
    Speech Disorders 269
    Language Disorders 270
    Cognitive Disorders 270
    Swallowing Disorders 272
Summary 272
Key Concepts 272
References 273

Chapter 12. Assessment and Treatment of Cognitive Disorders 275
Assessment of Cognitive Disorders 275
    Approaches to Assessment 276
    Test Batteries and Participation-Level Assessments 279
    Attention 279
    Executive Function and Awareness 281
    Memory 286
    Social Cognition 287
    Goal Attainment Scales 288
Treatment of Cognitive Disorders 291
    Approaches to Treatment 291
        Metacognitive Strategy Training 291

Generalized Attention 294
　　　Executive Function and Anosognosia................................ 296
　　　Memory.. 298
　　　Social Cognition 298
　Summary... 302
　Key Concepts 302
　References.. 302

Chapter 13. Assessment and Treatment of Dysarthria 307
and Dysphagia
　Assessment of Dysarthria and Dysphagia 307
　　Dysarthria 308
　　　Perceptual Assessment... 309
　　　Motor Assessment (Strength and Tone) 309
　　　Instrumental and Acoustic Assessment 309
　　Dysphagia 315
　　　Dysfunction by Phases of Swallowing............................. 315
　　　Dysfunction by Underlying Disease Processes 318
　　Cranial Nerve Exam.. 319
　　Oral Mechanism Exam.. 321
　　Intervention for Dysarthria.. 321
　　Intervention for Dysphagia.. 324
　Summary... 325
　Key Concepts 326
　References.. 326

Chapter 14. Diffuse Brain Damage... 329
　Diffuse Etiologies 329
　　Traumatic Brain Injuries 330
　　　Assessment... 333
　　　Intervention 336
　　Alzheimer Disease.. 338
　　　Assessment... 338
　　　Intervention 342
　　Multiple Sclerosis... 344
　　Prion Diseases 344
　　Metastatic Tumors.. 346
　Speech Disorders... 348
　Language Disorders... 348
　　Social Communication 348

Cognitive Disorders 350
Swallowing Disorders 350
Summary 352
Key Concepts 352
References 352
Resources 354

Index 355

Preface

Organization of This Book

Unlike most textbooks on this topic, ours is organized by anatomical systems and locations, not by disorder. We intentionally wanted to emphasize the interrelatedness of speech, language, cognition, and swallowing, and the complexity of presentation when damage to the brain occurs. We believe that students will benefit from understanding co-occurrence of deficits and the impact of deficits upon each other and learning these concepts from the beginning. We understand that this approach is different and may require a shift in the way instructors organize their thoughts and their courses.

This book is not intended to provide in-depth information on assessment and treatment of acquired communication and swallowing disorders. It would be many magnitudes bigger and heavier if it did! Although there are many other texts and resources that provide the level of detail and theoretical background needed for students to be able to put assessment and treatments into practice, our goal is to introduce the disorders and provide enough information about how they are typically assessed and treated to create a full understanding of the disorders.

How to Use This Textbook

Thank you for choosing *Acquired Neurogenic Communication Disorders: An Integrated Clinical Approach*. The intent of this tutorial is to briefly describe and demonstrate the organization of chapters, which integrate speech, language, cognition, and swallowing. Understanding the organization may help both course instructors and students to best utilize the resources.

Our **customized illustrations** help to solidify connections between brain anatomy, functions, and areas of damage. This is accomplished through:

- A variety of views and perspectives (superior/inferior, dorsal/ventral, sections—coronal-transverse-sagittal, frontal/lateral/posterior)
- Resections/Cutaway illustrations to visualize deep, hard to see/visualize structures

- Close-up (magnified) pull-out illustrations of small sections of a structure along with the broader view of the structure itself for context
- Structures in situ (within the larger structure, which is transparent to allow you to see the deeper structure)
- Schematics, depicting sequences or processes, and speech, language, cognition, and swallowing systems or networks
- Illustrations of brain imaging included to provide a basic distinction between neurotypical brains and those with various pathologies
- A variety of etiologies and pathologies included so you can see where damage exists
- Models of speech, language, cognition, and swallowing mapped directly onto brain structures

We have highlighted foundational concepts and terminology by **bolding keywords** throughout, as well as including Latin and Greek word origins and meanings.

Assessment and Intervention Tables: Provide a summary of common assessments and interventions for speech, language, cognition, and swallowing. While these are not intended to be exhaustive, the tables highlight many of the most commonly used approaches.

Concept Tables: Several tables include information about subtypes of disorders, components of complex functions (e.g., prosody, language, executive functions, discourse), and frameworks (e.g., WHO-ICF).

Systems-Based Clinical Approach chapter: This chapter is the cornerstone of the textbook. The idea is to break down the artificial silos created when there are separate courses or book chapters to address acquired neurogenic disorders of speech (e.g., motor speech disorders), language (e.g., aphasia and related disorders), cognition (e.g., cognitive communication disorders), and swallowing (e.g., dysphagia). Since these disorders co-occur in individuals with neurological damage, our integrated structure is purposeful to help readers see the connections and overlaps.

Table 6–2. Treatments for Deficits Associated With Frontal Lobe Damage

Domains	Recommended Practices	Description
Agitation and Behavioral Disinhibition	Validation therapy (Benjamin, 1995, Neal & Wright, 2003)	Affirms the individual's emotional state rather than correcting them. Redirects to a positive interaction or activity.
	Redirection and movement (Ponsford et al., 2023)	In response to agitation, redirect the individual to another activity. Movement through space and to different environments typically reduces agitation as well.
	Routines (Hoepner & Togher, 2022)	Establishing a daily schedule and routine to help with orientation and foster positive behaviors (reduce agitation).
Executive Dysfunction	Environmental modifications	Modify the physical environment to reduce distractions. Train partners to provide scaffolding and reduce demands. Educate staff and partners.
	Metacognitive strategy instruction (Kennedy et al., 2008; Palinscar, 1986; Ylvisaker, 2006)	Break tasks or problems down into smaller steps. Practice strategies in the context of meaningful activities.

> **BOXES. A place for applying learning.**
>
> **Key terminology and concepts**—Whenever there are numerous key terms necessary to understand broader concepts, a mini-glossary is included to define terms and concepts.
>
> **Clinical cases**—Clinical cases that integrate commonly co-occurring speech, language, cognition, and swallowing impairments are sprinkled throughout the book. The intent is to help readers recognize that disorders like aphasia, dysarthria, dysphagia, and cognitive communication disorders don't usually occur in isolation but rather together. Many cases include questions to provoke thinking about the overlap between speech, language, cognition, and swallowing.

Overview of Neuroanatomy chapter: This chapter is not intended to replace a full review of neuroanatomy and physiology; it is meant to serve as a refresher and reference for concepts that are expanded upon in later chapters.

Etiologies and Pathophysiology chapter: This chapter introduces readers to a range of etiologies for various acquired and progressive neurological disorders. Some less common etiologies that provide useful illustrations of cognitive or communication disorders are included along with the more common etiologies that SLPs are likely to have on their caseloads. Accessible discussions of pathophysiology (what the damage looks like and where it is located) help readers to understand potential consequences.

Neurorehabilitation chapter: This chapter is intended to provide frameworks for holistic assessment and intervention that are culturally sensitive and responsive.

System-Based chapters: These chapters organize locations and etiologies of damage by anatomically related systems, including prefrontal, left perisylvian, right perisylvian, posterior cortical, subcortical, brainstem, and cerebellar. Disorders that occur with damage/degeneration of the anatomical region are discussed.

Assessment and treatment for those disorders that are almost always linked to that region are covered (e.g., assessment and treatment of aphasia and apraxia of speech are included in the Left Perisylvian Area chapter).

Assessment and Treatment chapters: These chapters cover cognitive disorders, dysarthrias, and dysphagia, all of which can occur due to damage or disruption of various areas of the brain. Pulling them out reduces redundancies throughout the text, and also highlights to students that these disorders are not localizable.

The order of the chapters attempts to build upon concepts from one chapter to the next. That being said, we went back and forth on the best order several times—while some chapters were easy to place early or later in the sequence, others were a bit tricky. Instructors can choose to assign chapters in the order that best fits their conceptualization and teaching style. Each chapter has cross-references to others for more information, so you can easily find background or in-depth information if you teach the chapters in a different order.

Summary: Each chapter ends with a plain language summary that highlights key concepts within the chapter. Some learners may wish to begin by reading the summary and key concepts before delving into the content, and end by returning to it after reading the chapter.

Key concepts:

1. A bulleted list is included at the end of each chapter to highlight key concepts and learning outcomes.
2. For students: At minimum, you should be sure to understand these key concepts. If you don't, we suggest that you return to the chapter, consult resources provided by your instructor (recorded lectures/screencasts, animations, supplementary readings), and ask your peers/instructors clarifying questions.

References and Further Reading: In some cases, these items were referenced directly in the text, while others are just useful resources to augment your learning.

Disorder Videos: This textbook includes numerous videos of individuals with various acquired neurogenic disorders (e.g., aphasia, primary progressive aphasia (PPA), dysarthria, cognitive-communication disorders) and etiologies (stroke, Parkinson disease, traumatic brain injury) completing speech, language, cognitive, and swallowing tasks. Partners of individuals with PPA were also interviewed, to provide context for the videos of individuals with PPA.

Acknowledgments

We are deeply indebted to the artists who created the images for this book. Tatiana Gandlin is not only a gifted artist but also efficient and patient. We were thrilled that she was able to contribute to this book as we worked closely with her for our *Clinical Neuroscience for Communication Disorders* text, and value her ability to figure out what we wanted from our rough sketches and notes. Mariah Hoepner created beautiful and accurate images of imaging scans and brain pathologies. The images created by these two artists make the content accessible to readers in a way that words cannot accomplish alone.

Holly Baker (UH) and Annika Kornmann (UWEC) were invaluable in helping with the less glamorous work that goes into a book such as documenting illustrations and tables and finding and double-checking references. Holly Baker and Alyssa Hall (UWEC) created chapter test banks, flashcards, and indexing for the entire textbook.

Rob Mattison, a videographer and video production editor from UWEC, filmed and edited the supplementary videos with the help of his student, John Franklyn. The video productions are high resolution with excellent audio quality and eloquent transitions. The videos capture interviews and assessments of individuals with aphasia, primary progressive aphasia (PPA), traumatic brain injuries, Parkinson disease, mild cognitive disorder, and apragmatism. Additionally, partners of individuals with early and late stage PPA were interviewed to provide additional contexts. UWEC graduate students Gabby Djupstrom, Julia Wainio, and Karlee Whyte completed portions of the Talk Bank assessment protocols and interviews. We also wish to thank the individuals with neurogenic disorders and their partners for sharing their time and experiences.

Several others provided material or feedback that strengthened the quality of the book: Nancy Peterson and Clark (Friedreich's Ataxia case), Stephanie Daniels (review of dysphagia material), University of Houston students Aunza and Silvia (student-perspective feedback), and Shannon Sheppard and Alexandra Zezinka Durfee (right hemisphere images).

We'd also like to thank the many reviewers who provided feedback on either our original proposal or our book draft. We appreciate the time you set aside from your "real job" to read our work and provide helpful and insightful comments and recommendations. This book is better organized, less redundant, and clearer than it would have been without your input.

Reviewers

Plural Publishing and the authors would like to thank the following reviewers for taking the time to provide their valuable feedback during the manuscript development process. Additional anonymous feedback was provided by other expert reviewers.

Adrienne Bratcher, SLP.D, CCC-SLP, CBIST
Professor and Department Chair
Eastern New Mexico University
Portales, New Mexico

Miriam Carroll-Alfano, PhD, CCC-SLP
Associate Professor
Midwestern University
Glendale, Arizona

Zeth Everick Collom, MS, CCC-SLP
Instructor and Speech-Language Pathologist
West Texas A&M University
Canyon, Texas

Heidi Iwashita, PhD, CCC-SLP
Assistant Professor
Eastern Washington University
Cheney, Washington

Qiang Li, PhD
Assistant Professor
Fort Hays State University
Hays, Kansas

Joy McKenzie, EdD, MS, CCC-SLP
Associate Professor
St. Cloud State University
St. Cloud, Minnesota

Kelly Rutherford, EdD, CCC-SLP
Associate Professor
Marshall University
Huntington, West Virginia

Cindy M. Sendor, MA, CCC-SLP
Assistant Professor
California Baptist University
Riverside, California

Deborah Sharp, PhD, CCC-SLP/L
Associate Professor and Department Chair
State University of New York (SUNY)
University at Cortland
Cortland, New York

Karin Thomas, SLPD, CCC-SLP
Assistant Professor
Saint Mary's College
Notre Dame, Indiana

Bruce Wisenburn, PhD, CCC-SLP
Associate Professor
Marywood University
Scranton, Pennsylvania

To my Mom, Connie Lehman, for everything she's done over the past half-century that helped me to get to the point where I am today. If I listed everything the dedication would be longer than the rest of the book. And to Aunt Milly and Sheri who hosted my writing retreats and continue to provide unwavering support.

—PB

To my Mom and Dad, who instilled the values of showing kindness and respect to all people. This has been my compass and it ignited my passion for serving others, regardless of their personal beliefs and perspectives. Fortunately, they also taught me the value of spending time with family. There's nothing quite like time in a boat with your lifelong fishing partners to clear your mind and decompress the business of life. And to Carol, my lifelong partner for being my rock.

—JH

1
SYSTEMS-BASED CLINICAL APPROACH

Chapter Overview

Breaking Down the Silos
Models of Communication Systems
   What Is the Value in Models?
   Speech: DIVA (Directions Into Velocities of Articulators)
   Language: Dual Stream Model
   Cognition: ACT-R (Adaptive Control of Thought-Rational)
   Swallowing: IFSiP (Integrated Framework for Swallowing Processes)
Putting It All Together
Summary
Key Concepts
References

Breaking Down the Silos

A disorder-based approach to addressing acquired neurogenic disorders has been the predominant approach for many years. In this approach, specific acquired communication/swallowing disorders (e.g., aphasia, cognitive-communication disorders, executive dysfunction, motor speech disorders, and dysphagia) are discussed independently, in separate courses. While there are benefits to clearly separating out cognitive, language, speech, and swallowing disorders to emphasize the differences between them, it creates challenges for students who need to be prepared for clinical practice. Brain damage, regardless of the etiology, rarely affects language, speech, cognition, or swallowing independently. For instance, clients with a focal left hemisphere lesion rarely have only aphasia; most often they present with aphasia along with apraxia, dysarthria, and/or dysphagia. Likewise, a client with a TBI that causes prefrontal and diffuse axonal injury typically presents with not only executive dysfunction but also dysphagia, dysarthria, visuoperceptual impairments, and language/pragmatic impairments. The traditional siloed, disorder-based approach can leave students ill-equipped to make connections between concomitant disorders, which places them at a distinct disadvantage when preparing for assessment and treatment.

Case-based approaches integrate impairments that co-occur in real clients in a manner that is more representative of what we encounter in clinical practice. Instead of isolating communication/swallowing impairments typically addressed in our discipline, cases integrate other impairments typically addressed by related disciplines, such as occupational and physical therapy, respiratory therapy, social work, nursing, and medical subspecialties (Table 1–1). This allows learners to see the client (human being) more holistically. We have selected a couple of types of cases (horses and zebras) to highlight the integration and overlap of motor speech, language, cognition, and swallowing impairments present within the individuals we serve. Horses are the everyday cases that you are likely to encounter in most adult rehabilitation contexts. Zebras are rare diseases/disorders that are less likely to be encountered in clinical practice, but can eloquently demonstrate system overlaps. Case 1–1 represents a horse, as traumatic brain injuries are common. Case 1–2 represents a zebra, as corticobasal syndrome (CBS) is a rare degenerative disease.

Table 1–1. Disciplines Involved in Care of Patients With Neurogenic Disorders

Discipline	Primary Role
Occupational therapy	physical and cognitive abilities required for activities of daily living; body movement, particularly arms and hands
Physical therapy	body movement, particularly legs and back
Speech-language pathology	communication, cognition, and swallowing
Respiratory therapy	respiration, potentially tracheostomy care
Social work	mental & behavioral aspects of functioning, addiction, coordination of care
Nursing	address medical status, intake-output, medication administration, hygiene

Table 1–1. *continued*	
Discipline	Primary Role
Neurology	address diagnosis of underlying lesion or disease, some pharmacological interventions
Neuropsychology	cognition, predominantly assessment
Ear, Nose, & Throat (ENT)	assess cranial nerve function in oral, pharyngeal, and laryngeal structures
Gastroenterology	some gastroenterological diseases have a neurological component and vice versa
Radiology	neuroimaging, radiographic/fluoroscopic imaging for swallowing

As is apparent from these two cases, speech, language, cognition, and swallowing can all be affected by a single etiology or disease process. While these two cases both involve fairly widespread changes, co-occurrence is also common in relatively focal strokes. SLPs need to be aware of not only the variety of potential disorders/impairments related to a disease or location of damage, but also the influence of one impairment on another. As described in Case 1–1, the cognitive deficits (impulsivity and impaired attention) affected both swallowing and language, exacerbating the impact of each of those independently.

Models of Communication Systems

These cases highlight the importance of taking a connectionist, systems-based approach to learning about neurogenic disorders. Cortical and subcortical speech, swallowing, language, and cognitive systems are interconnected. Overlap exists between functional organization of these structures and the white matter tracts that connect multiple systems within the nervous system. This does not even address the complexity of sensory inputs and the reciprocal interplay between those inputs and outputs. Fear not, our intent here is not to scare you off but to try to simplify and integrate contemporary neuroscience and cognitive-linguistic sciences to demonstrate the interconnectedness of cognitive and language systems with motor and sensory systems. Given that connection, we hope to clearly illustrate why damage to brain

Case 1–1. Traumatic Brain Injury (The Horse)

Traumatic brain injuries (TBIs) result in a mix of focal and diffuse brain lesions. Collectively, these pathologies affect many brain structures. As such, many brain systems (motor speech, voice, language, cognition, and swallowing) are impacted.

Case Description: Dennis was an 18-year-old high school graduate when he sustained a TBI in a motorcycle accident. He was taking courses at the local technical college and working for a local concrete mason at the time of his injury. On his way home from work, he collided with a deer, sustaining numerous fractures (legs, arms, ribs, pelvis, jaw) and diffuse axonal injury (DAI). Because he was helmeted, there was no significant focal damage or hematomas, confirmed by an acute CT scan. DAI was presumed and later evidenced on an MRI scan. He was in a coma for a week. When he emerged from the coma his speech was marked by mixed dysarthria and breathiness (at least partially due to traumatic intubation for ventilation). He was disoriented to person (oriented only to self), place, time, and situation. His attention span was less than a minute without redirection from medical staff. He had moderate-to-severe oral and pharyngeal dysphagia, further compromised by his cognitive status and attention impairments. Throughout the following week of rehab, a broader picture of impairments emerged. Along with a lack of cohesive discourse, clearly compromised by cognitive status, he demonstrated frequent anomia and paraphasic errors (both semantic and phonemic). Mobility was impaired, compromised by numerous orthopedic fractures as well as bilateral weakness and incoordination (targeting of movements, timing, proprioception, and troubles gauging velocity and amplitude of movements). Gait could be described as mechanical and stiff (how you might think of Frankenstein's gait). Activities of daily living, including self-feeding and self-care (brushing teeth, combing hair, bathing, etc.), were compromised by weakness, orthopedic fractures, and incoordination.

Given this background on TBI and this case description, answer the following questions:

1. Identify systems affected by TBI, and any anatomical correlates.
2. Identify disorders that would typically be addressed by a speech-language pathologist. (Hint: think speech, language, cognitive, and swallowing subsystems.)
3. Identify disorders that would typically be addressed by a related profession and include the names of those disciplines (refer back to Table 1–1).

Case 1–2. Corticobasal Syndrome (The Zebra)

Corticobasal syndrome (CBS) is an acquired, neurodegenerative disease that affects cortical and subcortical brain structures. While it is a rare disorder that you may not encounter clinically, it provides a strong model for why it is important to integrate learning about systems, rather than isolating by specific impairments such as speech, language, cognition, or swallowing. CBS is characterized by the following clinical symptoms: asymmetrical motor impairments, prominent apraxia, unilateral muscle rigidity, and focal cortical syndromes (e.g., aphasia, executive dysfunction, memory impairments, sensory loss, and anosognosia). Limbic and homeostatic systems are also involved, resulting in excessive eating or drinking. Behavioral changes such as apathy, irritability, disinhibition, impulsivity, and other personality changes are common.

Case Description: The following case is drawn from a published case study on an individual with CBS and her spousal partner (Hoepner et al., 2015). Margaret was a departmental administrative assistant at a university prior to the onset of CBS. CBS is often characterized by early onset and in this case, Margaret was presumptively diagnosed with CBS by age 57, approximately five years following onset of symptoms. Her first symptoms appeared at age 52. These included vertigo and nausea, symptoms rarely documented in case-based research of CBS. These symptoms increased over time, while other symptoms such as difficulties with spelling, problem solving, short-term memory, and speech fluency began to emerge. Neuroimaging identified mild generalized cerebral atrophy and a stable pattern of diffuse, multifocal white matter disease. Note that such changes are fairly common in imaging of typically aging individuals with or without symptoms. As such, imaging did not aid in differential diagnosis. Within five years of onset, anomia became persistent. By eight years, verbalizations were limited to yes/no responses. At nine years post-onset, yes/no confusion was common and symptoms of anarthria began to emerge. By ten years (age 62), Margaret had no usable speech, could comprehend only simple messages, responded only gesturally (head nod/shake), neglected her right arm, and had limited coordination of her left arm due to apraxia. Her gestural communication was ineffective due to yes/no confusion in her use of head nods/shakes. Other impairments also present included visual and gaze difficulties, alien limb phenomena, and attention impairments.

Given this background on CBS and this case description, answer the following questions:

1. Identify systems affected by CBS, and any anatomical correlates.
2. Identify disorders that would typically be addressed by a speech-language pathologist. (Hint: think speech, language, cognitive, and swallowing subsystems.)
3. Identify disorders that would typically be addressed by a related profession and include the names of those disciplines (refer back to Table 1–1).

structures seldom causes discrete effects to one system (i.e., speech, language, cognition, swallowing). It is not fully possible to map brain regions and networks to cognitive and language functions (see, e.g., Poeppel, 2012) due to the complexity of the systems, interconnectedness of structures, and the limitations of any one mapping technology. Regardless of how structure (neurobiology) and function (speech, language, cognition, swallowing) are mapped (i.e., functional imaging of activation, lesion locations, electrophysiological techniques, streams/networks, long-term potentiation changes to synapse, immunocytochemistry), no single approach captures everything.

What Is the Value in Models?

Models are created to map out and illustrate components of a larger process, such as language or cognition. In some cases, component functions can be linked to brain regions and then used to make predictions that damage to specific brain regions will result in predictable changes in function. Unfortunately, things are not always quite so simple. Here we highlight four models, one each for speech, language, cognition, and swallowing. The purpose is to show the extensive networks involved in each of these processes, and the shared "real estate" as some of the areas involved overlap.

While numerous models of communication exist, we chose these four because they are integrative in nature. That is, they do not simply examine speech, sensorimotor, language, or cognitive functions in isolation but as interdependent functions of a unified neurological system. As a starting point, if you can grasp the principles of interdependency and integration across these subsystems, you will have an adequate basis for a clinical speech-language pathologist.

Speech: DIVA (Directions Into Velocities of Articulators)

Contrary to localizationalist models that identify a few discrete brain structures involved in speech, in reality, speech processes depend upon numerous brain structures. This includes motor (planning, initiation, refinement), kinesthetic, auditory, cognitive, and language areas. These structures are interdependent, speaking to the integrated nature of speech. For instance, motoric, phonological production is dependent on lexical access and comprehension, which are sensory and memory dependent.

The DIVA model maps the connections between these systems from the perspective of speech production/motor control (Guenther et al., 2006). Central to this model are three main principles: feedback, feedforward, and monitoring/adjustments (Figure 1–1). This accounts eloquently for the interplay between motor, sensory, and cognition/language systems. The feedback process is central to learning and adjusting. Most feedback is internal to the individual producing and hearing their own speech productions. This includes auditory and proprioceptive/kinesthetic feedback, which allows the individual to determine if the sound targets were produced correctly or if adjustment is needed. Once the auditory and somatosensory (proprioceptive/kinesthetic) targets are met, a map of articulatory placements for the speech sounds is formed. From this point forward, as long as the system does not change, a feedforward

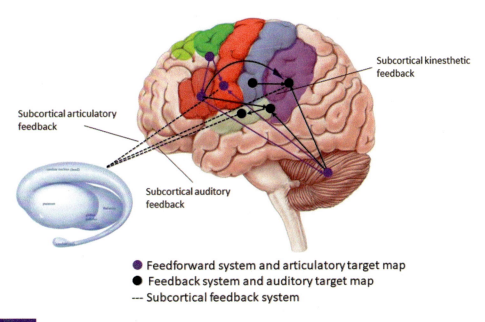

Figure 1–1. DIVA schematic.

mechanism guides articulatory placements. Only when there is a change in the mechanism due to structural or functional changes is there a need to return to feedback and mapping of placements in order to adjust and achieve the somatosensory and auditory target for the sound.

DIVA takeaways:

- Feedback = primarily internal kinesthetic placement feedback to achieve target sound productions
- Feedforward = pre-planning sequences of articulatory placements sensitive to production contexts such as coarticulation
- Monitoring and adjustments = altering articulator placements when there is structural or physiological change

Language: Dual Stream Models

Wernicke–Geschwind's classic model of language processing attempted to isolate a handful of left hemisphere structures as having a role in language comprehension and production (Tremblay & Dick, 2016). This model became obsolete when functional imaging made it evident that sound-based representations of speech are comprehended bilaterally, while both motor and comprehension structures have access to phonological coding.

According to the dual stream model of left hemisphere language (Hickock & Poeppel, 2000), language is processed through two bidirectional pathways, the dorsal and ventral streams (Figure 1–2). The **dorsal stream** carries information about **phonological processing**

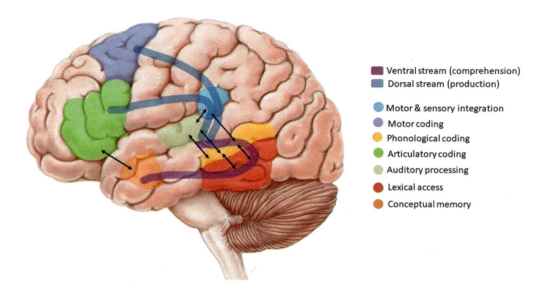

Figure 1–2. Simplified dual stream model.

Note: Dorsal stream is the "production" component and ventral stream is "comprehension." This figure is a modified version of Hickok, 2012 and G. Hickok's 2017 C-STAR lecture.

and the **motor aspects of speech**, including the mapping of phonological processes to articulation, connecting the frontal, parietal, and temporal lobes in order to convert voices to phonemes, retrieve words, repeat words, and articulate words. This pathway is also involved in learning new vocabulary. The **ventral stream** passes through the inferior fronto-occipital fasciculus (IFOF) and intratemporal networks, facilitating **semantic processing** (Chang et al., 2015). This includes lexical access and assigning meaning to words, and integration of phonological and semantic processing. The streams split just posterior to the auditory cortices where phonological access is present to both the dorsal and ventral streams. Sensory and motor integration appears to take place there too at the superior-parietal-temporal gyrus (SPT) (Hickok, 2012).

Lexical processing for complex sentences and discourse is not isolated to the temporal lobe. Syntactic processing, contextual semantics, and word selection associated with semantic memory are also carried out by the inferior parietal lobule and inferior frontal gyrus. This suggests that language comprehension and expression are integrated. Speech perception and comprehension rely heavily on the conceptual, memory interface and is thought to be processed bilaterally (Hickok & Poeppel, 2007). The right hemisphere has a role in interpreting and producing prosodic features, particularly emotional tone (Chang et al., 2015).

In support of this model, functional imaging of individuals with LH stroke indicates that damage to the dorsal stream results in production problems, while damage to the ventral stream results in comprehension problems (Bates et al., 2003; Fridriksson et al., 2016; Price et al., 2010).

Dual stream takeaways:

- Dorsal stream = motor production stream
- Ventral stream = semantics and comprehension stream
- Language production is left hemisphere dominant, while comprehension is bilateral
- Emotional prosody production and comprehension are right hemisphere dominant

Cognition: ACT-R (Adaptive Control of Thought-Rational)

Cognition is an incredibly complex and distributed set of processes. It encompasses language, memory, attention, and executive functions. Identifying a model for cognition that is both comprehensive and yet applied to brain structure correlates and behaviors is difficult. Cognition draws upon both hemispheres of the cerebrum, along with the basal ganglia, thalamus, and cerebellum. It also interfaces with both motor and sensory systems. The Adaptive Control of Thought-Rational (ACT-R), was initially devised as a theory to explain development and learning of mathematics. ACT-R is a unified theory of cognition, meaning it can address a full range of cognitive functions (not simply one, such as language, attention, memory, or executive functions alone). While no model is perfect in capturing all cognitive processes or anatomical correlates, ACT-R at least attempts to represent most cognitive functions.

ACT-R was developed through artificial intelligence and mapped to brain structures through imaging studies. ACT-R consists of five modules and a central production system (Figure 1–3). This model is a contemporary modification of Anderson's earlier work (Anderson et al., 2004; Borst & Anderson, 2015; Ritter et al., 2019). While not all variations of ACT-R models include the motor and perceptual modules, these systems are essential for processing the world around us (Ritter et al., 2019). The **visual module** identifies object characteristics

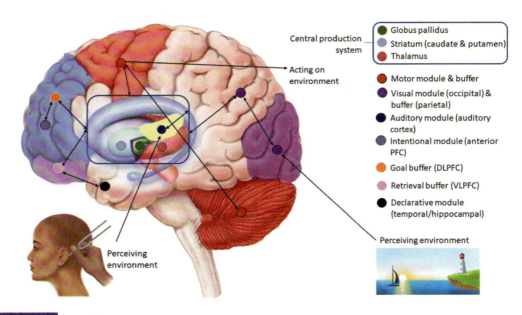

Figure 1–3. ACT-R model.

and locations in one's visual field, including face recognition. This takes place in the occipital and ventral temporal regions. The **aural module** deciphers acoustic information and is located in the superior temporal gyrus. The **intentional module**, found in the anterior prefrontal cortices, coordinates intention and goal-oriented behaviors. The **declarative module**, which includes the hippocampus, anterior medial temporal, and ventrolateral prefrontal cortex, carries out learning and retrieval. The **motor module**, composed of the pyramidal system and cerebellum, controls body movements. A **central production system**, made up of the basal ganglia and thalamus, coordinates the communication between and actions of these modules. Of course, this entire system interfaces with the environment, either perceiving stimuli or acting on the environment. The intent of the ACT-R model is to identify the systems and networks involved globally in cognitive processes. This includes cortical and subcortical, and sensory and motor cortices, along with specific cognitive substrates (i.e., memory, attention, executive functions, and visuospatial).

ACT-R takeaways:

- Sensory, motor, and cognitive functions are interconnected with the central production system and interdependent upon each other

Swallowing: IFSiP (Integrated Framework for Swallowing Processes)

While swallowing is a motoric function, it is impacted by sensory and cognitive factors. A four-stage swallowing model is commonly used, including oral preparatory, oral transport, pharyngeal, and esophageal phases. Typically, these are addressed only from a motoric standpoint. Muhle et al. (2020) examined the effects of motoric and cognitive dual tasks on oral-pharyngeal function. This was conducted with healthy participants with a mean age of 29 years old. Significant differences were noted on oral-pharyngeal swallowing safety during the motoric dual task (i.e., premature pharyngeal spillage and residue). Changes were also noted in the cognitive dual tasks, but they were not significant. Labeit et al. (2021) examined motoric and cognitive dual tasks on oral-pharyngeal function of individuals with Parkinson disease, identifying significant declines with both motor and cognitive dual tasks. This reminds us that oral-pharyngeal swallowing functions are not exclusively reflexive but require attention, which accounts for the dual task changes. Sensory functions are also often overlooked. This not only includes feeling foods within the mouth and pharynx but also tasting them. An integrated model of swallowing was not identified; therefore the integrated framework for swallowing processes (IFSiP) was our initial attempt to address this gap (Figure 1–4). The IFSiP model attempts to show the interdependency between cognitive, motor, sensory, and autonomic functions.

IFSiP takeaways:

- Swallowing involves attending to the act of eating, carrying out the complex motor functions associated with chewing and swallowing, and integrating sensory inputs and feedback

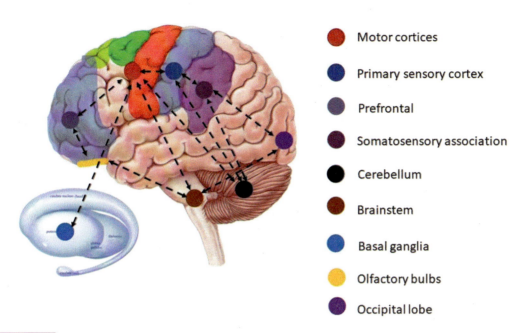

Figure 1–4. Integrated framework for swallowing processes (IFSiP).

- For individuals without differences/impairments to sight and taste, swallowing typically involves seeing the food and salivating in response, and smelling and tasting the food

Putting It All Together

Now that you've seen each of the four models, imagine overlaying them. Now imagine that a stroke occurs to damage even a small region of the brain within the illustrated models. It is immediately apparent that damage will interrupt the function of multiple systems. In addition, Figure 1–5 shows the interdependency between our four systems: speech, language, cognition, and swallowing. Even if one system escapes direct damage, the interconnectedness will have impacts on a person's ability to function. For example, prefrontal damage that affects primarily cognition will often negatively impact language and speech production.

Understanding the integrated, interdependent nature of neurological systems is crucial to addressing the comorbidity of speech, motor, language, and cognitive impairments in acquired neurogenic disorders. Considering these three mini-cases and drawing upon the integrated framework from Figure 1–5, respond to the questions associated with each case.

1. Jameson has an acquired apraxia of speech (AOS). Assume for a moment that this is somehow isolated to motor speech, with no direct changes to language or cognition. Even if that were possible or however unlikely, what are the downstream effects of increased demands of motor formulation and effort on language and cognition? How might his swallowing be affected?

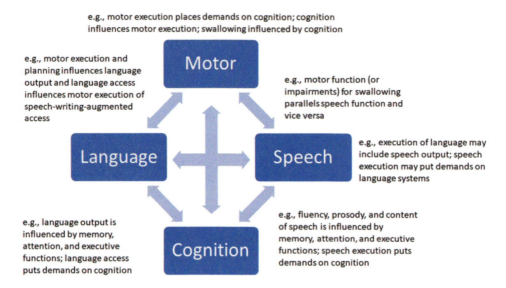

Figure 1–5. Integrative model of speech, motor, language, and cognition.

2. Rishi has spastic dysarthria with significant weakness. How might his swallowing be affected? Could there be effects related to effort on language and coordination?

3. Xiqu has ataxic dysarthria with poor motor coordination. How might his swallowing be affected? If Xiqu had an apraxia of speech instead of dysarthria, how might swallowing be affected?

4. Carmen has Alzheimer dementia. At this point, assume that she has good oral and pharyngeal strength, good laryngeal sensitivity, and a strong respiratory drive. Her language is relatively intact—she has decent auditory comprehension and no expressive aphasia. From a sensory standpoint, Carmen demonstrates oral agnosia, which impairs her ability to recognize food as food, particularly when it is lukewarm and has little texture and little flavor. She is disoriented to her living environment and frequently wanders through the residence. How, if at all, would swallowing be affected by cognition? How might language be affected by cognition?

5. Jose sustained a traumatic brain injury with diffuse axonal injury and some focal lesions. How likely (given the fact that there is damage spread throughout the cortex, subcortical structures, and brainstem) is it that cognition is the only subsystem affected? What other systems are likely to be affected and how?

✓ Summary

Speech, motor, language, and cognitive functions are never fully independent. Each affects the others, whether directly or indirectly. Due to the overlapping location of processes underlying domains of communication and swallowing, most patients/clients will have deficits in multiple domains. Learning about these domains in an integrated, rather than siloed approach, adds some complexity to the learning process while establishing a greater understanding of the interconnectedness and the reality of clinical practice.

Key Concepts

- The CNS is complex and highly interconnected. Most neurogenic diseases/disorders cause multiple impairments.
- In complex diseases that affect multiple brain regions and systems (e.g., TBI, CBS), speech, language, cognition, and swallowing are all affected.
- Discrete or focal damage also tends to produce some combination of speech, language, cognition, and swallowing impairments.
- Thorough assessment and treatment of patients with neurogenic diseases require collaboration between multiple disciplines.
- Cognition, language, speech, and swallowing are interconnected; an impairment in one can impact function in others.
- Models of speech, language, cognition and swallowing illustrate the interconnectedness and the various areas of the CNS involved. For instance, speech is not an exclusively motoric process but involves a variety of cortical and subcortical structures that may also be associated with language, cognition, and swallowing.

References

Anderson, J. R., Bothell, D., Byrne, M. D., Douglass, S., Lebiere, C., & Qin, Y. (2004). An integrated theory of the mind. *Psychological Review, 111*(4), 1036.

Bates, E., Wilson, S. M., Saygin, A. P., Dick, F., Sereno, M. I., Knight, R. T., & Dronkers, N. F. (2003). Voxel-based lesion–symptom mapping. *Nature Neuroscience, 6*(5), 448–450.

Borst, J. P., & Anderson, J. R. (2015). Using the ACT-R Cognitive Architecture in combination with fMRI data. In B. U. Forstmann & E.-J. Wagenmakers (Eds.), *An introduction to model-based cognitive neuroscience* (pp. 339–352). Springer.

Chang, E. F., Raygor, K. P., & Berger, M. S. (2015). Contemporary model of language organization: An overview for neurosurgeons. *Journal of Neurosurgery, 122*(2), 250–261.

Fridriksson, J., Yourganov, G., Bonilha, L., Basilakos, A., Den Ouden, D. B., & Rorden, C. (2016). Revealing the dual streams of speech processing. *Proceedings of the National Academy of Sciences, 113*(52), 15108–15113.

Guenther, F. H., Ghosh, S., Nieto-Castanon, A., & Tourville, J. (2006). A neural model of speech production. In J. Harrington & M. Tabain (Eds.), *Speech production: Models, phonetic processes and techniques* (1st ed., pp. 27–40). Routledge.

Hickok, G. (2012). The cortical organization of speech processing: Feedback control and predictive coding, the context of a dual-stream model. *Journal of Communication Disorders, 45*(6), 393–402.

Hickok, G., & Poeppel, D. (2000). Towards a functional neuroanatomy of speech perception. *Trends in Cognitive Sciences, 4*(4), 131–138.

Hickok, G., & Poeppel, D. (2007). The cortical organization of speech processing. *Nature Reviews Neuroscience, 8*(5), 393–402.

Hoepner, J., Sell, L., & Kooiman, H. (2015). Case study of partner training in corticobasal degeneration. *Journal of Interactional Research in Communication Disorders, 6*(2), 157.

Labeit, B., Claus, I., Muhle, P., Regner, L., Suntrup-Krueger, S., Dziewas, R., & Warnecke, T. (2021). Effect of cognitive and motor dual-task on oropharyngeal swallowing in Parkinson's disease. *European Journal of Neurology, 28*(3), 754–762.

Muhle, P., Claus, I., Labeit, B., Ogawa, M., Dziewas, R., Suntrup-Krueger, S., & Warnecke, T. (2020). Effects of cognitive and motor dual-tasks on oropharyngeal swallowing assessed with FEES in healthy individuals. *Scientific Reports, 10*(1), 20403.

Poeppel, D. (2012). The maps problem and the mapping problem: Two challenges for a cognitive neuroscience of speech and language. *Cognitive Neuropsychology, 29*(1–2), 34–55.

Price, C. J., Seghier, M. L., & Leff, A. P. (2010). Predicting language outcome and recovery after stroke: The PLORAS system. *Nature Reviews Neurology, 6*(4), 202–210.

Ritter, F. E., Tehranchi, F., & Oury, J. D. (2019). ACT-R: A cognitive architecture for modeling cognition. Wiley Interdisciplinary Reviews: *Cognitive Science, 10*(3), e1488.

Tremblay, P., & Dick, A. S. (2016). Broca and Wernicke are dead, or moving past the classic model of language neurobiology. *Brain and Language, 162*, 60–71.

2
OVERVIEW OF NEUROANATOMY AND NEUROPHYSIOLOGY

Chapter Overview

Overview
Structures and Regions
   Frontal Lobes
   Parietal Lobes
   Temporal Lobes
   Occipital Lobes
   Insula
   Subcortical Regions and Structures
     Subcortical White Matter
     Subcortical Structures
   Brainstem
     Cranial Nerves
   Cerebellum
Meninges and Ventricles
Blood Supply to the Brain
Neurophysiology
Typical Aging
Summary
Key Concepts
References

Overview

A solid knowledge of the major structures and regions of the nervous system is important for understanding communication and swallowing disorders caused by nervous system damage or degeneration. This brief overview serves as an orientation to the structures and regions important for communication (which, as it turns out, is nearly the whole brain). Details about specific regions and structures are provided in other chapters. Table 2–1 and Figure 2–1 provide a review of anatomical terminology.

The **central nervous system (CNS)** consists of the brain and spinal cord. The **peripheral nervous system (PNS)** consists of all of the nerves that extend out from the CNS. The PNS can be further subdivided into the **somatic** and **autonomic** systems. The somatic (Latin: *soma = body*) nervous system innervates skeletal muscles and other body systems that can generally be consciously controlled. The autonomic (from autonomy: working independently or involuntarily) system controls the involuntary systems of the body such as digestion, cardiac function, and respiration. The autonomic system includes both the **sympathetic** and

Table 2–1. Terms of Position and Orientation	
Superior: toward the top	**Inferior:** toward the bottom
Superficial: toward the surface	**Deep:** away from the surface
External: toward the surface	**Internal:** away from the surface
Medial: toward the midline (mesial, median) A medial view of the brain is one looking at a slice along, or close to, the midline.	**Lateral:** away from the midline; toward the side A lateral view of the brain is one looking from the right or left side.
Proximal: toward the point of attachment	**Distal:** away from the point of attachment
Dorsal (brain): top of head (superior) **Dorsal (body, from the neck down):** toward the backbone (posterior)	**Ventral (brain):** bottom of head (inferior) **Ventral (body, from the neck down):** toward the belly (anterior)
Rostral: toward the nose	**Caudal:** toward the tail
Central: toward the center	**Peripheral:** away from the center
Afferent: conducting inward or toward the central nervous system; sensory	**Efferent:** conducting outward or away from the central nervous system; motor
Ipsi-: same (ipsilateral = same side)	**Contra-:** opposite (contralateral = opposite side)

Source: Adapted from *Clinical Neuroscience for Communication Disorders: Neuroanatomy and Neurophysiology* (p. 11) by Blake, M. L. and Hoepner, J. K. Copyright © 2023 Plural Publishing, Inc. All rights reserved.

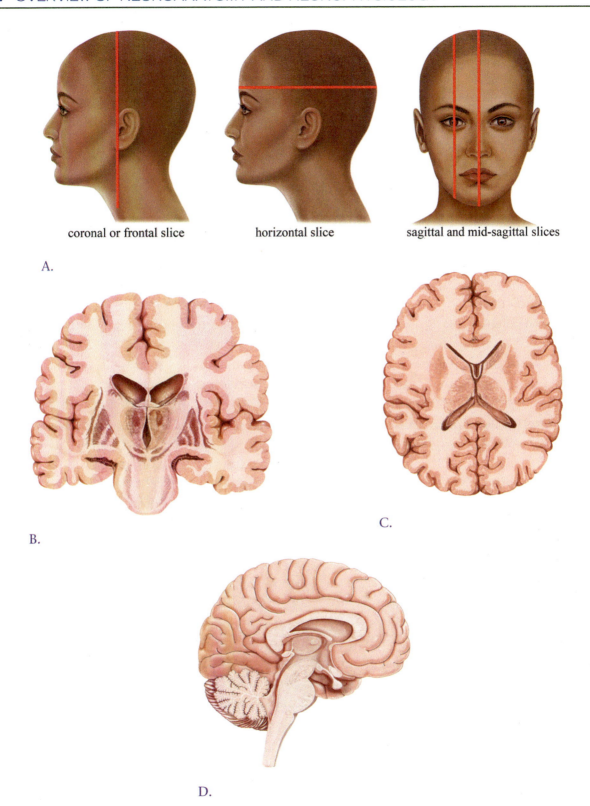

Figure 2–1. A. Planes of section shown on the head. B. Coronal (frontal) slice of the brain. C. Horizontal slice of the brain. D. Midsagittal slice of the brain showing the medial surface of the left hemisphere. From Blake & Hoepner (2023) *Clinical Neuroscience for Communication Disorders*, Figure 1–13, p. 13.

parasympathetic systems, which are responsible, respectively, for the "fight, flight, or freeze" and the "return to rest" responses. This text will focus primarily on the CNS since it is the site of control of communicative functions. Sensorimotor control over speech production and swallowing includes both CNS and PNS components; these will be described in Chapters 10 and 11.

Structures and Regions

What we call "the brain" is really three structures: the **cerebrum**, made up of the left and right hemispheres; the **brainstem**, which provides the connection between the cerebrum and the spinal cord; and the **cerebellum** (Latin: *little brain*), which extends posteriorly from the brainstem (Figure 2–2). All of these structures are made up of two types of cells: **neurons** and **glial cells** (plural: glia). Neurons, what we think of as "brain cells," receive and send signals and coordinate to create all thoughts, emotions, movements, etc. A typical neuron has three major components: the soma, or cell body, where processing occurs and signals are generated; dendrites, which receive signals (usually from other neurons); and a single axon, which transmits signals to other neurons or structures (Figure 2–3). The point of communication is called a **synapse**. Most axons are coated with a white fatty substance called **myelin** which speeds up the transmission of signals. Bundles of axons make up the **white matter** in the brain. Neuron cell bodies, because they have no myelin, appear darker, and make up the **gray matter** of the brain. The outer surface of the brain consists of cell bodies, and this region of gray matter is called the **cortex** (Latin: *bark*). There are other collections of cell bodies deep in the brain and brainstem that are called either **ganglia** or **nuclei** (Figure 2–4).

Neurons cannot function without the support of glial cells, which create structure, provide sustenance, and have cleaning functions (Figure 2–5). **Astrocytes** connect to both blood vessels and neurons and act as a filter, barring some substances from flowing from the bloodstream into the CNS. This system is called the **blood brain barrier**. There are several subtypes of **microglia**. Some aid in immune system responses; others clean up dead cells, such as after a stroke or other brain injury. **Oligodendrocytes** and **Schwann** cells create the myelin sheaths around axons. Oligodendrocytes are found in the CNS and Schwann cells in the PNS.

The cerebral hemispheres have many hills and valleys. A **gyrus** (plural: gyri) is a hill or elevated region while a **sulcus** (plural: sulci) or **fissure** is a valley or enfolding. Fissures tend to be deeper than sulci and divide the brain into distinct regions (Figure 2–6). However, the rules of naming are not consistently used. For example, the **sylvian fissure** is also known as the **lateral sulcus**. While there are some differences in sulci and gyri across people, the pattern is not random. There are some that are obvious across all human brains. These are used as landmarks and in some cases as borders for dividing regions. Some sulci and gyri have specific functions, even if they vary somewhat in size and shape across brains.

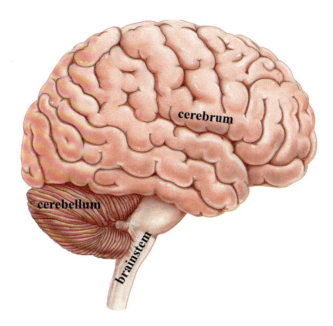

Figure 2–2. Major components of the "brain.".

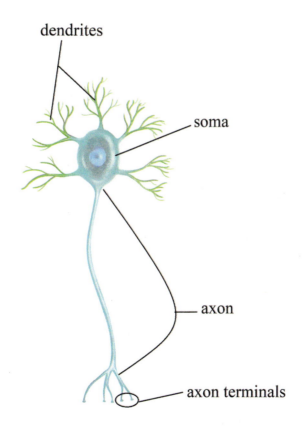

Figure 2–3. Components of a stereotypical neuron. From *Clinical Neuroscience for Communication Disorders: Neuroanatomy and Neurophysiology* (p. 14) by Blake, M. L. and Hoepner, J. K. Copyright © 2023 Plural Publishing, Inc. All rights reserved.

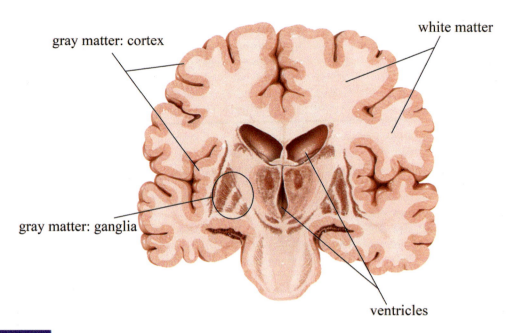

Figure 2–4. Gray and white matter in the brain. Adapted from *Clinical Neuroscience for Communication Disorders: Neuroanatomy and Neurophysiology* (p. 2) by Blake, M. L. and Hoepner, J. K. Copyright © 2023 Plural Publishing, Inc. All rights reserved.

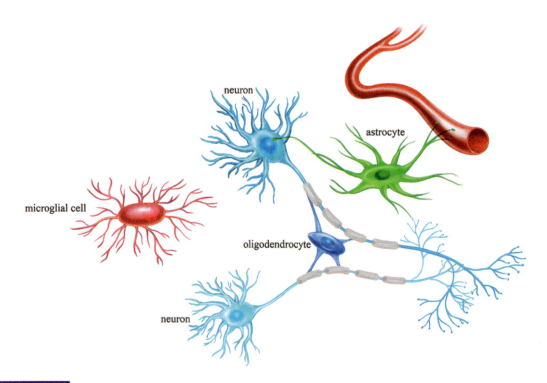

Figure 2–5. Neurons and glial cells. Adapted from *Clinical Neuroscience for Communication Disorders: Neuroanatomy and Neurophysiology* (p. 16) by Blake, M. L. and Hoepner, J. K. Copyright © 2023 Plural Publishing, Inc. All rights reserved.

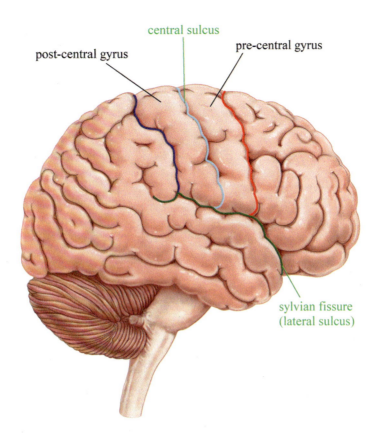

Figure 2–6. Landmarks on the lateral surface of the right hemisphere. Fissures/sulci are labeled in green; gyri are labeled in black. From *Clinical Neuroscience for Communication Disorders: Neuroanatomy and Neurophysiology* (p. 19) by Blake, M. L. and Hoepner, J. K. Copyright © 2023 Plural Publishing, Inc. All rights reserved.

Each hemisphere is divided into four major lobes—frontal, parietal, occipital, and temporal (Figure 2–7)—and the insula. Frontal lobes, logically, are the most anterior, at the front of the head. Posterior to these are the parietal lobes. The occipital lobes make up the posterior portion of the brain. The temporal lobes are inferior to the frontal and parietal lobes. Some readers may remember from their head and neck anatomy class that the lobes of the brain share names with the bones of the skull that overlay them.

All of the lobes are extensively connected to the others, and as described in Chapter 1 and will become clearer throughout the book, most functions are a result of interconnected regions. For example, the **perisylvian region** is the area of the brain surrounding the sylvian fissure (Figure 2–8). It includes the inferior frontal, inferior parietal, and superior temporal lobes. Most language and communication processing occurs in the perisylvian areas of the left and right hemispheres. Despite this interconnectivity, each lobe has primary control over certain functions. In the descriptions below, all regions are bilateral unless noted otherwise.

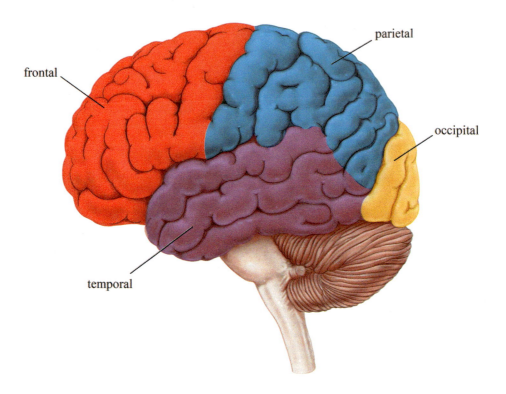
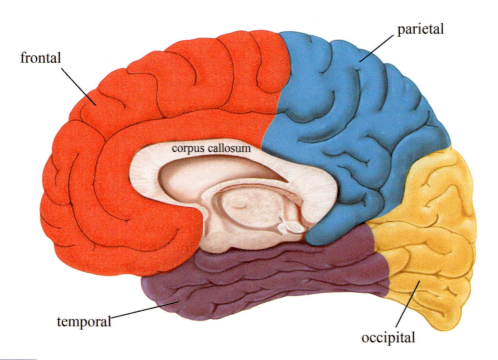

Figure 2–7. Lobes of the brain. From *Clinical Neuroscience for Communication Disorders: Neuroanatomy and Neurophysiology* (p. 6) by Blake, M. L. and Hoepner, J. K. Copyright © 2023 Plural Publishing, Inc. All rights reserved.

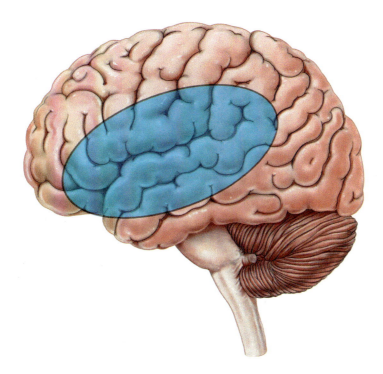

Figure 2–8. Perisylvian area of the left hemisphere.

Frontal Lobes

The frontal lobes have a leading role in cognition, motor control, and language (Figure 2–9). They are primarily responsible for higher-level cognition, also known as **executive functions** such as planning, organizing, reasoning, and judgment. Motor areas for planning, programming, and initiating movement are in the superior and posterior frontal lobes. Language production is controlled primarily in the inferior regions. The inferior left frontal lobe is important for language production such as finding the words you want to say and organizing them into syntactic structures. This region is often called **Broca's area**, named for neurologist Paul Broca who was one of the first to describe the function of this area. The inferior right frontal lobe is involved in production of emotional prosody which allows you to convey how you are feeling through your tone of voice. The **central sulcus** is the border between the frontal and parietal lobes. The sylvian fissure divides the frontal lobe from the temporal lobe.

Parietal Lobes

The parietal lobes (Figure 2–10) contain the primary sensory cortex, where signals conveying sensation from the body (pain, touch, temperature, body position and movement) all arrive. The superior parietal lobes, particularly in the right hemisphere, are important for body awareness and perception as well as attention and interpreting where items are in space and

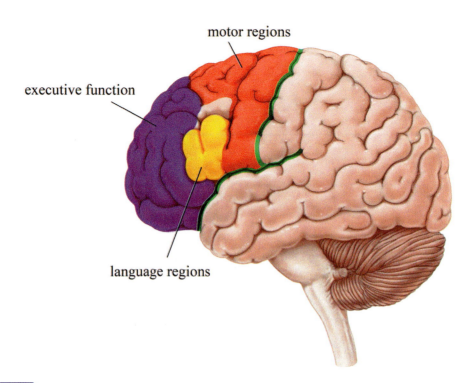

Figure 2–9. Functional regions of the frontal lobe.

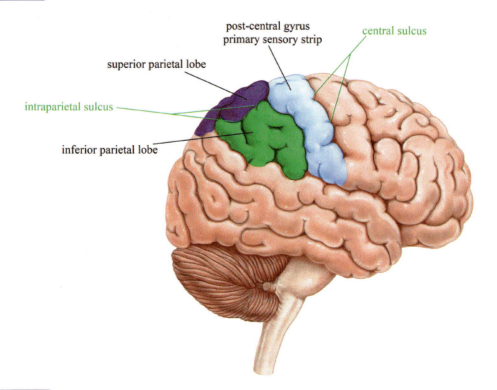

Figure 2–10. Regions of the parietal lobe shown on the right hemisphere. From *Clinical Neuroscience for Communication Disorders: Neuroanatomy and Neurophysiology* (p. 24) by Blake, M. L. and Hoepner, J. K. Copyright © 2023 Plural Publishing, Inc. All rights reserved.

in relation to oneself. These play an important role in orientation to movement and path finding. The inferior parietal lobes are important for comprehension. The sylvian fissure (lateral sulcus) separates the parietal from the temporal lobe. On the lateral side of the brain, there is no clear border between the parietal and occipital lobes.

Temporal Lobes

The temporal lobes (Figure 2–11) process auditory signals, aid in language comprehension, recognize visual images (e.g., faces, objects, colors, letters, and numbers), and are a primary site for memory storage. Deep in the temporal lobes is a structure called the **hippocampus** which is critical for forming new memories. The language functions are in the superior, posterior region where the temporal and parietal lobes meet. This is called the **temporo-parietal junction**. In the right side of the brain, this region is important for recognizing and interpreting emotional prosody. It is also part of the theory of mind network that helps in understanding other people's perspectives, beliefs, and emotions. In the left hemisphere, this region is important for auditory comprehension of words and sentences. This includes **Wernicke's area** as well as the **angular gyrus** and **supramarginal gyrus.** These latter two integrate auditory and visual language signals for reading and writing. As noted above, the sylvian fissure divides the temporal lobe from the frontal and parietal lobes. There is no clear border between the temporal and occipital lobes.

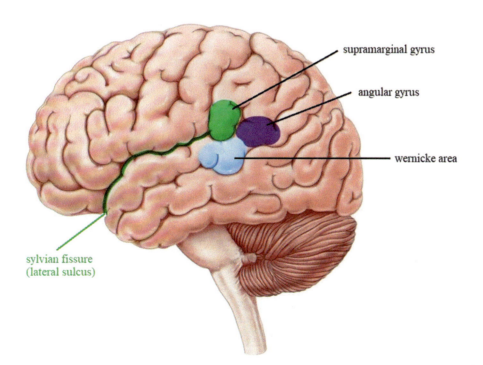

Figure 2-11. Regions of the temporal lobe shown on the left hemisphere.

Occipital Lobes

The occipital lobe is the primary site for visual processing (Figure 2–12). Signals from the eyes are transmitted to the occipital lobe where they undergo initial processing. From there, signals are sent to regions of the parietal and temporal lobes for further processing and interpretation. The dorsal stream to the parietal lobe (the "where" pathway) is important for spatial processing and localizing visual images in space, while the ventral stream to the temporal lobe (the "what" pathway) is for recognizing and interpreting visual images.

Insula

The insula is a section of cortex deep in the sylvian fissure (Figure 2–13). Sometimes it is referred to as the insular lobe because it consists of cortical tissue just like the other lobes. There are at least five different functions of the insula (Uddin et al., 2017). First, it is connected to the visceral sensorimotor system and involved in regulation of autonomic functions such as heart rate, blood pressure, and feelings from the digestive system as well as pain sensations from the body. Second, it has connections to a variety of special sensory systems including taste, smell, auditory, and vestibular systems. Third is its involvement in social cognition including theory of mind, emotions, and empathy. Fourth, the insula is part of the attentional

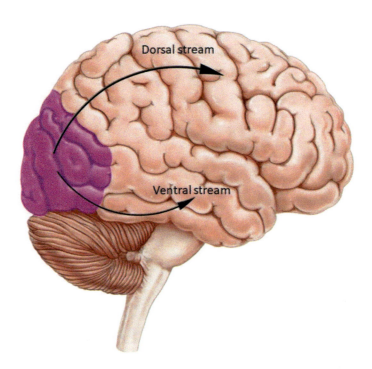

Figure 2–12. Dorsal and ventral visual streams.

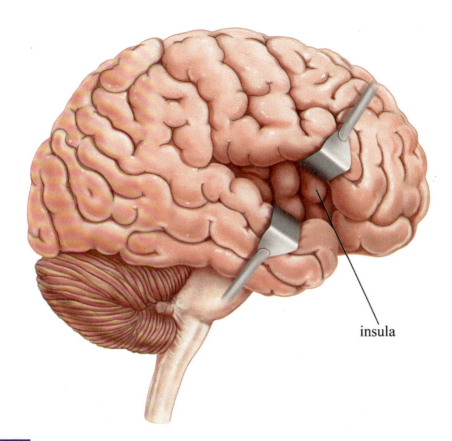

Figure 2–13. Lateral view of the insula deep to the sylvian fissure of the right hemisphere. Adapted from *Clinical Neuroscience for Communication Disorders: Neuroanatomy and Neurophysiology* (p. 20) by Blake, M. L. and Hoepner, J. K. Copyright © 2023 Plural Publishing, Inc. All rights reserved.

networks. Finally, it has a role in speech production, and damage to the insula can cause motor speech disorders.

Subcortical Regions and Structures

Subcortical White Matter

The subcortical white matter is made up of the myelinated axons of millions of neurons. These are variously called fasciculi, tracts, pathways, or, when they connect the right and left sides of the brain, commissures (Figure 2–14). Tracts can be classified based on what they connect. **Association tracts** connect areas within a hemisphere, **commissural tracts** connect the right and left hemispheres, and **projection tracts** connect the brain and brainstem/spinal cord.

There are a few association tracts that are of relevance for communication. In the left hemisphere language processes are dependent upon the **arcuate fasciculus** that connects parietal/temporal regions with the frontal lobes, the **uncinate fasciculus** that connects

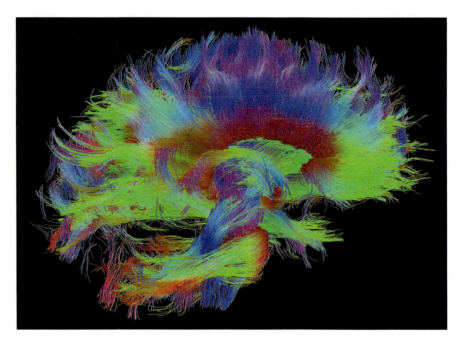

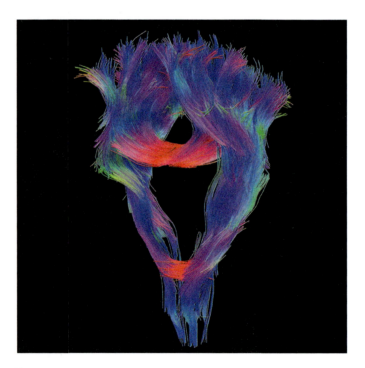

Figure 2–14. A. White matter tracts in the brain, brainstem, and cerebellum. B. White matter projection and commissural tracts. Courtesy of the USC Laboratory of Neuro Imaging and Athinoula A. Martinos Center for Biomedical Imaging, Consortium of the Human Connectome Project – http://www.humanconnectomeproject.org

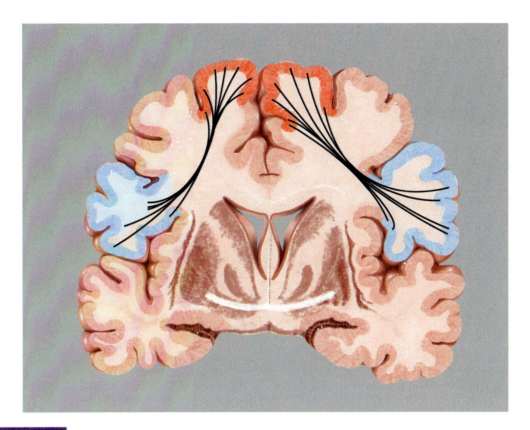

Figure 2-15. Frontal aslant tracts connecting superior frontal motor (red) to inferior frontal language (blue) areas.

anterior temporal to inferior frontal regions, and the **frontal aslant tract** which connects medial frontal motor areas to inferior frontal language areas (Figure 2-15). In the right hemisphere, prosodic processing relies on the **superior longitudinal fasciculus** connecting the parietal to the frontal lobe and the **inferior fronto-occipital fasciculus.**

The largest commissural tract is the **corpus callosum**, which connects the two hemispheres of the brain. It can easily be seen on a midsagittal cut of the brain (refer back to Figure 2-7B). Projection tracts include the **pyramidal tracts** which provide motor signals to the muscles of the head/neck and body, respectively, as well as sensory tracts that carry sensory signals (pain, touch, temperature, body position, and special senses) from the body to the brain.

Subcortical Structures

The **basal ganglia** are made up of several individual structures. The main ones are the caudate nucleus, putamen, and globus pallidus (Figures 2-16 and 2-17). All are collections of cell bodies that receive and send signals. Most of these structures are part of the motor system. The **thalamus** is another collection of cell bodies. It has multiple functions including processing

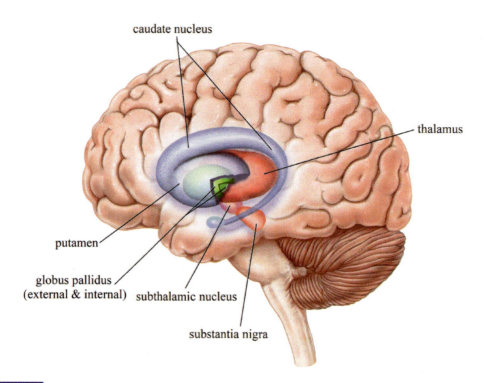

Figure 2–16. Basal ganglia and thalamus shown from lateral view of the left hemisphere. From *Clinical Neuroscience for Communication Disorders: Neuroanatomy and Neurophysiology* (p. 27) by Blake, M. L. and Hoepner, J. K. Copyright © 2023 Plural Publishing, Inc. All rights reserved.

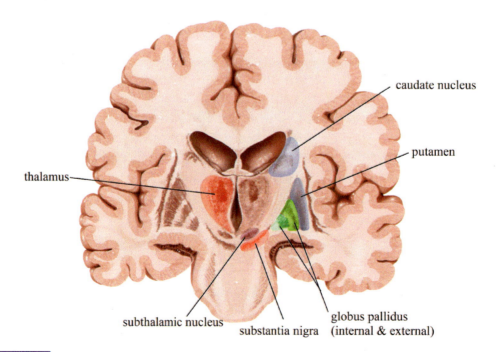

Figure 2–17. Subcortical structures in a coronal slice. Adapted from *Clinical Neuroscience for Communication Disorders: Neuroanatomy and Neurophysiology* (p. 27) by Blake, M. L. and Hoepner, J. K. Copyright © 2023 Plural Publishing, Inc. All rights reserved.

and relaying sensory signals from the body and the motor system, or to and from areas of the cortex and the brainstem to maintain consciousness, aid in language, and facilitate other cognitive processes.

Brainstem

Physically, the brainstem is the connection between the brain and the spinal cord. It is divided into three segments: the midbrain, pons, and medulla (Figure 2–18). All signals coming from the body pass through the brainstem to get to the brain and vice versa. Functionally, the brainstem keeps the body alive. Nuclei (groups of cell bodies) in the brainstem are responsible for maintaining and adjusting respiration and cardiac function. For example, when you are exercising, your heart rate and breathing both increase to bring in and circulate sufficient amounts of oxygen. Of prime interest to speech-language pathologists are the sensory and motor pathways for speech production and coordination of all the processes related to swallowing.

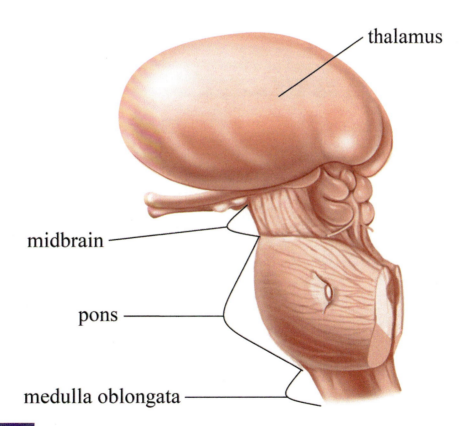

Figure 2–18. Lateral view of the brainstem with cerebellum removed. From *Clinical Neuroscience for Communication Disorders: Neuroanatomy and Neurophysiology* (p. 29) by Blake, M. L. and Hoepner, J. K. Copyright © 2023 Plural Publishing, Inc. All rights reserved.

Cranial Nerves

There are 12 pairs of cranial nerves (Table 2–2) that carry signals to/from structures of the head and neck. The first two, olfactory and optic, directly connect to the brain. All the rest enter/exit the CNS through the brainstem (Figure 2–19). Some have only sensory functions, such as the olfactory and optic nerves which carry signals related to smell and vision, respectively. Others are motor only, carrying only motor signals out to muscles. The oculomotor, trochlear, and abducens which control muscles of the eyes, are examples of motor-only cranial nerves. Yet others have both sensory (affective) and motor (effective) components.

Motor innervation through cranial nerves is primarily through the corticobulbar pathway (Figure 2–20) that begins in the cortex and ends in the brainstem (bulbar refers to the bulb-like shape of the brainstem). This provides a direct connection between the motor cortex and muscles. Upper motor neurons have cell bodies in the primary motor strip in the posterior frontal lobe. Their axons extend down through a section of white matter between the caudate nucleus and putamen called the internal capsule and continue down to the brainstem. Once in the brainstem, the axons decussate (cross over) to the opposite side and then synapse onto lower motor neuron cell bodies in cranial nerve nuclei.

Table 2–2. Cranial Nerves and Their Functions

CN	Name	Function
I	Olfactory	Special sensory for smell
II	Optic	Special sensory for vision
III	Oculomotor	Motor innervation of 4 of the 6 muscles of the eye
IV	Trochlear	Motor innervation of 1 of the 6 muscles of the eye
V	Trigeminal	Somatosensory for the face, dura, teeth, anterior tongue, mucous membranes of the mouth & nose
		Motor innervation of muscles of mastication and 1 velar muscle
VI	Abducens	Motor innervation of 1 of the 6 muscles of the eye
VII	Facial	Special sensory for taste for the anterior tongue
		Motor innervation of anterior salivary glands and muscles of facial expression
VIII	Auditory/Vestibular	Special sensory for hearing and balance
		Motor innervation of auditory hair cells

Table 2–2. *continued*		
CN	Name	Function
IX	Glossopharyngeal	Somatosensory for pharynx (including nasopharynx), posterior tongue
		Special sensory for taste from posterior tongue
		Motor innervation of the stylopharyngeous muscle and posterior salivary glands
X	Vagus	Somatosensory and motor for pharynx and larynx
		Pharyngeal branch: motor innervation of soft palate
		Superior laryngeal nerve • Internal branch: somatosensory from larynx above the vocal folds • External branch: innervation of cricothyroid muscle
		Recurrent laryngeal nerve: innervation of all intrinsic muscles of the larynx; somatosensory for region below the vocal folds
XI	Spinal accessory	Blends with vagus for motor innervation for velum, larynx; innervation of some neck muscles.
XII	Hypoglossal	Motor innervation of all intrinsic and 3 of 4 extrinsic tongue muscles

Sensory pathways can be divided into special senses and somatosensory functions. Special senses include taste, smell, vision, and hearing. Each of these has a unique pathway created by a specific series of neurons and synapses. Somatosensory pathways carry signals representing touch, pain, temperature, and proprioception (information about joint positions). Most somatosensory pathways have the same essential structure: First-order neurons with dendrites in muscles and joints extend into the spinal cord and synapse onto second-order neurons; axons of these neurons cross over to the opposite side and extend up to the thalamus where they synapse onto third-order neurons that extend to the primary sensory strip in the anterior parietal lobe. For the head and neck regions, the first-order neurons are the sensory component of the cranial nerves. They enter the brainstem and synapse onto second-order neurons in the respective cranial nerve nuclei. From there, signals are transmitted to the thalamus and from there to the primary sensory strip.

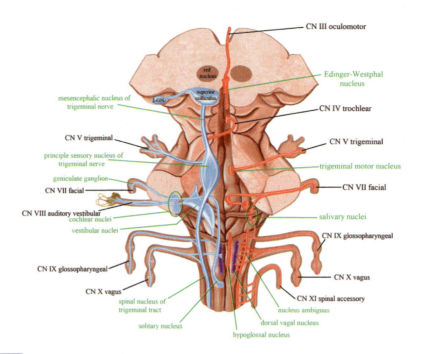

Figure 2–19. Cranial nerve nuclei for motor (red) and sensory (blue) pathways. LGN, lateral geniculate nucleus. From *Clinical Neuroscience for Communication Disorders: Neuroanatomy and Neurophysiology* (p. 175) by Blake, M. L. and Hoepner, J. K. Copyright © 2023 Plural Publishing, Inc. All rights reserved.

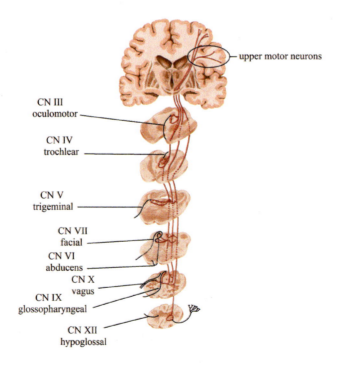

Figure 2–20. Corticobulbar pathways. Adapted from *Clinical Neuroscience for Communication Disorders: Neuroanatomy and Neurophysiology* (p. 174) by Blake, M. L. and Hoepner, J. K. Copyright © 2023 Plural Publishing, Inc. All rights reserved.

Cerebellum

The cerebellum lies posterior to the brainstem and inferior to the occipital lobe. It is attached to the brainstem by the superior, middle, and inferior cerebellar peduncles (Latin: *foot stalk*). Its primary function is in the motor system. For complex movements, the cerebellum coordinates signals to multiple muscles and muscle groups so the movements are appropriately timed and smooth, coordinated movement occurs. The cerebellum also receives sensory signals from the body; these are essentially reports on which muscles are moving, and where and when. These signals are compared to the initial plan for movement, to determine if the actual movement matched the intended movement. If there is not a match, signals from the cerebellum to the cortical motor areas adapt the movement so that successive attempts will be more successful. In this way, the cerebellum assists with error detection and motor learning. As you might suspect, the cerebellum is critically important for speech production, given the complex coordination of articulatory, pharyngeal, laryngeal, and respiratory systems required to produce even simple syllables and short strings of words or sentences.

There are three major functional regions of the cerebellum (Figure 2–21). The vestibulocerebellum of the flocculonodular lobe has connections to and from the vestibular system and cranial nuclei for the eye (oculomotor, trochlear, and abducens). It facilitates vestibular reflexes and eye movements that impact balance as well as movement planning, initiation, and timing. The connections with the vestibular system are used to coordinate limb movement for walking.

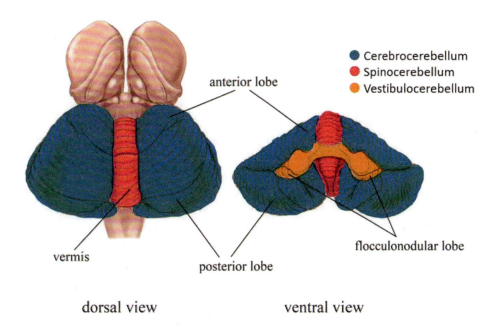

Figure 2–21. Dorsal and ventral views of the cerebellum. Adapted from *Clinical Neuroscience for Communication Disorders: Neuroanatomy and Neurophysiology* (p. 28) by Blake, M. L. and Hoepner, J. K. Copyright © 2023 Plural Publishing, Inc. All rights reserved.

The spinocerebellum is made up of the vermis and the medial cerebellar hemispheres. Somatosensory signals come in from the spinal cord through the spinocerebellar tracts, with additional inputs from the vestibular, visual, and auditory systems. Integration of these sensory inputs and the output to motor neurons in the spinal cord influence posture, locomotion, and adjustment to movement to keep us upright.

The cerebrocerebellum consists of the lateral cerebellar hemispheres which are connected to frontal lobe motor areas including the premotor and primary motor cortices. Due to these connections, the cerebrocerebellum influences motor planning and is responsible for coordination and timing of movements. It also is involved in cognitive functions.

Meninges and Ventricles

The CNS is protected by several structures and systems. Surrounding the brain and spinal cord is a set of three tissues called the **meninges** (Figure 2–22). The outer, most superficial tissue is the double layered **dura mater** (Latin: *tough mother*), which lies adjacent to the inner surface of the skull. The periosteal dural layer is closest to the skull bones; the meningeal dural layer is deeper and adjacent to the **arachnoid membrane**. Extending out from the arachnoid membrane are thin filaments of connective tissue called trabeculae that create the structure

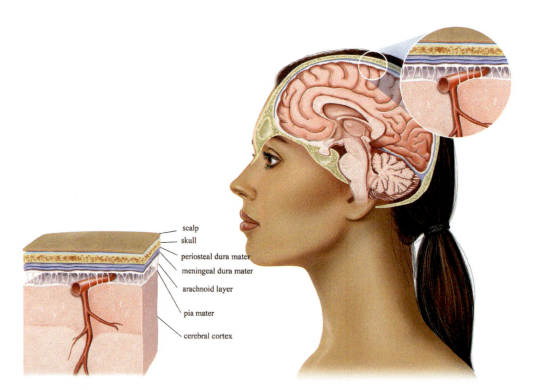

Figure 2–22. Meningeal layers. From *Clinical Neuroscience for Communication Disorders: Neuroanatomy and Neurophysiology* (p. 35) by Blake, M. L. and Hoepner, J. K. Copyright © 2023 Plural Publishing, Inc. All rights reserved.

for the **subarachnoid space**. The space is filled with **cerebrospinal fluid (CSF)**. The deepest layer of the meninges is the **pia mater** (Latin: *little mother*) which is a thin, translucent tissue that lies directly on the surface of the cortex. The meninges help to hold the brain in place so that it does not move within the skull. The presence of the CSF also aids in preventing movement of the brain. Imagine an egg inside a jar. If it were not tethered somehow (which is what the meninges do), it would easily hit the sides of the jar with nearly any movement. If the jar were filled with liquid (like the CSF within the meningeal layers), movement of the egg would be slowed because to hit the wall of the jar the egg would have to move fast enough and hard enough to displace the liquid. The meningeal layers cannot prevent all movement, as rapid acceleration/deceleration can cause the brain to move enough that it hits the inner surface of the skull, resulting in traumatic brain injury.

The **ventricular system** is a set of fluid-filled spaces and canals. There are four ventricles and a series of connectors between them (Figure 2–23). There are two C-shaped **lateral ventricles**, one in each hemisphere. Through the interventricular foramen of Monro, these are connected to the midline third ventricle which fills the space in between the right and left thalami. The **third ventricle** is connected to the fourth through the cerebral aqueduct which runs down through the brainstem. The midline **fourth ventricle** fills the space between the posterior brainstem and the cerebellum. There are four conduits out of the fourth ventricle: the spinal canal, two foramina of Luschka, and one foramen of Magendie.

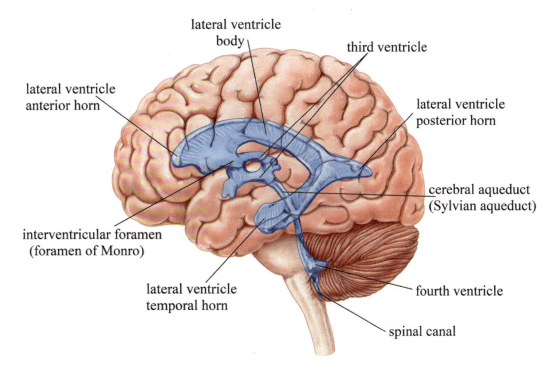

Figure 2–23. Lateral view of the ventricles in situ. Adapted from *Clinical Neuroscience for Communication Disorders: Neuroanatomy and Neurophysiology* (p. 38) by Blake, M. L. and Hoepner, J. K. Copyright © 2023 Plural Publishing, Inc. All rights reserved.

The fluid filling the ventricular system is CSF. It is produced by choroid plexus cells in the ventricles and flows from the lateral to the third and then to the fourth ventricle. From there, it can flow either down the spinal cord in the spinal canal, or through the foramina of Luschka and Magendie which connect to the subarachnoid space. CSF thus both fills spaces within the brain and surrounds the entire CNS. In addition to providing the cushioning protection, CSF provides a system for rapidly transmitting hormones throughout the CNS.

Blood Supply to the Brain

The brain requires a constant supply of blood to provide neurons and glia with the oxygen and glucose they need to survive. There are two sets of arteries that extend to the brain (Figure 2–24). Anteriorly are the right and left carotid arteries. These split into the **external carotid** that supplies blood to the face and scalp and the **internal carotid** that enters

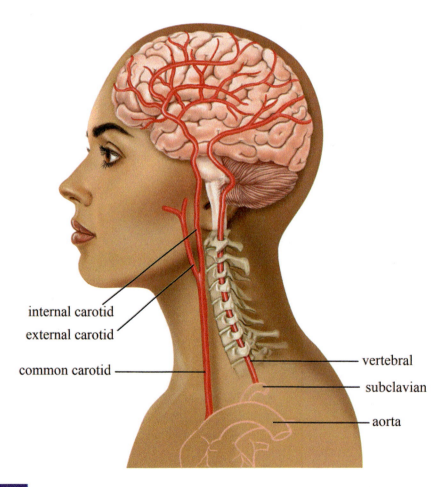

Figure 2–24. Arteries extending from the heart to the brain. From *Clinical Neuroscience for Communication Disorders: Neuroanatomy and Neurophysiology* (p. 219) by Blake, M. L. and Hoepner, J. K. Copyright © 2023 Plural Publishing, Inc. All rights reserved.

the cranium and supplies the majority of the brain. Posteriorly, the right and left **vertebral arteries** extend up through the vertebral column and supply the brainstem, cerebellum, and posterior and inferior regions of the brain.

At the base of the brain the main arteries feed into a structure called the **circle of Willis** (Figure 2–25). From this structure, three pairs of cerebral arteries exit to carry blood to the cerebral hemispheres (Figure 2–26). The **anterior cerebral artery (ACA)** extends anteriorly through the sagittal sulcus and then curves posteriorly along the medial surface of each hemisphere, supplying the medial frontal and parietal lobes. The **middle cerebral artery (MCA)** extends laterally through the sylvian fissure to supply the lateral surface of the frontal, parietal, and temporal lobes. Branches off the MCA supply some regions of the basal ganglia. The **posterior cerebral artery (PCA)** comes from the vertebral system. At the base of the pons, the left and right vertebral arteries fuse to form the **basilar artery**. Branches extend from the basilar to supply the brainstem and cerebellum. At the level of the midbrain, the

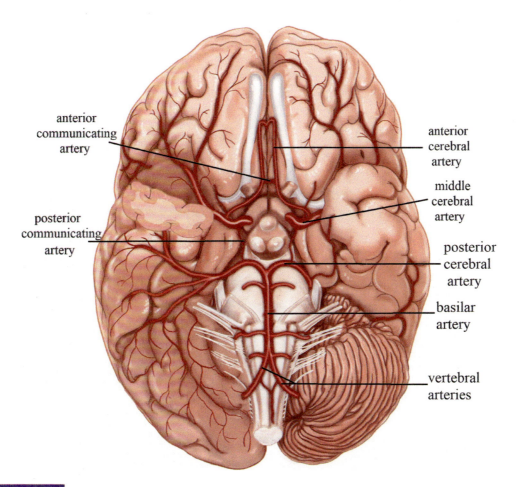

Figure 2–25. Circle of Willis in the context of the inferior surface of the brain. From *Clinical Neuroscience for Communication Disorders: Neuroanatomy and Neurophysiology* (p. 221) by Blake, M. L. and Hoepner, J. K. Copyright © 2023 Plural Publishing, Inc. All rights reserved.

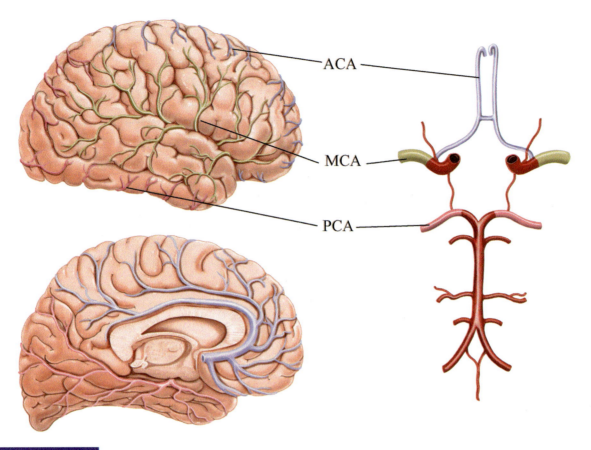

Figure 2–26. Cerebral artery branches on the lateral, medial, and inferior surfaces of the brain. Adapted from *Clinical Neuroscience for Communication Disorders: Neuroanatomy and Neurophysiology* (p. 222) by Blake, M. L. and Hoepner, J. K. Copyright © 2023 Plural Publishing, Inc. All rights reserved.

basilar artery splits into the right and left PCAs. The PCAs supply the inferior surface of the temporal lobe, the thalamus, and the occipital lobe.

Neurophysiology

All of the things you can do, from unconscious reflexes to deep thoughts and creativity, are a result of neuronal function. While it might seem like there must be hundreds or thousands of different signals neurons can send to do all these things, there are actually only two: **excitatory** and **inhibitory**. Essentially, any one neuron can only "tell" another neuron to send a signal (go) or to not send a signal (no go). The combination of thousands of go and no go signals coming from different functional areas and the patterns and timing of these signals create all of the abilities and functions of the brain.

Neurons communicate by using a combination of electrical and chemical signals. Within a neuron, signals generated in the soma and transmitted down the axon are electrical, and are created and driven by the exchange of charged particles called **ions**. This electrical signal is called an **action potential**. Once the action potential reaches the axon terminal at the end of an axon it triggers the release of chemicals called **neurotransmitters** (Table 2–3) stored in the axon terminal. The neurotransmitters are released into a small gap in between the axon terminal of the sending neuron and the dendrites or soma of the receiving neuron. This point of communication between neurons is called a synapse. At the synapse, the released neurotransmitters bind to **receptors** on the receiving neuron. This causes an electrical change

Table 2–3. Common Neurotransmitters

Neurotransmitter	Location	Function	Effects of Disruption
Gamma-amino butyric acid (GABA)	Cortex, hippocampus, cerebellum	Inhibitory effects and regulation	Huntington disease
Glutamate (Glu)	Various areas within the CNS	Fast synaptic transmission	Schizophrenia
Acetylcholine (ACh)	Neuromuscular junction	Voluntary movement; some involuntary movement	Myasthenia gravis, weakness, paralysis
	Frontal lobes, hippocampus	Cognitive networks, memory processes	Alzheimer disease
Dopamine (DA)	Basal ganglia	Motor system	Parkinson disease
	Frontal lobes, limbic system, reward centers	Reward behaviors, motivation	Gambling/sex addictions; cognitive deficits
Epinephrine	Sympathetic nervous system, through bloodstream	Increases heart rate, muscle activation, blood pressure, and sugar metabolism	Anxiety, depression, blood pressure changes (low levels) Tachycardia, hypertension, anxiety, weight loss, and excessive sweating (elevated levels)

continues

Table 2–3. continued

Neurotransmitter	Location	Function	Effects of Disruption
Norepinephrine (NE)	Brainstem (locus coeruleus), thalamus, cortex, limbic system	Attention & vigilance	Anxiety, depression, lethargy, inattention (low levels) Hypertension, sweating, irregular heartbeats, headaches (elevated levels)
	Sympathetic nervous system	Fight or flight response	
Serotonin (5-HT)	Various areas within the CNS	Sleep cycles, mood, modulation of pain input	Depression

in the receiving neuron. An excitatory change makes the receiving neuron more likely to generate an action potential and send a signal to a new target neuron (go). An inhibitory change makes that neuron less likely to generate an action potential (no go). Whether or not a signal is excitatory or inhibitory is based on the neurotransmitter and the receptor. Some neurotransmitters tend to create excitatory changes most of the time (e.g., acetylcholine), while others almost always are inhibitory (e.g., GABA), and still others can create either excitatory or inhibitory responses depending on the type of receptor on the receiving neuron (e.g., dopamine).

Typical Aging

While acquired neurogenic disorders can occur at any age, most of the patients and clients on a speech-language pathologist's (SLP) caseload will be adults. As with all systems and structures in the body, the CNS declines as part of the typical aging processes. Some neurons and glial cells die off, leaving atrophy of the cortex and enlargement of the ventricles. The glial cell lining of the ventricles begins to break down, allowing some CSF to leak into the brain tissue. Cognitive, communication, and swallowing changes can occur. The C-shaped principle of development and decline states that the structures that developed or matured last are the first to decline. As shown in Figure 2–27, these include the prefrontal lobes and anterior temporal regions. As a result, memory and attention decline, and language can become less precise

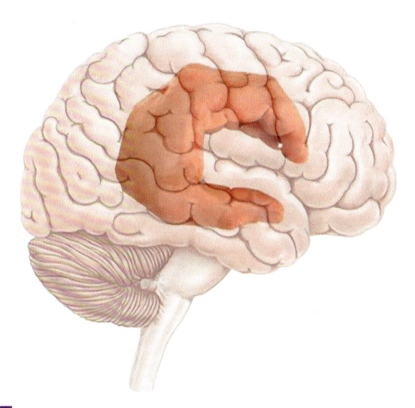

Figure 2–27. Principle of C-shaped development and degeneration. Regions at the tips of the C shape develop last and degenerate first.

but generally remains accurate. Peripheral changes in muscle physiology can impact speech and swallowing and decreases in hearing and visual acuity can impact communication. This all sounds bad, but the functional communication and cognitive changes associated with healthy aging processes should not affect one's basic daily activities. Changes that do impact such activities may be related to a disease process and should be evaluated by a physician.

⊘ Summary

A solid knowledge of brain anatomy and physiology is important for understanding how damage to the structures and systems can affect communication, cognition, and swallowing. Damage or dysfunction to different regions or structures results in different disorders and impairments. Any component of neuronal structure or function can be affected, including damage to the cell bodies or axons that results in neuronal death (stroke, traumatic brain injury); changes in the amount of neurotransmitter available (Parkinson disease); disruption of functions within the neuron (Alzheimer disease); or slowing of electrical transmission in the axon (multiple sclerosis). Pressure on the brain from tumors or excess CSF (causing hydrocephalus) can impact neurons' ability to function. Specific diseases and disorders that commonly affect communication and swallowing will be covered in more detail in Chapter 3. Typical speech, language, cognitive, and swallowing disorders related to damage to regions of the central nervous system will be covered in the rest of the chapters.

Key Concepts

- The two hemispheres are divided into four lobes and the insula. These each have some specific functions and are highly interconnected with other areas.
- Gray matter in the cortex, nuclei, and ganglia is made up of neuron cell bodies.
- White matter tracts/pathways are created by axons.
- The central nervous system is protected by the meningeal layers and ventricular system.
- Blood travels to the brain through two major artery systems. Three pairs of cerebral arteries (anterior, middle, and posterior cerebral arteries) carry blood to the cerebral hemispheres.
- Sensorimotor pathways are created by a series of neurons that transmit signals from the body to the brain (sensory) and from the brain to the body (motor).
- Aging is accompanied by slow decline of CNS structures and functions that can impact communication and swallowing to some degree.

Reference

Uddin, L. Q., Nomi, J. S., Hébert-Seropian, B., Ghaziri, J., & Boucher, O. (2017). Structure and function of the human insula. *Journal of Clinical Neurophysiology, 34*(4), 300–306. https://doi.org/10.1097/WNP.0000000000000377

3
ETIOLOGIES AND PATHOPHYSIOLOGY

Chapter Overview

Etiologies
   Stroke
   Anoxia and Hypoxia
   Tumors
   Traumatic Brain Injury
   Degenerative Diseases
      Dementias
      Parkinson Disease
      Huntington Disease
      Multiple Sclerosis
      Amyotrophic Lateral Sclerosis
   Infectious Diseases
Prevalence Patterns
Brain Imaging
   Anatomical/Structural Imaging
   Functional Imaging
Concepts for Understanding Effects of Brain Injury
Summary
Key Concepts
References

Etiologies

Acquired neurogenic communication and swallowing disorders result from a variety of sources, including interruption of oxygen or blood supply (anoxia, stroke), abnormal growths (tumor), traumatic injuries to the head/brain, degenerative diseases that alter the physiological processes of neurons, and infectious diseases. Each of these impacts the health and/or

Box 3–1 Latin/Greek Roots: Traditions of Nomenclature

Medical terminology is based on Latin and Greek. In general, Latin is the basis for anatomical terms and Greek is the basis for clinical terms. Table 3–1 contains common medical prefixes and suffixes. There are several traditions in naming. One is to use descriptive naming, referring to the shape (e.g., pars triangularis, shaped like a triangle), function (e.g., abducens cranial nerve which innervates the muscles that abduct the eye), or location (e.g., the superior temporal gyrus). Other names are based on the people who first (or most publicly) described a region/location/function/disease, or as a tribute to outstanding work in the field. This tradition has led to names for diseases such as Alzheimer and Parkinson, Broca's and Wernicke's language areas in the left hemisphere, the Sylvian fissure and sulcus of Rolando, etc.

Geographically specific names for diseases also sometimes occur due to famous people who develop diseases, such as the use of Lou Gehrig disease in the United States as a name for amyotrophic lateral sclerosis (ALS), also known as motor neurone disease (to which my friend from Wales says, "Who the heck is Lou Gehrig?").

Descriptive terminology is preferred by many because it provides useful information. It also avoids problems with naming after people: most names are of European white males; most discoveries are not made by a single person (e.g., there is a long-standing argument that Marc Dax and Paul Broca drew conclusions about the left inferior frontal language area at about the same time); and famous physicians, flawed like all humans, can be found to have beliefs or actions that no longer are acceptable (e.g., recent attention to Paul Broca's racist beliefs).

Table 3–1. Common Medical Prefixes and Suffixes.

Prefix	Meaning	Suffix	Meaning
A- or an-	without, not	-ac	pertaining to (e.g., cardiac)
Brady-	slow	-algia	pain
Cephalon-	pertaining to the head	-gnosis	knowledge
Cerebro-	pertaining to the brain (cerebrum)	-oid	resembling
Cerebello-	pertaining to the cerebellum	-ole	small, little

Table 3–1. continued

Prefix	Meaning	Suffix	Meaning
Contra-	opposing, opposite	-oma	tumor, mass, fluid
Cranio-	pertaining to the skull/cranium	-opsy	inspection, examination
Di-	Greek: two Latin: apart or separated	-osis	condition or disease
Dys- or dis-	disrupted, abnormal	-paresis	weakness
Hema- or Hemo-	related to the blood	-pathy	disease or negative condition
Hypo-	not enough, reduced, below normal	-phage or -phago or -phagia	relating to eating
Hyper-	too much, extreme, more than normal	-plegia	paralysis
Idio-	one's self	-plexy	stroke, seizure
Inter-	between, among	-ptosis	falling, drooping
Intra-	within	-rrhage or -rrhagia	burst, rapid flow
Ipsi-	same	-sclerosis	hardening
Myo-	pertaining to muscle	-stasis	stop, stand
Meyl-	pertaining to spinal cord or bone marrow	-stenosis	narrowing
Patho-	disease	-tension or -tensive	pressure
Per-	through	-tic	pertaining to
Peri-	surrounding or around	-tomy	cutting or incision

continues

Table 3–1. continued			
Prefix	Meaning	Suffix	Meaning
Phren- or Phrenic	relating to the mind	-trophy	development or nourishment
Poly-	many, multiple, a lot	-ula, -ule	small
Pre- or pro-	before or in front of		
Somato-	pertaining to the body		
Sub-	below, beneath, under		
Super- or supra-	above, in excess		
Sy-, syl-, sym-, syn-, sys-	similarity, belonging together		
Terato-	monster		
Thromb- or thrombo-	related to a blood clot		
Thym-	relating to emotions		
Toxi, toxo, toxico-	poison, toxin		
Uni-	one		
Vaso- or vasculo-	related to veins		
Ventriclo-	related to ventricles		

function of CNS neurons. The extent and location of the damage within the brain determines the type and severity of communication, cognition, and/or swallowing deficits.

Stroke

Strokes, or **cerebrovascular accidents (CVAs)**, are caused by interruption of the blood supply. Neurons have no mechanism for storing oxygen, so they rely on a continuous and consistent blood supply to deliver oxygen and glucose. Significant reduction in the cerebral blood flow for more than a few minutes will cause irreversible brain damage.

> ### Box 3-2 Be Fast
>
> The acronym BE FAST (Aroor et al., 2017) can aid in determining if someone is having a stroke. In the case of a stroke, the changes typically occur suddenly and on one side of the body.
>
> B—balance: difficulty with balance or coordination. Watch them attempt to stand or walk and ask if they feel dizzy
> E—eyes: loss of vision, double vision, or blurred vision
> F—face: drooping or asymmetry of the face. Ask them to smile & look for asymmetry
> A—arms: weakness or numbness on one side. Ask them to raise both arms & look for asymmetry
> S—speech: slurred speech or difficulty understanding speech. Ask them to repeat a sentence & see if they understand you and correctly repeat the sentence. Pay attention to articulation and word or sound errors.
> T—time: Call 911 immediately! The faster you get treatment, the fewer brain cells will die. Remember that "Time = Brain."

Every year strokes affect 15 million people worldwide (World Health Organization, 2023), with nearly 800,000 of them in the United States.. Three-fourths of these are first-time strokes (Centers for Disease Control and Prevention, 2022). It is estimated that 70% of cardiovascular disease events (e.g., stroke, heart diseases, peripheral artery disease) are directly related to moderate or poor cardiovascular health, and that improving such health has the potential to decrease the number of cardiovascular events by 1.2 to 2 million annually (Tsao et al., 2022). In addition to the impact on health and well-being, this would substantially reduce the economic impact, as the direct (e.g., hospitalization and medical treatment) and indirect (e.g., loss of wages) costs of stroke in the United States exceed $375 billion annually.

There are two major types of stroke: ischemic and hemorrhagic. **Ischemic** (Greek/Latin: *stopping blood*) strokes are caused by blockage in the arterial blood supply that prevents the oxygenated blood from reaching the neurons it supplies. Approximately 90% of strokes are ischemic. A **thrombotic ischemic stroke** occurs when internal carotid or cerebral arteries are narrowed by the buildup of fatty plaques on the internal surface of blood vessels and/or blood clots form within the cerebral arteries and block the flow of blood (Figure 3–1A). **Embolic ischemic strokes** are caused by blood clots that form somewhere in the body (e.g., deep vein thrombosis in the legs, or clots created in the heart by churning of the blood through the ventricles during atrial fibrillation), and travel through the bloodstream until they get wedged into a narrow artery within the brain (Figures 3–1B and C). Within minutes of insufficient oxygen, neurons will begin to die off. Neurons in the ischemic core are those that die due to lack of oxygen. Surrounding this core is a region called the **ischemic penumbra** (Latin: *almost shadow*) in which the neurons are getting just enough oxygen to survive, but

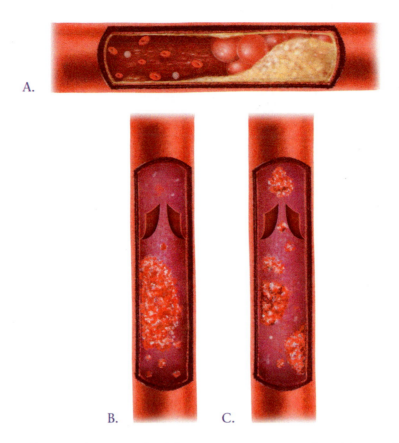

Figure 3–1. A. Fatty plaques inside an artery restrict blood flow. B. Blood clot forming in a blood vessel. C. Blood clot breaking off and flowing through blood vessel.

not enough to fully function (Figure 3–2). If blood flow can be restored, these neurons will be revived. If blood flow is not restored, the penumbra neurons also may die off, extending the size and extent of the stroke.

Hemorrhagic (Greek/Latin: *bleeding violently* related to a *break* or *burst*) strokes occur when a blood vessel tears or bursts and blood spills out (Figure 3–3). The resulting pool of blood is called a **hematoma**. When this occurs just under the skin, the hematoma is called a bruise; it is caused by a broken blood vessel (such as from stubbing your toe or getting your finger pinched in a door) and the resulting pool of blood. In the brain, descriptive labels are used based on the location (Figure 3–4). **Epidural hematomas** are typically caused by trauma and result in blood between the dura mater and the skull. **Subdural hematomas** occur between the dura mater and the arachnoid layers of the meninges and are most often due to traumatic injuries. **Subarachnoid hemorrhages** and resulting hematomas are between the arachnoid and pia mater. **Intracerebral hemorrhages** occur within the brain tissue, with blood spilling out around the neurons and glia. The latter two are most often caused by aneurysms, which are weak areas of the wall of blood vessels that break or burst (Figure 3–5). All of these hemorrhages fall under the category of **intracranial hemorrhages** since they

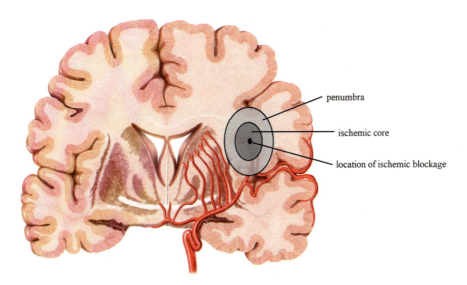

Figure 3–2. Ischemic core and penumbra. From *Clinical Neuroscience for Communication Disorders: Neuroanatomy and Neurophysiology* (p. 232) by Blake, M. L. and Hoepner, J. K. Copyright © 2023 Plural Publishing, Inc. All rights reserved.

> ### Box 3–3 "He's only mostly dead"
>
> Fans of the movie The Princess Bride will surely recall Miracle Max announcing that the hero Wesley was only "mostly dead" and could be restored to full health. Neurons in the ischemic penumbra are in a similar state. They cannot fully function, but can be revived if blood flow is restored. If you haven't seen the movie, we strongly suggest you do during your next break from studying neurogenic communication disorders.

occur within the cranium, and can cause increased intracranial pressure, which can have dire consequences. Remember that the skull is formed by fused bones; when there are extra substances (e.g., spilled blood) in or around the brain the skull cannot expand to accommodate them, and as a result the brain itself is compressed.

For intracerebral hemorrhages, brain damage occurs in three ways: first from the insufficient blood supply to regions distal from the burst blood vessel; second from the pressure on the neural tissue due to spilled blood, swelling, and inflammation; and third from **vasogenic cytotoxicity**, in which contents of the blood are toxic to the neurons and glial cells. Inflammation and swelling are normal healing processes of the body. Unfortunately, when these occur in the brain, they create additional problems due to the pressure within the enclosed bony skull.

Regardless of the type, strokes affect relatively focal areas of the brain, and any one ischemic stroke affects only one hemisphere of the brain. As a result, the communication and swallowing deficits can be predicted to some extent based on the specific location of

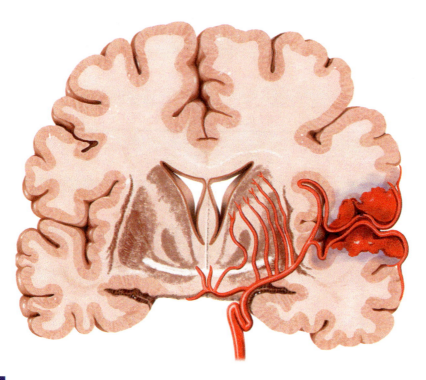

Figure 3–3. Intracerebral hemorrhagic stroke.

the damage. Beyond the focal area of damage, however, there can be additional brain areas affected. **Diaschisis** (Greek: *shocked through*) is a phenomenon in which there is reduced metabolism and neuronal function in a region of the brain remote from the damage. For example, a cerebellar stroke can be accompanied by reduced metabolism in the motor cortex of the frontal lobes. The remote area affected by diaschisis is always one that has neuronal connections to the lesion site, and the reduced function is due to damaged neurons no longer sending excitatory signals to the remote region. In the cerebellar example, there are cerebrocerebellar pathways connecting the cerebellum with the frontal lobe (see Chapter 11). When cerebellar neurons are damaged, they can no longer send signals to the frontal lobe. As a result, the frontal lobe neurons no longer receive these signals, so their function is reduced. In most cases, diaschisis is temporary. The resolution of the diaschisis is one explanation of spontaneous recovery that happens in the early days and weeks post stroke.

Anoxia and Hypoxia

Anoxia (no oxygen) is a loss of oxygen supply to the brain. **Hypoxia** (low oxygen) is a substantial reduction in oxygen supply. These occur either when blood flow is restricted, or when there is not enough oxygen in the blood that reaches the brain (Lacerte, Hays Shapshak, & Mesfin, 2023). Toxic anoxia occurs in the case of carbon monoxide poisoning. The carbon molecules take the place of oxygen in the bloodstream and because neurons cannot "breathe"

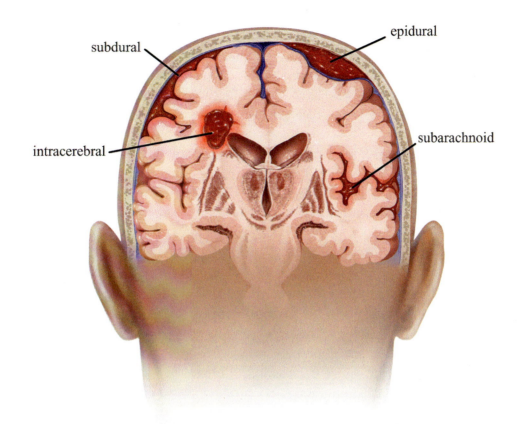

Figure 3-4. Hematomas in and around the brain.

Figure 3-5. Berry aneurysm: intact and bursting.

carbon, they start to die off. Anoxic anoxia occurs when the lungs are unable to bring in enough oxygen, so the blood continues to flow to the brain without carrying enough oxygen molecules. In some cases, there is insufficient oxygen in the environment such as at extreme elevations, near-drowning incidents, or asphyxiation (Greek: *stopping of the pulse;* oxygen deprivation that results in death). In other cases, the underlying problem is lung function, such as in asthma or chronic obstructive pulmonary disease (COPD). Stagnant anoxia occurs when blood supply, and as a result, oxygen supply, is limited. Heart attacks are a common cause of hypoxic-anoxic brain injury because there is insufficient blood pumped to the brain. Strokes also cause stagnant anoxia because they interrupt the blood supply. However, strokes are commonly considered a separate category of brain injuries (and will be in this book), because the anoxia is restricted to a single area and causes relatively focal damage while all the other types of hypoxia-anoxia result in generalized damage to the brain. The widespread effect on the brain impacts higher-level brain functions such as cognition and attention as well as coordinated movement. The brainstem is particularly sensitive to changes in oxygen, so loss of consciousness commonly occurs.

Tumors

Tumors are abnormal masses of tissue caused either by abnormally rapid reproduction of cells or cells that do not degenerate/degrade as they should. **Malignant** tumors are cancerous; **benign** tumors are not. Malignant tumors also can metastasize (Greek: *to rapidly move from one point to another*) which occurs when cells break off and travel through the blood supply or lymphatic system to new areas of the body and create tumors in that new area. Tumors occupy space, which is a critical characteristic in the CNS because any mass that develops within the cranium will put pressure on the brain due to the fused bones of the cranium that cannot expand in response to the growth of the tumor. Thus, both benign and malignant brain tumors can have devastating consequences.

Brain tumors are classified by their cellular makeup and/or their location (Figure 3–6). Gliomas affect glial cells, such as astrocytomas (astrocytes), oligodendrogliomas (oligodendrocytes), schwannomas (Schwann cells), ependymomas (ependymal cells) and glioblastomas. Meningiomas form in the meninges; medulloblastomas affect the medulla. The morphology of the tumor (whether it is encapsulated or if it has extensions), and the location in relation to important areas (language) or critical centers (brainstem cardiac and respiratory) and ease of access—all are considered in decisions about surgical removal.

Consequences of brain tumors depend on their location, the rate of growth, and responsiveness to treatments. Slow-growing tumors in the cerebral hemispheres can reach relatively large sizes before they cause lasting signs or symptoms because the brain adapts over time. Rapid-growing tumors, those that impact the blood supply, or those that impact the brainstem can have dramatic consequences even at small sizes. This is because they interrupt normal function before the brain can adapt or impact the functions of the brainstem that keep the body alive such as cardiac and respiratory functions. In some cases, **herniation** can occur when cerebral brain tissue is squeezed through the foramen magnum due to the added pressure of a tumor within the closed cranium. Midline shift occurs when left hemisphere structures are compressed past midline into the right side of the cranium or vice versa (Figure 3–7).

Treatments for tumors such as radiation and chemotherapy, while impacting the tumors themselves, also can have negative effects on brain function. Chemotherapy in particular has been linked to declines in cognitive function (commonly known as chemobrain), even

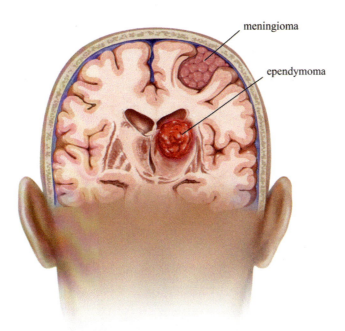

Figure 3–6. Meningioma and ependymoma. Note midline shift of thalamus.

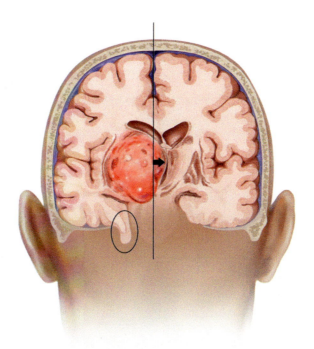

Figure 3–7. Glioblastoma causing herniation of medial temporal lobe (*circled*) and midline shift (*arrow*).

when it is used to target cancers outside of the brain, such as breast cancer (Mounier et al., 2020). Steroid-based palliative and short-term treatments for tumors also can have a negative impact on cognition (Dietrich et al., 2011).

Traumatic Brain Injury

Traumatic brain injuries occur when there is sudden impact to the brain, often causing movement of the brain within the cranium (Figure 3–8). In most cases TBI is a result of an external impact, such as a car accident, a sporting event (being hit by a ball or another athlete), or hitting one's head in a fall. Violent shaking (e.g., shaken baby syndrome) or intimate partner violence that includes blows to the head also can result in TBI. Additionally, blast injuries can cause TBI. The sudden, extreme change in air pressure caused by an explosion can radiate into the body and interrupt normal brain physiology. The term **concussion** is used for mild traumatic brain injuries that commonly (but not always) resolve within days or weeks. All of these are closed head injuries, in which the skull remains intact. Open head injuries, such as from a gunshot wound or shrapnel that pierces the skull, also fall under the category TBI. The damage from open head injuries is more likely to be focal, while diffuse brain injury is common with closed head injuries.

Two primary forms of damage occur with TBI. One is focal contusions caused by the brain hitting the inner surface of the skull. A contusion at the site of the impact is called the **coup** (Latin: *blow*) injury. If the impact was great enough to cause a rebounding of the

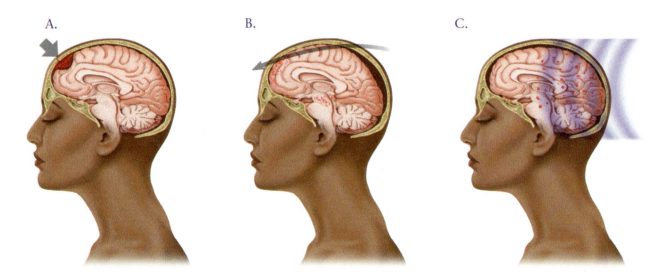

Figure 3–8. Mechanisms of traumatic brain injury. A. Focal impact with hematoma. B. Acceleration-deceleration injury to frontal and posterior regions. C. Blast injury causing diffuse injury.

> ### Box 3–4 Sex Differences in Brain Injury
>
> TBIs in young children (0–4 years old) and older adults (over 65) affect males and females similarly. In these age groups, TBIs are most often due to falls. Male and female children and older adults have similar risks due to physical development and aging processes. During the adolescent and early adult years, males traditionally were at greater risk, with a ratio of up to 4:1 compared to females, due to their greater participation in contact sports (think hockey and American football), extreme sports (e.g., rock climbing), and riskier driving behaviors. While there still is a difference in risk, it has decreased as women are drinking more alcohol and participating in more contact and extreme sports.
>
> Specifically for concussion, males and females are equally likely to incur concussions in limited contact activities such as baseball, gymnastics, skateboarding, and volleyball. In contact sports, males most often incur concussions in football and females in soccer (Sarmiento et al., 2019). The risk of concussion and TBI due to intimate partner violence more commonly affecting females has only recently started garnering attention.
>
> Unfortunately, treatment recommendations and public awareness are not keeping up with the changes in behavior. Sports concussion protocols for making return-to-play decisions are largely based on research with males and do not take into account factors that may impact females such as hormonal fluctuations, increased reporting of symptoms, and different timeline of recovery.
>
> The Pink Concussion group is a great resource for information about women and TBI. https://www.pinkconcussions.com
>
> Sarmiento, K., Thomas, K. E., Daugherty, J., Waltzman, D., Haarbauer-Krupa, J. K., Peterson, A. B., . . . Breiding, M. J. (2019). Emergency department visits for sports- and recreation-related traumatic brain injuries among children – United States, 2010–2016. *Morbidity and Mortality Weekly Report, 68*(10), 237–242. https://doi.org/10.15585/mmwr.mm6810a2. PMID: 30870404; PMCID: PMC6421963.

brain, a **contrecoup** injury can occur as the brain "bounces back" and hits the opposite wall of the skull. The second form of damage is **diffuse axonal injury** (DAI; also called traumatic axonal injury). The movement of the brain within the skull can cause stretching and tearing of axons as more dense areas move further and faster than less dense areas (Figure 3–9). DAI is more common with rotational than linear movement of the brain; a hit that causes the head to rotate usually results in more damage than one that causes either left-right or front-back movement.

Additional damage can occur in the hours and days after the injury. If there is damage to blood vessels, there will be hemorrhages and hematomas that not only interrupt the blood supply but also increase intracranial pressure. **Edema** (swelling) occurs as glial cells

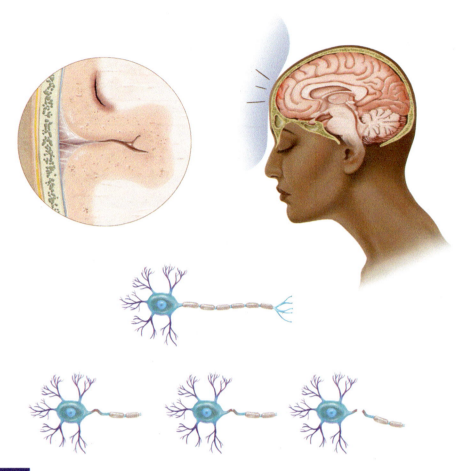

Figure 3–9. Traumatic brain injury causing axonal tearing and damage at the gray-white border.

migrate to the area to assist with the cleanup and recovery processes. This too, adds to intracranial pressure and impacts neurons' ability to function. **Excitotoxicity** occurs as excitatory neurotransmitters that spill out of the damaged neurons have a toxic effect on nearby neurons. The pressure on the CNS structures can obstruct the ventricular system causing hydrocephalus, and seizures can occur.

Blast injuries affect the brain in multiple ways (Bryden et al., 2019). First, the extreme change in air pressure interrupts the neuron physiology and can result in a mild TBI. The exact mechanism is unclear, but the pressure wave differentially affects air- and fluid-filled organs. The cerebrospinal fluid within the CNS and the extensive cerebrovascular system can be affected, and bubbles of gases are created from the fluid. Second, shrapnel from explosions that impact the head can cause open head injuries and focal damage to the brain. Third, if the person is pushed to the ground or against a solid object due to the blast wind, they can hit their head, causing another TBI. Finally, there can be damage caused by products of the explosion, such as inhalation of toxic gases that get into the bloodstream.

The effects of traumatic brain injury are varied. Focal contusions will cause relatively predictable deficits based on location. DAI and increased intracranial pressure result in a broad range of cognitive, speech, language, swallowing, and sensorimotor deficits. Concussions typically interrupt physiological processes that can recover within days or weeks without permanent damage to neurons. However, there can be lasting effects, particularly after multiple concussions.

Degenerative Diseases

There are many diseases that impact the function of neurons and glial cells. Here we will cover only those that most commonly affect communication and/or swallowing. In-depth discussions of the diseases and their effects on cognition, communication, and swallowing, are included in future chapters.

Dementias

Dementia is a general term for degenerative changes that primarily impact cognition. Two main types of dementia are proteinopathies and vascular dementias. Proteinopathies are characterized by abnormal collections of proteins in neurons that interrupt function and result in neuronal death. Each of the proteinopathies is characterized by damage to brain regions and the associated primary deficits (Table 3–2). Alzheimer disease is the most common type of dementia. Figures 3–10 and 3–11 illustrate the cortical and hippocampal degeneration and resulting atrophy that occurs with Alzheimer disease.

Vascular dementia is a result of changes to the cerebral vasculature (blood vessels) that cause small strokes (both infarcts and hemorrhages) as well as white matter damage. Blood vessels decrease in diameter each time they branch, so the most distal blood vessels are very small. This makes them susceptible to even small amounts of atherosclerotic buildup and tiny blood clots. Together these changes are commonly referred to as small vessel disease. White matter damage includes demyelination, astrocytosis, and damage to axons that ultimately leads to neuronal death. Early in their course, the small strokes can go unnoticed or cause limited deficits that may not have much impact on daily communication or activities. Over time, the amount of brain tissue affected by the strokes adds up, and the deficits become more noticeable either because of a reduction in plasticity, meaning the remaining tissue cannot compensate for the losses, or because a critical mass of neurons responsible for specific functions has been affected. The resulting cognitive, communication, and swallowing deficits depend on the location of the damage.

Reversible or pseudo-dementias are changes to cognitive function related to a treatable source. In older adults a common cause is polypharmacy, or the use of multiple prescription drugs that cause drug interactions. Other causes include depression, metabolic imbalances, infection, or inflammation. For each of these, once the underlying cause is addressed, cognitive deficits are reversed.

Parkinson Disease

Parkinson disease results from loss of dopaminergic neurons (neurons that produce or use the neurotransmitter dopamine) in the substantia nigra, a small nucleus in the upper midbrain (Figure 3–12). Initially, changes to the substantia nigra tend to be unilateral but eventually progress to bilateral degeneration of dopaminergic neurons. The reduction in dopamine in the basal ganglia circuits results in the characteristic changes in the motor system including reduction of movement (masked face, shuffling gait, soft voice, and imprecise articulation) and resting tremors. The motor deficits impact speech and swallowing. Cognitive deficits occur later in the disease as frontal lobe dopaminergic circuits are affected.

Table 3–2. Types and Pathologies of Proteinopathic Dementias

Classification	Subtypes	Cortical	Subcortical	Brain Regions Affected
Prion	Creutzfeld-Jacob disease (CJD)	✔	✔	cortex, basal ganglia, thalamus, cerebellum (potentially throughout CNS – primarily grey matter)
	Fatal Familial Insomnia (FFI)			
	Gerstmann-Sträussler-Scheinker disease (GSS)			
Alzheimer	Amnestic	✔		medial temporal lobe and entorhinal cortex
	Behavioral and dysexecutive	✔		prefrontal cortices, entorhinal cortex
	Logopenic primary progressive aphasia (PPA)	✔		left middle-posterior temporal gyrus, angular gyrus, precuneus, hippocampus, and left inferior parietal
	Visuoperceptive	✔		right inferior parietal, posterior temporal
	Posterior cortical atrophy	✔		parietal, occipital and occipito-temporal cortices

Table 3–2. *continued*

Classification	Subtypes	Cortical	Subcortical	Brain Regions Affected
Frontotemporal	Behavioral	✔		orbitomedial prefrontal cortices and anterior temporal lobes
	Non-fluent primary progressive aphasia (PPA)	✔		left inferior frontal gyrus, sma, motor strip, and insula
	Semantic primary progressive aphasia (PPA)	✔		anterior temporal lobe bilaterally (left > right)
	Frontotemporal dementia with motor neuron disease (FTD-MND)	✔		frontal and temporal lobes, hypoglossal nucleus motor neurons, and spinal motor neurons
	Cortico-basal degeneration (CBD)	✔	✔	superior fronto-parietal regions, primary motor and somatosensory cortices, anterior corpus callosum, putamen, and median substantia nigra
	Progressive supranuclear palsy (PSP)		✔	subthalamic nucleus, globus pallidus, striatum, red nucleus, substantia nigra, pontine tegmentum, oculomotor nucleus, medulla, and dentate nucleus

continues

Table 3–2. *continued*				
Classification	Subtypes	Cortical	Subcortical	Brain Regions Affected
Lewy-body	Lewy body dementia (LBD) Parkinson's dementia		✔	basal ganglia, subthalamic nucleus, substantia nigra, globus pallidus, and brainstem

Source: Clinical Neuroscience for Communication Disorders: Neuroanatomy and Neurophysiology (p. 242) by Blake, M. L. and Hoepner, J. K. Copyright © 2023 Plural Publishing, Inc. All rights reserved.

Huntington Disease

Huntington disease is a result of degeneration of inhibitory neurons in the caudate nucleus (Figure 3–13). The degeneration alters the balance between inhibitory and excitatory signals in the basal ganglia circuits and causes unwanted movements. The characteristic movements are "dance-like," complex choreiform movements. The changes to the motor system primarily impact speech and swallowing. Cognitive and behavioral changes also occur due to the connections between the basal ganglia and frontal lobes.

Multiple Sclerosis

Multiple sclerosis (MS) is an autoimmune disease in which the body's immune system attacks the oligodendrocytes that produce myelin in the CNS (Figure 3–14). The most common form of MS has a relapsing-remitting pattern in which there are periods of worsening symptoms (relapse) as the myelin is destroyed and neural function declines. These are followed by periods of remission in which the immune system relents, and some recovery occurs as oligodendrocytes re-myelinate axons. Over time, the amount of recovery that occurs during each remission period decreases, as axons become damaged by the repeated attacks on the myelin. CNS neurons have little ability to recover from damage, and thus die off. While myelin damage can occur anywhere within the CNS, damage often clusters in certain areas, including periventricular areas and optic pathways (Figure 3–15). Damage is further exacerbated when it expands beyond the white matter pathways, affecting adjacent areas through finger-like extensions of damage known as Dawson fingers (Figure 3–16).

Communication and swallowing deficits associated with MS are dependent upon the specific axon tracts that are affected, but often involve motor control of articulators; coordination of movement for speech and swallowing; and cognitive functions such as attention, memory, and executive function.

3 ETIOLOGIES AND PATHOPHYSIOLOGY

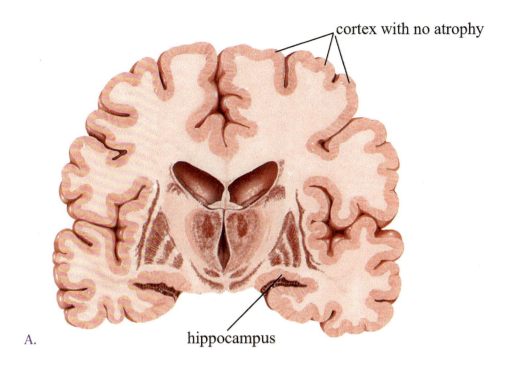

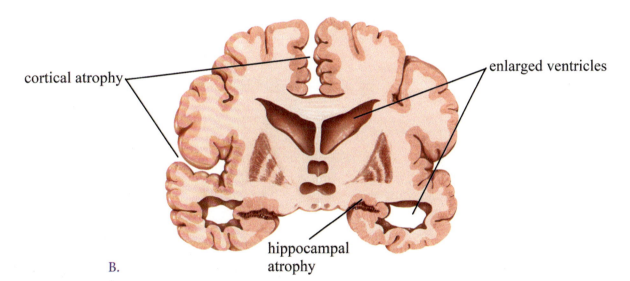

Figure 3–10. A. Coronal slices of healthy brain with no atrophy. B. Cortical and hippocampal atrophy. Adapted from *Clinical Neuroscience for Communication Disorders: Neuroanatomy and Neurophysiology* (p. 287) by Blake, M. L. and Hoepner, J. K. Copyright © 2023 Plural Publishing, Inc. All rights reserved.

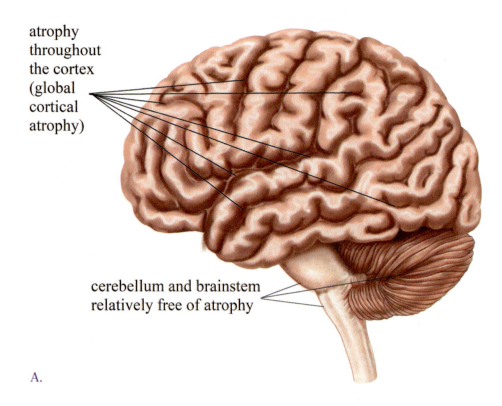

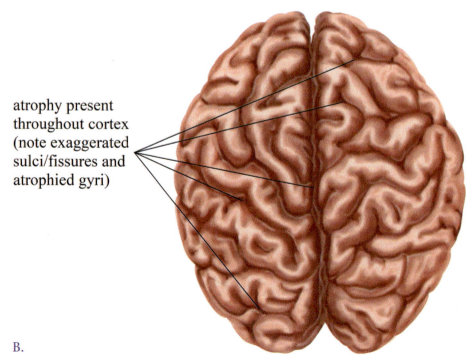

Figure 3–11. A. Generalized cortical atrophy seen in lateral views of the brain. B. Superior views of the brain. Adapted from *Clinical Neuroscience for Communication Disorders: Neuroanatomy and Neurophysiology* (p. 289) by Blake, M. L. and Hoepner, J. K. Copyright © 2023 Plural Publishing, Inc. All rights reserved.

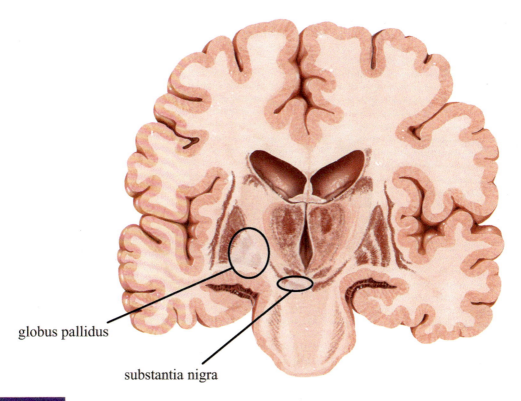

Figure 3–12. Degeneration of basal ganglia characteristic of Parkinson disease.

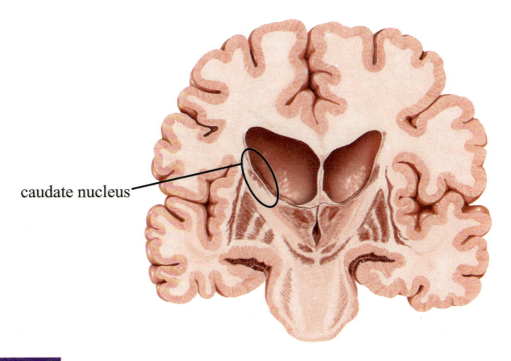

Figure 3–13. Degeneration of caudate nucleus characteristic of Huntington disease.

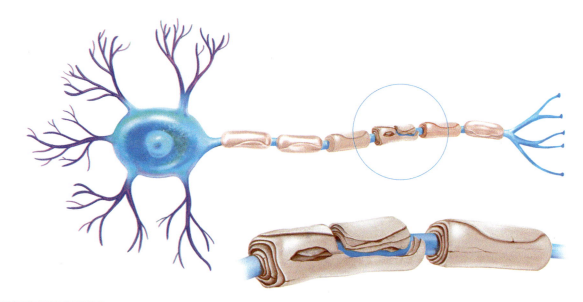

Figure 3–14. Degeneration of myelin characteristic of multiple sclerosis.

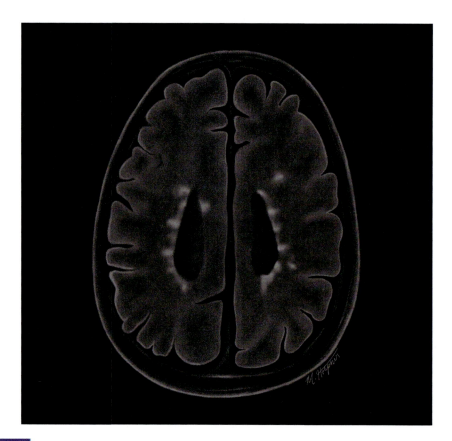

Figure 3–15. White matter lesions characteristic of multiple sclerosis.

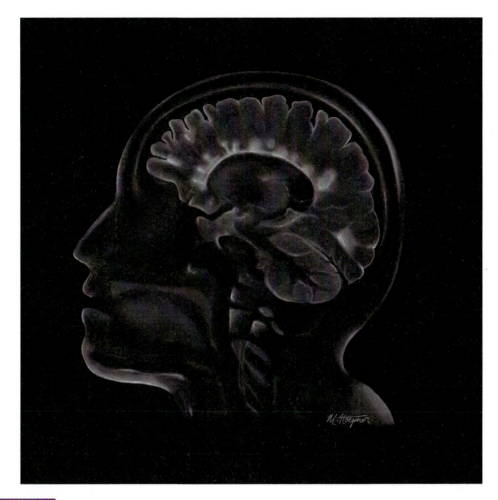

Figure 3-16. White matter lesions known as Dawson fingers characteristic of multiple sclerosis.

Amyotrophic Lateral Sclerosis

Amyotrophic lateral sclerosis (ALS), also known in the United States as Lou Gehrig disease and in the United Kingdom and elsewhere as motor neurone disease, is caused by progressive degeneration of both upper and lower motor neurons. In bulbar onset ALS, the cranial nerves are affected first, with early changes in speech, swallowing, and facial expression. In spinal onset ALS, the spinal nerves are affected first, with early changes in gross and fine motor control of the limbs. As the disease progresses, both bulbar and spinal systems will be affected. Muscle atrophy occurs as a result of loss of innervation (Figure 3–17). Essentially, if muscles never receive signals to contract, they will waste away. While the primary characteristics of ALS relate to movement, approximately 50% of people with ALS will develop cognitive deficits. These deficits typically affect executive functioning and language, particularly expressive language (both written and spoken).

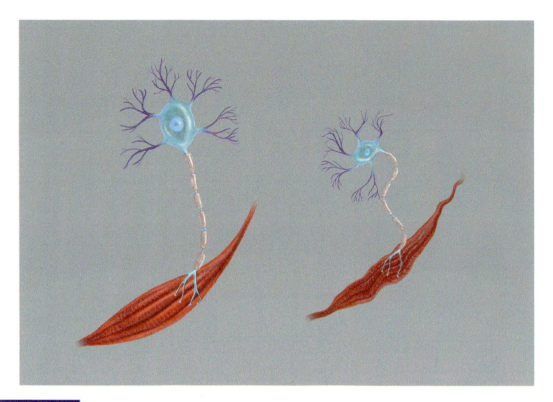

Figure 3–17. Healthy and degenerating neuron and muscle.

Infectious Diseases

Meningitis is an infection of the meninges (Mayo Clinic, n.d.). The infection causes inflammation that results in headache, stiff neck, confusion, and fever among other symptoms. Long-term meningitis can affect memory, learning, hearing, and movement. Meningitis is most often caused by viruses or bacteria. In the United States, viral meningitis is more common and tends to be less serious. Bacterial meningitis, while more rare, is more serious. Pneumococcal and meningococcal vaccines can prevent some forms of bacterial meningitis. In developing countries, tuberculosis also can cause meningitis.

Encephalitis is an inflammation of the brain (NINDS, 2023). Encephalitis can affect speech and language, cognition, and sensorimotor systems. Encephalitis can be caused by viruses, bacteria, parasites, or fungi. In the United States, most cases are related to the herpes simplex virus. There also are several varieties caused by mosquitoes including West Nile and Japanese encephalitis. It is a rare but serious consequence of COVID-19 (Siow et al., 2021).

Prevalence Patterns

The 2016 Global Burden of Diseases, Injuries, and Risk Factors Study (Feigin et al., 2019) examined the impact of 15 common neurological disorders (Tables 3–3 and 3–4). They focused on disability-adjusted life years (DALYs), which is the sum of the number of years

Table 3-3. Global Impact of 15 Neurological Disorders

	Primary Ages Affected	Primary Sex Affected*	Primary Impact: Years Lost Due to Death vs. Years With Disability
Stroke	60+ years	Males	Death + disability
Migraine		Females	Disability
Alzheimer & Other Dementias	80+ years		Death + disability
Meningitis	Children		Death
Epilepsy			Disability
Spinal Cord Injury			Disability
Traumatic Brain Injury		Males	Disability
Brain and Other CNS Cancer			Death
Tension-type Headache		Females	Disability
Encephalitis	Children		Death
Parkinson Disease		Males	
Other Neurological Diseases			
Tetanus	Children	Males	Death
Multiple Sclerosis		Females	
Motor Neuron Diseases		Males	

Note: *Male-dominated diseases had a Male: Female ratio of at least 1.5; female-dominated diseases had a ratio of less than 0.7. Overall, the Male: Female ratio is 1:15.

Source: Data from Feigin, V. L., Nichols, E., Alam, T., Bannick, M. S., Beghi, E., Blake, N., . . . Vos, T. (2019). Global, regional, and national burden of neurological disorders, 1990–2016: A systematic analysis for the Global Burden of Disease Study 2016. *The Lancet Neurology*, 18(5), 459–480. https://doi.org/10.1016/S1474-4422(18)30499-X

of life lost and the number of years lived with a disability. Stroke, migraine, and dementias were the largest contributors to DALYs. Meningitis and encephalitis had the largest impact on babies and children, while stroke and dementias were more prevalent in older adults. Headaches and migraines affected teens through middle-aged adults.

Within the United States, dementia (including Alzheimer disease) affects 2.9 million people, making it the fourth most prevalent neurological disorder and the leading cause of death among neurological disorders (Tsao et al., 2022).

Table 3–4. Incidence of and Risk Factors for Neurologic Diagnoses That Impact Communication and Swallowing

	Incidence or Prevalence – US	Incidence or Prevalence Worldwide	Racial/Ethnic Differences	Risk Factors
Stroke	795,000 annually	Prevalence: 101.5 million; 6.6 million deaths per year. Rates highest for Oceania, S.E. Asia, N. Africa, Middle East, E. Asia (https://professional.heart.org)	Black > White risk of first stroke Black > White death from stroke	Age, hypertension, high cholesterol, smoking, obesity, diabetes
Dementias	5.8–6.5 million	50–65 million cases per year; 60% in low-middle income countries (https://www.who.int)	Black > Hispanic > White dementia diagnosis White > Black > Hispanic death from dementia	Age, family history, poor cardiovascular health, traumatic brain injury
Traumatic Brain Injuries	1.5 million annually	50–60 million per year (estimate 50% of population will have TBI)*	Black, Hispanic disproportionately affected by TBI; Asians less affected	Age (babies, teens, older adults), sex (Males 2x females), alcohol/drug use, education, SES

Note: *Mollayeva, T., Mollayeva, S., & Colantonio, A. (2018). Traumatic brain injury: Sex, gender and intersecting vulnerabilities. *Nature Reviews: Neurology, 14,* 711–722. https://doi.org/10.1038/s41582-018-0091-y

Source: Data from CDC https://www.cdc.gov/stroke/facts.htm

Ethnic and racial disparities are present in the prevalence of neurological disorders. In the United States, underrepresented minorities (Black, Hispanic/Latino, Asian, Native American) are more likely to have strokes, TBIs, and dementias. Disparities in health care and social determinants of health will be covered in Chapter 5.

Brain Imaging

Understanding brain function and dysfunction relies both on behavioral observation and assessment as well as imaging to ascertain changes to the anatomy and physiology. Speech-language pathologists play a key role in assessing communication and swallowing from the behavioral perspective. While SLPs are not directly involved in brain imaging, the results of those tests can corroborate communication diagnoses and/or guide the plan for the diagnostic process. For example, knowing that a stroke occurred in the posterior left middle cerebral artery distribution should guide the SLPs decision to assess for aphasia, and particularly for receptive language abilities.

Most imaging techniques illuminate either anatomical or physiological changes. Structural, or anatomical, imaging shows structures, while functional imaging shows activity in the brain. Each technique has specific strengths and weaknesses and is selected based on the suspected medical diagnosis and the questions to be answered.

Anatomical/Structural Imaging

Computed Tomography (CT or CAT) scans use x-rays to reveal horizontal slices of the brain. Distinctions between regions with different densities are apparent (Figure 3–18). This allows discrimination of healthy brain tissue from ventricles and tumors, and the presence of blood such as in a hematoma. The relative size and position of structures can be evaluated to diagnose enlarged ventricles due to hydrocephalus, atrophy of cortical regions, and compression of brain tissue. Tumors, hematomas, and infarcted tissue also can be identified. CT scans are commonly used to check for hemorrhages when a patient arrives at a hospital with a suspected head injury or stroke.

A **Magnetic Resonance Imaging (MRI) scan** uses a strong magnet to cause re-orientation of hydrogen atoms in the brain, and then measures the radio frequency signal given off as the atoms return to their original position. The resulting image provides good spatial resolution of different types of tissues and substances (Figure 3–19). There are clear distinctions between gray and white matter, tumors and healthy tissue, and brain tissue versus fluid (e.g., blood or cerebrospinal fluid). For strokes and TBIs, MRIs are more accurate in the sub-acute phase than acutely. Various modifications of MRIs, including perfusion-weighted, diffusion-tensor imaging, and fractional anisotropy are used to highlight specific types of tissues or structures.

Angiograms involve the use of a contrast dye injected into the bloodstream. This dye shows up on x-ray images, allowing visualization of the arterial system (Figure 3–20). For neurological purposes, it is used to view the arteries that extend up to the brain, the circle of

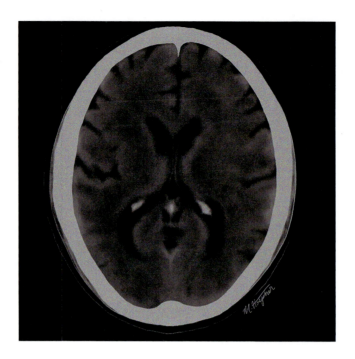

Figure 3–18. Illustration of computed tomography (CT) scan.

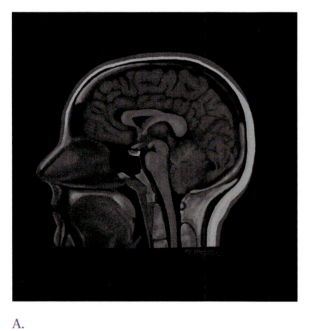

A.

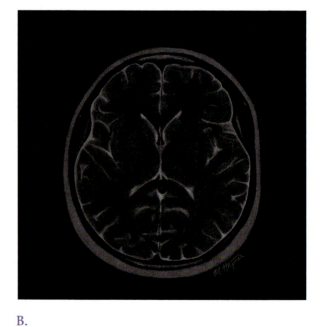

B.

Figure 3–19. A & B. Illustration of magnetic resonance imaging (MRI) scan.

Figure 3–20. Illustration of angiogram.

Willis and the cerebral arteries that supply blood to the brain. Angiograms are used to detect aneurysms and blockages in the blood flow due to atherosclerosis or ischemic clots.

Functional Imaging

Positron Emission Tomography (PET) scans measure the metabolism of the brain tissues (Figure 3–21). A radioactive tracer that attaches to glucose is injected into the bloodstream and the PET scan measures how much glucose is used in different regions of the brain. Glucose use increases with neuron activity and decreases when neurons are silent, thus revealing areas that are active versus not, or those that may be underperforming. PET scans have low spatial resolution so only general regions of activity can be detected (e.g., prefrontal, anterior temporal). PET scans can be used to diagnose some types of dementia.

Electroencephalograms (EEG) measure the electrical activity of the brain. Electrodes are placed on the skull and the electrical activity of neurons in various areas is measured. EEGs are particularly useful for diagnosing and identifying the source of seizures. They also can be used to diagnose sleep disorders.

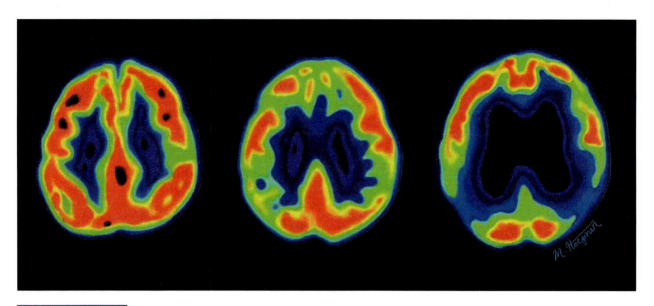

Figure 3–21. Illustration of a PET scan.

Near-infrared spectroscopy (NIRS) is a non-invasive technique that uses light waves in the near-infrared spectrum to indirectly measure brain activity. Molecules called chromophores absorb light which then can be tracked. Changes in concentration of specific chromophores, specifically oxyhemoglobin and deoxyhemoglobin, reflect changes in oxygenation and metabolism that are then interpreted as brain activity.

Functional MRI (fMRI) uses a combination of the fine resolution of the MRI anatomical scan with a measure of oxygen use during activity. The resulting images allow researchers to identify specific areas of the brain that are active during specific tasks. fMRI is used for research purposes to identify areas of the brain involved in, or critical for, specific functions, and to examine the activity of intact areas of the brain after a lesion that disrupts functioning. It is rarely used for medical diagnoses.

Concepts for Understanding Effects of Brain Injury

Several key concepts will recur throughout this book. The first is location. Many, but not all, communication functions can be linked to a region of the brain. Damage to cortical areas or networks connecting cortical areas often can result in predictable impairments in communication. This is especially apparent for motor speech and swallowing disorders because of the precise organization of sensorimotor systems. It is truer for basic language functions controlled by the left hemisphere than for pragmatic and other communicative functions lateralized to the right hemisphere. High-level cognitive functions are more diffusely distributed and require extensive connections to a variety of regions of the brain. While frontal lobes are commonly implicated, deficits are not easily localized to specific regions of damage.

A second concept is focal versus diffuse injuries. Focal injuries are more likely to have specific and predictable effects on communication or swallowing function. Diffuse injuries can impact many different aspects of communication and swallowing, particularly cognitive functions that either underlie communication and swallowing (e.g., attention) or the higher-level executive functions that are needed for complex communication or learning/remembering techniques for safe swallowing.

A third concept is the principle of C-shaped development and decline (refer back to Figure 2–27 in Chapter 2). In the brain, structures at the tips of the C-shape, including the prefrontal cortex and the anterior temporal poles, are the last to fully develop and the first to decline in aging. Thus, with increasing age executive functions, attentional control, and strategic memory decline while visual processing remains relatively intact.

A fourth concept is the time course or progression of a disease or disorder. Strokes and TBIs have a sudden onset followed by a protracted period of recovery. The expectation is that function will continue to improve over time with continued stimulation and use. Tumors have an increasing impact over time as they grow. If left untreated, the deficits can be expected to increase along with the tumor growth. However, treatment may stop the progression that would allow for restoration of function to some extent. Progressive diseases, as the name implies, will cause increasing degeneration of neurons and glial cells over time with an associated continuing decline of function. Treatments may be able to slow the progression, but rarely can they halt the progression or reverse the course. For SLPs, treatment for strokes and TBI will focus on restoring or compensating for deficits. In contrast, treatment for degenerative conditions typically focus on minimizing the impact of the disease on communication and establishing compensatory strategies for patients and families to maximize communication or swallowing function for as long as possible.

Summary

The central nervous system can be disrupted in many different ways. Some diseases or damage affect small regions while others have more extensive and diffuse effects. Depending on the size and location of damage, the consequences can be minimal or devastating. Understanding the causes of brain injury aids in predictions of the resulting deficits, the options for treatment, and the prognosis for recovery. Speech-language pathologists rely on doctors and other medical professionals for diagnosis of the neurological disease, and contribute to the impact on cognition, communication, and swallowing as well as the impact for participation in activities of daily living.

Key Concepts

- Brain damage can occur at any age and can affect various CNS structures, functions, and systems.

- Damage to neuronal function can occur suddenly (e.g., TBI, stroke) or gradually (progressive diseases or tumors).
- The location of damage is linked to the types of communication, cognitive, and swallowing deficits.
- Neuroimaging techniques can identify the location and etiology of brain injury.
- The impact of neurological diseases can be measured by both death and disability.

References

ALS Association. (2023). *Dedicated to finding a cure for ALS.* https://www.als.org/

Aroor, S., Singh, R., & Goldstein, L. B. (2017). BE-FAST (Balance, Eyes, Face, Arm, Speech, Time): Reducing the proportion of strokes missed using the FAST mnemonic. *Stroke, 48*(2), 479–481. https://doi.org/10.1161/STROKEAHA.116.015169

Bryden, D. W., Tilghman, J. I., & Hinds, S. R. (2019). Blast-related traumatic brain injury: Current concepts and research considerations. *Journal of Experimental Neuroscience, 13.* https://doi.org/10.1177/1179069519872213

Centers for Disease Control and Prevention. (n.d.). *Interactive atlas of heart disease and stroke.* https://nccd.cdc.gov/dhdspatlas/

Centers for Disease Control and Prevention. (2022). *Stroke facts.* https://www.cdc.gov/stroke/facts.htm

Dietrich, J., Rao, K., Pastorino, S., & Kesari, S. (2011). Corticosteroids in brain cancer patients: Benefits and pitfalls. *Expert Review of Clinical Pharmacology, 4*(2), 233–242. https://doi.org/10.1586/ecp.11.1

Feigin, V. L., Nichols, E., Alam, T., Bannick, M. S., Beghi, E., Blake, N., Culpepper, W. J. . . . Vos, T. (2019). Global, regional, and national burden of neurological disorders, 1990–2016: A systematic analysis for the Global Burden of Disease Study 2016. *The Lancet Neurology, 18*(5), 459–480. https://doi.org/10.1016/S1474-4422(18)30499-X

Lacerte M., Hays Shapshak A., & Mesfin F. B. (2023). Hypoxic brain injury. In: *StatPearls* [Internet]. StatPearls Publishing. https://www.ncbi.nlm.nih.gov/books/NBK537310/

Mayo Clinic. (n.d.). *Meningitis.* https://www.mayoclinic.org/diseases-conditions/meningitis/symptoms-causes

Mollayeva, T., Mollayeva, S., & Colantonio, A. (2018). Traumatic brain injury: Sex, gender and intersecting vulnerabilities. *Nature Reviews: Neurology, 14,* 711–722. https://doi.org/10.1038/s41582-018-0091-y

Mounier, N. M., Abdel-Maged, A. E. S., Wahdan, S. A., Gad, A. M., & Azab, S. S. (2020). Chemotherapy-induced cognitive impairment (CICI): An overview of etiology and pathogenesis. *Life Sciences, 258,* 118071.

National Institute of Neurological Disorders and Stroke (2023). *Encephalitis.* https://www.ninds.nih.gov/health-information/disorders/encephalitis

Pink Concussions. (n.d.). *Female brain injury from sports, violence, military service.* https://www.pinkconcussions.com/

Siow, I., Lee, K. S., Zhang, J. J. Y., Safari, S. E., & Ng, A. (2021). Encephalitis as a neurological complication of COVID-19: A systematic review and meta-analysis of incidence, outcomes, and predictors. *European Journal of Neurology, 28,* 3491–3502. https://doi.org/10.1111/ene.14913

Supporting Survivors of Abuse and Brain Injury Through Research. (n.d.). *Highlighting an invisible brain injury.* https://soarproject.ca/

Tsao, C. W., Aday, A. W., Almarzooq, Z. I., Alonso, A., Beaton, A. Z., Bittencourt, M. S., . . . Martin, S. S. (2022). Heart disease and stroke statistics—2022 update: A report from the American Heart Association. *Circulation, 145*(8). https://doi.org/10.1161/CIR.0000000000001052

World Health Organization. (2023). Stroke, cerebrovascular accident. https://www.emro.who.int/health-topics/stroke-cerebrovascular-accident/index.html

Resources

There are many organizations that provide information about specific neurogenic diseases and brain injury. These are just a few.

ALS Association: https://www.als.org/
American Stroke Association: https://www.stroke.org/en/
Brain Injury Association of America: https://www.biausa.org/
Brain Injury Services: https://braininjurysvcs.org/
CDC Interactive Atlas of Heart Disease and Stroke: https://nccd.cdc.gov/dhdspatlas/
CDC Stroke Facts and Data: https://www.cdc.gov/stroke/facts.htm
Huntington's Disease Society of America: https://hdsa.org/
Model Systems Knowledge Translation Center (information for traumatic brain injury, spinal cord injury, and burns): https://msktc.org/
National Multiple Sclerosis Society: https://www.nationalmssociety.org/
Pink Concussions: https://www.pinkconcussions.com/
SOAR (Supporting Survivors of Abuse and Brain Injury through Research) is a multi-disciplinary, community-engaged, research partnership between the University of British Columbia (UBC) – Okanagan and Kelowna Women's Shelter in Kelowna, British Columbia, Canada: https://soarproject.ca
University of Sydney Acquired Brain Injury Communication Lab:
https://www.sydney.edu.au/medicine-health/our-research/research-centres/acquired-brain-injury-communication-lab.html

4
COMMUNICATION, COGNITION, AND SWALLOWING

Chapter Overview

Definitions and Disorders
Speech
  Disorders of the Motor System
  Motor Speech Disorders
Language
  Disorders of Language
Is it Speech? Or Language? Or Both?
Cognition
  Attention
    Attention Networks
    Disorders of Attention
  Memory
    Disorders of Memory
  Executive Functions
    Disorders of Executive Function
  Awareness
    Disorders of Awareness
  Social Cognition
    Disorders of Social Cognition
Is it Language? Or Cognition? Or Both?
Swallowing
  Disorders of Swallowing
Summary
Key Concepts
References

Definitions and Disorders

In this book we use four categories of processes and disorders: speech, language, cognition, and swallowing. Much of the education for speech-language pathology is organized this way, especially in graduate school where you may have separate courses covering acquired disorders of language (e.g., aphasia), motor speech (e.g., apraxia, dysarthria), and swallowing (e.g., dysphagia). However, because of the interconnectedness of regions of the brain that control aspects of communication and swallowing and the typical patterns of brain damage or degeneration, the patients and clients served by speech-language pathologists rarely have impairments of only one area (speech, language, cognition, swallowing). Recall the overlap in location of the models in Chapter 1. Because of this, there are patterns of co-occurrence based on the regions or systems impacted by the disease/disorder. Each chapter in this book focuses on a region or system of the brain and covers the potential speech, language, cognition, and swallowing deficits that can occur when that region/system is damaged. This provides a more integrated approach to learning about neurogenic disorders because it is immediately apparent that patients and clients typically present with a combination of communication and swallowing deficits.

This chapter includes broad descriptions of speech, language, cognitive, and swallowing processes, followed by definitions and brief descriptions of acquired neurogenic disorders. In subsequent chapters, these disorders will be discussed in more detail within the integrated systems-based approach.

Speech

Speech involves the production and articulation of phonemes combined into strings to create words and sentences. Speech is evaluated based on the precision of articulation; the sequencing of phonemes; the fluency or flow of production; the intonation or melody (prosody); and characteristics of the voice such as loudness, quality, resonance, and pitch.

Speech production is dependent upon the sensorimotor systems. The motor system is responsible for planning, coordinating, programming, and initiating movement. The sensory system provides feedback that is used to monitor and evaluate the accuracy of production based on the location, rate, and range of movement as well as the resulting auditory signal, and to guide subsequent attempts if an error is detected.

Disorders of the Motor System

Different types of deficits that affect speech production occur based on the location of disruption within the motor system. **Paralysis** refers to a complete loss of muscular function. **Paresis** is muscular weakness. **Hemiparesis**, or "half weakness" refers to weakness of one side of the body. This occurs with damage to the cortical motor neurons and is often a consequence of a stroke affecting the lateral regions of a hemisphere. Weakness can be accompanied by either a reduction or increase in muscle tone. Reduced muscle tone is called **flaccidity**; flaccid muscles hang limply (due to lower motor neuron damage). Increased muscle tone is called **spasticity**; spastic muscles are stiff and tight (due to upper motor neuron damage).

Dystonia is the presence of unwanted muscle contractions that are repetitive or sustained. These create prolonged postures or twisting movements. **Ataxia** is a disruption of coordinated movement and targeting. Finally, **apraxia** is an impairment of coordinated purposeful movement caused by interruption of motor programming. All of these motoric disorders can affect various muscles or muscle groups in the body. When they affect the articulators (i.e., lips, tongue, velum, pharynx, larynx) and respiratory system, they have the potential to affect speech production.

Motor Speech Disorders

There are two major types of motor speech disorders: the **dysarthrias** and **apraxia of speech** (Table 4–1). Dysarthria is the collective term for speech disorders caused by disruption to the motor system. The various types of dysarthria are based on patterns of motor impairments, which in turn are related to the region of the motor system that is affected. **Flaccid dysarthria** is characterized primarily by muscle weakness. It is due to damage to lower motor neurons (LMNs). Muscles are flaccid because they receive no signals to contract, and so hang limply. **Spastic dysarthria** is caused by damage to upper motor neurons (UMNs) that result in increased muscle tone and stiffness. Cerebellar damage disrupts circuits responsible for coordinated movement of the articulators and results in **ataxic dysarthria**. **Hyperkinetic** and

Table 4–1. Lesion Location and Primary Characteristics of Motor Speech Disorders

Motor Speech Disorder	Lesion Location	Primary Characteristics
Flaccid dysarthria	lower motor neurons	flaccidity, muscular atrophy; slow, weak movements
Spastic dysarthria	upper motor neurons	spasticity, increased muscle tone, stiffness; slow, weak movements
Ataxic dysarthria	cerebellum	incoordination
Hyperkinetic dysarthria	basal ganglia	too much movement; uncontrolled, unwanted movements
Hypokinetic dysarthria	basal ganglia	not enough movement; small but fast movements
Apraxia of speech	left frontal motor cortices, left insula	impaired motor planning

hypokinetic dysarthria are characterized by too much and too little movement, respectively. These dysarthrias are due to damage to structures in the basal ganglia and midbrain. While the specific speech characteristics differ across the various types of dysarthria, in general, dysarthrias affect articulation, resonance, and prosody. Dysarthrias typically are not affected by linguistic characteristics. For example, short words (cat) will be just as easy or difficult to produce as long words (catastrophe).

Apraxia of speech (AOS) is an impairment of coordinated, purposeful movement of articulators to produce speech, caused by disruption to motor programming systems. AOS affects production of phonemes, words, and prosody. Shorter and phonologically simpler words (art) are more likely to be produced correctly than longer words (artillery). AOS often involves **articulatory groping** in which the person moves their articulators (e.g., lips, tongue) in attempts to get them into the correct position for production. Attempts to correct an incorrect production often are not successful.

Language

Languages are symbol systems used to convey meaning. Spoken and written languages are the most common, but gestural languages such as sign language are equally valid and relevant. Languages are characterized by form, content, and function. The form includes the rules for creating and combining components such as **phonology** (sound or signing hand position systems and rules for sound/position combinations), **morphology** (smallest meaningful language units and rules for combining those to create words), and **syntax** (rules for combining words or signs into phrases and sentences). **Semantics** are the content, the system for meanings of words and word combinations. The functional domain of language is called **pragmatics**, often referred to as the use of language in context. It includes **linguistic** (choice of words and syntactic structures), **paralinguistic** (prosody), and **extralinguistic** (non-verbal cues such as facial expression, gestures, and body language) components. Pragmatics are bound to the communicative context such that the same morphologically, syntactically correct production may be pragmatically appropriate in one context or situation but inappropriate in another.

Grice's (1975) four maxims of communication provide a succinct way of explaining effective and efficient pragmatic communication: you should tell the truth, provide just the right amount of information, provide relevant input, and be clear and efficient. Of course, we all break these "rules" often, such as when telling jokes, being sarcastic, making a story interesting and exciting, etc. In those cases, we choose to break a rule for a purpose. However, if someone consistently and unintentionally shared information that wasn't true, or was commonly vague or ambiguous, it would impact social interactions and relationships.

Languages have both expressive and receptive components: you must be able to both produce and understand a language for it to be a functional means of communication. The perisylvian region of both right and left hemispheres is heavily engaged in language. Other structures such as the thalamus and cerebellum also provide input for language processing.

> ### Box 4–1 Adjusting to Your Audience
>
> Your communication partners or audience are part of the context that should impact the linguistic aspects of pragmatics. Responding to a question in one of your classes and wanting to impress your fellow students and the instructor, or at least not wanting to "sound dumb," you may select vocabulary that you've learned in class (e.g., "phonemes" rather than "sounds") and use syntactically complex sentences. You may choose to give as complete an answer as you can, or you may choose to only provide the information that you're confident is correct. Later, at home, when you're talking to family or friends and sharing what you learned in class, you probably change your vocabulary to use the words you know they will understand (e.g., "sounds" rather than "phonemes"), you might use simpler sentences, and you may convey everything you learned or just the highlights based on your estimation of how long you'll be able to hold their attention. All of these are linguistic aspects of pragmatics.

For the vast majority of humans, language form (phonology, morphology, syntax) is controlled primarily by the left hemisphere, and function (pragmatics) is controlled predominantly by the right hemisphere. Both hemispheres contribute to content (semantics), with the left hemisphere having a larger role. This lateralization of language is stronger for males than females. Reversed lateralization, in which the roles of the hemispheres are switched, can occur, most often in left-handers (Packheiser et al., 2020; Somers et al., 2015).

Disorders of Language

Disorders of language can affect form, meaning, and/or function. Expressive and receptive language can be affected differentially: some people may have equally severe deficits in production and comprehension, while others may be more impaired in one than the other. The most common acquired language disorders are **aphasia** and **apragmatism**.

Aphasia is a language disorder associated primarily with damage to the left hemisphere perisylvian areas. It can affect production (word finding, ability to create grammatical sentences, repetition, and fluency of production) and comprehension (difficulty comprehending words and sentences). Both verbal (talking, listening) and written (writing, reading) production and comprehension are affected. Pragmatics generally are well preserved in aphasia. The two major types of aphasia are fluent and non-fluent. **Fluent aphasia** is characterized by smooth production and typical prosody, although the language produced often is vague, uninformative, and may contain **neologisms** (made-up words), sound errors, or word substitutions. The production impairments primarily affect semantics with spared morphology and syntax. This fluent production is combined with deficits in language comprehension. **Nonfluent aphasia** is characterized by hesitations, **anomia** (word finding deficits), **agrammatism** (syntactic deficits), and disrupted prosody. Semantics, morphology, and syntax are all affected. Language comprehension is relatively preserved. **Paraphasias**, or word errors, occur in both fluent and non-fluent aphasias. These can be semantic, in which a related word is substituted (e.g., cat for dog) or phonemic, in which a phoneme substitution results in the wrong word (e.g., log for dog). Other left-sided, acquired disorders of language affect specific domains: **alexia** is an impairment in reading, and **agraphia** is a writing disorder. Alexia and agraphia can occur with or without aphasia.

Apragmatism is a label for the communication disorders commonly associated with damage to the right side of the brain. As the name suggests, it affects the pragmatic aspect of language. It is "a disorder in conveying and/or comprehending meaning or intent through linguistic, paralinguistic and/or extralinguistic modes of context-dependent communication. The context includes (among other things) the conversational partner(s), environment, cultural considerations and goal of the interaction" (Minga et al., 2023, p. 656). **Linguistic apragmatism** is characterized by contextually inappropriate word choices; tangential, overpersonalized, or disorganized discourse; inefficient generation of inferences and use of questions; difficulty understanding non-literal language such as idioms or metaphors; and/or talking too much or too little. **Paralinguistic apragmatism** involves changes to production or comprehension of emotional or linguistic prosody that impedes effective communication of intended meaning. This is also called **aprosodia**. **Extralinguistic apragmatism** affects the efficient and appropriate use and interpretation of non-verbal communication such as facial expressions, gestures, and body language.

The term apragmatism was suggested by the International Right Hemisphere Collaborative, a group of right hemisphere clinicians and researchers, to define the pragmatic communication disorders commonly seen after RHD. However, the definition does not require that damage be restricted to the right hemisphere. Communication disorders resulting from traumatic brain injury (TBI), for example, may be labeled as apragmatism. A key to the use of the label is whether the communication challenge is primarily related to a pragmatic

Box 4–2 Pragmatics of Texting

Translating pragmatics into written communication (texting or writing):

Linguistics are the words and acronyms (IMHO, ICYMI)
Paralinguistics often are expressed with punctuation and capitalization (what?!!? u CANT b serious)
Extralinguistics are the emojis used either instead of words or in addition to them.
Paralinguistic and extralinguistic cues are used to emphasize the intended meaning that may not be immediately apparent just from the linguistics. Think about how you would interpret "good luck!" followed by a thumbs up, a wink, a smiley face, or an exploding head emoji.

Box 4–3 Right Hemisphere Communication Disorders

Communication disorders associated with right hemisphere brain damage started gaining recognition in the early 1970s. (Note that this is over 100 years after aphasia was named and described in the mid-1860s.) For many decades there was no agreed-upon label for such disorders. They were variously called *high-level language disorders, non-aphasic language disorders, right hemisphere syndrome,* and *cognitive-communication disorders*. In 2021, the International Right Hemisphere Collective proposed that the term *apragmatism* should be used as the standard label for these communication disorders. Since this terminology is recent, you may not come across it often. We hope that you will be the first of many generations of speech-language pathologists to learn the term apragmatism and to use it in your career.

Box 4–4 Anomia Versus Linguistic Apragmatism

Anomia is a common deficit in aphasia in which a person has difficulty finding words to express themselves. While everyone sometimes struggles to find the specific word they want ("I know what I want to say . . . it's kind of like X, but that's not the right word . . ."), anomia in aphasia is more pervasive and often affects everyday words like *dog* or *chair*. Anomia may be worse when someone is tired or emotional or engaged in a complex task, but otherwise it is not context-dependent.

The linguistic component of apragmatism is context-dependent. It occurs when someone does not select words that are appropriate for the context. This could appear as not substituting milder words for curse words when talking with an employer or child, or using job-related jargon regardless of whether you are talking to a colleague or someone with limited knowledge of the field.

language impairment (linguistic, paralinguistic or extralinguistic), or if it is a result of a cognitive deficit. In the latter case, where comprehension is reduced due to attention or memory deficits, or executive dysfunction impacts integration of information, a better label would be cognitive-communication disorder.

Is It Speech? Or Language? Or Both?

Prosody is the "melody" of speech created by changing pitch, timing, and loudness. Prosody is suprasegmental, meaning it is created over multiple speech segments or phonemes. It spans both speech and language. It is a part of speech because it is dependent on the sensorimotor systems; it is part of language because it is the paralinguistic piece of pragmatics in which meaning is conveyed through prosody.

Types of prosody are classified by their functions (Peppé, 2009; Table 4–2). **Grammatical prosody** is used to convey word-level and syntactic meaning, such as differentiating between nouns and verbs (CONvict versus conVICT), compound nouns and adjectival phrases (a hotdog versus a hot dog), and boundaries between clauses or phrases (Marilyn, said Sheri, is brilliant versus Marilyn said Sheri is brilliant). **Pragmatic prosody** is used to produce speech acts, such as rising intonation to differentiate a question from a statement; and to emphasize important information as with emphatic stress (MILLY is a nun versus Milly is a NUN). In many studies of prosody after stroke, grammatical and pragmatic prosody are lumped into a single category called linguistic prosody. **Emotional** or **affective prosody** conveys emotions, moods, and feelings.

Because prosody is part of both speech and language, prosodic deficits can occur in both speech and language disorders. Dysarthria, particularly ataxic dysarthria, and apraxia of speech can impact prosody because of altered timing of motor signals. Non-fluent aphasias can cause changes in prosody because of the hesitations and pauses related to word-finding deficits. Aprosodia, particularly emotional aprosodia, is a component of apragmatism.

Table 4–2. Types of Prosody

Type of Prosody	Meaning Conveyed	Examples
Grammatical	word-level meaning	Nouns versus verbs *CONvict* versus *conVICT* Compound noun versus adjectival phrase *hotdog* versus *hot dog*
	syntactic meaning	Clause boundaries *Marilyn, said Sheri, is brilliant* versus *Marilyn said Sheri is brilliant*
Pragmatic	Speech acts	Questions vs. statements versus directives *Dayvon ate the pizza.* versus *Dayvon ate the pizza?*
	Emphatic stress	Highlight important/novel information *MILLY [not Berta] is a nun.* *Milly is a NUN [not a teacher]*
Emotional/Affective	Conveying emotion or attitude (e.g., pride, boredom)	Elevated pitch, rate, and loudness expressing happiness; reduced pitch, rate, and loudness expressing sadness

Cognition

Cognition encompasses all forms of thinking. In cognitive psychology, language is considered one of the components of cognition, and thus the term cognition includes language. In speech-language pathology, we generally talk about language and cognition as separate (although interconnected) mechanisms, and consider language disorders such as aphasia and apragmatism to be separate from cognitive disorders. There are different ways to categorize cognitive functions. Here we categorize them in a way that is consistent with the types of cognitive disorders diagnosed and treated by SLPs.

The frontal lobes, specifically the prefrontal regions, are the primary drivers of executive function, with extensive networks and circuits connecting the frontal lobes to other areas of the brain. Memory (hippocampus) and attention (parietal lobes) primarily engage other regions of the brain, but these too have extensive connections throughout the CNS.

Attention

Attention is necessary for nearly all cognitive and communication functions. In order to remember someone's name, you have to pay attention when they introduce themselves. To learn a new task, you need to concentrate and focus attention on the steps of the process. To comprehend what someone is saying you need to listen to them and pay attention to what they're saying and how they're saying it. Four key concepts for understanding and evaluating attention are the speed of processing incoming information, the amount of information that can be processed (often referred to as attentional capacity), sustaining attention over time, and controlling attentional processes and allocating attention to different tasks or processes (Sohlberg et al., 2023). Attention can further be described in relation to modality: visuospatial, verbal, and auditory attention.

Two primary components of attention are sustained attention and attentional control. **Sustained attention** is the ability to maintain attentional focus over time. **Attentional control** is necessary for **selective, alternating,** and **divided attention**. Selective attention is needed to focus on one stimulus while ignoring others. Being able to study in a student center, coffee shop, or even in an apartment with others around requires selective attention. **Alternating attention** is rapidly shifting attention from one stimulus or action to another. Taking notes in class requires you to shift from auditory language comprehension to written production. You must time the switches carefully so that you don't miss what the instructor says. **Divided attention** allows you to do two things at once. It is only really possible when the two tasks are different—like a motor and a language task— and when one of the tasks is relatively automatic and doesn't require much attention. If you're trying to do two similar tasks, like listening and writing, you have to alternate attention. When people talk about "multi-tasking" they're referring to divided and alternating attention. Many people feel they are really good at multitasking, but typically they're successful only with the criteria described above: using different domains and at least one task is automatic. Otherwise, performance

Box 4–5 Test the Myth of Multitasking. [Task based on Nancy Napier's multitasking exercise]

You'll need the assistance of a partner for this lab. Draw two horizontal lines. Have your partner time you while . . .
  A. On one line write "I am a great multitasker"
  B. On the second line write the numbers 1–20 (1, 2, 3, etc. . . .)

Note the time it took.

Next, have your partner time you while you write "I am a great multitasker" but instead of writing it out completely, write one letter, then write one number on the line below, then another letter on line one, followed by the next number on line two. Repeat the cycle until you've written the entire sentence and each of the numbers. Reflect on your experience.

So, you'll write, "I-1-a-2-m-3 . . ."

Note the time it took to do the two tasks together compared to focusing attention on each individually. Also note whether there were errors in either of the two conditions.

Box 4–6 Forms of Attention in Daily Life

You're taking a break from studying to watch your favorite sports team (football, soccer, cricket, lacrosse, curling, take your pick!). You're in your apartment alone, so you're hanging out on the couch sustaining attention on the game/match. Then your roommate comes home, and cues up their favorite podcast while making a snack in the kitchen. You now switch to selective attention as you ignore the podcaster's voice and clattering of dishes in the adjoining room so you can still process the announcer's commentary. Your phone pings—it is your mom, asking about your day and about her plans to come for dinner. You are now alternating attention, reading and sending texts in between spurts of action in the game so that you don't miss anything. Realizing that you should clean up a bit before your mom arrives, you grab a dust rag and broom. You're now dividing your attention between cleaning and watching the game. Note that switching between texting and watching/listening to the game requires alternating attention, because you're moving back and forth between two language tasks. Divided attention is only really possible when the two tasks require different skills (e.g., motor and language), or one of them is so automatic that it does not take much attention at all. If you tried to divide your attention between the game and the texting you'd find that you missed information from one of the two—perhaps having to go back and replay the announcer's commentary—because dividing attention between two similar tasks (in this case two language tasks) is nearly impossible.

on one task will decrease significantly. Try singing to a song while reading or studying; you'll probably find that you don't remember anything about what you read/studied, or you stop singing when you focus on the reading task.

Attention Networks

Many regions of the brain are involved in attention, including the brainstem reticular system, thalamic, parietal, prefrontal systems, and the networks that connect these areas. Reticular functions control arousal, which is the most rudimentary level of attention. The thalamus serves as a regulator of global attention and parietal structures facilitate visuospatial attention processes. Higher-order attentional regulation is a function of the frontal lobes. Two of the networks are the **dorsal attention network (DAN)** and **ventral attention network (VAN)** (Figure 4–1). The DAN is responsible for sustained attention and focused attention toward the contralateral space. Therefore, the LH attends to the right side of space and vice versa. Pattern recognition and prediction are controlled by the DAN. This is often referred to as top-down visual processing. Recognition of stimuli with important, distinctive, or relevant features is a function of the VAN. This is often referred to as bottom-up processing. The DAN and VAN both originate posteriorly but project to the prefrontal cortices. Although these two networks are bilateral, the right hemisphere usually has a greater role in attention processing.

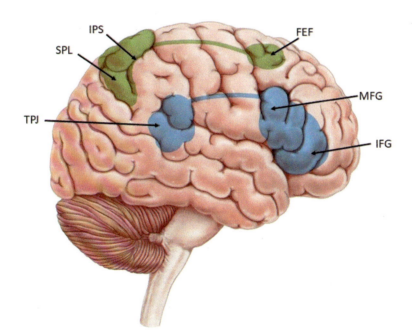

Figure 4–1. Regions in the dorsal (green) and ventral (blue) attention networks. FEF = frontal eye fields; IFG = inferior frontal gyrus; IPS = intraparietal sulcus; MFG = middle frontal gyrus; SPL = superior parietal lobe; TPJ = temporoparietal junction.

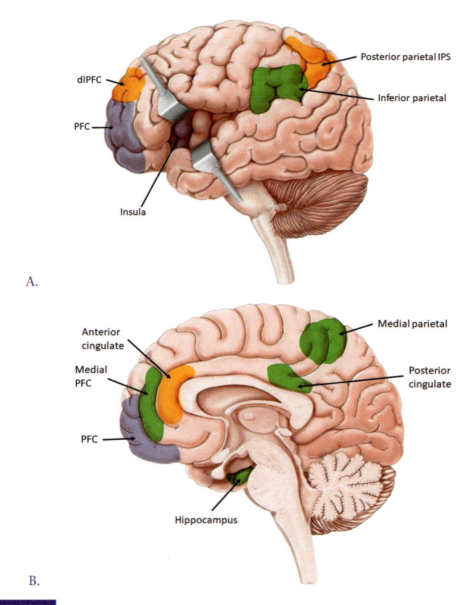

Figure 4–2. Central executive (orange), default mode (green), and salience (purple) attentional control networks on lateral (A) and medial (B) views. dlPFC = dorsolateral prefrontal cortex; IPS = intraparietal sulcus; PFC = prefrontal cortex.

In addition, there are three attentional control systems that regulate attention, including what we attend to and what we filter out or ignore: the **central executive network** (bilateral dorsolateral prefrontal cortices and lateral posterior parietal cortices), the **default mode network** (parietal and ventromedial prefrontal cortex), and the **salience network** (bilateral anterior cingulate and insular cortices) (Figure 4–2). The central executive network (CEN) is responsible for sustained attention, information processing, problem-solving, decision making, and working memory to facilitate goal-directed behaviors (Menon, 2011). It responds to external stimuli. The default mode network (DMN) operates when we are not focused on a task and simply letting our minds wander or think about our past and future. Perspective taking, introspection, and autobiographical memory formation are DMN functions. Finally, the salience network is responsible for directing our attention to salient stimuli and inhibiting (filtering) our attention from irrelevant stimuli. In that way, it is believed to have a role in switching attention between the default mode (fully intrinsic) and central executive (more extrinsic) networks.

Disorders of Attention

Attentional deficits present as difficulties focusing or concentrating and distractibility. Many people with brain injury describe how they used to be able to do more than one thing at once, but now they can only really focus on one thing and if they are interrupted they may not be able to easily re-focus. One specific attentional disorder is **unilateral neglect**. This is a deficit in which the brain fails to fully attend to sensory stimuli from a specific region of space, typically contralateral to the location of the lesion. Stimuli may be processed to some extent at an unconscious level. It usually occurs after damage to the right hemisphere, causing left unilateral neglect. People with unilateral neglect appear as if they cannot see things that are on the left side, but actually their visual system is intact and they are not able to consciously attend to things on that side. They may not realize when people come into their room if the door is to their left, they may not read words on the left side of the page, and they may write starting in the middle of the page instead of on the left side. Some may not comb their hair on the left side, or may not put their left arm into a shirt sleeve when getting dressed. Although unilateral neglect most often affects the visual modality, it can also reduce the use of one arm, hand, or leg (motor neglect); reduce response to sensory stimulation (e.g., pain, touch, temperature) on one side of the body (somatosensory neglect); or impair localization of sounds coming from one side (auditory neglect). For instance, an individual may bang their left shoulder on a door frame but not respond specifically to the pain in that shoulder. Likewise, upon hearing the voice of a person immediately to their left, they may turn to the right until they have found the source, rather than directly to the left side.

Memory

Memory includes the ability to encode, store, and retrieve information. Memory is classified by the type of information (e.g., events, facts, skills, and emotional associations) as well as how long information is stored (Figure 4–3). **Declarative memory**, also called explicit memory, includes events (**episodic memory**) and facts or details (**semantic memory**). This includes things you learn "on purpose" like when you study terms and concepts on flash cards. Remembering what you learned in your Intro to Communication Disorders courses would be semantic memories. Remembering activities you did or the study sessions you had with your friends in the library would be episodic memories. **Prospective memory** is the ability to remember to do things in the future. Remembering to talk to a friend after class or

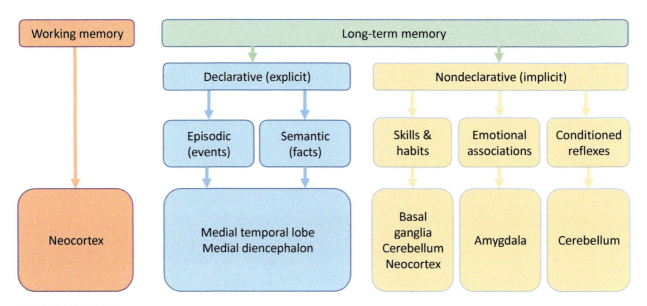

Figure 4–3. Memory systems and functions. From *Clinical Neuroscience for Communication Disorders: Neuroanatomy and Neurophysiology* (p. 205) by Blake, M. L. and Hoepner, J. K. Copyright © 2023 Plural Publishing, Inc. All rights reserved.

to call the vet once you get home are examples of prospective memory. **Metamemory** is a person's knowledge and understanding of their own memory abilities. Someone who knows that they have difficulty learning anatomical structures and because of this decides to try using various methods (labeling images, reading and paraphrasing descriptions, creating note cards, re-copying notes), would have good metamemory.

Nondeclarative memory, also called implicit memory, includes skills and habits, conditioned reflexes, and emotional associations. You might think of this as "learning by doing." Motor memory, or those movements or skills that you learned by practicing, are implicit memories. Often these are things you know how to do but would have a hard time explaining to someone else; it would be easier to show them than to tell them. The emotions you feel when you smell a scent from your childhood or a vacation to the mountains are also implicit memories.

Characteristics related to the time frame distinguish **short-term memory** from **long-term memory**. These are fairly intuitive: short-term memories are those that you hold onto for a few minutes. Long-term memories are those that are deeply encoded, and are from weeks, months, or years prior.

Working memory differs from other types primarily due to the processes involved. It involves remembering things for a short amount of time, but it differs from STM because it includes not only remembering information but also processing it in some way. For example, you can complete mental calculations (e.g., 356 + 431) thanks to working memory. You hold the numbers in your short-term memory and then process or manipulate them by adding them in your head, often with a mental visual image in your mind to aid calculation. Language comprehension relies heavily on working memory as you have to not only hold onto the words that someone is saying, but also interpret them in relation to the other words in the sentence, the syntactic structure, and the context of the interaction to be able to fully comprehend the message. Formulating a response requires you to take in all of that information and then generate a response that fits the conversation. Some researchers use STM and WM interchangeably. Others consider WM as an executive function. We will use them to refer to memory storage alone (STM) versus storage plus processing (WM).

Disorders of Memory

Memory deficits commonly affect short-term and working memory. **Amnesia** is a loss of memory, typically for a period of time. One example is **posttraumatic amnesia**, the inability to remember things that occurred during the time surrounding a TBI. Working memory and prospective memory deficits are not uncommon after stroke or TBI, but procedural memory is rarely impacted. Dementias affect short term memories first, and only later are long-term memories affected.

Executive Functions

Executive functions are the cognitive processes needed to create, carry out, and self-monitor goal-directed behaviors such as asking for a raise, figuring out how to get to work when your car breaks down, and learning new concepts or new skills. Executive functions help us respond to novel situations, when we need to think on the spot or make a plan for a situation we've never encountered before. Executive functions draw upon our knowledge base but they must adjust to the current demands and context. There are different opinions regarding what exactly should be included in the definition of executive function. We take a broad view and include a variety of high-level cognitive processes that support nonautomatic goal-driven

Box 4–7 Memories

Akiko was a retired teacher who had mild-moderate dementia. She lived with her husband who did the majority of the cooking, shopping, and monitored her medications. During a visit with her daughter-in-law, she asked questions about her grandchildren. When hearing that her granddaughter was 8, she related a story of when she taught 8-year-olds, providing details about her favorite student and the student who caused her the most trouble in class. She continued to describe a field trip they took. The conversation meandered from there to other general topics that were shared between the women. Then Akiko asked again about her grandkids and their ages. Upon finding out the age of her granddaughter, she re-told the same story about her teaching experiences. Akiko's long-term memories were preserved, and she was able to relate stories in sufficient detail. However, she was not encoding or storing short-term memories, so each time she heard that her granddaughter was 8 years old, it triggered the same long-term memory and she had no recollection that she had just told the story.

Table 4–3. Components of Executive Function and Characteristics of Deficits

Categories	Components	Characteristics of Deficits
Initiative	motivation, drive, creativity, shifting cognitive set, mental flexibility	apathy, unsure where to begin or how to proceed, difficulties considering or using different ways to do things, difficulties switching from one task or idea to another
Restraint	judgment, foresight, perseverance, delayed gratification, self-motivation, self-regulation, inhibition of thoughts and behaviors, concentration	engaging in risky behavior, not considering consequences or challenges, not staying on task, impulsivity, poor self-evaluation or estimates of performance, perseveration, interrupting others, distractibility
Order	planning, organization, sequencing, abstract reasoning, working memory, perspective-taking	disorganization; limited planning of activities or actions; problems with time lines; concrete, egocentric thoughts; difficulty holding onto information long enough to process it; difficulties with novel tasks; difficulties understanding other perspectives, feelings, or beliefs

behaviors, divided into three categories: initiative, restraint, and order (Table 4–3). Essentially, executive functions allow you to (a) do the things that are appropriate to meet goals, (b) not do things that are inappropriate, and (c) do things in a relevant, reasonable order.

Disorders of Executive Function

Executive dysfunction can affect any of the components of executive function. This can result in impulsivity, difficulty staying on task or completing tasks, poor self-monitoring and self-correction, apathy, disorganization, poor planning, and difficulty with reasoning. Typically multiple areas are affected, and deficits are more apparent with more complex or unfamiliar situations, or when there is a time pressure or emotional component.

Awareness

Self-awareness allows a person to recognize their abilities, strengths, and weaknesses. It allows one to detect when their performance or behavior is different (better or worse) than their typical, and recognize internal and external factors that affect performance or behavior. **Metacognition**, the awareness of one's own cognitive abilities, is one component of awareness. Metamemory, discussed above, is another.

Disorders of Awareness

Anosognosia (Greek: *lack of knowledge of disease*) is a disorder of awareness. People with anosognosia may not be aware of newly-acquired deficits, even when they are seemingly obvious, such as paresis of the left arm and leg. When asked about difficulties, such as why they cannot walk unaided they may **confabulate** and create a reason, such as "There's nothing wrong with my leg, but the physical therapist is so nice that I'm using the walker just to make her happy." When I asked a former patient with severe anosognosia and left-sided paresis to demonstrate her ability to stand up, she replied, "I can normally do it but not while you're watching me." Some will acknowledge knowing about a deficit without really accepting it: "My doctor keeps telling me that I can't drive anymore because of my vision, but I can see just fine and only drive to the grocery store anyway."

The label **Impaired Self-Awareness (ISA)** is commonly used in reference to awareness deficits caused by TBI. It is broader than anosognosia, and encompasses not only reduced awareness of a specific deficit, but also reduced appreciation or understanding of the consequences of deficits or ability to compensate for them. This includes someone who can say that they have difficulty with attention and remembering what they read, but does not appreciate that those deficits will make it difficult to return to work or school.

Social Cognition

Social cognition is "a set of cognitive processes that allow us to attend to, recognize, and interpret the broad contexts in which communication occurs. It includes recognition and interpretation of emotional/affective cues; **theory of mind**, and social inferential reasoning to integrate all of the components into a gestalt."[1] Empathy, the ability to understand and share other's emotions and feelings, is sometimes considered a component of social cognition. Social cognition is closely related to pragmatics, as they both are associated with communication in context.

Theory of mind (ToM) is the ability to understand that other people have their own thoughts, beliefs, knowledge base, feelings, and emotions, and that these may be different from your own. **Cognitive ToM** includes knowledge, thoughts, and beliefs. Understanding that your friend majoring in business does not know the difference between speech and language or phonemes and morphemes allows you to adjust what you say—we call this presupposition. Knowing that family members have political views that differ from yours also is part of cognitive ToM. **Affective ToM** includes feelings and emotions, such as understanding that

---

[1] Definition created by the International Right Hemisphere Collaborative: Margaret Blake, Petrea Cornwell, Ronelle Hewetson, Melissa Johnson, Jamila Minga, and Shannon Sheppard.

your sister may be upset or angry about losing her job, even if you feel relieved and glad because the job was not a good fit for her.

Disorders of Social Cognition

Social cognition deficits impact how people communicate and interact with others. Someone with poor cognitive ToM might believe that everyone has the same view on a topic, such as politics. That person says what they think without regard to other people's perspectives. Or it can relate to concrete thinking, like a child talking to a grandparent on the phone and pointing to an animal they see in the yard, not recognizing that their grandparents cannot see the deer. Impairments of affective ToM can include a disregard toward another person's feelings. This is not an intentional disregard, but rather a failure to consider the other person's feelings and that they might be different from their own. This could include not recognizing that taking something from another person (which makes you happy) will make the person you took it from feel sad.

Is It Language? Or Cognition? Or Both?

The label **cognitive-communication disorders** was initially coined to describe the communication deficits associated with TBI that are due primarily to cognitive impairments. As described in Chapter 2, TBIs commonly cause diffuse damage to many regions of the brain bilaterally and affect a variety of cognitive processes (e.g., executive function, attention, memory) that in turn impact communication.

Theory of mind and social cognition are typically considered aspects of cognition, but they have direct impacts on communication. These can fit under the cognitive-communication label, and overlap with some of the characteristics of apragmatism. For example, poor ToM would prevent someone who is an avid birder from understanding that their niece knows nothing about birds, and carry on a conversation-turned-monologue about bird species, their migration patterns, and deteriorating habitats, which is largely uninterpretable and possibly uninteresting to the niece.

Swallowing

Swallowing involves more than just the action of moving food or liquid from the mouth to the esophagus. It begins with seeing the food/liquid; salivating; retrieving it from the cup, straw, spoon, fork, or fingers; and then chewing and forming a bolus (a cohesive ball of masticated/chewed-up food or liquid). This is called the **oral preparatory phase**, as you prepare the food/liquid in the mouth. While much of this phase is automatic (we're not aware of what we're doing and don't have to think about it for it to work), we do have volitional control over this phase, meaning we can voluntarily stop, start, or modify these actions.

Once a bolus is formed, the **oral phase** can begin. The primary purpose of this phase is bolus transfer from the mouth to the pharynx. We do have some volitional control over this phase but it initiates an autonomic phase.

The autonomic **pharyngeal phase** moves the food or liquid bolus from the mouth to the esophagus, while protecting the airway. In order to do that, multiple functions must take place within this involuntary step. These four functions take place almost simultaneously. 1) Velopharyngeal closure—in which the soft palate elevates and closes off the velopharyngeal port between the pharynx and nasopharynx. This prevents the bolus from entering the nose and creates positive pressure to drive the bolus into the pharynx. This is also supported by oral closure and tongue retraction. 2) Hyolaryngeal excursion—the hyoid bone and thyroid cartilage elevate, which inverts the epiglottis so that it bends over the larynx and protects the airway. 3) Laryngeal adduction—the vocal folds come together (adduct) and the space above the vocal folds, called the laryngeal vestibule, tightens and shrinks to maintain positive pharyngeal pressures and prevent food from entering the larynx. 4) Pharyngeal contraction—the three pharyngeal constrictor muscles contract in sequence from top to bottom to move the bolus through the pharynx and into the esophagus. The fourth phase, the **esophageal phase**, is fully autonomic and involves transfer of the bolus to the stomach.

Disorders of Swallowing

Dysphagia is the label for disorders of swallowing. There are various classifications depending on the phase of swallowing affected: oral preparatory, oral/oropharyngeal, pharyngeal, or esophageal dysphagia. Changes to motor, sensory, and cognitive processes can result in dysphagia. Motor system deficits can interrupt the movement or coordination of the various structures that move a bolus of food or liquid from the oral cavity through the pharynx and over the larynx into the esophagus where it is transported to the stomach. If sensation is reduced, you may not feel the bolus and it can spill into the pharynx prematurely, or the laryngeal muscles may not contract in time to properly protect the airway. Dysphagia is often exacerbated by cognitive impairments, such as impulsivity which results in a person eating too much too fast, overwhelming the motor and sensory systems. A variety of neurogenic disorders result in dysphagia. This includes but is not limited to dementias, TBIs, cortical and subcortical strokes, and degenerative diseases such as Parkinson, Huntington, multiple sclerosis, and amyotrophic lateral sclerosis. Since speech is an overlaid function, disorders in speech tend to parallel disorders of swallowing. In fact, speech tasks and speech-related cranial nerve function can provide important insights into swallowing function. Dysphagia is often exacerbated by cognitive impairments.

Summary

The brain is a complex organ that controls nearly all functions of the body from the most basic to the most complex thoughts, behaviors and emotions. While the brain is highly interconnected there are some functions that are lateralized—controlled primarily by either the right or left hemisphere—and some that can be localized to regions within one or more lobes. Acquired neurogenic communication and swallowing disorders result from damage or disruption of the networks that control speech, language, cognition, and swallowing. Such disorders rarely occur in isolation. Rather, damage to the CNS disrupts multiple functions depending on the location of the damage and the neurons and circuits affected.

Key Concepts

- Apraxia of speech and dysarthria are disorders of motor speech. Different types of dysarthria are related to the region of the motor system that is affected.
- Language disorders include aphasia, alexia, and agraphia, typically caused by damage to the left hemisphere, and apragmatism, associated with damage to the right hemisphere.
- Cognitive disorders impact thinking and behavior through changes in attention, memory, and executive function. Disorders of social cognition specifically affect communication and interpersonal interactions.
- Dysphagia can affect any stage of swallowing from before the food enters the mouth to the point at which it enters the stomach. Swallowing is a complex process with both voluntary and involuntary stages.

References

Grice, P. (1975). *Logic and Conversation.* Academic Press.

Menon, V. (2011). Large-scale brain networks and psychopathology: A unifying triple network model. *Trends in Cognitive Sciences, 15*(10), 483–506.

Minga, J., Sheppard, S. M., Johnson, M., Hewetson, R., Cornwell, P., & Blake, M. L. (2023). Apragmatism: The renewal of a label for communication disorders associated with right hemisphere brain damage. *International Journal of Language & Communication Disorders, 58*(2), 651–666. https://doi.org/10.1111/1460-6984.12807

Packheiser, J., Schmitz, J., Arning, L., Beste, C., Güntürkün, O., & Ocklenburg, S. (2020). A large-scale estimate on the relationship between language and motor lateralization. *Scientific Reports, 10*(1), Article 1. https://doi.org/10.1038/s41598-020-70057-3

Peppé, S. J. (2009). Why is prosody in speech-language pathology so difficult? *International Journal of Speech-Language Pathology, 11*(4), 258–271. https://doi.org/10.1080/17549500902906339

Sohlberg, M. M., Hamilton, J., & Turkstra, L. S. (2023). *Transforming cognitive rehabilitation: Effective instructional methods.* Guilford Publications.

Somers, M., Aukes, M. F., Ophoff, R. A., Boks, M. P., Fleer, W., de Visser, K. C. L., . . . Sommer, I. E. (2015). On the relationship between degree of hand-preference and degree of language lateralization. *Brain and Language, 144,* 10–15. https://doi.org/10.1016/j.bandl.2015.03.006

5
FOUNDATIONAL KNOWLEDGE FOR NEUROREHABILITATION

> **Chapter Overview**
>
> Neural Plasticity
> Historical Context
> Framing Assessment and Intervention in Neurorehabilitation
> Rehabilitation Treatment Specification System (RTSS)
> Health Equity, Social Determinant of Health, Cultural/Ethnic Issues
>   Keeping Up With Terminology
>   Social Determinants of Health
>   Access to Care and Healthy Living
>   Education and Socialization
>   The Coin Model
> Summary
> Key Concepts
> References
> Resources

Neurorehabilitation is a systematic process designed to improve a person's well-being by reducing symptoms and increasing function after damage to or disease of the nervous system. After brain injury, changes to the nervous system—both positive and negative—are possible because neurons can adapt. To understand neurorehabilitation and current views on best practices, it is useful to know some of the history, how to map current knowledge to assessment and treatment practices, and how personal, system, and societal factors impact health, disease, and recovery.

Neural Plasticity

A central, foundational tenant of neurorehabilitation is that the interventions we deliver to clients will lead to improvements in their functional abilities. A primary driver for those improvements is **neural plasticity**, or the ability of the nervous system to change, specifically in response to stimuli and practice. Changes can occur in the structures, connections, and functions. Essentially, neurons can change their pattern of functions, make new connections, break existing connections, and alter the use of and response to neurotransmitters. Growth of new neurons, called **neurogenesis**, is also possible. Neural plasticity is greatest during childhood development, and is evident by the amount of learning that takes place. Although neural plasticity decreases with age, it never completely ceases.

Within neurorehabilitation, approaches are often divided into four categories: restorative treatments, compensatory strategies, assistive devices, and education. Restorative treatments, as the name suggests, are designed to restore (as much as possible) the type and level of function that a person had before brain injury. The remaining three approaches aim to improve everyday function by limiting the impact of impairments or deficits. Essentially, if a person is unable to produce speech effectively or efficiently, but an assistive device such as a computer can be used to produce what the person wants to say, then the negative effects of the impairment have been reduced even if the pre-injury speech ability is not regained. All of the approaches rely on neural plasticity. Restorative treatments directly aim to change neural processes to restore ability. For compensatory strategies and assistive devices, a person needs to learn new processes and skills to be able to use a strategy or device, which also require neural plasticity. To fully understand neurorehabilitation, one needs to understand principles of neural plasticity.

Kleim and Jones (2008) authored a seminal paper on the principles of experience-dependent neural plasticity in the disciplines of speech-language pathology and audiology. It is useful to highlight the term **experience-dependent** as the crux of adaptive neural change or recovery. The extent and nature of the recovery depends upon the person's experiences. In other words, the extent to which they participate in activities, and the types of activities they participate in, matter.

We know that neural plasticity is a key component of rehabilitation. That being said, not all activity is equal and not all neural plasticity is adaptive. Effective interventions are examined through research that follows a specific protocol and we should expect that quality of outcomes will relate to how accurately the intervention is implemented (this is called treatment fidelity). On the other hand, not every individual responds to interventions in the exact same way, so individual adjustments must be made to optimize treatment outcomes. Knowing which elements of an intervention must remain consistent and which ones can/should be altered for individuals requires a clear understanding of the intervention. To complicate this further, much of the research fails to identify a specific set of active ingredients and optional elements. The **rehabilitation treatment specification system (RTSS)** attempts to identify those elements and thus optimize treatment outcomes (optimize neural plasticity).

Box 5-1 Principles of Experience Dependent Neural Plasticity

- *Use it or lose it*—Our brains remodel based on the activity we engage in or fail to engage in.
- *Use it and improve it*—Again, our brains remodel based upon the activity we engage in and can improve, assuming we engage accurately. This relates to the old adages of practice makes perfect and practice makes permanent.
- *Specificity*—Treatment targets must be equivalent or at least as similar as possible to the behavior we hope to change. Thus, it is useful for interventions to be ecologically valid (likely to generalize to everyday activities) and authentic. Further, environment matters, as many behavior outcomes are context specific.
- *Repetition matters*—Errorless repetition = adaptive plasticity. Again, this relates to the adage practice makes permanent. Accurate practice results in adaptive plasticity changes but inaccurate practice can lead to maladaptive plasticity changes.
- *Intensity matters*—How much intervention is optimal? This relates to the concept of dosage of interventions along the recovery continuum. For instance, low intensity during acute recovery may be best, whereas the need for intensity often increases during subacute recovery.
- *Time matters*—When is optimum time for intervention? This relates to the concept of timing of interventions along the recovery continuum. Plasticity is not a single process, and some forms of plasticity function early while others function later. In general, early treatment after brain injury is important.
- *Salience matters*—This means the more personally relevant an action is, the more impact it is likely to have. This point emphasizes the importance of person-centered interventions and collaborative goal setting. It also relates to motivation and the need to establish relevance and purpose.
- *Age matters*—While younger brains are more adaptable, change remains possible across the lifespan. Further, some damage that occurs at critical points of development may not surface, in terms of behavioral impairments, until a later point in life. For instance, early damage to the frontal lobes may compromise executive functions but because executive functions are not expected to emerge until the pre-teen years, impairments may not be apparent until that time.
- *Transference matters*—Plasticity in response to training in one experience can positively influence acquisition of similar behaviors or skills. Generalization depends on authentic intervention in authentic contexts and personally relevant tasks.
- *Interference*—Plasticity in response to one experience can interfere with acquisition of other behaviors. One experience affects others and this can be constructive or deconstructive.

From Blake and Hoepner, 2023, pp. 266–267. Used with permission.

Historical Context

Historically, views of health and rehabilitation focused on the absence of disease and deficits. The medical (or biomedical) model is based on the discipline of medicine, where physicians focused on impairments and sought to "correct" health conditions that they encountered (WHO-ICF, 2001). This model views disability as a characteristic of the person, caused by disease, trauma, or other health conditions, and which requires medical care. Additionally, it purports that disease is a disorder of the structure or function of the body and therefore underlies all changes to health (Wade, 2015). While this model addresses the physical factors associated with diseases and other health conditions, it fails to address the whole human being. For example, a physical impairment such as hemiparesis can certainly restrict one's participation in physical activities but it is not the only factor of influence. Likewise, while repairing or addressing a physical impairment may address function, it is not exclusively responsible for degree of recovery.

In the 1990s, medical professions began to shift from an impairment focused medical model toward a biopsychosocial model. As the name suggests, the newer model takes into account not only biological factors (e.g., a brain injury), but also psychological and social aspects relevant to an individual that influence both the impact of the disease/damage and the recovery from it. The field of speech-language pathology experienced a parallel shift, particularly in medical speech-language pathology contexts.

To encourage consideration of the person with a health condition in the context of their life experience, the World Health Organization devised the International Classification of Functioning, Disability, and Health (WHO-ICF, 2001) (Figure 5–1). In this biopsychosocial framework, body structures and functions (i.e., physical status or impairment) and contextual factors (both environmental and personal) have the potential to affect a person's ability to participate fully in activities that they want and need to engage in. Note that physical status or impairments to status can serve as barriers or facilitators to participation. Likewise, the physical environment and/or partner environment can be either an obstacle or facilitator of participation. The physical environment includes (among other things) the temperature, lighting, surfaces, auditory and visual demands. The partner environment includes who the partner is, their relationship to the person, their attitudes, and addresses how partner interactions either support or impede participation. Finally, personal factors can be barriers or facilitators to participation. Personal factors include internal states (e.g., fatigue, hunger, thirst, pain), beliefs, attitudes, and motivation. An example of mapping a client to the WHO-ICF is shown in Figure 5–2.

The WHO-ICF model can be used to guide assessment and treatment, as shown in Tables 5–1 and 5–2. This structure aids in consideration of all relevant factors when determining a client's strengths and weaknesses as well as selecting goals and methods for achieving those goals.

In addition to the ICF model, the WHO (2022) now defines health as a state of optimal physical, psychological, and social well-being, rather than the absence of disease or disability. Well-being is defined as "the balance point between an individual's (biopsychosocial) resource

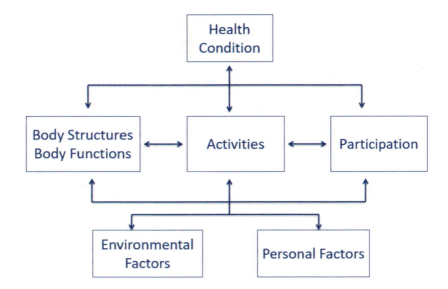

Figure 5–1. The WHO-ICF model for rehabilitation. *Source*: Adapted from World Health Organization. (2001). International classification of functioning, disability and health: ICF. World Health Organization. https://apps.who.int/iris/handle/10665/42407

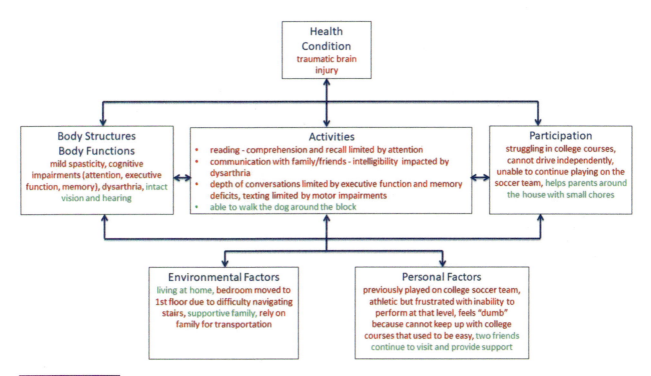

Figure 5–2. Mapping clients to the WHO-ICF model. *Note:* Factors in red are negative; factors in green are positive. *Source*: Reproduced from World Health Organization. (2001). International classification of functioning, disability and health: ICF. World Health Organization. https://apps.who.int/iris/handle/10665/42407

Table 5–1. Links Between WHO-ICF and General Assessment Principles

Domains	Recommended Practices	Considerations
Body Structures and Body Functions	Observations of function	Observe performance in different settings and conditions
	Non-standard assessments of function	Observe performance under different conditions and environments
	Standardized assessments of ability and impairments	Some standardized assessments have cultural and linguistic biases
Activity & Participation	Learn what the client wants and needs to do, as well as how participation is restricted	Can involve conversations or formal questionnaires such as the Sydney Psychosocial Reintegration Scale (SPRS), tangible value sorts (e.g., Talking Mats, Life Interest and Value (LIV) Cards, Activity Card Sort), etc. Select tools that are culturally representative
Personal Factors	Interview client	May require use of tangible sorts and communication supports to ensure a means of response
	Interview family	Allows you to learn additional information and corroborate the client's answers
	Tangible sorts of interests and values	Talking Mats, Life Interests and Value Cards (LIV Cards), Activity Card Sort (ACS), Personal value sorts
	Needs checklists	Ask about preferences for terminology and other cultural preferences
Environment	Examine how the physical environment either serves as a barrier or facilitator to participation	Environmental inventories like the ICF environmental factors, Environment and Communication Assessment Toolkit (ECAT), Craig Hospital Inventory of Environmental Factors (CHIEF)
	Examine how partners serve as a barrier or facilitator to participation	Partner interaction styles vary by culture

Table 5–2. Links Between WHO-ICF and General Intervention Principles

Domains	Recommended Practices	Description
Body Structures and Body Functions	Direct practice with clinician and client's own feedback	Engage the client in direct practice of the treatment targets, clinician prompts self-assessments with or without the support of video and audio review, clinician provides constructive feedback
Activity & Participation	Practice and use communication modalities within personally relevant activities (e.g., work, school, home, and community)	The clinician elicits information about the client's communicative contexts and needs. Practice functional communication tasks within those contexts.
Personal Factors	Address personal factors	The clinician elicits information about the client's interests, values, beliefs, motivations, and intrinsic state (pain, fatigue, hunger, etc.)
Environment	Communication partner training (CPT)	Train everyday communication partners on how to best support an individual with a communication disorder. Provide education.
	Environmental modifications	Modifications to the physical environment (e.g., reduce noise, decrease visual distractions, improve lighting, etc.)

pool and the (biopsychosocial) challenges faced" (Dodge et al., 2012, p. 230). Despite inroads to more holistic models of illness and intervention, the biomedical model of illness persists as the dominant model of illness in most of the world. It also strongly adheres to **Cartesian dualism**, the belief that the mind is separate from the body. This idea leads to the division of **organic** (caused by physical, biochemical or structural change) versus **non-organic** or **functional** (symptoms appear without identifiable or measurable physical, biochemical or structural change) disorders, failing to recognize any overlap or reciprocal influence of mind on body or vice versa. Consequences of adhering to this model include the beliefs that: (a) diseases have external causes and the person is not responsible, (b) treatments are also external and the person is a passive recipient, (c) ill persons should be cared for, and (d) the ill person should receive and follow treatments and advice.

Box 5–2 Definitions of WHO-ICF Terminology

Disability: Definitions differ through the lens of the medical model as opposed to a social model, which aligns with the WHO-ICF framework. All direct quotes are taken from the ICF Beginner's Guide (WHO-ICF, 2002).

> "The medical model views disability as a feature of the person, directly caused by disease, trauma or other health condition, which requires medical care provided in the form of individual treatment by professionals. Disability, on this model, calls for medical or other treatment or intervention, to 'correct' the problem with the individual."

> "The social model of disability, on the other hand, sees disability as a socially created problem and not at all an attribute of an individual. On the social model, disability demands a political response, since the problem is created by an unaccommodating physical environment brought about by attitudes and other features of the social environment."

Health condition: diseases, disorders, trauma, or other health conditions.

Body structures: "physiological functions of body systems (including psychological functions)."

Body functions: "anatomical parts of the body such as organs, limbs and their components."

Impairments: "problems in body function or structure such as a significant deviation or loss."

Activity: "the execution of a task or action by an individual."

Activity limitations: "difficulties an individual may have in executing activities."

Participation: "involvement in a life situation."

Participation restrictions: "problems an individual may experience in involvement in life situations."

Environmental factors: "make up the physical, social and attitudinal environment in which people live and conduct their lives" including: "social attitudes, architectural characteristics, legal and social structures, as well as climate, terrain and so forth."

Personal factors: "gender, age, coping styles, social background, education, profession, past and current experience, overall behaviour pattern, character and other factors that influence how disability is experienced by the individual."

Box 5-3 The Problem With Cartesian Dualism (aka, The Mind and Body Aren't Really Separate)

An eloquent example exists in our clinical work within individuals with executive dysfunction. Damage to the prefrontal cortex causes reduced working memory and executive dysfunction. In clinical contexts, where emotional demands are low, the environment is fairly controlled, and task complexity is fairly stable, consequences of the organic damage to the brain are often minimized. Conversely, in community contexts, emotions run high, environments can be complex, and task demands are less predictable. Because emotions and stress deplete working memory, performance can drop sharply. A biomedically minded practitioner may see this change or deficit in performance as purely functional, based in anxiety and other mental health dysfunction, rather than something structural or organic. Consequently, the practitioner may dismiss the organic cause rather than recognizing that it is likely both organic and nonorganic. A biopsychosocial minded practitioner is more likely to view this context-specific struggle as a product of impairment + environment + personal factors.

Box 5-4
Case 5-1. Friedreich Ataxia Case Illustration

Friedreich ataxia (FDRA) is a genetic disease that typically presents during puberty. FDRA is typically autosomal recessive, which results in a 25% chance of passing it along to an offspring (Figure 5–3A). Like diseases such as Huntington disease, it can sometimes be autosomal dominant, resulting in about a 50% chance of passing it along to an offspring (Figure 5–3B). It is the most common inherited ataxia. Predominant impairments include ataxia, dysarthria, sensory loss, muscle weakness, scoliosis, foot deformities, nystagmus, sensory loss, visual and hearing loss, diabetes mellitus, and cardiomyopathy (Reetz et al., 2015). Symptoms are progressive and begin quite mild but most individuals with FDRA lose the ability to walk by age 25 and die in their late 30s. Speech, swallowing, sensory, motor, language, and cognitive system impairments are all present.

Case Description: Making a connection to the human side of disease is crucial, as the effects are not solely on the individual and extend far beyond the physical changes. Therefore, this case frames FDRA from the perspective of a mom, more specifically a mom who works in rehabilitation herself.

"So, you've known forever that something is wrong with your child. You feel silly bringing it up anymore. And when you mention it to his primary care doctor, the doctor just shrugs. Eventually, others start to notice, and you return to various doctors

continues

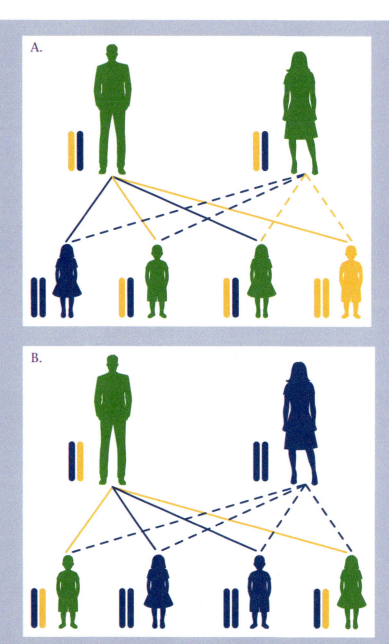

Figure 5–3. A. Familial inheritance of autosomal recessive diseases. *Note:* Each parent is a carrier with one recessive (yellow) gene with the FRDA mutation and one (blue) dominant gene. Children have a 50% chance of being carriers, and a 1 in 4 chance of either not inheriting the recessive mutated gene (blue child) or inheriting recessive genes from both parents (yellow child) and expressing the disease. B. Familial inheritance of autosomal dominant diseases. *Note:* The father has one dominant mutated gene (yellow) while the mother has none. The children have a 50% chance of inheriting the mutated gene and expressing it (green children) and a 50% chance of inheriting two genes with no mutation (blue children).

in earnest, neurologists conducting mini-neuro testing, physical therapy to strengthen his core, negative genetic tests, electromyography, 'weird' EKGs, never-ending questions, more shrugging of shoulders and no movement toward diagnosis. No closer to understanding why your child isn't walking correctly, why he has ataxia and it's getting worse. No playing sports, no running, no riding a bike. He's 12 years old.

"And then one day, someone smart and curious and interested says she might have an idea about his walking. She is an electrophysiologist, and, because of a secondary genetic finding on one more negative genetic test, we meet, she listens to our 11-year odyssey, and she asks to do a heart scan, an ECHO. I watch, knowing little, but even I can see his heart is not right. Now I know, in my gut, we are closer to an answer and the answer is not going to be good. 'I think I know what it is, I've seen it once before. Please run a test,' she says to the genetic counselor in the room, 'and in 21 days, we will know for sure.' The longest 21 days. Then the call on my father's birthday, Friedreich's Ataxia (FRDA or FA). Life just made a hard left and, despite the little voice in your head telling you, 'You were right,' you aren't prepared for the turn. He's 13 years old."

This comes from a mom who is a master level social worker, the resource queen of a prestigious neurorehabilitation center, a previous pediatric hospice social worker, whose job it is to help families like . . . hers. FDRA leads to progressive mitochondrial dysfunction, oxidative stress leading to cell death, particularly within the dorsal root ganglia of the spinal cord and the dentate nucleus of the cerebellum (Campuzano et al., 1997). By age 16, her son Clark has most of the impairments identified by Reetz et al. (2015) and will continue to develop more.

"He has no sensory input to his legs. He's had 3 cardioversions; we've been hospitalized 5 times. He has a heart monitor implanted in his chest; we now have an AED in our house. He sleeps with oxygen so his O_2 saturation stays above 80. He's recently diagnosed with anxiety and panic disorder; we're even paying out-of-pocket for a pharmacogenetic test to ensure we understand how his liver metabolizes medications to ensure proper dosing. Then there are things not yet officially attributed to FA. Clark has them all including urinary urgency, central and obstructive sleep apnea, neuropathic pain, and the FA parents' group continue to add to this list. We await his next scoliosis curve readings to see if a surgical rod is needed and Clark impatiently awaits a date for head and neck surgery to make his breathing less obstructed and dangerous.

"And yet somehow, we are truly thrilled that he has smaller GAA (DNA) repeats compared to others and is considered a 'slow progressor.' This should be good news because it means if a treatment comes, when a breakthrough finally comes, he may have more left to save than those children who have been wheelchair bound since the age of 9 or 10. Clark still walks, but not safely alone. He refuses a walker or cane and still does fairly well if you give him your elbow. He uses the walls and door frames at home.

continues

He goes to an alternative school because there was no way to navigate our large high school and that was if he would even agree to try. There is nothing worse than being obviously different in a world of angsty teens striving to be alike. He is comfortable on his computer in his room away from the in-person world. I want more for him than he has currently chosen for himself, but I'm so tired. I'm not proud to take the easy road in parenting sometimes, but I'm getting better at giving myself grace."

As you see, nestled within the descriptions of neurological impairments, there is a family, a teenager, and a psychosocial context.

Given background on FDRA and this case description, answer the following questions. Questions 1–3 focus on body structures and functions, while questions 4–8 address activity, participation, and contextual factors.

1. Identify systems affected by FDRA, and any anatomical correlates.
2. Identify disorders that would typically be addressed by a speech-language pathologist. (Hint: think speech, language, cognitive, and swallowing subsystems)
3. Identify disorders that would typically be addressed by a related profession and include the names of those disciplines.
4. Beyond physical impairments, what psychosocial factors are relevant to supporting Clark?
5. What are Clark's interests and what limits his participation in those activities?
6. What does he currently do and what does he want to do that he cannot?
7. How might different environments and people either serve as facilitators or barriers to his participation in his preferred activities?
8. How might his own thoughts, beliefs, and feelings affect his participation in his preferred activities?

Case descriptions by Nancy Peterson, MSW.

Framing Assessment and Intervention in Neurorehabilitation

Assessment and intervention for individuals with acquired neurogenic impairments are complex processes. Dr. Derick Wade, professor of neurological rehabilitation at Oxford University, has developed rehabilitation frameworks based on a holistic, biopsychosocial model (Figure 5–4). Dr. Wade contends that while biological impairments are often the emphasis of physician- and clinician-directed acute care and rehabilitation, people (patients, clients, families) are primarily interested in social function (Nair & Wade, 2003). Shifting

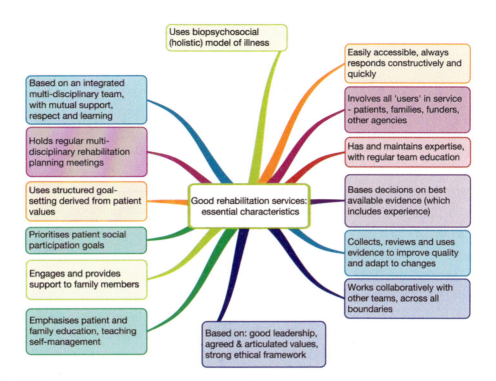

Figure 5–4. Wade's characteristics of good rehabilitation services. Copyright 2016. Derick Wade. May reproduce freely, with acknowledgement.

the dominant biomedical model requires more than shifting what rehabilitation disciplines believe. While the WHO-ICF (2001) framework is broadly known and gaining support in rehabilitation disciplines, the biomedical model remains a stronghold of the medical care system, including many medical subdisciplines. Further, it is the implicitly held standard for many persons and families who receive care in medical systems. To address this paradigm shift, Wade (2016) identifies elements of "good" rehabilitation services, beginning with being guided by a holistic, biopsychosocial model. While Wade suggests that a transdisciplinary team (i.e., where teammates carry out some roles of other disciplines—an SLP may assist with transfers and a PT may provide supported conversation to a person with aphasia) is best suited to manage the complexities of neurorehabilitation, he acknowledges that a multi-disciplinary team (i.e., where disciplines work together as a team but stick to their own disciplinary roles) is the standard of practice in current medical settings. What distinguishes an integrated multi-disciplinary team from what Wade (2016) refers to as "an accidental group of people who all happen to see the same person from time to time" (p. 4) are the factors identified in Figure 5–4. This framework is foundational for beginning our discussion of assessment and intervention in rehabilitation. Wade and Halligan (2017) argue that addressing these holistic factors improves health care outcomes.

In a typical neurorehabilitation context, our patients or clients present with a particular problem(s). This begins a rehabilitation process (cycle) with various actions needed from the rehabilitation team (Wade, 2016) (Figure 5–5, a modified version of Wade's rehabilitation process). **Assessment** includes identifying problems, impairments, and disabilities, formulating causes and influences, and identifying prognosis and potential goals. Effective, biopsychosocial-minded assessment includes identification of pathology (e.g., oral, facial, laryngeal weakness or damage), impairments (e.g., linguistic, cognitive, speech/voice, swallowing, etc.), activities (including restrictions to access), participation (including interests and altered roles), personal context (values, beliefs, motivation, stress, motivation, internal factors), and physical and social environments. In addition to the limitations and weaknesses, strengths should also be identified. **Goal setting** should include short, medium, and long-term goals that are personally relevant, time sensitive, challenging, and measured. Those goals should be based on prognosis and patient input. **Intervention** includes both supportive care and treatment (therapy). Of course, that intervention process must address several variables (Figure 5–6, a modified version of Wade's rehabilitation "intervention" process). Finally, **evaluation** measures progress/current status against the goals that were set, consider any new information, and new opportunities or goals (which leads back to further assessment or goal achievement). You can think about evaluation as progress monitoring and continuous improvement. Like intervention, evaluation is a multi-component process (Figure 5–7, a modified version of Wade's rehabilitation "evaluation" process).

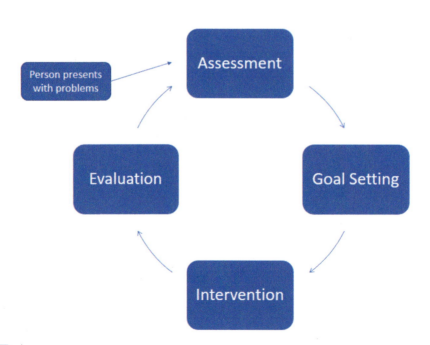

Figure 5–5. Simplified rehabilitation process. Copyright 2016. Modified from Derick Wade. May reproduce freely, with acknowledgement.

Figure 5-6. Expansion of intervention process. Copyright 2016. Modified from Derick Wade. May reproduce freely, with acknowledgement.

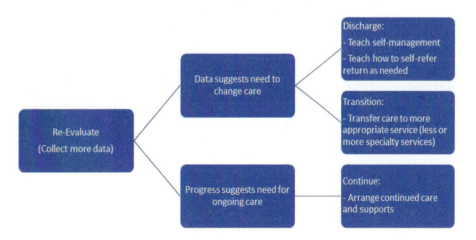

Figure 5-7. Expansion of diagnostic process. Copyright 2016. Modified from Derick Wade. May reproduce freely, with acknowledgement.

Box 5–5 Collaborative Goal Setting Tools

A number of excellent collaborative goal models exist in speech-language pathology and related disciplines (Haley et al., 2019; Hersh et al., 2012; Turkstra, 2021; Wilson et al., 2009). Brief descriptions of these models follow.

- FOURC (Haley et al., 2019): The FOURC or four Cs model describes a process for choosing communication goals given the support of tangible topic sorts, such as the Life Interests and Values (LIV) Cards (Haley et al., 2010; Haley et al., 2013). The use of tangible topic sorts allows individuals with cognitive and language impairments to self-select goal areas and prioritize them through the use of ranking and rating scales. Clients are involved in measuring their own outcomes.
- SMARTER goals (Hersh et al., 2012): SMARTER goals are intended to emphasize development of client-centered goals that can be framed as objectively measured SMART goals (Specific, Measurable, Achievable, Relevant, and Time-Bound). SMARTER goals are *shared* (client-centered but address clinician identified needs), *monitored* (measured/assessed by both the client and clinician), *accessible* (clients have tools to select their own goals, such as tangible topic sorts), *relevant* (valued by the client), *transparent* (link goal targets and outcomes in client-friendly terms), *evolving* (changing as priorities and needs change), and *relationship-centered* (acknowledging personhood and fostering therapeutic alliance, agreed upon by all parties).
- Goal mapping (Turkstra, 2021): Goal maps use backward mapping toward the client's broad goals (e.g., they want to be able to accomplish X). Clinicians help the client to map each of the steps needed to accomplish that larger goal. This allows clients to see when they reach incremental steps and to understand the process involved in reaching the broader goal. Like the FOURC and SMARTER goals, self-measurement of incremental and final outcomes is part of this process. This process also aligns with the RTSS by isolating targets and matching them to specific outcome measures.
- Formulations (Wilson et al., 2009): Formulations establish a framework for better understanding a client's abilities/impairments, interests/values, and goals. Collaborative development of goals ensures that clinician and client are on the same page, not just drawing goals from assessment outcomes but on interests and values.
- Goal attainment scales are another mechanism that engages clients in the process of goal setting and measurement (Hoepner et al., 2021; Malec, 1999; Turner-Stokes, 2009). Because the goals are set collaboratively with the clients and worded in an objective manner that clients can rate, they become more familiar with their goals and increments of progress toward goals.

Rehabilitation Treatment Specification System (RTSS)

The RTSS is a framework for systematically classifying rehabilitation treatments (Hart, Kozlowski, et al., 2014; Hart, Tsaousides, et al., 2014; Hart et al., 2019). The RTSS conceptual framework makes the link between treatment theory and ingredients, helping the clinician to understand how and why specific treatment approaches work (Turkstra et al., 2016).

To more specifically describe and organize what really goes into treatments, the RTSS draws upon theory to identify three key parts: targets, ingredients, and mechanisms of action (Hart et al., 2014; Turkstra et al., 2016; Whyte et al., 2014) (Figure 5–9). First, you must identify what you are attempting to change, the **treatment target**. Targets are a specific component of a client's function that the client and clinician directly want to change or improve. In pharmacological interventions, the target is a physiological change (e.g., cessation of headache) and the **active ingredient** is the chemical formula for the medication that achieves this target. While cessation of the headache is the immediate target, the overall treatment aim is likely broader, such as allowing the person to participate in daily activity

> ### Box 5–6 Good Rehab is a Lot Like a Good Cookie
>
> Let's use the metaphor of baking to explore why not all treatments are the same. Have you ever made cookies based on an old family recipe? Grandma makes the best cut out cookies for the holidays but you don't get to see grandma as often as you'd like or eat her cookies as often either. So, last holiday season you got smart and made copies of all of grandma's best cookie recipes, including the cut out cookies. You know all of the ingredients and just how long to bake each cookie. Sadly, when you mix up the ingredients and bake them, they're nothing like grandma's cookies. With tears streaming down your face, you ask the question, "WHY?" Grandma's recipe, much like descriptions of a treatment approach, includes the overt ingredients and instructions. What her recipe doesn't include are all of the other things grandma implicitly knows to do but did not write on the recipe (like mix the wet ingredients first, gently fold in the dry ingredients, don't overagitate the mix once flour has been added, and grandma's oven runs a little hot so she bakes at 400 instead of 425 . . . oh, and add a pinch of love). This is similar to the way rehabilitation happens. We all follow the basic recipe but some of us have the unwritten recipe. Learning that recipe requires one of two things: (1) experience and (2) a more complete, nuanced "grandma" recipe. This is where the RTSS comes in. John Whyte describes grandma's special ingredients as the black box of rehabilitation. Sure, we know the basic ingredients of an intervention, but do we know everything else that goes into effective interventions? Some of them, like grandma's baking, have to do with general practices of good clinicians. See Figure 5–8 for a visual of what may go into the black box of unspoken ingredients.

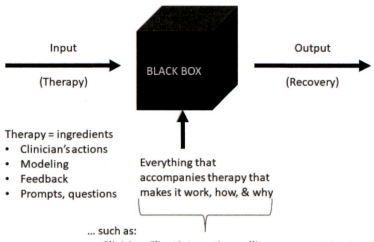

Figure 5–8. What is in the black box?

or improve their quality of life. In neurorehabilitation, the **target** may be something like improved comprehension, accurate articulation of a sound or word, a safe swallow, ability to recall a task, and the like. In many cases, this is equivalent to the client or clinician's short-term goals. A clear understanding of the targets directly influences which ingredients are used and how, which is essential to maximize benefits (Turkstra et al., 2016). In neurorehabilitation, **ingredients** are the clinician's actions and the materials they use to make changes in the target behavior. These are selected to directly impact the treatment **targets** (short term or micro-goals). Typical **treatment aims** are connected to the client or clinician's long-term goals, such as improved communication or quality of life (long-term or macro-goals). The targets are steps toward achieving the aims. **Mechanisms of action** for interventions are typically not visible or tangible (Hart et al., 2018; Meulenbroek et al., 2019) . Short-term targets, ingredients, and mechanisms of action collectively predict achievement of a treatment aim. Since many treatments are implemented with the ultimate goal of reaching the treatment aim (e.g., better interactions with family and friends, better quality of life), we must accurately identify all of the targets, ingredients, and mechanisms of action necessary. Often, multiple targets and ingredients are necessary to reach a treatment aim.

As addressed in Figure 5–8, the mechanism of action (i.e., what is in the black box or grandma's secret ingredients) is not as easy to isolate. A target is the most proximal functional change caused by the active ingredients' mechanism of action (Whyte & Turkstra,

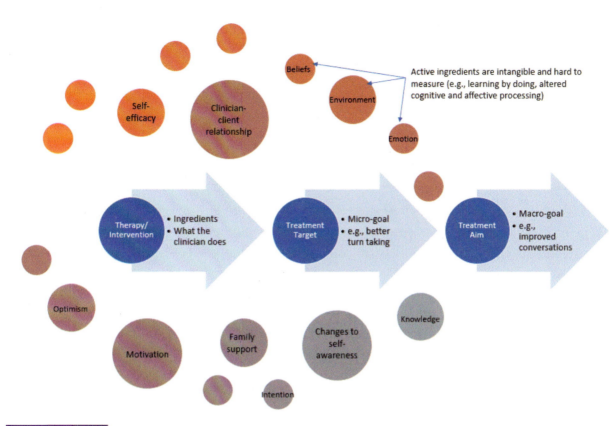

Figure 5–9. From ingredients to goal achievement.

Box 5–7 The Trouble With Standardized Assessments

Let's say that your treatment target is reading age-appropriate and personally interesting materials. You work on a variety of reading tasks following a specific reading intervention. To examine whether the client has met the goal, you conduct a reading assessment. The reading assessment includes reading single words, phrases, and paragraphs; matching words to images; comprehension tasks; etc. The test may give you subscores, which would allow you to more directly measure the outcome or it may give you a total, composite score, which assesses all of the elements and doesn't truly reflect the one piece you actually wish to measure for the treatment target. Further, it does not address other factors that contribute to reading success, such as attention, cognitive endurance, motivation, and more.

Here's another example. Let's say your treatment target is self-regulation, an element of executive function. Your standardized assessment includes a number of executive function measures, including working memory tasks, problem solving and reasoning tasks, inhibition, shifting set, etc. Parsing out or extrapolating self-regulation from a

continues

> composite of those measures is daunting, perhaps impossible. This creates a challenge in determining what data you use to assess whether the client met the treatment target.
>
> These scenarios are true for therapy as well as for research outcome measures. The moral of the story is that both researchers and clinicians need to do a better job of isolating what we measure and matching it to what we are purporting to measure.

2021). In order to determine whether the client has achieved the target, you must select a way to measure it. Outcome measures ideally should be a direct indication of the target. Unfortunately, the outcome measures that are typically used to measure target achievement are often composite measures, which include multiple skills, some of which are unrelated to the target. In these cases the extent to which performance improves on outcome measures is not a true indication of meeting the target. If you are interested, Behn et al. (2023) mapped treatment targets, aims, and mechanisms of action to a treatment approach. You may find the framework useful for mapping what your treatments are intended to change.

Health Equity, Social Determinants of Health, Cultural/Ethnic Issues

Recent geopolitical events coupled with health inequities exposed through the COVID-19 pandemic have caused many institutions to reevaluate health inequities, underlying contributors to those disparities, and their own role in contributing to or perpetuating these injustices. Identifying inequities, searching for causes, and acknowledging and reconsidering long-held beliefs about health, health care systems, public health, and societal inequities is necessary to move toward health equity.

Keeping Up With Terminology

The terminology and narratives we use can contribute to perpetuating health inequities and injustice. Medicine, for example, has a history of patriarchal narratives that promote traditional race and gender norms. These exist alongside the biomedical model and together put power and decision making in the hands of physicians. Narratives such as these can become **deep narratives** (sometimes referred to as malignant narratives) that over time have become deeply entrenched and have the potential to create harm, undermine public health, and be a barrier to health equity. The Race Forward organization (https://www.raceforward.org/) describes the development of deep narratives as starting with words and images that are used to create stories. Multiple stories that all represent the same belief or idea collectively become a narrative that explains a problem, its causes, and the solutions. Once this narrative has been repeated over and over across time and generations, it becomes what we come to take for granted as "the way things are and always have been," and which influence our values and our behaviors.

The Race Forward organization suggests that we need to be intentional about promoting stories and messages that align with the values we want to promote. The Centers for Disease Control (CDC), American Medical Association (AMA) and the Association of American Medical Colleges (AAMC) Center for Health Justice all have created resources for selecting and using terminology. Accepted terminology changes rapidly, especially when there are active societal conversations about values. Readers are encouraged to check websites for recommended terminology. Some current principles for selecting terms include:

- Avoid stigmatizing adjectives that serve as a blanket, proxy term for a broad range of individuals, such as "vulnerable" or "high risk" (Katz et al., 2020).
- Avoid dehumanizing language such as disabled, handicapped, or demented, and respect neurodiversity by describing differences rather than disorders (see Box 5–8).
- Remember that there are many subpopulations, and avoid blanket terms that include large, heterogeneous groups when you are talking about individuals.
- Avoid terms with a potentially violent connotation.
- Avoid unintentional blaming and focus on a person's choices (not to wear a mask) rather than their failure to conform to others' choices (anti-masker).

Box 5–8 Terminology Changes

When we (the authors) started teaching, there was a strong focus on "person-first language" that recommended avoiding labels based on a condition or disease, such as "aphasic" or "brain injured" patients. This labeling convention was designed with the best of intentions, to keep clinicians and others thinking about the person, and not defining them by a disease or disorder. Some groups started pushing back, arguing that their so-called "condition" was an integral part of who they were, and they didn't appreciate outsiders making decisions about labels. Two notable examples are the Deaf community and autistic people. People in the Deaf community do not see their deafness as a disability. Many are proud to be Deaf, and calling them "people with hearing impairment" or with "a hearing loss," instead of seeming more kind, actually highlights the presence of a deficit instead of identifying a key characteristic (which is not negative) of who they are. Similarly, many autistic people prefer to be called autistic because that is who they are. Terminology around autism continues to change, as "autism spectrum disorder" is in some settings changing to "autism spectrum condition" because many on that spectrum do not perceive themselves as having a disorder, but rather a different way of thinking and communicating. Some like person-first language. Some do not. The best thing to do is pay attention to how people introduce themselves or ask about their preferred descriptors.

Social Determinants of Health

The WHO defines social determinants of health as "non-medical factors that influence health outcomes. They are the conditions in which people are born, grow, work, live and age, and the wider set of forces and systems shaping the conditions of daily life" (World Health Organization, 2023). These include patient, provider, system, and policy level factors. **Patient level factors** include health literacy; trust of health and social systems; access to medical care, healthy foods, and safe areas for exercise; treatment preferences and adherence to medical recommendations; and prior experiences, especially experiences of discrimination. **Provider level factors** include prejudice and implicit bias, cultural competency, cross-racial and cross-ethnic interactions/experiences, and underrepresentation of minority groups in provider roles. **System and policy level factors** include access to medical care, quality of that care, resource allocation, insurance policies, cultural norms and values, and structural racism. As will be seen below, these factors are not independent. For example, access and trust are commonly lower for people in historically marginalized groups who also may experience cultural or language differences between themselves and health care providers.

Access to Care and Healthy Living

Access to health care involves having doctors, clinics, or hospitals nearby, but also having transportation and time off from work to access them, insurance to cover the costs, and being able to communicate with them and understand the information they provide. The latter includes not only the language(s) in which the information is conveyed but also the level at which it is conveyed.

In the United States, the interaction between access and race/ethnicity has received increasing attention. A survey of 30 studies of stroke care indicated that in general, Whites were more likely to (a) use emergency services, (b) arrive at a hospital within three hours of stroke symptom onset, and (c) receive the gold-standard pharmacological treatment for stroke compared to Black, Asian, and Hispanic groups (Ikeme, 2022). People from historically minoritized and marginalized groups, including Black and Hispanic/Latino groups, are disproportionately affected by TBI. This is true for both children and older adults, and for mild as well as more severe TBIs. Discrepancies affect quality of care, also. They have longer wait times to see medical personnel, receive fewer referrals for relevant care as well as fewer total hours of treatment. They have poorer functional outcomes and community re-integration and increased level of disability (Brenner et al., 2020). Discrepancies also occur for dementias: People from these historically marginalized groups tend to be diagnosed with dementia later in the course of the disease, and experience greater cognitive decline (Quinones et al., 2020). They also report lower health-related quality of life.

Social determinants of health include the access to healthy food options, including the number of grocery stores, convenience stores, and fast-food restaurants. In four major cities in the United States, average neighborhood income is inversely related to the density of convenience stores and in low-income neighborhoods, the percentage of neighborhood population that identifies as White is inversely related to the density of fast-food restaurants (Tsao et al., 2022).

Research shows that high-intensity and high-dosage rehabilitation facilitates recovery. This is true for all sorts of communication and cognitive disorders. Unfortunately, that regimen is not accessible to everyone who needs it. It requires money, both for the therapy and for the time needed. To engage in long-term, intensive therapy, a patient needs to be able to re-allocate their time from their caregiving, job, housekeeping, or other responsibilities. It also assumes that there are no additional medical issues that might derail or delay recovery. Gabby Giffords, the congresswoman from Arizona who became aphasic after a gunshot wound to the head (see Chapter 7, Box 7–5) has experienced a substantial improvement in her aphasia over more than a decade. There are many factors that likely had an impact: her high level of education, her strong family support, and her perseverance and determination, but also the resources that allow her to work with experts in aphasia and to continue rehabilitation long after medical insurance stops paying for it (see Fridriksson, 2020 for more comments).

Education and Socialization

Level of education is related to the ability to understand health care information and instructions. The more education you have, the easier it is to understand what your doctor is saying. But this is not the sole determinant. Someone with a high-school education who has family members with stroke may have a better understanding of the condition than someone with advanced education who has never been exposed to stroke personally. Additionally, health literacy is not all or none. Someone living with diabetes may have a very good understanding of their condition and may be able to communicate with a physician at a high level. However, they may need simpler language and more detailed descriptions of traumatic brain injury.

Education is beneficial not only for communicating about health conditions, but also for overall brain function. Routine engagement in cognitively demanding tasks and thinking about things in new, creative ways improves brain function and provides some protection against the consequences of aging and damage to the brain. This is called **cognitive reserve.** The higher your cognitive reserve, the longer you'll be able to maintain function for daily activities in the face of aging or damage to the brain (Figure 5–10). Imagine that your overall brain function can range from 0–100, the average adult functions around 80, and difficulties with everyday tasks occur if the functional level drops below 50. If you can increase your functional level to 90, then if you incur a stroke or TBI that drops your functioning by 30, you will still be above the cut-off for impairments in daily life. This does not mean that highly educated people are immune to the effects of brain injury; rather, they have a "cushion" that includes the ability to think creatively and develop or use strategies. This may help them adjust to mild or moderate declines in neural functioning in order to maintain daily functions.

Cognitive reserve is one explanation for why higher levels of education are related to lower risk of dementias. Formal education is not the only source of increasing cognitive reserve. Routinely engaging in cognitively stimulating activities includes learning of any sort: learning a new language, skill, hobby, etc. People who actively use more than one language have greater cognitive reserve than monolinguals. Those who work in jobs that require

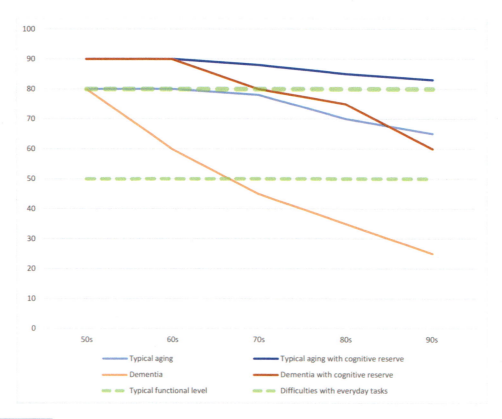

Figure 5–10. The purported effects of cognitive reserve.

problem solving or creative thinking are better off than those whose work is repetitive and requires little critical or creative thinking.

Socialization is a very important, but commonly overlooked, factor. The CDC reports that the risk of premature death is significantly increased by social isolation. This is true for all causes of death, and the increased risk is comparable to that related to obesity and smoking. Social isolation increases risk of stroke by over 30% and dementias by 50% (Centers for Disease Control, 2020b)

The Coin Model

Nixon (2019) developed the **Coin Model** to explain how systems such as health care can perpetuate social and health inequities (Figure 5–11). Oppression creates structural and systemic vulnerability. **Structural vulnerability** describes the risk that an individual or group has for poor health outcomes related to socioeconomic, political, and cultural hierarchies. **Systemic vulnerability** refers to a group of individuals who have difficulty achieving or sustaining livelihood. System and policy level factors may constrain one's ability to access health care services and prevention through healthy diet, environments, and activity. This

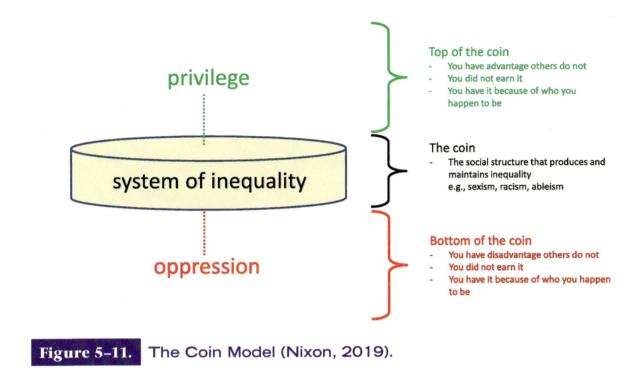

Figure 5–11. The Coin Model (Nixon, 2019).

includes individuals we encounter in rehabilitation settings because of social determinants of health. In this case, non-medical factors have the potential to influence or exacerbate health outcomes. These factors include food insecurity or lack of easy access to healthy foods; marginal, unstable or precarious housing; lack of proper medical care and insurance; co-existing mental health challenges; substance use; domestic, gender-based, and/or intimate partner violence; involvement in the criminal justice system; and/or refugee or asylum seeker status. Often differences in health literacy, quality or access to education and developmental habilitation or support make them susceptible as adults and limit their ability to access and effectively use the health care system as adults.

Summary

Effective neurorehabilitation is a complex process. It begins with understanding principles of neuroplasticity and making applications to evidence-based interventions. The RTSS model provides a framework for considering the ingredients, targets, and aims for evidence-based interventions to meet the needs of individual clients. A holistic, biopsychosocial approach is necessary to ensure that one's approach is person centered. This requires learning about the desires, needs, and values of the individual with whom you're working. Further, this requires an understanding of cultural and personal differences, including how to identify them and address them within intervention.

Key Concepts

- Neural plasticity is crucial to recovery and central to our rehabilitation goals. Participation in the right types of personally relevant activities and evidence-based intervention tasks can optimize functional outcomes following onset of a neurogenic disorder.
- The WHO-ICF model is a holistic, biopsychosocial model for health, which is intended to replace the impairment-focused medical model.
- The RTSS provides a framework for applying theory, research evidence, and broad clinical knowledge and skills to rehabilitation. Understanding the treatment targets, ingredients, mechanisms of actions, and aims is critical to achieving optimal outcomes.
- Wade's expanded biopsychosocial model for rehabilitation provides a detailed framework of the essential elements of effective rehabilitation services. Wade also provides a framework for the processes of rehabilitation, from assessment to progress monitoring and goal achievement.
- Several prominent medical organizations have developed guidelines for appropriate terminology and narratives for health equity.
- Access to health and health care can be enabled or restricted due to non-medical factors at the patient, provider, societal, and policy levels.
- Education and socialization are beneficial to maintaining health and recovering from diseases or disorders.
- Systems can perpetuate oppression and reduced access for care for some while providing a privilege to others.

References

Academy of Neurologic Communication Sciences & Disorders. (2023). *ANCDS podcasts*. https://www.ancds.org/public-podcasts

Academy of Neurologic Communication Sciences & Disorders. (2023). *Practice resources*. https://www.ancds.org/practice-resources

American Medical Association and Association of American Medical Colleges. (2021) *Advancing health equity: Guide on language, narrative and concepts*. ama-assn.org/equity-guide

American Speech-Language-Hearing Association. (2023). *About ASHA's special interest groups*. https://www.asha.org/sig/about-special-interest-groups

American Speech-Language-Hearing Association. (2023). *Cultural responsiveness*. https://www.asha.org/practice-portal/professional-issues/cultural-responsiveness/

American Speech-Language-Hearing Association. (2023). *The practice portal*. https://www.asha.org/practice-portal

Behn, N., Hoepner, J. K., Meulenbroek, P., Hart, J., & Capo, M. (2023). Core components of project-based intervention after acquired brain injury: Delivering meaningful groups online. *International Journal of Language and Communication Disorders*. https://doi.org/10.1111/1460-6984.12834

Blake, M. H., & Hoepner, J. K. (2023). *Clinical neuroscience for communication disorders* (pp. 266–267). Plural Publishing.

Brenner, E. K., Grossner, E. C., Johnson, B. N., Bernier, R. A., Soto, J., & Hillary, F. G. (2020). Race and ethnicity considerations in traumatic brain injury research: Incidence, reporting, and outcome. *Brain Injury, 34*(6), 801–810.

Campuzano, V., Montermini, L., Lutz, Y., Cova, L., Hindelang, C., Jiralerspong, S., . . . Koenig, M. (1997). Frataxin is reduced in Friedreich ataxia patients and is associated with mitochondrial membranes. *Human Molecular Genetics, 6*(11), 1771–1780.

Center for International Rehabilitation Research Information & Exchange. (2021). *Cultural competence.* http://cirrie-sphhp.webapps.buffalo.edu/culture

Centers for Disease Control. (2020a). *Culture, language, and health literacy.* https://www.hrsa.gov/about/organization/bureaus/ohe/health-literacy/culture-language-and-health-literacy

Centers for Disease Control. (2020b). Social Determinants of Health and Alzheimer's Disease and Related Dementias. https://www.cdc.gov/aging/disparities/social-determinants-alzheimers.html.

Dodge, R., Daly, A. P., Huyton, J., & Sanders, L. D. (2012). The challenge of defining wellbeing. *International Journal of Wellbeing, 2*(3), 222–235.

Fridriksson, J. (2020). Gabby Giffords and the lack of access to aphasia therapy. C-STAR ChitChat. https://cstar.sc.edu/gabby-giffords-and-the-lack-of-access-to-aphasia-therapy/

Haley, K. L., Cunningham, K. T., Barry, J., & de Riesthal, M. (2019). Collaborative goals for communicative life participation in aphasia: The FOURC model. *American Journal of Speech-Language Pathology, 28*(1), 1–13.

Haley, K. L., Womack, J., Helm-Estabrooks, N., Caignon, D., & McCulloch, K. (2010). *Life interests and values cards.* University of North Carolina.

Haley, K. L., Womack, J., Helm-Estabrooks, N., Lovette, B., & Goff, R. (2013). Supporting autonomy for people with aphasia: Use of the Life Interests and Values (LIV) cards. *Topics in Stroke Rehabilitation, 20*(1), 22–35.

Hart, T., Dijkers, M. P., Whyte, J., Turkstra, L. S., Zanca, J. M., Packel, A., & Chen, C. (2019). A theory-driven system for the specification of rehabilitation treatments. *Archives of Physical Medicine and Rehabilitation, 100*(1), 172–180.

Hart, T., Kozlowski, A. J., Whyte, J., Poulsen, I., Kristensen, K., Nordenbo, A., & Heinemann, A. W. (2014). Functional recovery after severe traumatic brain injury: An individual growth curve approach. *Archives of Physical Medicine and Rehabilitation, 95*(11), 2103–2110.

Hart, T., Tsaousides, T., Zanca, J. M., Whyte, J., Packel, A., Ferraro, M., & Dijkers, M. P. (2014). Toward a theory-driven classification of rehabilitation treatments. *Archives of Physical Medicine and Rehabilitation, 95*(1), S33–S44.

Health Resources & Services Administration. (2022). *Culture, language, and health literacy.* https://www.hrsa.gov/about/organization/bureaus/ohe/health-literacy/culture-language-and-health-literacy

Hersh, D., Worrall, L., Howe, T., Sherratt, S., & Davidson, B. (2012). SMARTER goal setting in aphasia rehabilitation. *Aphasiology, 26*(2), 220–233.

Hoepner, J. K., Sievert, A., & Guenther, K. (2021). Joint video self-modeling for persons with traumatic brain injury and their partners: A case series. *American Journal of Speech-Language Pathology, 30*(2S), 863–882.

Ikeme, S., Kottenmeier, E., Uzochukwu, G., & Brinjikji, W. (2022). Evidence-based disparities in stroke care metrics and outcomes in the United States: A systematic review. *Stroke, 29*(2), 670–679.

International classification of functioning, disability, and health: ICF. (2001). World Health Organization.

International classification of functioning, disability, and health: ICF. (2002). World Health Organization.

Katz, A. S., Hardy, B. J., Firestone, M., Lofters, A., & Morton-Ninomiya, M. E. (2020). Vagueness, power and public health: Use of 'vulnerable 'in public health literature. *Critical Public Health, 30*(5), 601–611.

Kleim, J. A., & Jones, T. A. (2008). Principles of experience-dependent neural plasticity: implications for rehabilitation after brain damage. *Journal of Speech, Language, and Hearing Research, 51*(1), S225–S239. https://doi.org/10.1044/1092-4388(2008/018)

Malec, J. F. (1999). Goal attainment scaling in rehabilitation. *Neuropsychological Rehabilitation, 9*(3–4), 253–275.

Meulenbroek, P., Ness, B., Lemoncello, R., Byom, L., MacDonald, S., O'Neil-Pirozzi, T. M., & Moore Sohlberg, M. (2019). Social communication following traumatic brain injury Part 2: Identifying effective treatment ingredients. *International Journal of Speech-Language Pathology, 21*(2), 128–142.

Nair, K. S., & Wade, D. T. (2003). Life goals of people with disabilities due to neurological disorders. *Clinical Rehabilitation, 17*(5), 521–527.

NeuroBITE. (2022). *NeuroRehab evidence resource.* https://neurorehab-evidence.com/web/cms/content/home

Nixon, S. A. (2019). The coin model of privilege and critical allyship: Implications for health. *BMC Public Health, 19*(1), 1–13.

Quiñones, A. R., Kaye, J., Allore, H. G., Botoseneanu, A., & Thielke, S. M. (2020). An agenda for addressing multimorbidity and racial and ethnic disparities in Alzheimer's disease and related dementia. *American Journal of Alzheimer's Disease & Other Dementias, 35,* 1533317520960874.

Reetz, K., Dogan, I., Costa, A. S., Dafotakis, M., Fedosov, K., Giunti, P., . . . Schulz, J. B. (2015). Biological and clinical characteristics of the European Friedreich's Ataxia Consortium for Translational Studies (EFACTS) cohort: a cross-sectional analysis of baseline data. *The Lancet Neurology, 14*(2), 174–182.

SpeechBITE. (n.d.). *Speech pathology database for best interventions and treatment efficacy.* https://speechbite.com

Tsao, C. W., Aday, A. W., Almarzooq, Z. I., Alonso, A., Beaton, A. Z., Bittencourt, M. S., . . . Martin, S. S. (2022). Heart Disease and Stroke Statistics—2022 Update: A Report From the American Heart Association. https://doi.org/10.1161/CIR.0000000000001052

Turkstra, L. S. (2021). Goal maps. Spain Rehabilitation Speech Pathologists. Unpublished manuscript. Used with permission.

Turkstra, L. S., Norman, R., Whyte, J., Dijkers, M. P., & Hart, T. (2016). Knowing what we're doing: Why specification of treatment methods is critical for evidence-based practice in speech-language pathology. *American Journal of Speech-Language Pathology, 25*(2), 164–171.

Turner-Stokes, L. (2009). Goal Attainment Scaling (GAS) in rehabilitation: A practical guide. *Clinical Rehabilitation, 23*(4), 362–370.

Wade, D. T. (2015). Rehabilitation–a new approach. Overview and Part one: The problems. *Clinical Rehabilitation, 29*(11), 1041–1050.

Wade, D. (2016). Rehabilitation–a new approach. Part three: The implications of the theories. *Clinical Rehabilitation, 30*(1), 3–10.

Wade, D. T., & Halligan, P. W. (2017). The biopsychosocial model of illness: A model whose time has come. *Clinical Rehabilitation, 31*(8), 995–1004.

Whyte, J., Dijkers, M. P., Hart, T., Zanca, J. M., Packel, A., Ferraro, M., & Tsaousides, T. (2014). Development of a theory-driven rehabilitation treatment taxonomy: Conceptual issues. *Archives of Physical Medicine and Rehabilitation, 95*(1), S24–S32.

Whyte, J., & Turkstra, L. S. (2021). Building a theoretical foundation for cognitive rehabilitation. *Brain, 144*(7), 1933–1935.

Wilson, B. A., Gracey, F., Evans, J. J., & Bateman, A. (2009). *Neuropsychological rehabilitation: Theory, models, therapy and outcome.* Cambridge University Press.

World Health Organization. (2001). International classification of functioning disability and health.

World Health Organization. (2002). Towards a common language for functionary, disability and health: ICF beginner's guide.

World Health Organization. (2023). Social determinants of health. https://www.who.int/health-topics/social-determinants-of-health

Resources

Evidence-Based Practice

Academy of Neurologic Communication Sciences & Disorders (ANCDS) Practice Guidelines and Podcasts
https://www.ancds.org/practice-resources
https://www.ancds.org/public-podcasts

American Speech-Language-Hearing Association (ASHA) Practice Portal and Special Interest Groups
https://www.asha.org/practice-portal
https://www.asha.org/sig/about-special-interest-groups

NeuroBite and SpeechBite Evidence Resources
https://neurorehab-evidence.com/web/cms/content/home
https://speechbite.com

Cultural Competence and Responsiveness

American Speech-Language-Hearing Association (ASHA) Cultural Responsiveness
https://www.asha.org/practice-portal/professional-issues/cultural-responsiveness/#collapse_2

American Medical Association and Association of American Medical Colleges. (2021) Advancing Health Equity: Guide on Language, Narrative and Concepts.
ama-assn.org/equity-guide

CDC, Culture, Language, and Health Literacy
https://www.hrsa.gov/about/organization/bureaus/ohe/health-literacy/culture-language-and-health-literacy

Center for International Rehabilitation Research Information & Exchange (CIRRIE) Cultural Competence Resources
http://cirrie-sphhp.webapps.buffalo.edu/culture

6
PREFRONTAL LOBES

Chapter Overview

Diseases and Disorders of the Frontal Lobes
   Traumatic Brain Injury
   Frontotemporal Dementia
      Assessment
      Frontal Damage Treatment
Speech Disorders
Language Disorders
   Discourse
Cognitive Disorders
   Attention
      Impairments to Attention
   Memory
   Executive Functions
   Awareness
Swallowing Disorders
Summary
Key Concepts
References

Diseases and Disorders of the Frontal Lobes

The prefrontal lobes (the anterior-most regions) are primarily responsible for higher-level cognition. Damage to right and left prefrontal regions tend to have similar effects, and thus we cover them together. Some common acquired neurogenic disorders that produce prefrontal damage include traumatic brain injuries (TBIs), anterior cerebral artery (ACA) strokes, and frontotemporal dementias (social, behavioral variant). The cognitive and communication consequences of these disorders are fairly consistent despite the differences in etiology and progression.

Traumatic Brain Injury

While many traumatic brain injuries are characterized by diffuse damage throughout the cerebrum, focal damage to the prefrontal cortices is a hallmark of many TBIs. This is in large part because there are bony projections on the floor of the skull adjacent to the inferior frontal and temporal lobes (Figure 6–1). Prefrontal dysfunction, characterized by executive dysfunction, impaired social communication, and impaired behavioral regulation are common impairments. Additional information about TBIs will be discussed further in Chapter 14 along with other injuries and diseases that cause diffuse damage.

Frontotemporal Dementia

Frontotemporal dementia (FTD) or Pick disease is sometimes discussed as a variant of primary progressive aphasias (PPA). As a frontal or behavioral variant (FTD-bv), the primary concerns are impairments to executive function and behavioral regulation. Onset is typically between the ages of 40 and 65 but it can begin earlier or later. Patterns of cortical atrophy in FTD

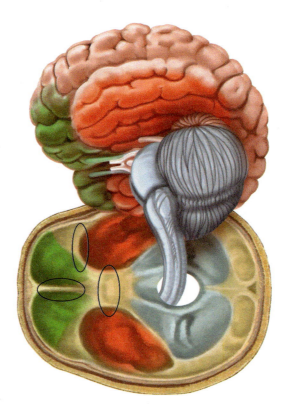

Figure 6–1. Bony projections adjacent to prefrontal (green) and anterior temporal (red) structures. Adapted from *Clinical Neuroscience for Communication Disorders: Neuroanatomy and Neurophysiology* (p. 33) by Blake, M. L. and Hoepner, J. K. Copyright © 2023 Plural Publishing, Inc. All rights reserved.

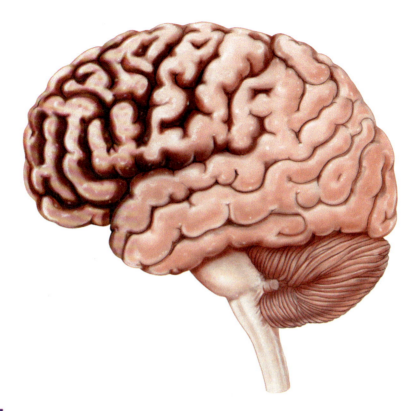

Figure 6–2. Brain atrophy typical of frontotemporal dementia.

include the anterior frontal lobe and anterior temporal lobe (Figure 6–2). Executive function impairments include impaired judgment, disinhibition, apathy, loss of empathy and interest in others, as well as declines in personal hygiene, perseverative and compulsive behaviors, pica (eating non-food items), emotional withdrawal, distractibility, agitation, and socially inappropriate behaviors. Individuals with FTD and amyotrophic lateral sclerosis (ALS) share pathology. However, ALS is a milder and more slowly progressing variant with regard to pathology. Prevalence of FTD among individuals with ALS ranges from 22% to 48% (Murphy et al., 2007), whereas about 15% of individuals with FTD show the classic signs of ALS and more show subtle lower motor neuron (LMN) signs (Lomen-Hoerth et al., 2002).

Assessment

Differential assessment of FTD primarily focuses on prefrontal functions (executive functions and social cognition). The primary intent is to distinguish FTD from Alzheimer disease (AD) and PPA variants of FTD. A number of assessments addressed in Chapter 11 are relevant, including The Awareness of Social Inferencing Test (McDonald et al., 2002). Brief overviews of two FTD-specific assessments are provided in Table 6–1.

Table 6–1. Assessments for Frontotemporal Dementia		
Test/Authors	Domains	Notes
Frontal assessment battery (FAB; Slachevsky et al., 2004)	Prefrontal functions	Includes six subtests that examine conceptualization and abstract reasoning, mental flexibility, motor programming and executive control of action, resistance to interference, inhibitory control, and environmental autonomy.
Social Cognition and Emotional Assessment (SEA; Funkiewiez et al., 2012)	Prefrontal function	Includes five subtests that examine orbitofrontal functions, including identification of facial emotions, a reversal/extinction task, a behavioral control task, a theory of mind test, and an apathy scale.

Frontal Damage Treatments

Behavior dysregulation or disinhibition is not uncommon after frontal lobe damage, and is a key symptom of FTD. There are several treatments that aid in minimizing the impact of such impairments on daily life. As shown in Table 6–2, these can include establishing and keeping set routines and redirecting to positive activities or interactions. Validation therapy, used not only for FTD but also other dementias, involves supporting the person's emotional state rather than correcting them and re-orienting them to reality.

Treatments for executive dysfunction include environmental manipulation and metacognitive strategies. These are discussed in more depth in Chapter 12.

Speech Disorders

Generally speaking, speech disorders are not directly associated with prefrontal functions. As will be covered in more detail in the next two chapters, apraxia of speech (Chapter 7) and dysarthrias (Chapters 7 and 8) are related to damage in the superior and posterior motor regions of the frontal lobe (e.g., premotor, supplementary motor, and primary motor areas). That is not to say that prefrontal functions have no influence on speech. Impulsivity may lead to issues with speaking rate and content clarity. This can present similarly to cluttering behaviors and exacerbate dysarthria and cause language clarity issues. Speech fluency is sometimes disrupted by formulation. Deficits in self-monitoring, common in prefrontal dysfunction, may lead to poor awareness and limited adjustments on the part of the speaker.

Table 6–2. Treatments for Deficits Associated With Frontal Lobe Damage

Domains	Recommended Practices	Description
Agitation and Behavioral Disinhibition	Validation therapy (Benjamin, 1995, Neal & Wright, 2003)	Affirms the individual's emotional state rather than correcting them. Redirects to a positive interaction or activity.
	Redirection and movement (Ponsford et al., 2023)	In response to agitation, redirect the individual to another activity. Movement through space and to different environments typically reduces agitation as well.
	Routines (Hoepner & Togher, 2022)	Establishing a daily schedule and routine to help with orientation and foster positive behaviors (reduce agitation).
Executive Dysfunction	Environmental modifications	Modify the physical environment to reduce distractions. Train partners to provide scaffolding and reduce demands. Educate staff and partners.
	Metacognitive strategy instruction (Kennedy et al., 2008; Palinscar, 1986; Ylvisaker, 2006)	Break tasks or problems down into smaller steps. Practice strategies in the context of meaningful activities.

Further, impaired perspective taking and theory of mind may decrease the likelihood of checking-in with one's communication partner to see if they understood.

Language Disorders

Aphasia (left perisylvian area damage) and apragmatism (right perisylvian area damage) affect core aspects of language. Prefrontal damage interrupts or exacerbates these core functions often because of impairments of cognitive functions that underlie language processes. The resulting communication disorders can be called cognitive-communication disorders as communication is impaired because of impairments in working memory, executive function, and/or social cognition.

Discourse

There is ample evidence that discourse is impaired following prefrontal damage due to traumatic brain injury and other causes (Byom & Turkstra, 2012; Douglas et al., 2007; Elbourn et al., 2019; Hartley & Jensen, 1992; Nielsen et al., 2020; Steel et al., 2017; Steel et al., 2015). Discourse production is often described as egocentric, tangential, perseverative, disorganized, and disinhibited, and there are problems with interruptions, word finding, lack of presupposition, lost train of thought, turn taking, and topic maintenance. Some people may be verbose, while others are terse or perfunctory. Discourse comprehension is compromised by impaired processing of linguistic, paralinguistic, and/or extralinguistic elements, including affective and linguistic prosody, emotion recognition, and inferences. This is true across the spectrum of discourse genres (Table 6–3). Generally speaking, the more complex and variable the genre of discourse, the more challenges are encountered. Measures of discourse often follow Grice's (1975) maxims of communication and common problems encountered by individuals with prefrontal damage often represent a problem with one of these linguistic skills (described in Chapter 4 and Table 8–2). Impairments to coherence and cohesion are also common.

Cognitive Disorders

Attention

As described in Chapter 4, there are several attentional networks. Our focus here is on attentional control systems that regulate attention, including what we attend to and what we filter out or ignore. As a reminder, the **central executive network (CEN)** is for sustained attention, information processing, problem-solving, decision making, and working memory to facilitate goal-directed behaviors (Menon, 2011). The **default mode network (DMN)** is engaged when we are letting our minds wander or thinking about our past and future; and the **salience network** is responsible for directing our attention to salient stimuli and inhibiting (filtering) our attention from irrelevant stimuli.

Impairments to Attention

Stroke, traumatic brain injury, and some dementias (e.g., FTD) can cause significant impairments to attention. Both selective attention and attentional control (for selective, alternating, or divided attention) can be affected. The degree of attention impairment varies widely

Table 6–3. Common Strengths and Challenges Across Discourse Genres

Genre	Strengths	Challenges
Monologic (e.g., think Jimmy Kimmel or Jimmy Fallon)	Self-directed and little interruption from others Can be fairly scripted	Presupposition and matching audience background knowledge can be difficult Knowing how much to say is a challenge
Descriptive (e.g., picture or object description)	Can draw on in-the-moment observations	May overlook details or important information, may have difficulty distinguishing salient from unimportant information May not be sure how much information to provide – either overshooting and providing too much or undershooting and providing too little
Procedural (e.g., making a sandwich, completing a complex task)	Procedural memory is a function of the basal ganglia and cerebellum so it often remains fairly intact	May be impaired by sequencing problems The more complex the procedure, the harder it will be to organize thoughts in a coherent manner
Narrative (e.g., retelling a personal story or a written or oral story)	Supported by implicit knowledge of story grammar and story elements	Compromised by memory difficulties Coherence is compromised by working memory impairments Sequencing order can be challenging
Expository (e.g., teaching someone)	Can draw upon declarative knowledge	May struggle with how much information to share and may err on the side of too much information/too many details or not enough information

continues

Table 6–3. continued		
Genre	Strengths	Challenges
		May struggle with presupposition, not taking the other person's knowledge and experiences into account. This plays right into the struggle with not knowing how much information to share, as they have not taken into account what the person knows/does not know
Persuasive	Can make strong arguments to support their point of view or perspective.	May struggle with presupposition and perspective taking necessary to persuade another
Conversation (i.e., can range from quick exchanges to extended or in-depth discussions)	Generally OK with superficial exchanges or familiar topics and people.	Relies heavily on working memory from a comprehension/listening and expression/responding standpoint
		Cohesion of thought is a challenge as it requires creating an internal plan and hierarchy to content, which is heavily dependent on executive functions
		Turn taking is challenging, as it often requires shifting set and perspective along with processing the communication partner's message and responding
		Requires perspective taking and presupposition regarding the communication partner

depending on the size of lesion and structures/networks affected. Impairments to frontal attention networks include difficulty shifting from intrinsic attention (DMN) to extrinsic attention (CEN). Since novel tasks and novel problem-solving place the highest demands on these frontal attention networks, information processing, problem-solving, decision making, and goal-directed behaviors are impaired.

Box 6–1 Chocolate Factories and Sushi Restaurants

Attentional control networks play a critical role in the interface between what's going on inside of our heads (intrinsic mode—default mode network [DMN]) and how we react extrinsically (central executive network [CEN]) and our ability to shift between intrinsic and extrinsic modes (salience network [SN]). All of us have a limited capacity for attention, working memory, and executive functions, particularly when we're engaged in novel problem solving. New situations place higher demands on CEN, as opposed to overlearned tasks that can function in default mode. Two classic TV skits, the classic Lucy and Ethel at the chocolate factory and the more contemporary Drake and Josh at the sushi restaurant, exemplify two of those high-demand, novel problem-solving situations. It's amazing to recognize that with enough time and practice, Lucy, Ethel, Drake, and Josh would probably be able to do these tasks while carrying on light conversations.

Take a few minutes to check out these two videos:
- Lucy and Ethel at the chocolate factory: https://youtu.be/NkQ58I53mjk
- Drake and Josh at the sushi factory: https://youtu.be/kkQXYbXZYW4

Memory

The ventromedial and orbitomedial portions of the PFC are responsible for working memory. Because this area is so commonly affected in TBI, even individuals with mild TBI experience reductions in processing speed and working memory (Dean & Sterr, 2013). These impairments to working memory compromise communication and pragmatics, which rely heavily on being able to listen and respond appropriately to communication partners (Murray et al., 2001; Tran et al., 2018). Impaired memory is also associated with reduced self-awareness (Ownsworth et al., 2019).

Executive Functions

Impairments to executive function are referred to as **executive dysfunction** or **dysexecutive syndrome**. Since executive functions are interdependent and complex, it is difficult to truly separate elements and impairments. Table 6–4 attempts to explain the typical types of impairment associated with each function.

Awareness

Awareness is a higher-level function, carried out by a complex network of sensory and prefrontal structures. As described in Chapter 4, problems with recognizing one's own deficits is referred to as **anosognosia**. While the term anosognosia typically is used in the context of a specific deficit (e.g., anosognosia for hemiparesis or for unilateral neglect),

Table 6–4. Executive Function Impairments

Impairments to Restraint	
Judgment	• Not taking into account potential safety concerns related to a task and/or environment • Not taking into account or being aware of any physical or cognitive impairments that may alter abilities (anosognosia)
Foresight	• Not anticipating potential challenges that will arise or making appropriate adjustments based on those anticipated challenges
Perseverance & Persistence	• Failing to stay on task in the face of struggle with task difficulty • Off-task behaviors
Delayed Gratification	• Choosing the immediate reward over long-term goals • Impulsive decision making, based in the moment or without forethought • This can relate to addictive behaviors (e.g., gambling, online shopping, pornography, etc.)
Self-Monitoring	• Evaluating one's own performance in the moment and making online adjustments if needed • Overestimation of performance/abilities or underestimation of challenges • Note that it is possible to self-monitor without self-regulating (e.g., individuals with executive dysfunction will say, "I know I shouldn't say this but..." and then they do say it) • Vague or overly specific explanations
Self-Regulation	• Failure to restrain thoughts, behaviors, and communication • Verbose speech, hypersexuality, emotional lability, inappropriate physical and/or social behaviors, failing to follow the typical rules of conversation • Struggles to emotionally regulate
Inhibition of Thoughts and Behaviors	• This is very closely related to self-regulation • Saying exactly what is on your mind, regardless of the consequences • Interruptions and tangential thoughts • Perseverative thoughts and behaviors • Topic repetitiveness • Rumination on negative thoughts

Table 6-4. *continued*	
Concentration	• This is a function of attention control systems, including selective and sustained attention on a specific task • Distractibility and lack of focus • Lost train of thought
Impairments to Initiative	
Motivation	• Apathy • Not knowing where to begin and difficulty initiating complex tasks • Speech can be terse and very restricted
Drive	• Closely related to motivation, perseverance/persistence, and concentration, and foresight (related to long-term goals or plan)
Creativity	• Closely related to mental flexibility, results in a lack of ability to consider alternate ways of thinking and doing • Note that disinhibition of thought actually increases creative thoughts at times
Shifting Cognitive Set	• This is often measured by tasks that require you to shift between one rule to another (e.g., Spordone Attention Battery—alternating subtraction by 3 and 5; FAS word fluency—shifting between words that start with f, a, and s; Stroop tasks—shifting between color, shape, word rules) • Difficulty transitioning between one conversational topic and another
Mental Flexibility	• Not being able to consider alternative ways of completing a task • This tends to go along with egocentrism (i.e., "this is the way I would do it," disregarding alternatives)
Personality	• Changes to interactions, including flat affect or hyper affective and emotionally labile (shifting from happy, to flat and uninterested, to angry, etc.)
Impairments to Order	
Abstract Reasoning	• Struggle to think through things that are intangible/not concrete • A tendency to think more concretely about tasks • Thought processes are often egocentric

continues

Table 6–4. *continued*

Impairments to Order	
Working Memory	• Difficulty with comprehension and expressive language • Reduced emotional regulation • Difficulty with thinking and problem solving in the moment
Perspective Taking & Theory of Mind	• Not being able to recognize or understand another person's perspective • Doing things without consideration or recognition of another person's experience or feelings • Thinking that because you see something or know something or believe something that everyone else sees, knows, and believes the same thing • Poor presupposition—not considering the audience when telling a story (e.g., "And then Phyllis did this!" and the partner is thinking, who is Phyllis?) • Not providing adequate background information or going into too much detail about something that the communication partner already knows about • Impaired reciprocity in conversations—never asking the communication partner how their day was or what they think
Planning	• Impulsively jumping into doing rather than pre-planning and making sure everything is ready for the task • Failure to recognize how much time the task will take, what resources are necessary, to account for whether they have previous experience with the task or not, and other situational demands (e.g., distractions)
Organization	• Discourse lacks cohesion and a clear direction, the person seems to be talking in circles or simply wandering through thoughts • Tasks entered haphazardly and consequently is less efficient and may miss elements of the task • Jumping from task to task without purpose and failing to prioritize required tasks
Sequencing	• Problems completing tasks in the correct order or not completing all of the steps • Can affect even relatively simple tasks (e.g., not being able to make a peanut butter and jelly sandwich)

Box 6–2 The Difference Between Knowing and Doing

Individuals with executive dysfunction often do and say things that would be considered uncharacteristic for them prior to the brain injury/disease. The phenomenon of knowing versus doing is a common challenge for these individuals. Outside of the moment, when they are not affected by task demands, emotional demands, time pressure, and internal states (hunger, fatigue, pain), they often know and would choose the most sensible option. However, within context, faced with all of those demands, they frequently do and say things, despite "knowing" better. Let's consider a few mini-cases where this phenomenon is at play.

1. Cassie is a 12-year-old with a TBI who comes home after a long day of school. She's doing well in school, after transitioning back following a moderate TBI a few months ago and is looking forward to returning to basketball, once she shows that she can handle a full load of courses. She rides the bus home. She knows her neighbors well and her best friend lives three houses away. Today she arrives at her house on a very cold winter afternoon and realizes that she is locked out of the house. Outside of this moment, if asked what she would do if she were ever locked out of her house, she would likely say she could go to her friend's house or ask a neighbor for help or to use their phone. So, Cassie "knows" what to do. Instead, her response was a bit different. She didn't choose one of those options but instead pounded her fists on and kicked the door until it dented, threw a tantrum about how it was someone else's fault, and ultimately did not get inside until her mom arrived some 40 minutes later. Why could she not do what she knew to do?

2. Janet is a 42-year-old woman who sustained a moderate TBI as an unhelmeted rider on a motorcycle. Prior to her accident she held an executive position in a small company. She was unable to return to that position. Due to financial challenges related to medical expenses and the loss of her job, she now drives an old, unreliable vehicle and could scarcely pay to keep it working properly. One day, on a shopping trip, her car started smoking. She pulled immediately into the vacant end of a department store parking lot and quickly got out. At that point, smoke became flames and it appeared that she made a good in-the-moment decision. That is when she realized that her purse and cell phone remained in the car. Asked outside of this moment, "If your car is on fire and you realize that your purse and cell phone are still inside, what would you do?" she would have replied, "Let it burn, it's not worth taking a chance." But, on the day of the incident, her actions were different. She opened the door and reached back into the car before becoming overwhelmed by the smoke. Fortunately, she was pulled out by a passerby moments later. Why did she not do what she knew to do?

Of course, these are fairly extreme examples, but the phenomenon of knowing versus doing plays out in small ways on a regular basis for individuals with TBI.

impaired self-awareness (ISA) encompasses multiple deficits and the consequences of those deficits. ISA is a common phenomena following prefrontal damage (Fleming & Strong, 1999; Hart et al., 2004; Ownsworth, Debois, et al., 2006; Ownsworth, Fleming, et al., 2006; Sherer et al., 2003). People with ISA frequently underestimate their struggles and overestimate their abilities (Douglas, 2010; Douglas et al., 2007a, 2007b, 2016). In some cases, they can list off their weaknesses or impairments, but do not understand the functional consequences. For example, they may be able to tell you that they have visual problems due to brain injury, but then talk about how they can't wait to get home so they can drive again. Decreased self-awareness is associated with less motivation for rehabilitation (Fleming et al., 1998). Basically, if you do not recognize that something is wrong, you will be unlikely to make any adjustments or be motivated to change your behavior.

Swallowing Disorders

Dysphagia that occurs after PFL damage is most often related to cognitive impairments, as the motor and sensory systems are controlled by more posterior regions of the frontal lobes. Impulsivity can lead to a rapid rate of intake and large bites or drinks. Impaired attention, including lack of focus, limited persistence and endurance, and distractibility can lead to incidents of choking. Because attention and focus tend to vary/fluctuate throughout the day, safety and status at one meal may not be predictive of the rest of the day. Agitation is common among those with acute prefrontal damage, which can result in limited intake as well. Certain foods, textures, temperatures, and smells can exacerbate that agitation. Simply having too many items present on the tray or table can be overwhelming.

Summary

The prefrontal lobes are critical for higher level thinking and their extensive connection to other areas of the brain make them an important contributor to communication and swallowing. Damage to PFL results in cognitive-communication disorders. Traumatic brain injury and some dementias are common etiologies of PFL damage. Assessment and treatment most often focus on attention, memory, executive function, awareness, and discourse-level communication.

Key Concepts

- The prefrontal lobes are critical for cognitive functions such as executive function, attention, and memory.
- Etiologies that cause diffuse damage, such as TBI and dementias, are the most common causes of prefrontal lobe damage.

- Cognitive-communication disorders are common, as discourse and speech are affected by executive dysfunction and disruptions to attention and memory.
- Swallowing disorders with prefrontal lobe damage most often result from the cognitive disorders.

References

Byom, L. J., & Turkstra, L. S. (2012). Effects of social cognitive demand on Theory of Mind in conversations of adults with traumatic brain injury. *International Journal of Language and Communication Disorders, 47*(3), 310–321.

Dean, P. J., & Sterr, A. (2013). Long-term effects of mild traumatic brain injury on cognitive performance. *Frontiers in Human Neuroscience, 7,* 30.

Douglas, J. M. (2010). Using the La Trobe Communication Questionnaire to measure perceived social communication ability in adolescents with traumatic brain injury. *Brain Impairment, 11*(2), 171–182.

Douglas, J. M., Bracy, C. A., & Snow, P. C. (2007a). Measuring perceived communicative ability after traumatic brain injury: Reliability and validity of the La Trobe Communication Questionnaire. *The Journal of Head Trauma Rehabilitation, 22*(1), 31–38.

Douglas, J. M., Bracy, C. A., & Snow, P. C. (2007b). Exploring the factor structure of the La Trobe Communication Questionnaire: Insights into the nature of communication deficits following traumatic brain injury. *Aphasiology, 21*(12), 1181–1194.

Douglas, J. M., Bracy, C. A., & Snow, P. C. (2016). Return to work and social communication ability following severe traumatic brain injury. *Journal of Speech, Language, and Hearing Research, 59*(3), 511–520.

Elbourn, E., Kenny, B., Power, E., Honan, C., McDonald, S., Tate, R., . . . Togher, L. (2019). Discourse recovery after severe traumatic brain injury: Exploring the first year. *Brain Injury, 33*(2), 143–159.

Fleming, J., & Strong, J. (1999). A longitudinal study of self-awareness: Functional deficits underestimated by persons with brain injury. *The Occupational Therapy Journal of Research, 19*(1), 3–17.

Fleming, J. M., Strong, J., & Ashton, R. (1998). Cluster analysis of self-awareness levels in adults with traumatic brain injury and relationship to outcome. *The Journal of Head Trauma Rehabilitation, 13*(5), 39–51.

Grice, H. P. (1975). Logic and conversation. In P. Cole, J. L. Morgan (Eds.), *Syntax and Semantics, Vol. 3, Speech Acts* (pp. 41–58). Academic Press.

Hart, T., Sherer, M., Whyte, J., Polansky, M., & Novack, T. A. (2004). Awareness of behavioral, cognitive, and physical deficits in acute traumatic brain injury. *Archives of Physical Medicine and Rehabilitation, 85*(9), 1450–1456.

Hartley, L. L., & Jensen, P. J. (1992). Three discourse profiles of closed-head-injury speakers: Theoretical and clinical implications. *Brain Injury, 6*(3), 271–281.

Lomen-Hoerth, C., Anderson, T., & Miller, B. (2002). The overlap of amyotrophic lateral sclerosis and frontotemporal dementia. *Neurology, 59*(7), 1077–1079.

McDonald, S., Flanagan, S., & Rollins, J. (2002). *The Awareness of Social Inference Test (TASIT)*. Pearson Assessment.

Menon, V. (2011). Large-scale brain networks and psychopathology: A unifying triple network model. *Trends in Cognitive Sciences, 15*(10), 483–506.

Murphy, J. M., Henry, R. G., Langmore, S., Kramer, J. H., Miller, B. L., & Lomen-Hoerth, C. (2007). Continuum of frontal lobe impairment in amyotrophic lateral sclerosis. *Archives of Neurology, 64*(4), 530–534.

Murray, L. L., Ramage, A. E., & Hopper, T. (2001). Memory impairments in adults with neurogenic communication disorders. *Seminars in Speech and Language, 22*(2), 129–138.

Nielsen, A. I., Power, E., & Jensen, L. R. (2020). Communication with patients in post-traumatic confusional state: Perception of rehabilitation staff. *Brain Injury, 34*(4), 447–455.

Ownsworth, T., Desbois, J., Grant, E., Fleming, J., & Strong, J. (2006). The associations among self-awareness, emotional well-being, and employment outcome following acquired brain injury: A 12-month longitudinal study. *Rehabilitation Psychology, 51*(1), 50.

Ownsworth, T., Fleming, J., Doig, E., Shum, D. H., & Swan, S. (2019). Concordance between the Awareness Questionnaire and Self-Awareness of Deficits Interview for identifying impaired self-awareness in individuals with traumatic brain injury in the community. *Journal of Rehabilitation Medicine, 51*(5), 58–61.

Ownsworth, T., Fleming, J. M., & Hardwick, S. (2006). Symptom reporting and associations with compensation status, self-awareness, causal attributions, and emotional wellbeing following traumatic brain injury. *Brain Impairment, 7*(2), 95–106.

Sherer, M., Hart, T., & Nick, T. G. (2003). Measurement of impaired self-awareness after traumatic brain injury: A comparison of the Patient Competency Rating Scale and the Awareness Questionnaire. *Brain Injury, 17*(1), 25–37.

Steel, J., Ferguson, A., Spencer, E., & Togher, L. (2015). Language and cognitive communication during post-traumatic amnesia: A critical synthesis. *NeuroRehabilitation, 37*(2), 221–234.

Steel, J., Ferguson, A., Spencer, E., & Togher, L. (2017). Social communication assessment during post-traumatic amnesia and the post-acute period after traumatic brain injury. *Brain Injury, 31*(10), 1320–1330.

Tran, S., Kenny, B., Power, E., Tate, R., McDonald, S., Heard, R., & Togher, L. (2018). Cognitive-communication and psychosocial functioning 12 months after severe traumatic brain injury. *Brain Injury, 32*(13–14), 1700–1711.

7
LEFT HEMISPHERE PERISYLVIAN REGION

Chapter Overview

Diseases and Disorders of the Left Hemisphere
Speech Disorders
    Dysarthria
    Apraxia of Speech (AOS)
        Assessment
        Treatment
    Primary Progressive Apraxia of Speech (PPAOS)
Language Disorders
    Aphasia
        Global Aphasia
        Mixed Transcortical Aphasia
        Non-Fluent Aphasia
        Transcortical Motor Aphasia
        Fluent Aphasia
        Transcortical Sensory Aphasia
        Conduction Aphasia
        Anomia
    Disorders of Reading and Writing
        Alexia and Agraphia
        Gerstmann Syndrome
        Surface Dyslexia/Dysgraphia
    Degenerative and Progressive Aphasias
        Primary Progressive Aphasia (PPA)
    Assessment
        PPA Specific Assessments (PPA)
    Intervention
Cognitive Disorders
    Attention
    Memory

> Executive Functions
> Anosognosia
> Non-Linguistic Cognitive Impairments in Post-Stroke Aphasia
> Degenerative and Progressive Cognitive Disorders
> Swallowing Disorders
> Motor/Weakness Related
> Sensory Related
> Cognition/Attention Related
> Summary
> Key Concepts
> References

As described in Chapter 4, for most people the perisylvian region of the left hemisphere (LH) has primary control of basic language functions such as word finding, phonology, morphology, and syntax. While LH processes are integrated, different regions have been identified that have primary roles in language (Figure 7–1). Lesions to specific areas or the white matter tracts that connect them have predictable effects on language. In this chapter, we address assessment and treatment of disorders that are most commonly, or exclusively, related to LH perisylvian area damage, such as aphasia and apraxia of speech (AOS). For those disorders that can occur from damage to other regions of the brain, such as attentional deficits or dysarthrias that occur after LH or right hemisphere (RH) damage, assessment and treatment will be covered in Chapters 12 and 13.

Diseases and Disorders of the Left Hemisphere

The LH can be damaged relatively focally by strokes or tumors. Degenerative diseases that have a LH focus often initially present as aphasia or AOS, with increasing cognitive impairments as the disease progresses. Focal contusions can occur with traumatic brain injuries (TBIs), but typically those are accompanied by diffuse axonal injury. TBIs and dementias will be covered in detail in Chapter 14 because they affect multiple areas and systems, not solely the LH.

Speech Disorders

Lesions to the motor strip and/or premotor and supplementary motor areas can lead to speech impairments. Since these structures share the same blood supply distributions, it is not unusual to have concomitant dysarthria and AOS.

Box 7-1 Language Dominance

The left hemisphere (LH) has traditionally been called the "dominant hemisphere" due to the fact that for the vast majority of humans, it primarily controls basic language functions such as word finding, phonology, morphology, and syntax. While the label was initially coined to refer to dominance for language, the associated "non-dominant" label for the right hemisphere (RH) implicitly (and sometimes explicitly) has been interpreted as "less important overall." This idea encompasses the prevalence and preference for right-handedness. Given the contralateral sensori-motor control, the left hand is controlled by the RH, which is another indicator that it is less important than the LH. As described in Chapter 4, the RH has important contributions to language and communication and is just as relevant to dysarthria and dysphagia as the LH. The notion of LH dominance suggests that the ability to find a word is more important than using the word appropriately in context, and that pragmatics is less important for communication than syntax. Anyone who has tried to communicate with someone who doesn't understand their language may disagree, for extralinguistic (non-verbal) and paralinguistic (prosodic) cues often are more than enough to establish a connection and to make basic wants, needs, and emotions known.

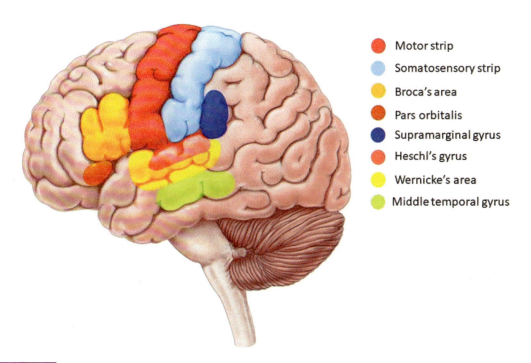

Figure 7-1. Left hemisphere perisylvian areas associated with language.

Dysarthria

Unilateral upper motor neuron dysarthria (UUMN) is the most likely form of dysarthria caused by left cortical lesions. Damage to upper motor neurons within the motor strip (primary motor cortex; Figure 7–2) occurs with strokes that affect the superior branch of the middle cerebral artery (MCA) (Figure 7–3). The speech deficits are primarily related to weakness but sometimes spasticity and incoordination are present (Duffy, 2019). Articulation, phonation, and prosody are disrupted. Articulatory errors are relatively consistent, given the primacy of weakness as a contributor to imprecise articulation. However, speech patterns can be hard to distinguish from spastic and ataxic dysarthria. Assessment and treatment of dysarthrias are covered in Chapter 13.

Apraxia of Speech

Impaired volitional control of muscles for initiating speech in the absence of muscle weakness is called **apraxia of speech (AOS)**. This is an impairment in motor planning, often caused by damage to the **premotor** and **supplementary motor area (SMA)**. The **frontal aslant tract (FAT)** connects Broca's area (also known as pars opercularis and pars triangularis in both hemispheres) to the premotor and SMA (refer back to Figure 2–15). Damage to the ventral-posterior portion of the FAT and anterior arcuate fasciculus consistently predicts the presence

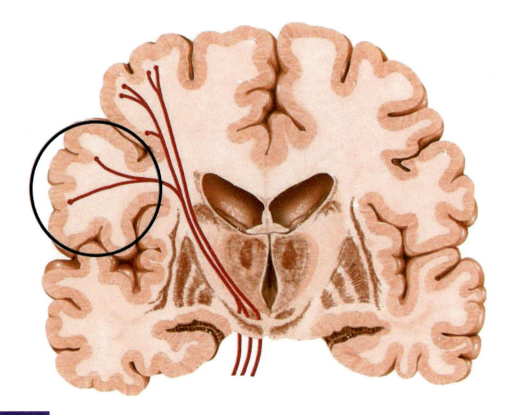

Figure 7–2. Site of lesion for unilateral upper motor neuron (UUMN) dysarthria.

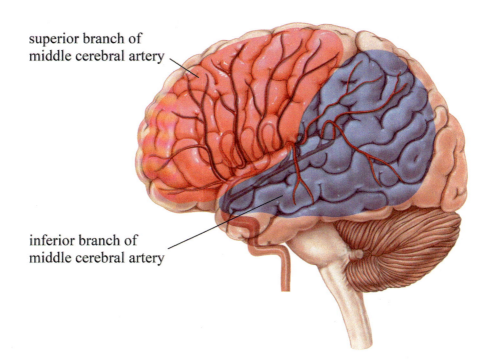

Figure 7–3. Superior and inferior branches of the middle cerebral artery (MCA) in the left hemisphere. From *Clinical Neuroscience for Communication Disorders: Neuroanatomy and Neurophysiology* (p. 225) by Blake, M. L. and Hoepner, J. K. Copyright © 2023 Plural Publishing, Inc. All rights reserved.

of AOS (Chenausky et al., 2020). In some cases, damage to the insular cortex is also present. **Articulatory groping** (labored attempts to achieve articulatory placement) and inconsistent sound production errors (phoneme substitutions, additions, prolongations, slow rate of speech, repetitions, and distortions) are the primary consequences of AOS.

Assessment

A primary goal in the assessment of AOS is differentiating between apraxia and dysarthria or aphasia. The American Speech-Language-Hearing Association (ASHA) Practice Portal provides an excellent table on differentiating characteristics of these three impairments (Table 7–1). Assessment of AOS involves eliciting speech—phonemes, syllables, words, sentences, and discourse—and examining motor control, articulation, prosody, and patterns of errors (Table 7–2). A complete evaluation should go beyond speech production to consider activity and participation, environmental and personal factors, and quality of life.

Treatment

The Academy of Neurogenic Communication Disorders and Sciences' (ANCDS) acquired apraxia of speech writing group published treatment guidelines in 2006 and an update in

Table 7–1. Characteristics of Apraxia of Speech (AOS), Dysarthria, and Aphasia

Characteristic	Apraxia of Speech (AOS)	Dysarthria	Aphasia
Muscle weakness	No	Yes	No
Articulatory deficits	Yes	Yes	No
Prosodic deficits	Yes	Yes	No
Language processing deficits	No	No	Yes
Consistent error patterns	No	Yes	No
Groping for articulatory postures	Yes	No	No

Note: Reprinted with permission from the ASHA Practice Portal.
https://www.asha.org/practice-portal/clinical-topics/acquired-apraxia-of-speech/#collapse_5

Table 7–2. Summary of Apraxia Assessments

Domain(s)	Test/Authors	Description
Body structure and body function	Apraxia Battery for Adults–Second Edition (ABA-2; Dabul, 2000)	Assesses diadochokinetic rate, effects of word length, limb apraxia and oral apraxia, latency time, utterance time for polysyllabic words, repeated trials test, inventory of articulation, and characteristics of apraxia
	Apraxia of Speech Rating Scale (ASRS; Strand et al., 2014)	Assesses presence and severity of distortions, AMRs, rate, sound prolongations, and syllable repetitions
	Oral mechanism exam	Examines strength and agility of movements, employs commands that are sensitive to apraxia
	Non-speech oral praxis includes diadochokinetic rates, including alternating motion rates (AMRs; e.g., /kuhkuhkuh/) and sequential motion rates (SMRs; e.g., /puhtuhkuh/)	SMRs are particularly sensitive to apraxia, as shifting between articulatory placements is difficult for individuals with apraxia

Table 7–2. *continued*

Domain(s)	Test/Authors	Description
	Speech samples for perceptual assessment (conversational speech, sustained vowels)	Used to examine listener perceptions of rate, prosody, and stress
	Speech samples for instrumental assessment (conversational speech, sustained vowels)	Used to examine acoustic characteristics such as voice onset time, rate, prosody and stress
	Motor speech planning including a range of motoric complexity (Duffy, 2013)	Comparisons between various articulatory positions and production manners, multisyllabic words and consonant clusters, stressed versus unstressed words, automatic versus propositional speech, and imitated versus prompted speech
Activity and participation	Communication Confidence Rating Scale (CCRS; Babbitt et al., 2011)	Self-rated communication confidence rating scales for a variety of communicative contexts
Environment	Assessment for Living with Aphasia (ALA; Kagan et al., 2007)	Designed for aphasia, but applicable to AOS. A pictographic, self-report measure of aphasia-related quality-of-life scaffolded by clinician interviewer
Personal Factors	Basic Outcome Measure Protocol for Aphasia (BOMPA; Kagan et al., 2020)	Designed for aphasia, but applicable to AOS. Assesses participation in conversation, quality of life related to living with aphasia, and aphasia severity
Quality-of-life	Stroke and Aphasia Quality of Life Scale (SAQOL-39; Hilari, Byng, Lamping, & Smith, 2003)	While an acquired apraxia of speech quality of life measure does not exist currently, many researchers use the SAQOL-39

Table 7–3. Summary of ANCDS Guidelines for Apraxia Interventions

Recommended Practices	Description
Articulatory Kinematic Interventions	These impairment-based approaches focus on improving articulator movements and positioning to improve speech production accuracy
Rate and/or Rhythm-Based Interventions	These impairment-based approaches use tones or metronomes to produce a rhythm model for clients to follow, often in conjunction with visual feedback and phonemic or placement cues
Intersystemic Facilitation and Reorganization	This impairment-based approach uses different modalities, such as gesture instead of verbal or gestures to augment verbal productions
Alternative and Augmentative Communication (AAC)	When apraxia is so severe that there is limited usable speech, AAC can be used to supplement verbal communication

2015 (Ballard et al., 2015; Wambaugh et al., 2006). They identified four types of recommended practices: articulation, rate/rhythm, intersystemic reorganization, and **alternative and augmentative communication (AAC)** (Table 7–3). Most of these target the impairment level, with the goal of restoring motor control. AAC can be used to supplement verbal communication.

Primary Progressive Apraxia of Speech (PPAOS)

While PPAOS shares many of the impairments associated with AOS following stroke, it is a degenerative and progressive disorder. AOS frequently occurs in conjunction with aphasia, whereas a key criterion in PPAOS is the absence of aphasia. Josephs et al. (2012) identified PPAOS as a discrete disorder, distinct from primary progressive aphasia (PPA) and corticobasal syndrome (CBS). Average age of onset is approximately a decade later than PPA (Josephs et al., 2006). Gray and white matter atrophy in the premotor and supplementary motor areas is the primary diagnostic feature. Generally speaking, individuals with PPAOS perform within normal range on global cognitive assessments, although this may change during late phases of the disease. PPAOS often progresses to mutism. Assessment practices are similar for stroke-related AOS and PPAOS. Due to the degenerative nature of the disease, treatment can include some restorative approaches to maximize the speech function, but should also include AAC to ensure that the person maintains communication for as long as possible in the face of the progression of disease.

Language Disorders

Language disorders can occur due to a variety of etiologies in the LH, including trauma, stroke, tumor, and degenerative diseases. Impairments range from discrete, affecting one particular aspect of language, to more generalized, affecting multiple aspects of language and cognition.

Aphasia

Aphasia is an acquired language disorder that affects comprehension and production. Typically, multiple modalities of language are affected but not equally. Aphasia can occur as the result of a stroke that produces focal damage to language structures in the brain. Alternatively, it can occur due to trauma, which is generally less discrete and may affect additional cognitive functions. Tumors and degenerative diseases can also result in aphasia symptoms but may or may not be as discrete. Aphasias are often associated with disruption to discrete blood supply regions (Figure 7–4). Specifically, the superior and inferior branches of the MCA distributions are implicated (refer back to Figure 7–3). **Non-fluent** aphasias are characterized by reduced fluency of language production with relative sparing of comprehension, and are associated with disruptions of the superior MCA branches and are sometimes referred to as **motor aphasias**. Damage to the inferior MCA branches results in **fluent** aphasias in which production is smooth and easy, but comprehension is affected; these are sometimes called **sensory aphasias**. Subtypes of fluent and non-fluent aphasias are based on the patterns of

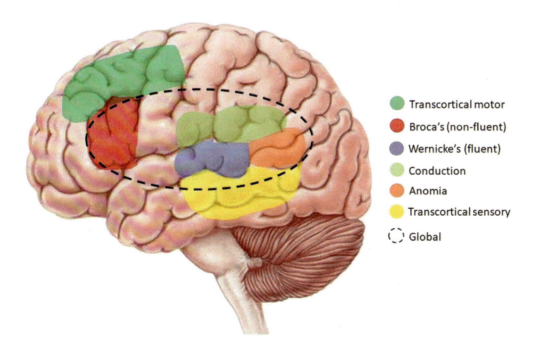

Figure 7–4. Lesion areas by aphasia type.

Table 7–4. Types of Aphasia and Language Characteristics			
	Fluent?	Good Comprehension?	Good Repetition?
Global Aphasia	No	No	No
Mixed Transcortical	No	No	Yes
Broca	No	Yes	No
Transcortical Motor	No	Yes	Yes
Wernicke	Yes	No	No
Transcortical sensory	Yes	No	Yes
Conduction	Yes	Yes	No
Anomic	Yes	Yes	Yes

Source: Clinical Neuroscience for Communication Disorders: Neuroanatomy and Neurophysiology (p. 247) by Blake, M. L. and Hoepner, J. K. Copyright © 2023 Plural Publishing, Inc. All rights reserved.

relatively spared versus impaired language functions, including fluency, comprehension, and the ability to repeat words and sentences (Table 7–4).

Global Aphasia

Global aphasia occurs when the majority of left MCA distribution and perisylvian structures are affected. The uncinate fasciculus, anterior and long segments of the arcuate fasciculus, and corticospinal tract are disrupted. The result is a mix of motor, language expression, language comprehension, and sensory impairments. Verbal output is often absent or limited to stereotypic or neologistic words, resulting in no functional speech. Verbal **stereotypic** words could be a real word or a **neologism** (nonsense word). In either case, the word is often repeated as if it were the only word available (e.g., "yep, yep, yep" or "gabong, gabong, gabong"). All modalities of language are impaired, including verbal, written, and gestural. Severe right-sided hemiparesis is also present.

Mixed Transcortical Aphasia

Mixed transcortical aphasia occurs when there is damage to the MCA watershed region (Figure 7–5). Because the watershed region includes the most distal and small diameter vessels at the outskirts of the MCA distribution, small vessel disease is often a contributing etiology. Overall, verbal output is non-fluent, characterized by perseverative, stereotypic utterances and **phonemic paraphasias**. Articulation is very effortful, as motor planning and gross motor functions are disrupted. Naming is severely impaired, given damage to posterior parietal and

Box 7-2 Yes-No Confusion

Impairments to comprehension can result in yes-no confusion. For instance, if a person named Juan is asked, "Is your name Juan?" they may respond with a "no." Sometimes other modalities are more or less accurate. For instance, although they responded verbally with a "no," they may nod "yes" or point to a written choice for "yes," rather than no. Additionally, responses may become perseverative. When asked, "Is your name Juan?" they may respond "yes" but subsequently respond "yes" when asked if their name is Carlos.

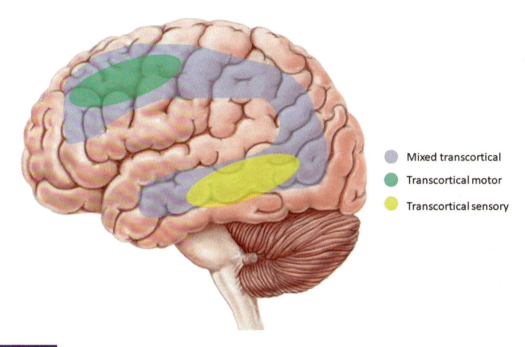

Figure 7–5. Transcortical aphasia lesions.

temporal regions responsible for lexical and semantic functions. Comprehension is severely impaired; however, repetition remains intact.

Non-Fluent Aphasia

Damage to portions of the superior MCA branch results in **non-fluent** aphasia, sometimes referred to as Broca's aphasia or motor aphasia. Specifically, lesions involving the left inferior frontal gyrus and inferior areas of the precentral gyrus result in non-fluent aphasias. Verbal expression is the primary impairment, subsequent to deficits in motor planning for speech, syntax, and grammar. Expression of nouns and verbs (content words) is typically retained,

Box 7-3 Cinderella Story Produced by A Person with Non-Fluent Aphasia

PWA: +" Cinderella Cinderella Cinderella.
PWA: because.
PWA: &-um &+w &-um dancing dancing.
PWA: &+r &-um &+t &+f wish upon a star.
PWA: if you witch upon a star.
PWA: &-um &-um [gestures sky] shhhh@o.
PWA: one time one time
PWA: oh wow wonderful, beautiful! [gestures dress]
PWA: hm &-um
PWA: um who is it? who is it? who is it?
PWA: &-um &-um &-um go &-um dancing dancing dancing &-uh &-um big tall man.
PWA: &-um &+w &+w &-um &+t one time beautiful.
PWA: one time.
PWA: oh oh oh!
PWA: bye!
PWA: running running.
PWA: fall down flipper &+n &-um.
PWA: &+t oo one time.
PWA: who is it?
PWA: um um um
PWA: go um
PWA: who is it?
PWA: who is it?
PWA: who is it?
PWA: um back um um um dancing um
PWA: wh sh um b um slippers slipper [reaches to foot]
PWA: wh married and married.
PWA: f um promise.
PWA: wh witch upon a tar. witch upon a tar.
PWA: and slipper dancing.
PWA: um t w um married.

Transcript from AphasiaBank. https://aphasia.talkbank.org/

Box 7–4 Non-Fluent Aphasia Terminology

Functors: Functional words like articles, prepositions, and conjunctions.

Telegraphic: A holdover term from the days of sending telegrams, where customers paid for each word, so they would often limit messages to nouns and verbs to reduce cost. The result of telegraphic speech is broken fluency and prosody, due to the lack of connecting words.

Telegrammatic: Again, a holdover term related to the elimination of connecting words and syntax, resulting in strings of nouns and verbs.

Agrammatic: Lacking grammatical components of sentences and phrases.

Box 7–5 Gabby Giffords

Senator Gabby Giffords became aphasic after a gunshot wound to the left side of her brain in 2011. Her recovery has been extensively documented in the press and in a documentary, "Won't Back Down." Typical of non-fluent aphasia, her production was limited but her comprehension was relatively preserved. Initially, production was limited to 1- and 2-word phrases. Over many years, she has improved substantially, but still, 11 years later, faces the challenges of aphasia: "*Aphasia* really sucks—the words are there in my brain, I just can't get them out!"

while functional words (functors) like articles, prepositions, and conjunctions, are often excluded. As a result, speech is **telegraphic** and telegrammatic (or **agrammatic**). Repetition is impaired given damage to anterior and long segments of the arcuate fasciculus. Comprehension is relatively preserved.

Transcortical Motor Aphasia

Transcortical motor aphasia is a relatively rare syndrome that involves a disruption to the tracts between the SMA and Broca's area (Figure 7–5). This falls within the anterior cerebral artery (ACA) and MCA watershed region. Motor impairments are severe, particularly initiation of speech. Verbal expression is marked by simplified grammar, echolalia, and buccofacial apraxia. **Echolalia** involves perseverative repetition of words and phrases. Impaired ability coordinating and carrying out facial movements such as smiling, raising eyebrows, and pursing lips together on command is called **buccofacial** or oral-facial apraxia. Acutely, the individual is often mute. Comprehension is relatively preserved and repetition remains intact.

Fluent Aphasia

Disruptions to portions of the inferior MCA branch (refer back to Figure 7–3) lead to **fluent** aphasia, also known as Wernicke's aphasia or sensory aphasia. Prosody and fluency are preserved in spite of limited inclusion of nouns and verbs. Impaired comprehension is the hallmark of fluent aphasia, especially acutely. Because language comprehension is bilaterally represented, comprehension may improve to some extent subacutely. Although syntax and functors remain relatively intact, semantics are impaired. The net effect is low content quality.

Box 7–6 Cinderella Story Produced by a Person With Fluent Aphasia

Clinician: Now tell me as much of the story of Cinderella as you can. Tell me the story. What happens?
PWA: she's the ʃeɪz@u hadta do with her.
PWA: then the kɛnz@u of them do that.
PWA: &-uh bad things on a things xxx to do it bad bad bad.
PWA: after thing little thing [gestures playing piano] bingbingbing@o a thing of this.
PWA: the other one, [gestures dress] one can see it on the thing.
PWA: they went for.
PWA: they can looking for.
PWA: with the big one or things a good one that sees [gestures fairy godmother].
PWA: +" oh we xxx pchoo@o [gestures poof].
PWA: +" you can do it.
PWA: +" when do you go?
PWA: xxx to do it boom_boom_boom_boom@o.
PWA: she sees it [pantomimes seeing dress].
PWA: the ball was rewound and we like (th)em.
PWA: we're gonna get it.
PWA: &-uh (.) and she's +"/.
PWA: +" [looks at watch] oh I gotta go.
PWA: +" [points to watch] it's gonna go .
PWA: fit it back.
PWA: launch the thing on [reaches for shoe].
PWA: gone and lost of it.
PWA: one here for looking of it.
PWA: put that on the bad thing.
PWA: with something it [gesturing repeat] sawed it.

PWA: she saw it.
PWA: [shakes head 'no'] I don't remember that one.
PWA: but &-uh when you say it she'll be looking to get it.
PWA: the bin [gestures big] one [reaches high] what sayin(g) of it +"/.
PWA: +" now I can't say it.
PWA: the next one [gestures side to side] you can't see the two ones to do it.
PWA: they should be doing.
PWA: it's &-uh not doing it.
PWA: it should be the one guy is doing this.
PWA: the two guys +"/.
PWA: +" well ‡ I should do it!
PWA: +" &-uh I can't get it.
PWA: +" can't get it.
PWA: now she says +"/.
PWA: +" well ‡ I'll try to + . . .
PWA: +" I could get it!
PWA: +" it's me the xxx one!
PWA: now he's gonna tell the one +"/.
PWA: +" you get the matter.
PWA: +" we gang [gestures upwards] away back again.
PWA: am I saying it?
Clinician: yeah yeah and then what happened?
PWA: +< good.
Clinician: what's the ending?
PWA: she got it!
PWA: the other thing you got it right here.

Transcript from AphasiaBank. https://aphasia.talkbank.org/

Box 7-7 Fluent Aphasia Terminology

Jargon: neologistic or non-words that replace content words.

Semantic paraphasia: substituting a word with a similar meaning as the target word (e.g., apple for orange, son for daughter, husband for wife).

Pronoun confusion: a form of semantic paraphasia, where pronouns are mixed up (e.g., he for she, him for her, etc.).

Transcortical Sensory Aphasia

Transcortical sensory aphasia is also relatively rare and occurs following damage to the posterior inferior MCA distribution, including the angular gyrus and middle temporal gyrus (Figure 7–5). This falls within the posterior cerebral artery (PCA) and MCA watershed region. Speech is fluent and retains its melodic line but semantics are severely impaired, resulting in **empty speech** and possibly **echolalia**. Semantic paraphasias are common and speech is highly perseverative. Auditory comprehension is impaired, as is reading comprehension. Repetition is preserved.

Conduction Aphasia

Impaired repetition is the hallmark of **conduction** aphasia. Damage to the left supramarginal gyrus and posterior segment of the **arcuate fasciculus** as well as optic radiations underlie these impairments. While comprehension and propositional expression is intact, repetition is severely impaired. Repetition becomes increasingly difficult as you move from single words to multiple words. Attempts to repair repetition errors are unsuccessful, often marked by **phonemic paraphasias** (phonological substitutions that are similar to the target word—e.g., fog for dog).

Anomia

Simply stated, **anomia** means no name (Latin a = *without*, nomen = *name*). Anomic aphasia results in word finding difficulties. A variety of lesion sites can result in word finding difficulties, although it is most often associated with inferior parietal and posterior temporal lobe lesions. **Circumlocution**, or talking around the word you are trying to find, is common (e.g., "I had to take my . . . my . . . pet, he barks . . . wag tail . . . yes! Dog for a walk"). Efficient circumlocutions can be functional, substituting descriptions or alternative words for the target words. Alternatively, some circumlocutions can become protracted and confusing, losing the intent of the initial target expression.

Disorders of Reading and Writing

Alexia is a term for a group of reading disorders. **Agraphia** is a term for writing disorders. These can co-occur, or can appear separately depending on the location of the brain damage (Figure 7–6A, B). They also can affect letters and words separately.

Alexia and Agraphia

Pure alexia (pure word blindness) is caused by damage to optic radiations or the visual cortices. Sometimes associated damage to the arcuate fasciculus and/or Wernicke's area is also present. This results in the inability to comprehend orthographic (written) words or letters despite

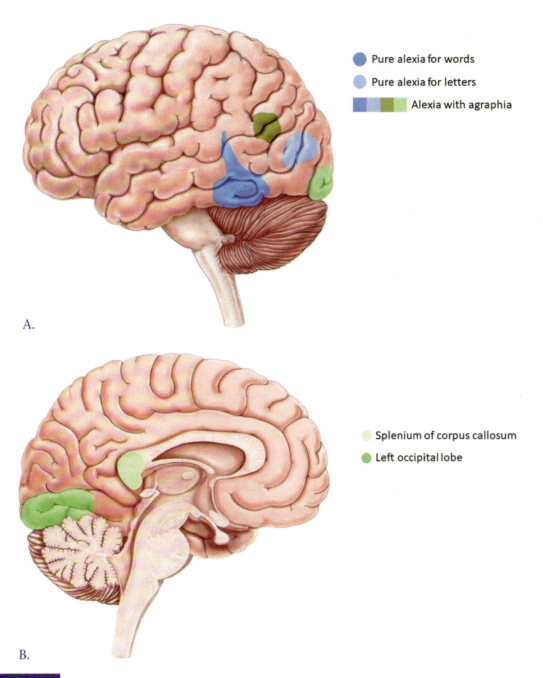

Figure 7–6. Typical lesions for forms of alexia and agraphia shown on (A) lateral and (B) medial regions of the brain.

intact vision. Individuals sometimes retain the ability to recognize and read iconic words in their iconic form. For example, they may not be able to read "coca-cola" if it were typed or handwritten, but could read the classic red and white Coca-Cola logo.

Alexia without agraphia is caused by damage to the left PCA with damage to the posterior region of the corpus callosum and left occipital lobe. It results in right hemianopia (loss of one half of the visual field). Hemianopia is discussed further in Chapter 9. The individual retains good listening comprehension and can write to dictation. However, oral reading and reading comprehension are severely impaired.

Alexia with agraphia is usually associated with conduction aphasia and often associated with more extensive parietal damage. This results in problems with writing, which is worse at the grapheme (letter) level than the word level. Problems with reading also are worse at the grapheme (letter) level than the word level. Typically, it does not impact habitual or iconic words. For instance, a former client, Marjorie, was asked to write her own signature, which she could do fairly automatically. When asked to write the name of a friend, she said, "That will be easy, my best friend's name is Marjorie!" but when she wrote it, it was illegible—suggesting that it was a different representation than her own name.

Gerstmann Syndrome

Gerstmann syndrome is associated with lesions to the angular gyrus, inferior parietal lobule, and white matter pathways. This is almost always associated with LH lesions to these areas but can occur with RH lesions. Left PCA strokes are the most common etiology (see Chapter 9). Impairments include finger agnosia, right-left confusion, acalculia, and agraphia without alexia. Finger agnosia affects both sides of the body, impairing the ability to name one's own fingers (e.g., pinky, index finger, thumb). Acalculia disrupts the ability to perform even simple mathematical calculations. Individuals with agraphia without alexia can copy but are unable to write spontaneously.

Surface Dyslexia/Dysgraphia

Surface dyslexia and agraphia are characterized by difficulty reading and writing words with atypical spelling. Patients/clients will spell and pronounce them as if they followed typical rules. For instance, "knew" would be spelled "new," and "through" would be spelled "threw." "Knife" would be pronounced "kuh-naif" and "ewe" would be pronounced "ee-wee."

Degenerative and Progressive Aphasias

Several variants of frontotemporal dementias exist (refer back to Table 3–2), three of which are language variants. While the three language variants will be discussed in this section, it is noteworthy that all begin as primarily language impairments but progress to include cognitive impairments consistent with dementias.

Primary Progressive Aphasia (PPA)

Primary progressive aphasia (PPA) is a form of frontotemporal dementia, characterized by changes to language comprehension and expression. There are three distinct language variants, including logopenic, non-fluent/agrammatic, and semantic (Figure 7–7). The fourth,

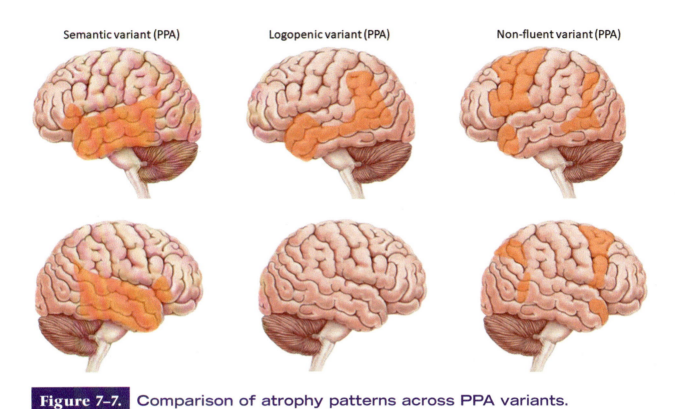

Figure 7-7. Comparison of atrophy patterns across PPA variants.

behavioral (frontal) variant was covered in Chapter 6. Like stroke-induced aphasia, initial consequences are typically limited to language impairments but cognition declines over time. The **logopenic variant** of PPA is characterized by anomia, semantic paraphasias, circumlocution, pausing to retrieve words, and impaired repetition. This variant most closely parallels stroke-based anomia. Spoken and written grammatical impairments, AOS, and broken speech fluency and prosody are characteristics of the **non-fluent PPA variant**. Non-fluent PPA most closely parallels stroke-based, non-fluent (Broca's) aphasia. The **semantic variant** is characterized by difficulty comprehending both spoken and written language, loss of word meaning and lexical access, surface dyslexia and dysgraphia, impaired knowledge of how objects are used, and impaired naming. The semantic variant of PPA most closely parallels stroke-based fluent aphasia. **Semantic dementia** is distinct from other primary progressive aphasias but still within the spectrum of frontotemporal dementias. When the semantic variant of PPA extends to include additional problems recognizing faces and objects, as well as more behavioral impairments, that typically indicates semantic dementia.

Assessment

Comprehensive assessment of language functions for aphasia includes items for all modalities of language. Bedside assessments of language address modalities with everyday objects and simple sentences (see Box 7–8). Standardized aphasia assessments generally follow a

Box 7-8 The Bedside Language Exam

1) Spontaneous speech
    a) Fluency
    b) Prosody
    c) Grammar and meaning
    d) Paraphasias (semantic, phonemic, yes/no confusion, pronoun confusion)
    e) Articulation
    f) Picture descriptions (e.g., park scene, cookie theft)
2) Naming
    a) Confrontation naming (line drawings and/or objects)
    b) Responsive naming (cloze sentences, color of an apple)
    c) Naming objects and parts (e.g., pen, pen tip, eraser, etc.)
    d) Nouns, verbs, proper nouns, colors, etc.
3) Comprehension
    a) Simple to complex commands
    b) Yes/No questions
    c) Multiple choice questions
    d) Point-to objects
    e) Syntax dependent meaning
4) Repetition
    a) Single words
    b) Multisyllabic words
    c) Simple sentences
    d) Complex sentences
5) Reading
    a) Reading aloud (greeting cards, paragraphs, more lengthy and complex passages)
    b) Reading comprehension (signs, medication labels and instructions, sentences, paragraphs)
6) Writing
    a) Printing one's name and address
    b) Signature
    c) Copy a sentence (e.g., The quick red fox jumped over the lazy dog)
    d) Spontaneous sentence
7) Gestures
    a) Yes/no, okay
    b) Pantomime

Table 7–5. Summary of Select Language and Aphasia Assessments

Domain(s)	Test/Authors	Description
Impairment (Speech, Naming, Comprehension, Repetition, Reading, Writing)	Bedside Evaluation Screening Test (BEST-2; West, Sands, & Ross-Swain, 1998)	Screening of language and aphasia for bedside assessment in acute care
Impairment (Speech, Naming, Comprehension, Repetition, Reading, Writing, Gesture)	Bedside Form of the Western Aphasia Battery (Kertesz, 2006)	Addresses linguistic and nonlinguistic domains of communication relevant to acute aphasia
Impairment (Speech, Naming, Comprehension, Repetition, Reading, Writing, Gesture)	Boston Assessment of Severe Aphasia (BASA; Helm-Estabrooks, Ramsberger, Morgan, & Nicholas, 1989)	Measures preserved linguistic and nonlinguistic communication in severe or global aphasia
Impairment (Speech, Naming, Comprehension, Repetition, Reading, Writing)	Boston Diagnostic Aphasia Examination (BDAE-3; Goodglass, Kaplan, & Barresi, 2000)	Assesses naming, comprehension (auditory, visual, and gestural), processing, expression (writing, speech, and working memory)
Impairment (Naming)	Boston Naming Test (BNT-2; Goodglass, Kaplan, & Weintraub, 2000)	Assesses confrontation naming of line drawings
Impairment (Speech, Naming, Comprehension, Repetition, Reading, Writing)	Burns Brief Inventory of Communication and Cognition (Burns, 1997)	Includes a left hemisphere specific test that addresses all domains of language and aphasia
Impairment (Speech, Naming, Comprehension, Repetition, Reading, Writing)	Quick Assessment for Aphasia (Tanner & Culbertson, 1999)	Addresses language domains associated with aphasia
Impairment (Reading comprehension)	Reading Comprehension Battery for Aphasia (RCBA-2; LaPointe & Horner, 1998)	Addresses reading comprehension across words, sentences, paragraphs, and functional reading (i.e., signs, medications, advertisements, etc.)

continues

Table 7–5. *continued*

Domain(s)	Test/Authors	Description
Impairment (Speech, Naming, Comprehension, Repetition, Reading, Writing)	Western Aphasia Battery (WAB-R; Kertesz, 2006)	Addresses a broad range of linguistic and non-linguistic skills affected by aphasia
Activity & Participation	Communication Activities of Daily Living, 3rd Edition CADL-3 (Holland et al., 2018)	Addresses reading, writing, numbers and calculations; social interactions; functional communication; humor, metaphor, and absurdities and internet basics
Activity & Participation	Multimodal Communication Screening Task for Aphasia (MCST-A; Garrett & Lasker, 2005)	Multimodality and AAC assessment for individuals with severe aphasia
Personal factors	Communication Confidence Rating Scale (CCRS; Babbitt et al., 2011)	Self-rated communication confidence rating scales for a variety of communicative contexts
Environment, Personal factors	Assessment for Living with Aphasia (ALA; Kagan et al., 2007)	A pictographic, self-report measure of aphasia-related quality-of-life scaffolded by clinician interviewer
Participation, environment, personal factors, impairment	Basic Outcome Measure Protocol for Aphasia (BOMPA; Kagan et al., 2020)	Assesses participation in conversation, quality of life related to living with aphasia, and aphasia severity
Participation, personal factors	Stroke and Aphasia Quality of Life Scale (SAQOL-39; Hilari et al., 2003)	Self-rated quality of life scale

Note: *Impairment aligns with the WHO-ICF body structures body functions.

Box 7–9 A Move Toward Culturally Sensitive and Representative Stimuli

In recent years, there has been an intentional shift to making assessment stimuli more representative of our increasingly diverse caseloads. The 21st century cookie theft is a good example, as the former version perpetuated gender and racial stereotypes (Figure 7–8; Berube et al., 2019). As new assessments are developed and existing assessments are updated, there is a trend toward more diverse and inclusive stimuli. It is noteworthy that some of the older assessments still include stimuli that perpetuate stereotypes and are culturally insensitive. Bernstein-Ellis et al. (2021), concerned with culturally insensitive stimulus items on the Boston Naming Test–2 (Goodglass, Kaplan, & Weintraub, 2000; e.g., one of the items was a noose), petitioned the publisher to change the stimulus items and authored an ASHA Leader paper on the topic. The publisher responded by updating the test and providing alternate stimuli, available for free, to replace the concerning stimuli. The Bernstein-Ellis team is to be applauded for this important advocacy and others are encouraged to take similar steps when they recognize similar concerns in assessment tools.

Figure 7–8. Modern Cookie Theft picture. Used with permission of ASHA from Stealing Cookies in the Twenty-First Century: Measures of Spoken Narrative in Healthy Versus Speakers With Aphasia, Berube et al. (2019), *American Journal of Speech-Language Pathology*, Vol 28, used with permission.

Table 7–6. Assessments Designed for Primary Progressive Aphasia (PPA)		
Domain(s)	Test/Authors	Description
Body Functions and Body Structures	Sydney Language Battery (SydBat; Savage et al., 2013)	This assessment examines picture naming, word comprehension, semantic association, and repetition. Designates PPA subtypes
Body Functions and Body Structures	Repeat and Point Test (RPT; Hodges et al., 2008)	This assessment is intended to differentiate between semantic and nonfluent variants. Patients are asked to repeat multisyllabic words and point to those words versus semantic and phonological foils

similar format and range of modalities as bedside examinations. A summary of commonly used aphasia assessments and the domains they address is included in Table 7–5.

PPA Specific Assessments (PPA)

Stroke-based aphasia batteries are commonly adapted and used for assessment of PPA. Unfortunately, these measures may not be sensitive to early changes in PPA. Recently, a systematic review identified nine assessments that could be modified for the assessment of PPA (Battista et al., 2017). Two of those assessments were designed to evaluate severity and progression in PPA (Hodges et al., 2008; Savage et al., 2013) (Table 7–6).

Intervention

A number of evidence-based interventions exist to address the consequences of aphasia. Some address specific language modalities, while others take a broader approach. There are two main intervention approaches: **Life Participation Approach to Aphasia** intervention (LPAA, Chapey et al., 2000; sometimes referred to as social approaches or social-consequence approaches) and impairment-based interventions.

LPAA approaches focus on life goals of the person with aphasia. They use a collaborative approach that involves not only an SLP and the person with aphasia, but also their family or friends. In contrast, impairment-based approaches are targeted toward specific language impairments such as naming outside of the communication context, with the goal of improving language and communication. It is important to recognize that LPAA and impairment-based approaches are not necessarily mutually exclusive and can be used simultaneously. The use of person-centered targets can make impairment-based interventions more functional and aligned with a LPAA approach. Table 7–7 provides a summary of recommended practices by

Table 7–7. Summary of Select Intervention Approaches for Aphasia

Domains	Recommended Practices	Description
LPAA APPROACHES		
Communication partner training (CPT), partner supports	Supported Conversation Approaches (SCA; Kagan et al., 2001)	Supportive strategies to increase comprehension (written key words, slower rate, visual supports, etc.) and strategies to ensure a means of response or participation (written choice, rating scales, pictographs, etc.).
Environmental modifications	Communication Partner Training (CPT; Simmons-Mackie et al., 2016)	Educates partners about aphasia, trains them to use support strategies (e.g., SCA), alter their own communication behaviors (e.g., rate, complexity), and modify the environment.
CPT	Conversational coaching (Hopper et al., 2002)	Clinician coaches partner to use multimodality communication support strategies and CPT.
Multimodality communication training, CPT	Conversation therapy (Best et al., 2016; Simmons-Mackie et al., 2014)	Focuses on improving conversations between individuals with aphasia and their partners, within groups, and directly with the clinician (one-on-one).
Groups, strategy training	Project-based interventions (Behn et al. 2023; Behn et al., 2021)	Uses self-selected projects as the authentic context for addressing communication and cognitive goals.
Strategy training	Group interventions (Elman, 2007; Lanyon et al. 2018)	A variety of tasks include strategy development, socialization and peer support, participation-focused tasks, and impairment-based interventions across modalities.
LPAA or impairment, oral expression and compensatory supports	Script training (Goldberg et al., 2012; Youmans et al., 2005)	Co-development and refinement of scripts for routine conversations. Script practicing to increase fluency of expression.

continues

Table 7–7. *continued*		
Domains	Recommended Practices	Description
IMPAIRMENT-BASED APPROACHES		
Oral expression and multimodality communication	Promoting Aphasia Communication Effectiveness (PACE; Davis, 1980, 2005)	Modalities can either be constrained or open, often employs barrier tasks to practice sending and receiving messages, encourages multimodality communication (verbal, gestural, writing, pantomime, drawing, etc.).
Oral expression	Melodic Intonation Therapy (MIT; Norton et al., 2009)	Uses the melodic line and prosodic flow of singing to facilitate verbal expression and increased fluency. Moves from singing words and phrases to fading toward more natural speech.
Impairment, oral expression	Response Elaboration Training (RET; Kearns, 1985)	Uses picture description and reinforcement models from clinicians to expand telegraphic verbal responses by adding additional words.
Impairment, oral expression and naming	Semantic Feature Analysis (SFA; Boyle, 2010)	Training a retrieval schema by identifying semantic features related to the target word.
Impairment, oral expression and naming	Verb Network Strengthening Therapy (vNEST; Edmonds, 2014)	Training a retrieval schema by identifying the people performing actions and the people being acted upon.
Impairment, oral expression and naming	Constraint Induced Aphasia Therapy (CIAT; Wang et al., 2020)	This approach forces use of the verbal modality, constraining use of other modalities like writing or gesturing.
Impairment, reading	Oral Reading for Language in Aphasia (ORLA; Cherney, 2010)	Focuses on reading sentences rather than single words in order to improve intonation, prosody, and reading fluency. Clinicians model then use choral reading fading to independent reading.

Table 7–7. continued

Domains	Recommended Practices	Description
Impairment, writing	Copy and Recall Training (CART; Orjada & Beeson, 2005)	Retraining functional words and orthographic representations. Supports single word naming, writing, and reading functions.
Impairment, writing	Anagram and Copy Therapy (ACT; Beeson et al., 2002)	Retraining writing of single words and their orthographic representations. Uses letter tiles in the form of anagrams. Clients rearrange the letters to form the target words.

intervention domains. While this is not a comprehensive list, it provides a good representation of commonly used intervention approaches.

Cognitive Disorders

Because cognition is dependent on both hemispheres, subcortical structures, and networks, it is a little challenging to think of it in isolation. Here we point out distinctions and specific roles of the LH in cognitive functions. A full discussion of assessment and treatment of attention, memory, executive function, and social cognition is provided in Chapter 12.

Attention

Attentional deficits are common after LH damage, particularly if the prefrontal and parietal cortices are affected. Impairments to attention also have been identified after left perisylvian lesions that cause aphasia (Helm-Estabrooks, 2002; Murray, 2012; Ramsey et al., 2017; Schumacher et al., 2019).

Memory

Few studies directly compare memory impairments in left and right hemisphere strokes directly but primary findings of those studies emphasize that verbal memory is more impaired in LH strokes versus visual memory in RH strokes (e.g., Campos et al., 2010; Philipose et al., 2007). According to a large-scale meta-analysis, activation for verbal working memory is equally distributed across the left and right frontal lobes, but there is more left than right parietal, and more right than left cerebellar activation (Emch et al., 2019).

While visuospatial memory is thought to be an RH dominant function, there is some evidence that changes to spatial memory exist in LH stroke. This is thought to relate to the use of subvocal, verbally-mediated strategies to support visual memory. About 28% of individuals with left-sided stroke demonstrated impaired performance on spatial digits forward and about 16% had difficulty with spatial digits reversed (Paulraj et al., 2018). Further, there was no difference in performance for those who had aphasia versus those who did not. Impairments in spatial digit span were associated with the left fronto-parietal network, which connects the somatosensory cortex, supramarginal gyrus, lateral prefrontal cortex, and the frontal eye fields (Paulraj et al., 2018). Similarly, Hachioui et al. (2014) identified visual memory (83% at 3 months; 78% at 1 year) as the most common cognitive impairment in post-stroke aphasia (left-sided lesions) and the least frequent visual perception and construction (19% at 3 months; 14% at 1 year).

Executive Functions

The LH is believed to regulate analytical processes, so it has a crucial role in making online adjustments, repairs, shifting cognitive set, and inhibiting responses to proactive interference (Garavan et al., 2002). As described in Chapter 6, many executive functions are not lateralized to left or right hemispheres, but are controlled by networks spanning the frontal lobes. Impairments to executive functions have been identified in LH stroke with aphasia (Helm-Estabrooks, 2002; Murray, 2012; Ramsey et al., 2017; Schumacher et al., 2019). In an effort to identify which executive functions have the greatest influence on communication, Gonçalves et al. (2018) conducted a systematic review of executive function subtest performance for persons with aphasia. They established that a relationship exists between working memory and several linguistic functions, including narrative and conversational discourse, writing abilities, and grammatical comprehension.

Anosognosia

Anosognosia after LH stroke is most common in fluent aphasia. While the individual with fluent aphasia has poor comprehension, low semantic content, and uses jargon speech that is sometimes non-communicative, they do not recognize this deficit, at least early on in their recovery. Anosognosia can also occur with diffuse damage to the LH following TBI and is common with bilateral atrophy to the posterior temporal and parietal regions present in Alzheimer dementia (Figure 7–9).

Non-Linguistic Cognitive Impairments in Post-Stroke Aphasia

The concept of verbally mediated strategies seems to have relevance to many cognitive functions in LH stroke. An interesting study of cognitive impairments in post-stroke aphasia revealed significantly lower orientation, visual perception, spatial perception, visuomotor organization, thinking operation, and attention scores in those with post-stroke aphasia

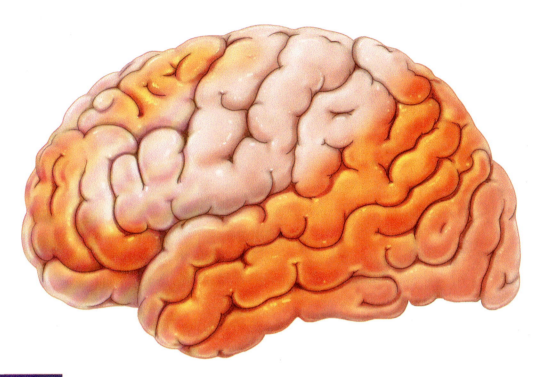

Figure 7–9. Typical pattern of degeneration in Alzheimer disease shown on the left lateral hemisphere. Darker shading indicates more atrophy and lighter shading less atrophy. Adapted from *Clinical Neuroscience for Communication Disorders: Neuroanatomy and Neurophysiology* (p. 290) by Blake, M. L. and Hoepner, J. K. Copyright © 2023 Plural Publishing, Inc. All rights reserved.

than those without aphasia (Yao et al., 2020). Further, individuals with non-fluent aphasia had more severe impairments than those with fluent aphasia, particularly orientation and spatial perception. Speaking to the complexity of interdependency of cognitive and language systems, it is difficult to truly separate cognition and language. Schumacher et al. (2019) cross-examined language and cognitive impairments in individuals with post-stroke aphasia (Figure 7–10). Not surprisingly, as aphasia severity increases, cognitive impairments increase. Perhaps more surprising is that some aphasia types appear more susceptible to cognitive impairments. Performance on language and non-language measures suggests that cognitive impairments in post-stroke aphasia cannot be reduced to a simple relationship. Rather, types of cognitive impairment vary by the location and severity of aphasia impairments.

Degenerative and Progressive Cognitive Disorders

While many dementias are bilateral, there are specific consequences associated with LH damage. As discussed earlier in this chapter, some conditions like primary progressive aphasias, are primarily, or at least initially, LH diseases. Once the degeneration extends beyond the LH, cognitive assessment and treatment methods such as those discussed in Chapter 12 can be adapted based on the co-existence of language and cognitive deficits.

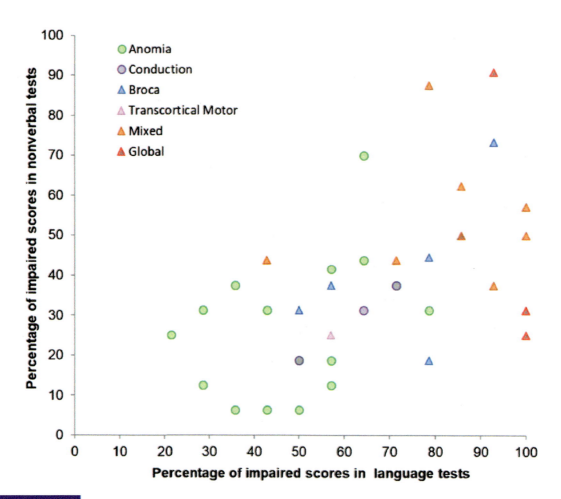

Figure 7–10. A comparison of impairments on non-linguistic to linguistic assessments. Rahel Schumacher, Ajay D Halai, and Matthew A Lambon Ralph, Assessing and mapping language, attention and executive multidimensional deficits in stroke aphasia, *Brain*, Volume 142, Issue 10, October 2019, Pages 3202–3216, https://doi.org/10.1093/brain/awz258 © The Author(s) (2019). Published by Oxford University Press on behalf of the Guarantors of Brain. This is an Open Access article distributed under the terms of the Creative Commons Attribution License (http://creativecommons.org/licenses/by/4.0/), which permits unrestricted reuse, distribution, and reproduction in any medium, provided the original work is properly cited.

Swallowing Disorders

Dysphagia may occur as the result of LH damage. The location of damage will predict the nature of impairments. Motor, sensory, and cognitive impairments are all possible. Assessment and treatment of dysphagia are covered in Chapter 13.

Motor/Weakness Related

Damage to the left primary motor cortex can lead to weakness and spasticity, which affects oral, pharyngeal, and laryngeal functions. This can result in unilateral oral and pharyngeal phase dysphagia. Strokes or TBI are the most likely causes of this type of damage, although it can occur with a number of neurological diseases as well. Damage to the premotor and SMA regions can also result in oral phase impairments, such as swallowing apraxia. This is an impairment to motor planning and execution, not caused by weakness or sensory impairments.

Sensory Related

Sensory impairments relate to damage in the primary somatosensory strip. This can result in oral, pharyngeal, and laryngeal sensory impairments. Sensory impairments may lead to food residuals on the tongue, palate, lateral buccal sulcus, or pharynx. Sensory impairments to the larynx may contribute to an increased risk for aspiration. Parietal damage can also lead to **oral agnosias**, where food is not recognized as food. This leads to holding food in the mouth without swallowing, spitting out food, and/or rumination (perseverative chewing or simply moving food around with the tongue without intent to swallow). Oral agnosias are a common impairment in Alzheimer disease.

Cognition/Attention Related

Fatigue and impaired global attention are common consequences of acute LH stroke and brain injury. The primary consequence is not paying attention to the process of eating or even falling asleep while eating. Like sensory impairments, decreased awareness on the affected side of the mouth may lead to pocketing of residuals in the right lateral buccal sulcus. If prefrontal damage is present, impulsivity may lead to a rapid rate of intake and/or large bites or drinks, which put the individual at risk for choking and aspiration. See Chapter 6 for more about prefrontal regions.

✅ Summary

For SLPs, the left perisylvian area is best known for its role in language and motor speech programming, and damage typically results in some form of aphasia and/or apraxia of speech. The type of aphasia is diagnosed based on patterns of preserved and impaired language abilities, and can be roughly mapped out onto areas of the perisylvian region. Degenerative diseases that begin in the left perisylvian areas initially present with aphasia or AOS (PPA or PPAOS). Due to the interconnectivity of the brain, cognitive disorders also can occur after LH lesions. Dysarthrias and dysphagia can occur after LH damage that impacts motor regions and pathways, but also after damage to RH, subcortical, brainstem, and cerebellar regions and pathways.

🔑 Key Concepts

- The left hemisphere is the primary region for many language functions including semantics, syntax, phonology, and morphology.
- The anterior left hemisphere regions are more important for language production while the posterior regions are more important for language comprehension.
- Speech motor programming is housed in the LH, and damage to this system can cause apraxia of speech.
- Unilateral upper motor neuron dysarthria can occur after damage to LH motor regions and pathways. Aphasia is a language disorder caused by damage to the brain, most often the left perisylvian regions.
- Types of aphasia are characterized by patterns of strengths and weaknesses in comprehension, repetition, and fluency of production.
- Primary progressive aphasia is due to degenerative diseases that initially impact the left hemisphere; subtypes occur due to localization of the degeneration.
- Cognitive impairments of attention, memory, and executive function can occur after focal LH damage but are often overlooked in the presence of aphasia.
- Fluent aphasia often co-occurs with anosognosia which makes the person not aware of their language disorder.
- Swallowing disorders can be primarily linked to changes in motor, sensory, or cognition.

References

American Speech-Language-Hearing Association. (n.d.). *Acquired apraxia of speech*. (Practice portal). http://www.asha.org/practice-portal/clinical-topics/acquired-apraxia-of-speech

Babbitt, E. M., Heinemann, A. W., Semik, P., & Cherney, L. R. (2011). Psychometric properties of the Communication Confidence Rating Scale for aphasia (CCRSA): Phase 2. *Aphasiology, 25*(6–7), 727–735.

Ballard, K. J., Wambaugh, J. L., Duffy, J. R., Layfield, C., Maas, E., Mauszycki, S., & McNeil, M. R. (2015). Treatment for acquired apraxia of speech: A systematic review of intervention research between 2004 and 2012. *American Journal of Speech-Language Pathology, 24*(2), 316–337.

Battista, P., Miozzo, A., Piccininni, M., Catricala, E., Capozzo, R., Tortelli, R., . . . Logroscino, G. (2017). Primary progressive aphasia: A review of neuropsychological tests for the assessment of speech and language disorders. *Aphasiology, 31*(12), 1359–1378.

Beeson, P. M., Hirsch, F. M., & Rewega, M. A. (2002). Successful single-word writing treatment: Experimental analyses of four cases. *Aphasiology, 16*(4–6), 473–491.

Behn, N., Hoepner, J. K., Meulenbroek, P., Hart, J., & Capo, M. (2023). Core components of project-based intervention after acquired brain injury: Delivering meaningful groups online. *International Journal of Language and Communication Disorders*. Advance online publication.

Behn, N., Marshall, J., Togher, L., & Cruice, M. (2021). Reporting on novel complex intervention development for adults with social communication impairments after acquired brain injury. *Disability and Rehabilitation, 43*(6), 805–814.

Berube, S., Nonnemacher, J., Demsky, C., Glenn, S., Saxena, S., Wright, A., . . . Hillis, A. E. (2019). Stealing cookies in the twenty-first century: Measures of spoken narrative in healthy versus speakers with aphasia. *American Journal of Speech-Language Pathology, 28*(1S), 321–329. https://doi.org/10.1044/2018_AJSLP-17-0131

Bernstein-Ellis, E., Higby, E., & Gravier, M. (2021). Responding to culturally insensitive test items. *ASHA Leader, 26*(4), 26–27.

Best, W., Maxim, J., Heilemann, C., Beckley, F., Johnson, F., Edwards, S. I., . . . Beeke, S. (2016). Conversation therapy with people with aphasia and conversation partners using video feedback: A group and case series investigation of changes in interaction. *Frontiers in Human Neuroscience, 10*, 562.

Boyle, M. (2010). Semantic feature analysis treatment for aphasic word retrieval impairments: What's in a name? *Topics in Stroke Rehabilitation. 17*(6), 411–422.

Burns, M. S. (1997). *Burns Brief Inventory Of Communication and Cognition*. Psychological Corporation.

Campos, T. F., Barroso, M. T. M., & De Lara Menezes, A. A. (2010). Encoding, storage and retrieval processes of the memory and the implications for motor practice in stroke patients. *NeuroRehabilitation, 26*(2), 135–142. http://doi.org/10.3233/NRE-2010-0545

Chapey, R., Duchan, J. F., Elman, R. J., Garcia, L. J., Kagan, A., Lyon, J., & Mackie, N. S. (2000). Life participation approach to aphasia: A statement of values for the future. *ASHA Leader, 5*(3), 4–6. https://doi.org/10.1044/leader.FTR.05032000.4

Chenausky, K., Paquette, S., Norton, A., & Schlaug, G. (2020). Apraxia of speech involves lesions of dorsal arcuate fasciculus and insula in patients with aphasia. *Neurology Clinical Practice, 10*(2), 162–169. https://doi.org/10.1212/CPJ.0000000000000699

Cherney, L. R. (2010). Oral Reading For Language In Aphasia (ORLA): Evaluating the efficacy of computer-delivered therapy in chronic nonfluent aphasia. *Topics in Stroke Rehabilitation, 17*(6), 423–431.

Dabul, B. (2000). *ABA-2: Apraxia Battery for Adults*. Pro-Ed.

Davis, G. A. (1980). A critical look at PACE therapy. *Clinical aphasiology: Proceedings of the Conference 1980*, pp 248–257. BRK Publishers.

Davis, G. A. (2005). PACE revisited. *Aphasiology, 19*(1), 21–38.

Duffy, J. (2013). *Motor Speech Disorders: Substrates, Differential Diagnosis, and Management* (3rd ed.). Elsevier Health Sciences.

Duffy, J. R. (2019). *Motor Speech Disorders E-Book: Substrates, Differential Diagnosis, and Management*. Elsevier Health Sciences.

Edmonds, L. A. (2014). Tutorial for Verb Network Strengthening Treatment (VNeST): Detailed description of the treatment protocol with corresponding theoretical rationale. *Perspectives on Neurophysiology and Neurogenic Speech and Language Disorders, 24*(3), 78–88.

Elman, R. (2007). Introduction to group treatment of neurogenic communication disorders. In *Group treatment of neurogenic communication disorders: The expert clinician's approach* (pp. 196–204). Plural Publishing.

Emch, M., Von Bastian, C. C., & Koch, K. (2019). Neural correlates of verbal working memory: An fMRI meta-analysis. *Frontiers in Human Neuroscience, 13*, 180.

Garavan, H., Ross, T. J., Murphy, K., Roche, R. A., & Stein, E. A. (2002). Dissociable executive functions in the dynamic control of behavior: inhibition, error detection, and correction. *Neuroimage, 17*(4), 1820–1829.

Garrett, K. L., & Lasker, J. P. (2005). *The Multimodal Communication Screening Test for Persons with Aphasia (MCST-A)*.

Goldberg, S., Haley, K. L., & Jacks, A. (2012). Script training and generalization for people with aphasia. *American Journal of Speech-Language Pathology*.

Gonçalves, A. P. B., Mello, C., Pereira, A. H., Ferré, P., Fonseca, R. P., & Joanette, Y. (2018). Executive functions assessment in patients with language impairment: A systematic review. *Dementia & Neuropsychologia, 12*, 272–283.

Goodglass, H., Kaplan, E., & Barresi, B. (2000). *Boston Diagnostic Aphasia Examination (BDAE-3)*. Psychological Corporation.

Goodglass, H., Kaplan, E., & Weintraub, S. (2000). *Boston Naming Test–2*. Pro-Ed.

Hachioui, H., Visch-Brink, E. G., Lingsma, H. F., van de Sandt-Koenderman, M. W., Dippel, D. W., Koudstaal, P. J., & Middelkoop, H. A. (2014). Nonlinguistic cognitive impairment in poststroke aphasia: a prospective study. *Neurorehabilitation and Neural Repair, 28*(3), 273–281.

Helm-Estabrooks, N. (2002). Cognition and aphasia: a discussion and a study. *Journal of Communication Disorders, 35*(2), 171–186.

Helm-Estabrooks, N., Ramsberger, G., Morgan, A., & Nicholas, M. (1989). *Boston assessment of severe aphasia (BASA)*. Chicago: Riverside.

Hilari, K., Byng, S., Lamping, D. L., & Smith, S. C. (2003). Stroke and Aphasia Quality of Life Scale-39 (SAQOL-39): Evaluation of acceptability, reliability, and validity. *Stroke, 34*, 1944–1950.

Hodges, J. R., Martinos, M., Woollams, A. M., Patterson, K., & Adlam, A. L. R. (2008). Repeat and point: differentiating semantic dementia from progressive non-fluent aphasia. *Cortex, 44*(9), 1265–1270.

Holland, A. L., Wozniak, L., & Fromm, D. (2018). *Cadl-3: Communication activities of daily living* (3rd ed.). Pro-Ed.

Hopper, T., Holland, A., & Rewega, M. (2002). Conversational coaching: Treatment outcomes and future directions. *Aphasiology, 16*(7), 745–761.

Josephs, K. A., Duffy, J. R., Strand, E. A., Machulda, M. M., Senjem, M. L., Master, A. V., & Whitwell, J. L. (2012). Characterizing a neurodegenerative syndrome: primary progressive apraxia of speech. *Brain, 135*(5), 1522–1536.

Kagan, A., Black, S. E., Duchan, J. F., Simmons-Mackie, N., & Square, P. (2001). Training volunteers as conversation partners using "Supported Conversation for Adults With Aphasia" (SCA). *Journal of Speech, Language, and Hearing Research, 44*(3), 624-638.

Kagan, A., Simmons-Mackie, N. N., Shumway, E., Victor, J. C., & Chan, L. (2020). Development and evaluation of the Basic Outcome Measure Protocol for Aphasia (BOMPA). *International Journal of Speech-Language Pathology, 23*, 258–264.

Kagan A., Simmons-Mackie, N., Rowland A., Huijbregts, M., Shumway, E., & McEwen, S. (2007). *The Assessment for Living with Aphasia*. Aphasia Institute.

Kearns, K. P. (1985). Response elaboration training for patient initiated utterances. In R. H. Brookshire (Ed.), Clinical Aphasiology Conference Proceedings (pp. 196–204). BRK.

Kertesz, A. (2006). *Western aphasia battery-revised (WAB-R)*. Pro-Ed.

Lanyon, L., Worrall, L., & Rose, M. (2018). Combating social isolation for people with severe chronic aphasia through community aphasia groups: consumer views on getting it right and wrong. *Aphasiology, 32*(5), 493–517.

LaPointe, L. L., & Horner, J. (1998). *RCBA-2: Reading comprehension battery for aphasia*. Pro-Ed.

Murray, L. L. (2012). Attention and other cognitive deficits in aphasia: Presence and relation to language and communication measures. *American Journal of Speech-Language Pathology, 21*(2), S51–S64. https://doi.org/10.1044/1058-0360(2012/11-0067

Norton, A., Zipse, L., Marchina, S., & Schlaug, G. (2009). Melodic intonation therapy: shared insights on how it is done and why it might help. *Annals of the New York Academy of Sciences, 1169*(1), 431–436.

Orjada, S., & Beeson, P. (2005). Concurrent treatment for reading and spelling in aphasia. *Aphasiology*, *19*(3–5), 341–351.

Paulraj, S. R., Schendel, K., Curran, B., Dronkers, N. F., & Baldo, J. V. (2018). Role of the left hemisphere in visuospatial working memory. *Journal of Neurolinguistics*, *48*, 133–141.

Philipose, L. E., Alphs, H., Prabhakaran, V., & Hillis, A. E. (2007). Testing conclusions from functional imaging of working memory with data from acute stroke. *Behavioural Neurology*, *18*(1), 37–43.

Ramsey, L. E., Siegel, J. S., Lang, C. E., Strube, M., Shulman, G. L., & Corbetta, M. (2017). Behavioural clusters and predictors of performance during recovery from stroke. *Nature Human Behaviour*, *1*(3), 1–10.

Savage, S., Hsieh, S., Leslie, F., Foxe, D., Piguet, O., & Hodges, J. R. (2013). Distinguishing subtypes in primary progressive aphasia: Application of the Sydney language battery. *Dementia and Geriatric Cognitive Disorders*, *35*(3–4), 208–218.

Schumacher, R., Halai, A. D., & Lambon Ralph, M. A. (2019). Assessing and mapping language, attention and executive multidimensional deficits in stroke aphasia. *Brain*, *142*(10), 3202–3216.

Simmons-Mackie, N., Savage, M. C., & Worrall, L. (2014). Conversation therapy for aphasia: A qualitative review of the literature. *International Journal of Language & Communication Disorders*, *49*(5), 511–526.

Strand, E. A., Duffy, J. R., Clark, H. M., & Josephs, K. (2014). The Apraxia of Speech Rating Scale: A tool for diagnosis and description of apraxia of speech. *Journal of Communication Disorders*, *51*, 43–50.

Tanner, D., & Culbertson, W. (1999). *Quick Assessment for Aphasia*. Oceanside: Academic Communication Associates.

Wambaugh, J. (2006). Treatment Guidelines for Apraxia of Speech: Lessons for Future Research. *Journal of Medical Speech-Language Pathology*, *14*(4), 317–321.

Wang, G., Ge, L., Zheng, Q., Huang, P., & Xiang, J. (2020). Constraint-induced aphasia therapy for patients with aphasia: A systematic review. *International Journal of Nursing Sciences*, *7*(3), 349–358.

West, J. F., Sands, E. S., & Ross-Swain, D. (1998). *Bedside Evaluation Screening Test*. Pro-Ed.

Yao, J., Liu, X., Liu, Q., Wang, J., Ye, N., Lu, X., . . . Zhang, Y. (2020). Characteristics of non-linguistic cognitive impairment in post-stroke aphasia patients. *Frontiers in Neurology*, *11*, 1038.

Youmans, G., Holland, A., Muñoz, M., & Bourgeois, M. (2005). Script training and automaticity in two individuals with aphasia. *Aphasiology*, *19*(3–5), 435–450.

8
RIGHT HEMISPHERE PERISYLVIAN REGION

Chapter Overview

Diseases and Disorders of the Right Hemisphere
Speech Disorders
Language Disorders: Apragmatism
   Linguistic Aspects: Production
   Linguistic Aspects: Comprehension
   Paralinguistic Aspects: Aprosodia
   Extralinguistic Aspects
   Assessment of Apragmatism
   Treatment of Apragmatism
      Linguistic and Extralinguistic Apragmatism
      Paralinguistic Apragmatism: Aprosodia
      Discourse and Pragmatics
Cognitive Disorders
   Attention
      Unilateral Neglect
         Assessment of Unilateral Neglect
         Treatment of Unilateral Neglect
   Memory
   Executive Function
   Anosognosia
   Social Cognition
Swallowing Disorders
   Motor/Weakness Related
   Sensory Related
   Cognition/Attention Related
Summary
Key Concepts
References

The right hemisphere (RH) plays a critical role in speech, language, cognition, and swallowing. Unfortunately, its role in language has been underestimated and largely ignored since at least the 1860s when the language abilities of the left hemisphere (LH) were discovered. The perpetuation of the idea (both implicitly and explicitly) that the RH has little or no contribution to communication has resulted in a decided imbalance within medicine including the field of speech-language pathology (SLP) which is severely detrimental to people with right hemisphere brain damage (RHD).

Hillis and Tippett (2014) surveyed caregivers of people with stroke to ask what deficit domains were most concerning to them. As shown in Table 8–1, there were a variety of concerns about physical, cognitive, and communication domains resulting from either right or left hemisphere strokes. What is particularly striking is that while LH strokes caused caregiver concerns in 7 of the 12 areas, RH strokes affected 11 of the 12 areas. This indicates that RH strokes have broad impacts. Appropriate assessment and treatment are critical because the

Table 8–1. Percentage of Caregivers Who Rated Domains as Either in Their Top 5 Concerns or At Least Moderately Important

Domain	Percentage of Caregivers With Concerns	
	Right Hemisphere Stroke	Left Hemisphere Stroke
Word Retrieval	0	57
Reading	36	50
Writing/Spelling	43	71
Memory	43	50
Energy/Fatigue	43	50
Mood	43	57
Walking	29	36
Prosody	29	0
Empathy	50	0
Spatial Attention	29	0
Other Cognitive	43	0
Personality/Behavior	43	0

Note: Data from Hillis & Tippett, 2014.

cognitive and communication deficits affect participation-level outcomes and make maintaining relationships difficult (Hewetson, 2018, 2021).

This chapter will cover a variety of speech, language, cognition, and swallowing disorders associated with RHD. Assessment and treatment will be covered for those disorders and impairments that are most commonly the result of RHD, such as apragmatism and visuospatial neglect. For those disorders and impairments that can occur from damage to other areas, such as dysarthria, dysphagia, and many cognitive deficits, assessment and treatment will be covered in Chapters 12 and 13.

Diseases and Disorders of the Right Hemisphere

Focal damage to the RH can occur from strokes or tumors. Degenerative diseases may initially begin on one side of the brain before the degeneration spreads to the opposite side. For example, frontotemporal dementias (FTDs) with a predominant RH onset cause deficits in empathy, affect, recognition of emotional facial expression, and interpretation of intended meaning (Gainotti, 2019), while those with a LH onset are typically diagnosed as primary progressive aphasias (see Chapter 7). Etiologies that cause widespread damage, such as traumatic brain injuries (TBIs) or multiple sclerosis (MS) typically present with signs/symptoms of both left and right hemispheric damage.

Speech Disorders

Damage to, or degeneration of, the right motor regions can result in dysarthria, primarily unilateral upper motor neuron (UUMN) dysarthria. The presentation is similar to that from LH damage, with the exception that the motor deficits will be on the left side of the face and articulators instead of the right. Assessment and treatment are the same as for any dysarthria (see Chapter 13). Clinicians should keep in mind the communication and cognitive disorders described in the following sections may co-occur with UUMN dysarthria.

Apraxia of speech is rare after RHD, as the speech motor planning and control centers are localized on the left side of the brain for the majority of the population.

Language Disorders: Apragmatism

The primary language disorder associated with RHD is **apragmatism**. There are occasional cases of **crossed aphasia** in which a right-handed patient develops aphasia as a result of a RH stroke. In these cases, it appears that the localization of primary language abilities is in the RH. For crossed aphasia, traditional aphasia assessments would be appropriate (see

Chapter 7). Additional assessments of attention and prosody would be warranted as it is possible that some traditional RH functions might also be affected.

As described in Chapter 4, apragmatism is a disorder of pragmatics, or the use of language within context. It can be subdivided into **linguistic** (words and grammatical structures) **paralinguistic** (prosody) and **extralinguistic** (nonverbal communication) components.

Linguistic Aspects: Production

Conveying intended meanings relies on selecting the words that best communicate what we want to say, putting those words into grammatical structures that are appropriate for the situation and our intent, choosing how much or how little information to share, and organizing sentences into a response (Table 8–2). The following are examples of deficits that have been reported. But most of these have been shown to be impaired in some studies, and in some people with RHD, but not in others. There are no clear patterns or key impairment(s) that are diagnostic of linguistic apragmatism. SLPs need to conduct a broad evaluation to determine what linguistic areas might have been affected.

In terms of word choice, people with RHD may use less emotionally charged words (see review in Blake, 2003). Instead of saying that they had a "fantastic" day, they may say it was "good." Looking at an image of space from the James Webb telescope they may say it is "pretty" while others would call it "stunning," "gorgeous," or "beautiful beyond words." Note that the word choices are not due to anomia; the problem is not with retrieving the

Table 8–2. Grice's Maxims for Efficient and Effective Communication and Examples of Disorders

Maxim (Linguistic Skill)	Definition and Purpose	Presentation of Disorders
Quality	Share only what you believe to be true or what you have evidence for	Exaggerated, hyperbole, fantastical descriptions
Quantity	Provide enough information but not more information than is necessary	Redundancies, repetition, verbosity or too brief and terse (paucity)
Relation	Be sure your contribution is relevant	Digressing away from topic, tangential topics
Manner	Be brief and orderly and avoid obscurity and ambiguity, be clear and efficient	Vague, oblique

words they want to say but rather selecting a word with affective or emotional connotation. Some people may produce fewer key elements or main ideas during discourse (Bartels-Tobin & Hinckley, 2005; Marini et al., 2012). Their descriptions may be less specific. In a picture description task, they may say "there is fruit in the bowl" instead of "there are grapes and apples in the bowl."

Use of pronouns or other referents can also be affected (Balaban et al., 2016). In retelling the story of Cinderella, they may use pronouns without clarifying whom they're referring to. Or they may make errors that are not corrected (Stockbridge et al., 2019), causing confusion on the part of the listener. **Cohesion** refers to linguistic ties between adjacent sentences through pronouns and their referents and use of connectors such as "but" and "and." Introducing a person (e.g., Cinderella) and then later referring to that person as "she" is an

---

Box 8–1 They? They Who?

Read this excerpt from a retelling of the Cinderella story by a person with RHD.

*There was a girl named Cinderella who had two evil stepsisters. And **they**[1] were invited to a ball and so **they**[2] got dressed and went off to the ball. **She**[3] was left behind to clean up and basically take care of the house. [RHDBank]*

If you're familiar with the story, you know that **they**[1] refers to Cinderella and her two stepsisters, but that **they**[2] refers only to the stepsisters, because Cinderella did not get to go with them to the ball (although she too got dressed for it). You also know that **She**[3] refers to Cinderella. The shared knowledge between the speaker and the listener allows you to understand the intended meaning despite the ambiguous pronouns.

Try this example:

*There was a boy named Diego who had two best friends. And **they**[1] were invited to go fishing so **they**[2] gathered their rods and tackle boxes and went to the lake. **He**[3] was left behind to mow the lawn.*

In this case, without prior knowledge, there is no way to tell who **they**[1] or **they**[2] refer to—the friends only, Diego and both friends, or Diego and one friend; or if there are different combinations of people referred to by **they**[1] and **they**[2] as in the Cinderella example. You also do not know which person was left to mow the lawn. When the listener does not share the same knowledge as the speaker, and the speaker does not realize or account for the difference, communication breakdowns occur. The understanding that others may have different knowledge from your own is part of theory of mind, discussed later in the Social Cognition section.

example of discourse cohesion. If Cinderella was not initially named, or if there were multiple females and it wasn't clear which one "she" referred to, then the discourse would have poor cohesion.

The amount of information conveyed can vary widely across people with RHD. Some exhibit **verbosity** in which they talk a lot and provide overly long responses. Others have **paucity of speech** in which responses are very short. In either case, the content of the responses may or may not be appropriate or relevant. With verbosity of speech, sometimes the person talks a lot but stays on topic and the response is relevant to the conversation. In other cases, they may share too much information, may share information that is inappropriate to the setting or communication partner, or the response may be tangential and disorganized such that they get off topic and after a while you're not quite sure what they're talking about. Similarly with paucity of speech, the short answers can be appropriate and relevant, but may or may not be complete. Or they can be off-target or inappropriate.

As described above, after RHD discourse can be disorganized, tangential, and/or overpersonalized (Blake, 2006; Marini, 2012). These can be measured by the amount of coherence, or how well the ideas or information fit together. **Local coherence** is a measure of the relatedness of adjacent sentences. Each subsequent sentence or idea in a discourse should build upon previous sentences. **Global coherence** relates to whether all the sentences/ideas fit into the same theme. An example of local coherence without global coherence is provided in Box 8–2. Tangential information can affect both local and global coherence if seemingly random ideas are stuck in but are not related to the overall gist or theme. Overpersonalization also can occur after RHD. One example from a Cinderella story retelling is a man who introduced the evil stepsisters and then compared himself to Cinderella and his older sisters

---

Box 8–2 Global and Local Coherence

This story contains good local coherence but poor global coherence. Each sentence is related to the previous one, but they do not all fit a single topic.

Kristy went grocery shopping on Thursday morning. She saw that the grocery carts were strewn around the front entrance. The carts had been blown around by a major windstorm. The wind speed had exceeded 50 miles an hour. The severity of the storm made it the worst weather event in the past 25 years in the small town. The town was known for its beautiful weather and mild climate. Summer was the most profitable time in the town for the tourism industry. The easy access to boating and water activities as well as the tradition of good food were a huge draw.

From *The Right Hemisphere and Disorders of Cognition and Communication: Theory and Clinical Practice* (p. 49) by Blake, M. L. Copyright © 2018 Plural Publishing, Inc. All rights reserved.

to the stepsisters. Needless to say, any interruption to coherence creates challenges for communicating and understanding intended meaning.

RH stroke can also affect one's ability to ask questions. In a series of studies, Minga (2020, 2022) found that people with RHD asked fewer questions than people without brain injury, and the types of questions asked were less likely to gather relevant information. The differences in question-asking were related to executive function abilities. Questions are an important component of conversation and information exchange, and these changes have the potential to impact communication efficiency and effectiveness.

Linguistic Aspects: Comprehension

After RHD, some people have difficulty generating inferences, correctly interpreting non-literal language such as idioms, metaphors, and sarcasm, and efficiently determining the contextually-appropriate meaning of ambiguous words and phrases (see Blake, 2018 for a review).

One model to explain these deficits is the fine coding versus coarse coding model (Beeman, 1998). According to this model, LH language processing focuses on fine coding, or determining word and sentence meaning, quickly landing on and selecting the most common meaning of words and sentences. The RH, in contrast, uses a coarse coding process in which multiple possible meanings of words, phrases, and sentences are generated, including both concrete and abstract meanings. These are all kept active for a period of time until the LH selects the most appropriate. Within this model, if the RH is damaged, then it cannot activate and maintain the alternative meanings or features, particularly those that are distantly related to the primary meaning or feature. For example, *wrinkled* is a potential feature of *shirt*, but it isn't a core feature. This affects inference generation, in which secondary or distant meanings or features often are needed to link words or phrases together. If someone says, "I didn't plan on having to iron this morning, but I need this shirt to match my suit," you probably generated the inference that the shirt was wrinkled. If you didn't generate that inference, then the exchange might not make any sense. Coarse coding deficits have been used as an explanation for RHD difficulties with interpreting non-literal language such as idioms, metaphors, and sarcasm or irony in which the intended meaning is not the literal meaning. The intended meaning of *a flood of e-mail* has nothing to do with excessive water, but rather that there were many, many emails that arrived in a short amount of time. Understanding the intended meaning requires considering multiple meanings of words and word combinations.

A second explanation of RHD linguistic comprehension deficits is the suppression deficit hypothesis (Tompkins et al., 2015). According to this hypothesis, after the coarse coding process occurs and multiple potential meanings or interpretations are activated, contextual cues are used to determine the most appropriate meaning and all others are suppressed or inhibited. For example, if you hear "She picked up the spade," you may think she is either gardening or playing cards. When you then hear "She dug a hole," the "cards" meaning of spade is suppressed or inhibited, so that the most likely meaning (shovel) is the most active meaning in your brain. RHD can affect the efficiency of this suppression process, so that the person has too many possible interpretations active at once, which affects overall comprehension accuracy. Several sentences later, they may wonder where the card game comes in, leaving them a bit confused about the conversation.

Paralinguistic Aspects: Aprosodia

Aprosodia is an impairment of comprehension and/or production of linguistic or emotional prosody. Impairments of prosody can occur after either LH or RH cortical damage, but emotional aprosodia is much more common after right than left hemisphere lesions (Stockbridge, 2022; Ukaegbe, 2022). Remember from Chapter 4 that prosody can be considered both part of speech and part of language. Aprosodia is an impairment of the paralinguistic component of language.

Expressive aprosodia is a deficit in which a person has difficulty in effectively manipulating prosody to convey their intended meaning. Their voice may sound flat and monotone. It may seem like they are talking fast, because they are not using the typical prosodic changes that signal breaks, boundaries, or important information. They may seem disinterested or as if they have no feeling about the topic at hand because they are not expressing emotion or mood. Grammatical, pragmatic, and emotional prosody are dissociable, meaning that they can be impaired independently. Someone may be able to use grammatical prosody and effectively convey speech acts and emphatic stress but be unable to convey emotion through their tone of voice.

No single component of prosody—timing, pitch, or loudness—is consistently affected in expressive aprosodia (Weed & Fusaroli, 2020). It may be that these components are too intertwined in our interpretation of meaning to be able to clearly separate out the effect of any one of them in isolation. For example, small changes in timing and loudness that are not large enough to show up as a clear deficit in either area alone might add together so that the intended meaning is not clearly conveyed.

Receptive aprosodia is a deficit in which a person has difficulty in recognizing or interpreting prosody used by others. People with receptive aprosodia may have difficulty understanding if someone is asking a question or making a statement; or misinterpret who said what (e.g., Marilyn, said Sheri, is brilliant versus Marilyn said Sheri is brilliant); or not understand the key detail someone is trying to convey (e.g., DAYVON ate the pizza versus Dayvon ate the PIZZA). They may not be able to use prosody to determine if someone is angry, sad, or bored. Receptive emotional aprosodia may co-occur with emotional facial recognition deficits, compounding the difficulty in interpreting another person's emotions or feelings. It also may co-occur with emotional semantic deficits, such as matching words to emotions (e.g., stench and putrid are related to disgust), or inferring emotion from a sentence (She practically danced down the steps = joyful) (Sheppard et al., 2021).

The RH is highly interconnected and has few obvious "centers" of processing. While there are not clear subtypes based on location of lesion, there are some patterns. Damage to anterior, frontal lobe regions and dorsal pathways are more likely to cause expressive aprosodia, while damage to posterior regions (e.g., parieto-temporal junction) and ventral pathways more commonly result in receptive aprosodia (Figure 8–1A, –D).

Extralinguistic Aspects

Extralinguistics are the non-verbal aspects of communication. They include facial expressions, eye contact, body language and gestures. There is much less research on deficits to the extralinguistic aspects of apragmatism compared to linguistic and paralinguistic components. But they are critical components of communication.

Both production and interpretation of facial expression, especially emotional expressions, can be reduced after RHD. Some people may not easily convey their emotions while others can produce appropriate facial expressions but have difficulty in interpreting others' expressions. Some people will have difficulty with both production and interpretation. While this may seem like a relatively unimportant ability, one study found that receptive facial expression deficits were associated with poorer marital satisfaction (Blonder et al., 2012). Imagine that your best friend or life partner suddenly stopped being able to read your mood or emotions. The communication between the two of you would change dramatically and likely would cause misinterpretations, hurt feelings, and perhaps the impression that the other person doesn't care for you in the same way they did before.

The impact of reduced facial expression production is likely heightened when combined with expressive emotional aprosodia. When these co-occur, the person cannot easily express mood or emotion without words. It is important to remember that people still feel emotions, but they cannot easily express them.

Appropriate eye contact also can be affected after RHD (Mackenzie et al., 1997). People may not use eye contact to express interest in a person or a conversation, or to signal turn-taking. Sometimes they may use too much eye contact, which typically leads to the communication partner feeling uneasy or uncomfortable.

Gestures can also be reduced (Cocks et al., 2007), with fewer iconic gestures—those that indicate actions, positions, or size and shape of an object. Gesture use also may be reduced during emotionally charged communication exchanges.

Assessment of Apragmatism

One of the major challenges of assessing and diagnosing apragmatism is that there is a wide range of pragmatic behaviors that are accepted within any society or culture. Looking back over the characteristics of apragmatism, you can probably think of at least one, and probably several people in your family or social circle who fit into the descriptions. Perhaps an uncle

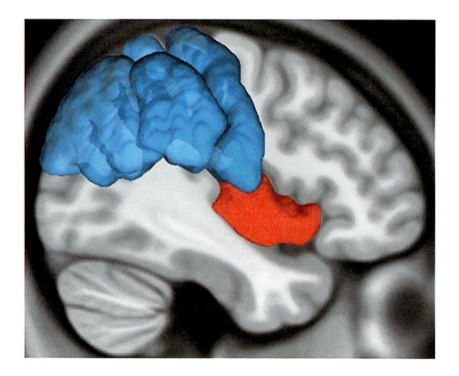

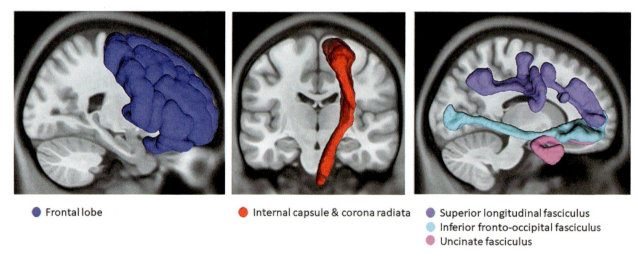

Figure 8–1. Right hemisphere regions associated with A. expressive, B. receptive, C. expressive or receptive aprosodia, and D. the dorsal and ventral streams. Based on data from Durfee and Sheppard, 2022. Figure courtesy of Alexandra Zezinka Durfee and Shannon Sheppard.

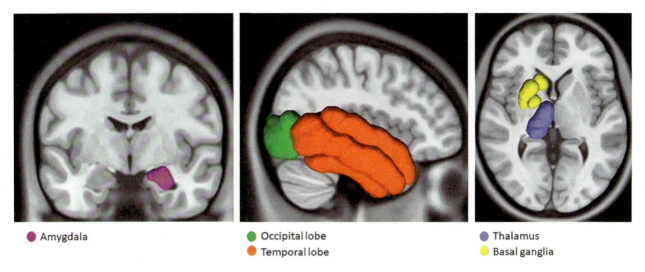

- Amygdala
- Occipital lobe
- Temporal lobe
- Thalamus
- Basal ganglia

C.

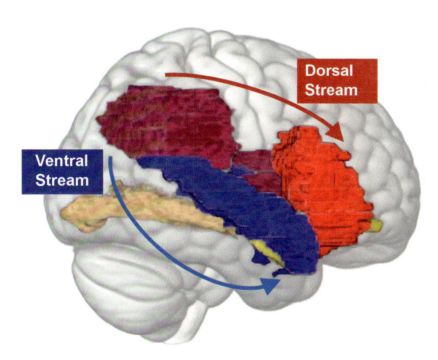

D.

Figure 8–1. *continued*

> ### Box 8–3 Timothy Omundson
>
> Timothy Omundson is an actor known for roles such as Carlton Lassiter in *Psych* and King Richard in *Galavant*, as well as smaller roles in *Xena: Warrior Princess, Deadwood, Judging Amy, Jericho,* and *This Is Us*. He had a right hemisphere stroke in 2017. Interviews before and after the stroke show the impact of paralinguistic and extralinguistic apragmatism. Pre-stroke his voice and face were very expressive. He was entertaining and genuinely seemed like a fun person to talk to. Post-stroke his jokes fell flat because his timing was off, and his facial expressions seemed forced. His linguistic abilities appear fine, but the prosody and non-verbal components of communication no longer appear easy and fluid. Watching interviews at different times shows ongoing recovery of these abilities.
>
> In *This Is Us* he played a character who had a stroke. In exchanges with his neighbor Kate, he comes off as gruff, uncaring, and mean. In the episode "Sorry" when Kate visits, he says (with flat prosody) that he's happy she came. She doesn't believe it because of the way he said it. He explains: "Ever since the stroke I've trouble (sic) making my voice and face express empathy and gratitude. Doesn't mean I don't have any."
>
> (Fogelman, D., Mastai, E., Freeman, E. (Writers), Asher, R. (Director). (2019, November 12). Sorry (Season 4, Episode 8) [Sorry]. In D. Fogelman, I. Aptaker, E.Berger, J. Requa, G. Ficarra, K. Olin, C. Gogolak, J. Rosenthal & S. Beers (Executive Producers), This Is Us. Rhode Island Ave. Productions; Zaftig Films; 20th Television).

who talks too much, shares too much, and makes every conversation about himself. Or a friend who rarely expresses emotions, and you're never quite sure what she's feeling. Unlike aphasia for which we can identify a fairly clear cut-off for language abilities we expect in a literate adult, there are no such cut-offs for pragmatics and apragmatism. As noted in the definition of apragmatism, the context of the communication exchange dictates what is appropriate. Someone who is open and shares extensively might be deemed appropriate in conversations with a spouse but not in conversations with their boss. Societal and cultural norms and expectations make the situation even more complicated. In some cultures, eye contact is not appropriate between people of different sexes or different positions on the social hierarchy. In others, sharing personal information is taboo except with the closest of family members. Diagnosing apragmatism, then, requires finding out how the person communicated prior to the RHD, and considering their cultural background as well as the culture and society in which they are living.

There are several standardized assessments for aspects of apragmatism (see Table 8–3). Several of these were created for people with traumatic brain injury, but may be appropriate for people with focal damage to the RH. In addition, there are various methods for analyzing discourse samples obtained from conversations, storytelling or retelling, and procedural discourse in which someone is asked to explain how to do something. These include clinical discourse analysis (Damico, 1991), main concept analysis, conversational analysis (Schlegloff et al., 1978), exchange structure analysis (Berry, 1981), and systemic-functional linguistics (Togher et al., 1999).

Table 8–3. Select Assessments Appropriate for Apragmatism

Test/Authors	Areas Included	Notes
Standardized Assessments		
Assessment Battery for Communication (ABaCo; Angeleri et al., 2012)	Linguistic: production & comprehension of communication acts Paralinguistic: prosody, facial expression & gesticulation; basic communication, emotions, contradictions between paralinguistic & linguistic content Extralinguistic: production & comprehension of gestures Context scale: communication within Grice's maxims and social norms Conversational scale: turn-taking, following topic threads	Authors include facial expression and gesticulation in paralinguistics; extralinguistics include only gestures Examiner–clinician interactions and videos used
Discourse Comprehension Test (DCT; Brookshire & Nicholas, 1997)	Linguistic reading and auditory comprehension for short scenarios, including main ideas and details both explicitly stated and implied	

continues

Table 8–3. *continued*

Test/Authors	Areas Included	Notes
Standardized Assessments		
Functional Assessment of Verbal Reasoning and Executive Strategies (FAVRES; MacDonald, 2005)	Linguistic verbal reasoning, discourse, comprehension	Also includes executive functions such as reasoning, planning, organizing, problem solving and generating rationales for responses
Montreal Evaluation of Communication (MEC; Joanette et al., 2004; 2015)	Linguistic: production & interpretation of idioms, metaphors, and speech acts; story comprehension & retelling; conversation Paralinguistic: production & interpretation of emotional and linguistic prosody Extralinguistic: facial expression and eye contact during conversation	Designed for people with RHD (French, Portuguese, and English versions available)
Voicemail Elicitation Task (VET; Meulenbroek & Cherney, 2019)	Linguistic: use of politeness markers in workplace communication	Role-playing voicemail task includes providing information and making requests to people with different social relationships (subordinate, superior, colleague, friend)
Questionnaires & Checklists		
Adapted Kagan Scales (Togher et al., 2010)	Rating scales for clinicians to assess communicative participation and competence; competence includes client's abilities and how communication partner supports and facilitates communication	Adapted for people with TBI from original scales for aphasia Domains of pragmatics are not separated out but scoring takes into account verbal and non-verbal contributions Interactions in different contexts and with different purposes can be scored individually

Table 8–3. *continued*		
Test/Authors	Areas Included	Notes
Questionnaires & Checklists		
Cognitive Communication Checklist for Acquired Brain Injury (CCCABI; MacDonald, 2015)	Screening checklist Linguistic: auditory comprehension, discourse production Extralinguistic: production of appropriate facial expression, eye contact, gestures, and tone of voice	Designed for people with TBI Checklist can be completed by SLP or other medical/rehabilitation professional Prosody is included as "tone of voice" with other non-verbals
Communicative Participation Item Bank (CPIB; Baylor et al., 2013)	Assesses how a person's "condition" interferes with communication in a variety of settings and conditions	Domains of communication are not separated out; answers can help identify what situations are challenging
LaTrobe Communication Questionnaire (LCT; Douglas et al., 2000)	Linguistic, Paralinguistic & Extralinguistic Assesses perceived communication ability from perspective of person with brain injury and communication partners Linguistic: based on Grice's Maxims of Quality (accuracy), Quantity (amount), Relation (relevance), and Manner (presentation, organization, turn-taking)	Designed for people with TBI. Forms available for patient (self) and other (regular communication partner) Comparison between self and other can yield information about awareness of deficits
Pragmatic Rating Scale (PRS; Iwashita & Sohlberg, 2019)	Linguistic—relevance, clarity, organization, initiation, cohesion, quantity	Designed for evaluation of conversation

continues

Test/Authors	Areas Included	Notes
Table 8–3. *continued*		
	Questionnaires & Checklists	
	Paralinguistic—intonation and stress patterns	
	Extralinguistic – eye contact, body language, facial expression, gestures	
	Interactional communication, including turn-taking and repairing communication breakdowns	
Profile of Pragmatic Impairment in Communication (PPIC; Linscott et al., 1996; Hays et al., 2004)	Linguistic, Paralinguistic & Extralinguistic Assesses conversational interactions; content, style, organization, etc.	Original assessment was named the Profile of Functional Impairment in Communication
Social Communication Skills Questionnaire Adapted (McGann et al., 1997; Adapted by Dahlberg et al., 2006)	Linguistic, Paralinguistic, Extralinguistic Self-report questionnaire about communication abilities	Includes behavioral responses and affective/emotional responses in conversations (e.g., controlling temper when others express differing opinions)

Treatment of Apragmatism

There are limited options for treatments specifically designed for communication disorders associated with RHD. Most of the treatments appropriate for linguistic and extralinguistic aspects of apragmatism were initially designed for adults with TBI. This doesn't mean they are not useful, but since TBI typically causes widespread deficits in cognition that impact communication (see Chapter 13) some treatments may focus on the underlying cognitive issues more than specific language deficits. All treatments should be contextualized, meaning they should take place in naturalistic communicative settings.

Linguistic and Extralinguistic Apragmatism

For linguistic and extralinguistic apragmatic production, the best available evidence is from group treatment programs in which structured conversations and storytelling are used to increase awareness of deficits in modes of communication and interpretation of intended meaning is facilitated through use of contextual cues and integration of linguistic, extralinguistic, and paralinguistic cues (Braden et al., 2010; Dahlberg et al., 2007; Gabbatore et al., 2014).

Linguistic apragmatic comprehension treatments typically involve metacognitive strategies in which patients/clients break down a comprehension task into steps where progress can be monitored along the way. One such strategy is Preview, Question, Read, Summarize, and Test (PQRST) (Robinson, 1970). The names of the steps are intuitive: first, Preview what is to be comprehended, be it an article, story, or some other text; Question the purpose and what the goal is—to summarize, to expand knowledge, to learn new material, etc.; Read it and Summarize what was read; and then Test or review the information. By replacing Read with Listen, the same strategy can be used for auditory comprehension, such as listening to a TED Talk, podcast, conversation, or some other discourse. The Strategic Memory and Reasoning Training (SMART) (Anand et al., 2011; Chapman & Mudar, 2014) is a more in-depth metacognitive strategy. Shown in Table 8–4, the steps involve inference, paraphrasing, and abstracting.

Contextualization treatment involves focusing on the context and the cues provided to deduce the intended meaning. This approach has not yet been tested for efficacy or

Table 8–4. SMART Metacognitive Strategy

Process	Description
Inhibiting	identify information that is not immediately relevant and remove it
Organizing/Managing	identify main ideas or themes and put related ideas together
Inferencing	generate inferences and links between main ideas and themes and develop abstract, deeper meanings
Paraphrasing	restate the information in your own words
Synthesizing	combine ideas or themes to generate the gist of the material
Integrating	integrate gist with pre-existing knowledge such as world knowledge or information from related material; can include multiple perspectives
Abstracting/Generalizing	summarize the gist and generalize information to other contexts or situations

Note: Based on Anand et al., 2011.

effectiveness, but is based on research that shows that people with RHD can use strong contextual cues to determine meaning, and that focusing on contextual cues can increase the efficiency of coarse coding processes (Blake & Lesniewicz, 2005; Blake et al., 2015). This approach can be used for idioms, metaphors and other non-literal language, or ambiguous words or phrases (Table 8–5).

Paralinguistic Apragmatism: Aprosodia

Expressive emotional aprosodia can be treated with a cognitive-affective hierarchical approach in which three cues are initially present: the name of an emotion, a written description of the appropriate prosody (e.g., sad prosody is low-pitched and slow), and a picture of the accompanying facial expression. The patient first matches the emotion with the correct prosody and facial expression, and then produces a sentence using the emotional prosody with all three cues visible. The treatment proceeds with removing the cues one by one—first the description, then the name of the emotion, and finally the facial expression—with the client producing a sentence each time with the target prosody (Leon et al., 2005; Rosenbek et al., 2006).

A motoric-imitative hierarchical approach has also shown to be effective (Leon et al., 2005; Rosenbek et al., 2006). In this approach, the clinician models emotional prosody by producing an emotionally laden sentence with appropriate prosody and facial expression (e.g., "I got the job!" in a happy tone of voice and facial expression) and then the clinician and client produce it in unison. The clinician reduces the support over a series of steps, moving from unison production to repetition, then removing facial and prosodic cues and asking the client to reproduce the target sentence with appropriate prosody.

The Recognition and Expression of Affective Communication Treatment (REACT) is a new treatment being developed (Durfee & Sheppard, 2022). It involves the use of both explicit (conceptual, top-down) and implicit (perceptual, bottom-up) cues. Examples of explicit cues include asking the patient/client to list the prosodic features along with the emotion conveyed in the speaker's tone of voice (recognition) or providing prosodic cues along with the emotion (expression). Examples of implicit cues include asking the patient/client to identify the emotion when a congruent emotional scene is present (recognition) or repeating the sentence with the same prosody as given in a model (expression). The paradigm also includes a trial of expression feedback wherein the patient/client produces the emotional prosody, the production is recorded by the examiner, and the patient/client and clinician listen to the production together to evaluate if the production was accurate or not, and if not, how the production could be changed to sound more emotional. Early evidence suggests this treatment may be effective for improving both expressive and receptive emotional aprosodia.

Discourse and Pragmatics

There are several treatments and programs created for people with TBI that address discourse and pragmatic aspects of communication more generally (Table 8–6). The Work-Related

Table 8–5. Example of the Contextualization Process for Ambiguous Words or Phrases

Step 1	Present ambiguous word and ask for different meanings.[1]	"Tell me the different meanings of the word 'spring'" [season, stream of water, metal coil]
Step 2	Put the word into a sentence context and discuss the meanings that would be appropriate. Provide different contexts for different meanings; some contexts may still leave some ambiguity.	"If I said 'When he took apart the clock he lost the spring,' what meanings would be appropriate? [coil] "What if I said 'he went fishing in the spring?' [season/stream of water]. "What if I said 'he liked to hunt in the winter but he went fishing in the spring?'" [season]
Step 3	Ask client to highlight/underline the cues that led to his/her choice of interpretation.	"When he took apart the <u>clock</u> he lost the spring." • A clock is a mechanical device with metal coils "He went <u>fishing</u> in the spring." • You fish in a body of water • You can fish in the spring season "He liked to hunt in the <u>winter but</u> he went fishing in the spring." • Contrast with winter leads to interpretation of "season" meaning
Step 4	Ask client to provide context that will support different meanings, highlighting the cues that support the intended meaning.	"The word is SPRING. Make up a sentence using the 'season' meaning of the word SPRING." "Now make up a new sentence using the 'stream of water' meaning of the word SPRING."

From *The Right Hemisphere and Disorders of Cognition and Communication: Theory and Clinical Practice* (p. 88) by Blake, M. L. Copyright © 2018 Plural Publishing, Inc. All rights reserved.

Note: [1] While listing multiple meanings will not directly address either suppression or coarse coding deficits, in this case the client is asked to list the meanings so that they can then be embedded into different contexts. The focus of the treatment is using context to determine the appropriate meaning.

Table 8–6. Sample of Treatments for Pragmatic Communication

Treatment	Areas Addressed	Notes & Key Studies
Communication Partner Training (TBI Express, TBI conneCT)	Training communication partners to recognize communication patterns and styles that can support or negatively impact the other's ability to participate to their fullest extent	Rietdijk et al., 2019; Rietdijk et al., 2020; Sim et al., 2013; Togher et al., 2016 Videos available at: https://www.sydney.edu.au/medicine-health/our-research/research-centres/acquired-brain-injury-communication-lab/tbi-express.html
Video Modeling	Clients and communication partners video natural exchanges (e.g., conversations at home) and then discuss patterns and styles that support or negatively impact the communication exchange	Can facilitate awareness of communication strengths and weaknesses of both partners. Douglas et al., 2019; Douglas et al., 2014; Hoepner & Olson, 2018; Hoepner et al., 2021
Work-Related Communication Training Approach (WoRC)	Focuses on politeness markers for workplace communication	Used in concert with voicemail elicitation task Meulenbroek & Cherney, 2019

Communication Training Approach (WoRC; Meulenbroek & Cherney, 2021) is specifically designed to help people with pragmatic aspects of communication such as politeness markers with the overarching goal of facilitating return to work or success in workplace situations.

Another important area of any communication approach is training the communication partner. Since communication relies on a minimum of two people, the actions of both contribute to the success of any interaction. When you are working with patients/clients with acquired communication disorders, you have to consider that their family members, caregivers, and friends are also impacted by the communication challenges. Their behaviors and responses to the patient/client have a huge role in whether or not an interaction is successful and/or efficient. Communication Partner Training is designed to help the partner understand the challenges and change their own communication style to facilitate meaningful, efficient, appropriate interactions. For example, it is easy for family members to turn conversations into quizzes ("Remember when I told you about Auntie Preeti's visit to India? Last week? Over dinner? Remember I dropped the plate of naan while setting the table?"), which are rarely fruitful or satisfying for either partner. Training can help them to provide necessary details or information needed to keep a conversation going and to support the other's ability to participate ("Auntie Preeti's visit to India sounded so exciting! What would you want to do if we went to India?").

Cognitive Disorders

Cortical strokes in the RH can affect attention, executive function, awareness, memory, and social cognition. These deficits can co-occur with apragmatism and increase the negative impact on social interactions and daily life. Assessment and treatment of cognitive disorders for the most part will be covered in Chapter 12, as the concepts and tools are useful not only for disorders associated with cortical RH lesions, but also for frontal lobe and diffuse damage.

Attention

Attentional deficits are common after RHD, and include both sustained attention and attentional control. Attentional deficits have widespread impacts on everyday functions and communication. You have to be able to focus attention to follow conversations, understand instructions for physical therapy, or make scrambled eggs for breakfast. Even something as routine as getting ready for work in the morning requires at least some attention. If you get distracted during that routine, you may miss a step in the process. Sustained attention is needed for any task or activity that lasts a few minutes or more. In a conversation, if you fail to sustain attention you might miss information or the punchline to a joke. Alternating and divided attention are required for more complex tasks like driving or for carrying on a conversation while making breakfast.

Attentional deficits are caused not only by impairments in the "amount" of attentional resources but also in the allocation of those resources. After a brain injury, activities that used to be automatic and require little attention suddenly require more attention. For example, making tea may require additional attention if you have hemiparesis and can use only one hand. The extra attention directed toward the teabag distracts from completing other steps in the process such as filling the teapot with water or turning on the stovetop to heat the water.

Box 8-4 Conversations Require Lots of Attention

Claudia Osborne, a Doctor of Osteopathic Medicine, experienced a TBI from a bike accident. She had difficulty following and participating in conversations, especially if several people were involved. She explains it like this: "When I was with Marcia and my other friends, the pace of their activity and conversation was too fast. I was always off balance, scrambling to follow, fatigued from trying to guess an answer or sort out where to focus my attention. In seeking a way out of my confusion, I asked too many questions. I bred irritation, disappointment, and sometimes incredulity" (Osborne, 2000, p. 216). She goes on to describe a conversation in which the topic flowed from a mutual friend to President Bill Clinton to a celebrated author. She was always one step behind, and left the conversation thinking that Bill Clinton was being compared to William Faulkner.

Box 8-5 Neglect Terminology

Because the visual domain and the left side of space are most commonly affected, those are usually inferred. The term "neglect" can be assumed to mean unilateral left visuospatial neglect. "Left neglect" almost always is used to refer to visuospatial neglect. Other terms such as hemispatial neglect or unilateral neglect are assumed to mean left visuospatial neglect unless otherwise specified (e.g., right neglect). Unfortunately, the label "neglect" is a misnomer. In order to neglect something, there has to be a level of awareness that it exists and a choice (conscious or unconscious) not to do anything about it. People with neglect do not consciously process items in the affected side of space. Their brains essentially are not telling them that there is something in that space.

Unilateral Neglect

Unilateral neglect is a specific form of directed attentional deficit. It most often affects the contralateral region of space such that damage to the RH impairs attention to stimuli in the left side of space. This occurs most frequently in the visual domain (visuospatial neglect), although auditory, tactile, and olfactory neglect are possible. Right neglect due to LH damage is possible, but when it occurs it is less severe and is more likely to resolve without treatment.

With left visuospatial neglect, a patient will act as if they do not see things in the left side of space. They may not read words on the left side of a page, will not realize they have a cup of chai or coffee if it is set to the left side, and may bump into the left side of a door frame as they move through it. Importantly, visuospatial neglect is not a visual deficit. The eyes are fine and the pathways from the eyes to the occipital lobe are intact. The impairment occurs because of damage to attentional networks that are supposed to process signals that capture things in a region of space.

Visuospatial neglect can affect communication in several ways. First, reading and writing will be affected. These can be called **neglect dyslexia** and **neglect dysgraphia**, respectively. Second, people with visuospatial neglect may not include people in conversations if those people are standing off to the left side, or even to the left of another person in the conversation. Finally, because unilateral neglect is an attentional disorder, there may be other general attentional deficits that impact comprehension and production.

Auditory and olfactory neglect are rare, in part because sensory signals from both sides of space are processed in both sides of the brain. For example, sounds coming from the left side of space are processed by both the left and right ears and in the left and right hemispheres. While auditory neglect does not impair hearing sounds from one side, it can affect the ability to localize sounds coming from the affected side of space.

Tactile neglect presents as reduced identification or response to touch on the affected side of the body (with RHD, this would be the left side), above and beyond any hemisensory deficit that prevents touch perception. Someone with hemisensory loss may not perceive touch on their left hand because of damage to the primary sensory strip in the parietal lobe. This is a sensory deficit, not neglect. If they have mild hemisensory loss and should be able to feel deep pressure but do not consciously register or respond to that pressure, that would be tactile neglect.

Most forms of neglect affect sensory domains, but motor neglect also can occur. This is a reduced use of movement above and beyond any motoric deficit. Similar to the description of hemisensory loss, someone with hemiparesis may have difficulty with left-handed movements due to motor deficits. If they do not use their arm/hand for any task, even movements which are possible for them, they may have motor neglect.

There are three main types of visuospatial neglect: personal, peripersonal, and extrapersonal. Personal neglect affects one's own body. Patients may comb only the hair on the right side, shave only the right side of their face, and/or dress only the right side of the body. Peripersonal neglect affects the region around the body, within an arm's reach. Peripersonal neglect affects reading, writing, eating, and many speech-language tasks such as naming objects or pictures (Figure 8–2). Extrapersonal neglect affects the area beyond an arm's reach. Recognizing visitors in your room, finding the TV on the wall, navigating down a hallway and through a door all can be affected by extrapersonal neglect. The three types can occur together or separately. Some people may have personal neglect but not peri- or extrapersonal. Others may have two of the three types or even all three.

Additionally, there are two ways that the "left side" can be defined. In viewer-centered neglect, left is defined by the person's visual field, so that they do not attend to things to the left of their midline. In contrast, for stimulus-centered neglect (sometimes called object-centered

Figure 8–2. Potential effects of peripersonal unilateral visuospatial neglect: eating food. From *Clinical Neuroscience for Communication Disorders: Neuroanatomy and Neurophysiology* (p. 257) by Blake, M. L. and Hoepner, J. K. Copyright © 2023 Plural Publishing, Inc. All rights reserved.

neglect), the patient will omit the left side of items regardless of where they appear in the visual field. Figure 8–3 shows stimulus-centered neglect in a scene copying task in which the left side of each item is missing.

Unilateral neglect is not an all-or-none phenomenon. The severity of neglect can appear to change throughout the course of the day and will be more severe with some tasks or in some environments compared to others (Figure 8–4). More complex tasks or images/stimuli that are more visually complex will tend to make neglect look more severe. Interesting or emotionally laden stimuli on the affected side will draw attention and make the neglect look less severe. If the person is fatigued or in pain, neglect will be more severe. Think about when

Figure 8–3. Scene copying A. stimulus item and B. stimulus-centered neglect.

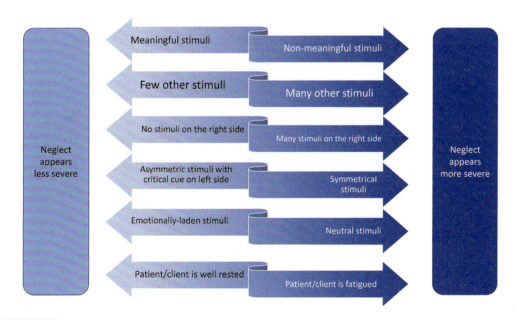

Figure 8–4. Factors that increase or decrease the apparent severity of unilateral neglect.

Table 8–7. Select Assessments of Unilateral Neglect

Test/Authors	Areas Included	Notes
Apples Test of the Birmingham Cognitive Screening (Bickerton et al., 2011)	peripersonal, viewer- and stimulus-centered	Cancellation task
Balloons Test (Edgeworth et al., 1998)	peripersonal, viewer-centered	Cancellation task
Behavioural Inattention Test (BIT; Wilson et al., 1987)	peripersonal, viewer-centered	Cancellation, line bisection, copying and drawing tasks; also functional tasks including menu reading, coin counting, and picture identification
Catherine Bergego Scale (CBS; Azouvi et al., 1996; 2003)	personal, peripersonal, and extrapersonal	Clinician observation of daily activities
Line Bisection Test (Schenkenberg et al., 1980)	peripersonal, viewer-centered	Paper-pencil task

you have to pay attention to something—it is easier when you are interested, well-rested, and there are few distractors. Because neglect is an attentional disorder, anything that makes focusing attention more difficult for people without brain injury will impact those with brain injury and neglect, and often the negative impact is much greater.

Assessment of Unilateral Neglect

Assessment of unilateral neglect typically involves paper/pencil tasks such as line cancellation, line bisection, copying, and drawing tasks. Picture description tasks also can be used. Most assessments are for peripersonal, viewer-centered visuospatial neglect. Scores are based on how many items the patient misses on the left side of the page. Several virtual reality assessments have been developed to test more realistic settings such as crossing a busy street. These assessments also more often assess extrapersonal neglect. A list of common tests of visuospatial unilateral neglect are provided in Table 8–7.

Treatment of Unilateral Neglect

Approaches to treatment of neglect can be divided into top-down, explicit treatments and bottom-up or implicit approaches. When working with a client, a mixture of these can be used.

Top-down treatments involve explicit cues and strategies for scanning the visual field. These include external or clinician-driven cues such as strategies and self-talk to "start on left," "look to the left." They also include strategies such as running a finger along the boundary of the page to establish the extent of the area the client needs to view. Bottom-up treatments work to draw a client's attention to the neglected space. This can include using meaningful, asymmetric, or emotional stimuli or using a red line or other bright marker on the left side of a page. Most treatments show some effectiveness, but none is consistently and substantially better than another (Bowen et al., 2013; Pernet et al., 2013; Yang et al., 2013).

Visual scanning treatments are primarily top-down, and involve repeated practice starting in the upper left corner of a page and scanning from left to right then back to the next line on the left—as you do in reading. Bottom-up cues can be used (e.g., a red line in the left margin), and the task can be made more or less challenging by manipulating the various factors that impact neglect (refer back to Figure 8–4). Other bottom-up approaches involve sensory stimulation, such as vibration to the neck region or visuomotor treatments in which movement of a limb or the head are paired with visual scanning.

Another approach to neglect is prism glasses, which are designed by neuro-ophthalmologists (Champod et al., 2018; Yang et al., 2013). One half of the lenses are prisms that shift items in the visual field to the ipsilesional region (most often, the right side). When asked to touch the target objects in front of them, they initially reach too far to the right, and have to correct their reach by moving their hand leftward. After repeated trials, the shift becomes more and more automatic, until they are reaching directly to the target objects. When the prism glasses are removed, their first reach to the target object now will overshoot to the left, and over repeated reaches they will adapt. This activity causes the person to reach into the neglected region of space, and can have temporary, and sometimes long-lasting amelioration of unilateral neglect.

Memory

Memory deficits occur in up to 50% of patients with stroke (Snaphaan & De Leeuw, 2007). Encoding, storage, and retrieval processes can be affected, as can all types of memory (Table 8–8). There are few studies that directly compare memory after RH versus LH stroke, but visual memory is more often affected after RH damage and verbal memory after LH damage. Assessment and treatment are covered in Chapter 12.

Executive Function

Few studies specifically address EF deficits after RH stroke. Despite this, executive functions are commonly assessed, and deficits commonly diagnosed, by SLPs (Ramsey & Blake, 2020). This is probably in part because SLPs have access to a variety of cognitive assessments and have educational and clinical experience with executive functions, so they assess and treat what they know.

Table 8–8. Memory Deficits After Stroke

Type of Memory	Deficit Example	Other Characteristics
Declarative	Difficulties recalling facts, names, places, etc. Poor use of strategies for encoding or retrieval	RHD = more difficulty with visual memory LHD = more difficulty with verbal memory
Episodic	Descriptions of autobiographical events can be missing details or have incorrect details	LHD descriptions may have more depth and details than RHD
Working Memory	Difficulty with simultaneous storage & processing; may lose details or have errors in processing	No clear difference in LHD versus RHD
Prospective Memory	Forget to do things in the future; forgetting is less likely for personally-relevant or meaningful things	May co-occur with deficits of attention and executive function
Metamemory	Over- or underestimating any memory abilities. Some people can be accurate about some types of memory (e.g., declarative recall) but not others (e.g., complex medication schedules)	Overestimation is more common, and co-occurs with deficits in executive function, attention, language, and visuoperception Underestimation can co-occur with disorders of affect

RHD = right hemisphere damage, LHD = left hemisphere damage

EF deficits that have been related to RHD include generative thinking, organization, and strategy use. People with RHD generate fewer ideas and can have more perseverations (see review in Lezak et al., 2004). In verbal problem-solving tasks they may not identify missing information, and they are less likely to monitor their responses or accurately judge their performance. Language and communication can be disorganized with poor integration of details.

Anosognosia

Anosognosia is relatively common after RHD and is one of the most well-known deficits. This is often called denial of deficits, but that label is not accurate. If you deny the existence of something, it means you have some experience of it but refuse to believe it. In anosognosia, the brain is not properly processing the loss of function, so the person is not consciously aware of it.

RHD can cause anosognosia for physical, cognitive, and communication deficits and disorders. With anosognosia for hemiplegia, someone may verbally report that their body is fine, that they have no difficulty walking, and might refuse to use a wheelchair or walker. Others may blame poor performance on factors other than a newly acquired deficit. Someone might say that they didn't do well on a memory task because they weren't really trying, because the noise in the room distracted them, or that they were never very good at that kind of thing in the first place. Anosognosia for neglect is very common; most patients with neglect are not aware that they are not fully processing the environment around them.

There are different levels of awareness. Explicit awareness is when you can specifically acknowledge or describe the deficits, such as being able to say that your left arm is weak. Implicit awareness occurs when you cannot report a deficit, but you unconsciously adapt your behavior. Someone with implicit awareness of hemiparesis may not try to get out of their wheelchair without assistance even though they cannot report that they have weakness of their left leg. Some awareness is task specific. Someone with memory impairment may be able to accurately state that they have difficulty remembering names but inaccurately believes that they do not have memory issues related to taking medication. Finally, there is awareness of the implications of deficits. Someone with unilateral neglect may be able to say that they have trouble seeing things to their left but may not be aware of the consequences, like that they will not be able to drive safely.

Anosognosia is not an all-or-none phenomenon. Some people can be aware of some deficits sometimes or in some situations, but not be aware of other deficits at any time. Awareness can fluctuate across domains (e.g., physical, cognitive). Generally speaking, people with RHD are more likely to be aware of physical deficits than they are of communication or cognitive deficits. This is in part because physical deficits are more concrete/objective, and communication and cognition are more abstract/subjective. Figure 8–5 shows a variety of factors that also can impact levels of awareness (based on Toglia & Kirk, 2000). Anosognosia will seem to be worse when the person is tired or emotional. It may appear milder for activities or tasks that are meaningful to the person, or that they are motivated to improve.

As described earlier in the section on attention, anosognosia commonly co-occurs with unilateral visuospatial neglect. Over time, some people may be able to report that they have unilateral neglect, but may not be able to actively compensate for it; they still may "lose" their glasses and not search for them on the left side of the table.

Social Cognition

Social cognition deficits associated with RHD include theory of mind (ToM) and empathy. The networks responsible for these abilities are bilateral. Regions in the right hemisphere are shown in Figures 8–6A and B. Recent studies suggest that over 50% of people with RH strokes have ToM deficits in the acute stage (Schnur et al., 2021). These deficits might cause

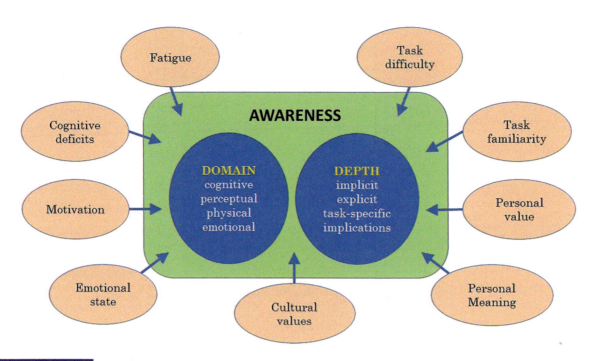

Figure 8–5. Factors influencing awareness.

apragmatism; if a speaker is not aware of the level of knowledge or perspective of their communication partner, it can affect the words they choose, or how much background they provide. It also may lead to misinterpretation of what the partner says.

Empathy can be thought of as a combination of ToM and emotion recognition and processing, in which a person not only understands that other people can have emotions and feelings that differ from their own, but they also can share those emotions. It's like the difference between knowing that a friend may be angry because they did poorly on an exam, and feeling bad about the grade with them. Referring back to Table 8–1, half of caregivers of people with RHD are concerned about the change in empathy. Looking carefully, you'll notice that there isn't any other area that 50% of RH caregivers agree upon as problematic. This indicates that this particular deficit has significant effects on caregivers.

Social inferential reasoning refers to integrating the multiple communication and contextual cues into a whole. This can include facial expression, expressions of emotion (e.g., crying, laughing), the setting in which the event is occurring, and what the person says.

Deficits in social cognition can impact relationships; people have fewer friends and a reduction of emotional closeness with family and spouses (Hewetson et al., 2021). More work is needed to understand what components of social cognition impact relationships and how best to help people with RHD and their families.

Hewetson and colleagues (2021) interviewed people with RHD and their spouses or family members and found four main themes related to deficits in social cognition. First, there can be reduced awareness of deficits and reduced motivation to engage in social activities. The

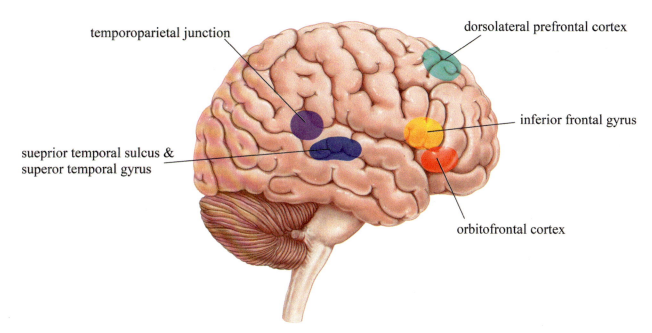

A.

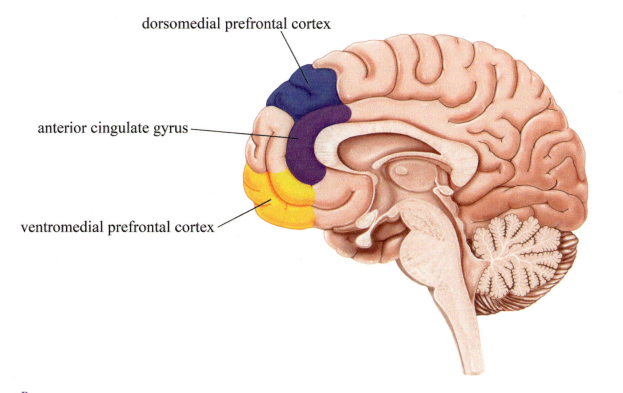

B.

Figure 8–6. A & B. Right hemisphere areas involved in cognitive (cool colors) and affective (warm colors) theory of mind. From *Clinical Neuroscience for Communication Disorders: Neuroanatomy and Neurophysiology* (p. 249) by Blake, M. L. and Hoepner, J. K. Copyright © 2023 Plural Publishing, Inc. All rights reserved.

anosognosia can cause frustration for family members because the person with RHD is not aware that their communication or social engagement is different than it used to be. This can lead to increasingly difficult social interactions. Reduced motivation may be linked to a second theme: the spouse as facilitator of social activities. Many spouses found that if they did not initiate interactions or activities, they wouldn't happen. A third theme was changes in communication. People could come across as rude or uncaring, not know what to talk about with others, or find it difficult to communicate well in emotional or stressful situations. Few people with RHD in this study received adequate education or treatment for their communication problems. Finally, issues with social cognition, specifically theory of mind, negatively impacted communication and, as a result, social interactions.

Swallowing Disorders

As with perisylvian LH damage, dysphagia due to RH damage can be related to motor, sensory, and/or cognitive deficits. Assessment and treatment are covered in Chapter 13.

Motor/Weakness Related

As with the motor pathways controlling speech, the right and left hemispheres of the brain equally contribute to the motoric aspects of swallowing, and dysphagia is equally likely to occur after RH or LH damage. The eventual outcomes—recovery versus persistent dysphagia or death, are similar regardless of side of damage. There may be differences in the type of dysphagia as RHD more often affects the pharyngeal phase of swallow while LH damage more often causes oral discoordination (Suntrup et al., 2015).

Sensory Related

As with LH strokes, RH strokes can result in reduced sensation, as in hemi-sensory loss due to interruption of sensory neurons taking pain, touch, and temperature information to the brain. When this happens, a person may not feel food left in their mouth, or may not feel a bolus of food or liquid passing into the laryngeal cavity.

Cognition/Attention Related

It seems logical that deficits in cognition and attention might impact swallowing and have negative consequences for dysphagia. Unfortunately, there are few studies overall, and of those that have been done, few clearly find a relationship. People with anosognosia for dysphagia may be more likely to engage in unsafe behaviors such as trying to swallow too much too quickly.

Summary

The RH is important for communication, primarily in the pragmatics domain. Apragmatism is the label for deficits in linguistic, paralinguistic, and/or extralinguistic components. A key component of assessment is talking with clients' family members or friends to determine what communication behaviors are new and apragmatic, and which ones are just part of who the person was prior to the brain injury. Dysarthria can occur if damage occurs to RH motor regions or pathways. Cognitive deficits affect attention, memory, executive function, and awareness. Unilateral neglect and anosognosia are notable consequences of RHD.

Key Concepts

- The right hemisphere plays an important role in communication in context, especially pragmatics.
- Unilateral upper motor neuron dysarthria is the most common form of dysarthria related to unilateral RH damage.
- Apragmatism is a communication disorder that affects the efficient and appropriate use of linguistic, paralinguistic, and extralinguistic aspects of communication.
- Expressive emotional aprosodia is usually linked to anterior RH lesions while receptive emotional aprosodia is more common after posterior RH lesions.
- There are limited options for assessment and treatment specifically for apragmatism, but a variety of options developed for TBI are available.
- Attention, memory, and executive function deficits can occur with RH damage.
- Unilateral visuospatial neglect is a classic sign of RH damage; the extent and severity of neglect can fluctuate and is dependent upon internal and external factors.
- Anosognosia, reduced awareness of deficits, often occurs and can fluctuate based on internal and external factors.
- Deficits in theory of mind and empathy impact relationships and create burdens for caregivers.
- Swallowing disorders can be related to sensorimotor deficits as well as cognitive deficits, specifically anosognosia.

References

Anand, R., Chapman, S. B., Rackley, A., Keebler, M., Zientz, J., & Hart, J., Jr. (2011). Gist reasoning training in cognitively normal seniors. *International Journal of Geriatric Psychiatry*, *26*(9), 961–968.

Angeleri, R., Bosco, F. M., Gabbatore, I., Bara, B. G., & Sacco, K. (2012). Assessment Battery for Communication (ABaCo): Normative data. *Behavior Research Methods, 44*, 845–861.

Azouvi, P., Marchal, F., Samuel, C., Morin, L., Renard, C., Louis-Dreyfus, A., . . . Bergego, C. (1996). Functional consequences and awareness of unilateral neglect: Study of an evaluation scale. *Neuropsychological Rehabilitation, 6*(2), 133–150.

Azouvi, P., Olivier, S., De Montety, G., Samuel, C., Louis-Dreyfus, A., & Tesio, L. (2003). Behavioral assessment of unilateral neglect: Study of the psychometric properties of the Catherine Bergego Scale. *Archives of Physical Medicine and Rehabilitation, 84*(1), 51–57.

Balaban, N., Friedmann, N., & Ariel, M. (2016). The effect of theory of mind impairment on language: Referring after right hemisphere damage. *Aphasiology, 7038*(1066), 1–38.

Bartels-Tobin, L. R., & Hinckley, J. J. (2005). Cognition and discourse production in right hemisphere disorder. *Journal of Neurolinguistics, 18*(6), 461–477.

Baylor, C., Yorkston, K., Eadie, T., Kim, J., Chung, H., & Amtmann, D. (2013). The Communicative Participation Item Bank (CPIB): Item bank calibration and development of a disorder-generic short form. *Journal of Speech, Language, and Hearing Research, 56*(4), 1190–1208.

Beeman, M. (1998). Coarse semantic coding and discourse comprehension. In *Right hemisphere language comprehension: Perspectives from cognitive neuroscience* (pp. 255–284).

Berry, M. (1981). Towards layers of exchange structure for directive exchanges. *Network, 2*(1), 23–32.

Bickerton, W. L., Samson, D., Williamson, J., & Humphreys, G. W. (2011). Separating forms of neglect using the Apples Test: Validation and functional prediction in chronic and acute stroke. *Neuropsychology, 25*(5), 567–580.

Blake, M. L. (2003). Affective language and humor appreciation after right hemisphere brain damage. *Seminars in Speech and Language, 24*(2), 107–120.

Blake, M. L. (2006). Clinical relevance of discourse characteristics after right hemisphere brain damage. *American Journal of Speech-Language Pathology, 15*(3), 256–267.

Blake, M. L. (2018). *The right hemisphere and disorders of cognition and communication: Theory and clinical practice*. Plural Publishing Inc.

Blake, M. L., & Lesniewicz, K. (2005). Contextual bias and predictive inferencing in adults with and without right hemisphere brain damage. *Aphasiology, 19*(3–5), 423–434.

Blake, M. L., Tompkins, C. A., Scharp, V. L., Meigh, K. M., & Wambaugh, J. (2015). Contextual Constraint Treatment for coarse coding deficit in adults with right hemisphere brain damage: Generalisation to narrative discourse comprehension. *Neuropsychological Rehabilitation, 25*(1), 15–52.

Blonder, L. X., Pettigrew, L. C., & Kryscio, R. J. (2012). Emotion recognition and marital satisfaction in stroke. *Journal of Clinical and Experimental Neuropsychology, 34*(6), 634–642.

Bowen, A., Hazelton, C., Pollock, A., & Lincoln, N. B. (2013). Cognitive rehabilitation for spatial neglect following stroke. *Cochrane Database of Systematic Reviews, 7*.

Braden, C., Hawley, L., Newman, J., Morey, C., Gerber, D., & Harrison-Felix, C. (2010). Social communication skills group treatment: A feasibility study for persons with traumatic brain injury and comorbid conditions. *Brain Injury, 24*(11), 1298–1310.

Brookshire, R. H., & Nicholas, L. E. (1997). *Discourse Comprehension Test*. BRK Publishers.

Champod, A. S., Frank, R. C., Taylor, K., & Eskes, G. A. (2018). The effects of prism adaptation on daily life activities in patients with visuospatial neglect: A systematic review. *Neuropsychological Rehabilitation, 28*(4), 491–514.

Chapman, S. B., & Mudar, R. A. (2014). Enhancement of cognitive and neural functions through complex reasoning training: Evidence from normal and clinical populations. *Frontiers in Systems Neuroscience, 8*, 69.

Cocks, N., Hird, K., & Kirsner, K. (2007). The relationship between right hemisphere damage and gesture in spontaneous discourse. *Aphasiology, 21*(3–4), 299–319.

Dahlberg, C. A., Cusick, C. P., Hawley, L. A., Newman, J. K., Morey, C. E., Harrison-Felix, C. L., & Whiteneck, G. G. (2007). Treatment efficacy of social communication skills training after traumatic brain injury: A randomized treatment and deferred treatment controlled trial. *Archives of Physical Medicine and Rehabilitation*, 88(12), 1561–1573.

Dahlberg, C., Hawley, L., Morey, C., Newman, J., Cusick, C., Harrison-Felix, C., & Coll, J. (2006). Social communication skills training after traumatic brain injury. *The Journal of Head Trauma Rehabilitation*, 21(5), 425.

Damico, J. S. (1991). *Some general comments about clinical discourse analysis.* https://userweb.ucs.louisiana.edu/~jsd6498/damico/damico-cda.html

Douglas, J. M., Knox, L., De Maio, C., & Bridge, H. (2014). Improving communication-specific coping after traumatic brain injury: Evaluation of a new treatment using single-case experimental design. *Brain Impairment*, 15(3), 190–201.

Douglas, J. M., Knox, L., De Maio, C., Bridge, H., Drummond, M., & Whiteoak, J. (2019). Effectiveness of communication-specific coping intervention for adults with traumatic brain injury: Preliminary results. *Neuropsychological rehabilitation*, 29(1), 73–91.

Douglas, J. M., O'Flaherty, C. A., & Snow, P. C. (2000). Measuring perception of communicative ability: The development and evaluation of the La Trobe Communication Questionnaire. *Aphasiology*, 14(3), 251–268.

Durfee, A. Z. & Sheppard, S. M. (2022). *Lecture: Neural correlates of aprosodia in RHD and treatment implications.* Academy of Neurologic Communication Disorders and Sciences Educational & Scientific Meeting.

Edgeworth, J., Robertson, I. H., & McMillan, T. M. (1998). *The Balloons Test.* Pearson Assessment.

Gabbatore, I., Sacco, K., Angeleri, R., Zettin, M., Bara, B. G., & Bosco, F. M. (2014). Cognitive pragmatic treatment: A rehabilitative program for traumatic brain injury individuals. *Journal of Head Trauma Rehabilitation*, 30(5), E14–E28.

Gainotti, G. (2019). The role of the right hemisphere in emotional and behavioral disorders of patients with frontotemporal lobar degeneration: An updated review. *Frontiers in Aging Neuroscience*, 11, 55.

Grice, H. P. (1975). Logic and conversation. In *Speech Acts* (pp. 41–58). Brill.

Hays, S.-J., Niven, B. E., Godfrey, H. P. D., & Linscott, R. J. (2004). Clinical assessment of pragmatic language impairment: A generalisability study of older people with Alzheimer's disease. *Aphasiology*, 18(8), 693–714.

Hewetson, R., Cornwell, P., & Shum, D. (2018). Social participation following right hemisphere stroke: influence of a cognitive-communication disorder. *Aphasiology*, 32(2), 164–182.

Hewetson, R., Cornwell, P., & Shum, D. H. (2021). Relationship and social network change in people with impaired social cognition post right hemisphere stroke. *American Journal of Speech-Language Pathology*, 30(2S), 962–973.

Hillis, A. E., & Tippett, D. C. (2014). Stroke recovery: Surprising influences and residual consequences. *Advances in Medicine*, 1–10. http://doi.org/10.1155/2014/378263

Hoepner, J. K. & Olson, S. E. (2018). Joint video self-modeling as a conversational intervention for an individual with traumatic brain injury and his everyday partner: A pilot investigation. *Clinical Archives of Communication Disorders*, 3(1), 22–41.

Hoepner, J. K., Sievert, A., & Guenther, K. (2021). Joint video self-modeling for persons with traumatic brain injury and their partners: A case series. *American Journal of Speech-Language Pathology*, 30(2S), 863–882.

Iwashita, H., & Sohlberg, M. M. (2019). Measuring conversations after acquired brain injury in 30 minutes or less: A comparison of two pragmatic rating scales. *Brain Injury*, 33(9), 1219–1233.

Joanette, Y., Ska, B. & Côté, H. (2004). *Protocole Montréal d'evaluation de la communication.* Ortho Edition.

Joanette, Y., Ska, B., Côté, H., Ferré, P., LaPointe, L., Coppens, P., & Small, S. (2015). *Montreal Protocol for the Evaluation of Communication (MEC)*. ASSBI Resources.

Leon, S. A., Rosenbek, J. C., Crucian, G. P., Hieber, B., Holiway, B., Rodriguez, A. D., . . . Gonzalez-Rothi, L. (2005). Active treatments for aprosodia secondary to right hemisphere stroke. *Journal of Rehabilitation Research and Development, 42*(1), 93–102.

Lezak, M. D., Howieson, D. B., & Loring, D. W. (2004). *Neuropsychological evaluation*. Oxford University Press.

Linscott, R. J., Knight, R. G., & Godfrey, H. P. D. (1996). The Profile of Functional Impairment in Communication (PFIC): A measure of communication impairment for clinical use. *Brain Injury, 10*(6), 397–412.

MacDonald, S. (2005). *Functional Assessment of Verbal Reasoning and Executive Strategies*. CCD Publishers.

MacDonald, S. (2015). Cognitive Communication Checklist for Acquired Brain Injury (CCCABI): An SLP screening and referral tool. CCD Publishing.

Marini, A. (2012). Characteristics of narrative discourse processing after damage to the right hemisphere. *Seminars in Speech and Language, 33*(1), 68–78.

Marini, A., & Urgesi, C. (2012). Please get to the point! A cortical correlate of linguistic informativeness. *Journal of Cognitive Neuroscience, 24*(11), 2211–2222.

McGann, W., Werven, G., & Douglas, M. M. (1997). Social competence and head injury: A practical approach. *Brain Injury, 11*(9), 621–628.

Meulenbroek, P., & Cherney, L. R. (2019). The Voicemail Elicitation Task: Functional workplace language assessment for persons with traumatic brain injury. *Journal of Speech, Language, and Hearing Research, 62*(9), 3367–3380.

Meulenbroek, P., & Cherney, L. R. (2021). Computer-based workplace communication training in persons with traumatic brain injury: The work-related communication program. *Journal of Communication Disorders, 91*, 106104.

Minga, J., Fromm, D., Devane-Williams, C., & MacWhinney, B. (2020). Question use in adults with right-hemisphere brain damage. *Journal of Speech, Language, and Hearing Research, 63*(3), 738–748. https://doi.org/10.1044/2019_JSLHR-19-00063

Minga, J., Fromm, D., Jacks, A., Stockbridge, M. D., Nelthropp, J., & MacWhinney, B. (2022). The effects of right hemisphere brain damage on question-asking in conversation. *Journal of Speech, Language, and Hearing Research : JSLHR, 65*(2), 727–737. https://doi.org/10.1044/2021_JSLHR-21-00309

Osborne, C. L. (2000). *Over my head: A doctor's own story of head injury from the inside looking out*. Andrews McMeel Publishing.

Pernet, L., Jughters, A., & Kerckhofs, E. (2013). The effectiveness of different treatment modalities for the rehabilitation of unilateral neglect in stroke patients: A systematic review. *NeuroRehabilitation, 33*(4), 611–620.

Ramsey, A., & Blake, M. L. (2020). Speech-language pathology practices for adults with right hemisphere stroke: What are we missing? *American Journal of Speech-Language Pathology, 29*(2), 741–759.

Rietdijk, R., Power, E., Attard, M., Heard, R., & Togher, L. (2020). Improved conversation outcomes after social communication skills training for people with traumatic brain injury and their communication partners: A clinical trial investigating in-person and telehealth delivery. *Journal of Speech, Language, and Hearing Research, 63*(2), 615–632.

Rietdijk, R., Power, E., Brunner, M., & Togher, L. (2019). A single case experimental design study on improving social communication skills after traumatic brain injury using communication partner telehealth training. *Brain Injury, 33*(1), 94–104.

Robinson, F. P. (1970). *Effective study*. Harper and Row.

Rosenbek, J. C., Rodriguez, A. D., Hieber, B., Leon, S. A., Crucian, G. P., Ketterson, T. U., . . . Gonzalez Rothi, L. J. (2006). Effects of two treatments for aprosodia secondary to acquired brain injury. *Journal of Rehabilitation Research and Development, 43*(3), 379–390.

Sacks, H., Schegloff, E. A., & Jefferson, G. (1978). A simplest systematics for the organization of turn taking for conversation. In J. Schenkein (Ed.), *Studies in the organization of conversational interaction* (pp. 7–55). Academic Press.

Schnur, T. T., Ding, J., & Blake, M. (2021). Understanding others requires right temporoparietal and inferior frontal regions. *BioRxiv.* Advance online publication.

Schenkenberg, T., Bradford, D. C., & Ajax, E. T. (1980). Line bisection and unilateral visual neglect in patients with neurologic impairment. *Neurology, 30*(5), 509.

Sheppard, S. M., Stockbridge, M. D., Keator, L. M., Murray, L. L., & Blake, M. L. (2022). The company prosodic deficits keep following right hemisphere stroke: A systematic review. *Journal of the International Neuropsychological Society, 28*(10), 1075-1090.

Sim, P., Power, E., & Togher, L. (2013). Describing conversations between individuals with traumatic brain injury (TBI) and communication partners following communication partner training: Using exchange structure analysis. *Brain Injury, 27*(6), 717–742.

Snaphaan, L., & De Leeuw, F. E. (2007). Poststroke memory function in nondemented patients: A systematic review on frequency and neuroimaging correlates. *Stroke, 38*(1), 198–203.

Stockbridge, M. D., Berube, S., Goldberg, E., Suarez, A., Mace, R., Ubellacker, D., & Hillis, A. E. (2021). Differences in linguistic cohesion within the first year following right- and left-hemisphere lesions. *Aphasiology, 35*(3), 357–371.

Stockbridge, M. D., Sheppard, S. M., Keator, L. M., Murray, L. L., Blake, M. L., Right Hemisphere Disorders Working Group, & Evidence-Based Clinical Research Committee. (2022). Aprosodia subsequent to right hemisphere brain damage: A systematic review and meta-analysis. *Journal of the International Neuropsychological Society, 28*(7), 709–735.

Suntrup, S., Kemmling, A., Warnecke, T., Hamacher, C., Oelenberg, S., Niederstadt, T., . . . Dziewas, R. (2015). The impact of lesion location on dysphagia incidence, pattern and complications in acute stroke. Part 1: Dysphagia incidence, severity and aspiration. *European Journal of Neurology, 22*(5), 832–838. https://doi.org/10.1111/ene.12670

Togher, L., Hand, L., Code, C., & McDonald, S. (1999). Exchanges of information in the talk of people with traumatic brain injury. *Communication Disorders Following Traumatic Brain Injury, 113,* 146.

Togher, L., Power, E., Tate, R., McDonald, S., & Rietdijk, R. (2010). Measuring the social interactions of people with traumatic brain injury and their communication partners: The adapted Kagan scales. *Aphasiology, 24*(6–8), 914–927. http://doi.org/10.1080/02687030903422478

Togher, L., McDonald, S., Tate, R., Rietdijk, R., & Power, E. (2016). The effectiveness of social communication partner training for adults with severe chronic TBI and their families using a measure of perceived communication ability. *NeuroRehabilitation, 38*(3), 243–255.

Toglia, J., & Kirk, U. (2000). Understanding awareness deficits following brain injury. *NeuroRehabilitation, 15*(1), 57–70. http://search.ebscohost.com/login.aspx?direct=true&db=cin20&AN=2003055532&site=ehost-live

Tompkins, C. A., Lei, C.-M., & Zezinka, A. (2015). The nature and implications of right hemisphere language disorders. In A. E. Hillis (Ed.), *Handbook of Adult Language Disorders: Integrating Cognitive Neuropsychology, Neurology, and Rehabilitation* (pp. 491–517). Psychology Press.

Ukaegbe, O. C., Holt, B. E., Keator, L. M., Brownell, H., Blake, M. L., & Lundgren, K. (2022). Aprosodia following focal brain damage: What's right and what's left? *American Journal of Speech-Language Pathology, 31*(5S), 2313–2328.

Weed, E., & Fusaroli, R. (2020). Acoustic measures of prosody in right-hemisphere damage: A systematic review and meta-analysis. *Journal of Speech, Language, and Hearing Research, 63*(6), 1762–1775.

Wilson, B. A., Cockburn, J., & Halligan, P. W. (1987). *Behavioural Inattention Test.* Pearson Assessment.

Yang, N. Y. H., Zhou, D., Chung, R. C. K., Li-Tsang, C. W. P., & Fong, K. N. K. (2013). Rehabilitation interventions for unilateral neglect after stroke: A systematic review from 1997–2012. *Frontiers in Human Neuroscience, 7,* 1–11.

9

CORTICAL POSTERIOR REGIONS

Chapter Overview

Diseases and Disorders of the Posterior Hemispheres
Visual Pathways
   Visual Field Cuts
   Visual Processing Disorders
   Assessment and Treatment of Visual Disorders
Speech Disorders
Language Disorders
Cognitive Disorders
   Visuoperception
   Visuocontruction
   Spatial Cognition
   Assessment and Treatment of Cognitive Disorders
Posterior Damage Syndromes
Swallowing Disorders
Summary
Key Concepts
References

Diseases and Disorders of the Posterior Hemispheres

The occipital lobe and posterior parietal and temporal lobes receive blood supply primarily through the vertebrobasilar arterial system (refer back to Chapter 2). The vertebral arteries branch off the subclavian artery above the heart, extend up the neck through the transverse foramen of the cervical vertebrae, and enter the skull through the foramen magnum. At the base of the pons the right and left vertebral arteries fuse to form the basilar artery. The basilar artery bifurcates (splits into two) at the superior extent of the brainstem into the right and

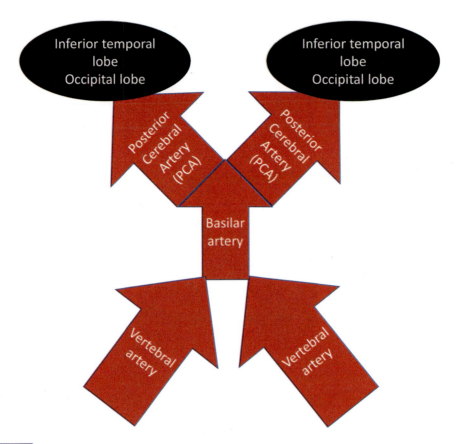

Figure 9–1. Schematic of the vertebrobasilar blood supply.

left posterior cerebral arteries (Figure 9–1). These take blood to the occipital lobe, inferior and posterior temporal lobe, and posterior parietal lobe.

Posterior strokes account for approximately 15–20% of cerebral strokes (Handelsmann et al., 2021). They occur more often in males than females and are more likely than anterior circulation strokes to be related to diabetes than to atherosclerosis and cardiac embolisms. Posterior circulation strokes are more likely to be misdiagnosed than anterior/carotid strokes, primarily due to the screening tools used. The original FAST acronym for identifying potential strokes (Face, Arms, Speech, Time) misses many posterior strokes that do not affect language or cause hemiparesis. In a 2017 study, over 14% of people with posterior stroke passed the "FAST test." The updated acronym, BE FAST (Aroor, 2017; refer to Chapter 2) adds Balance and Eyes to capture cerebellar or brainstem damage and visual field cuts, reducing the number of missed strokes to approximately 4%. Additionally, the items on the National Institutes of Health Stroke Scale (NIHSS) used to quickly assess the extent of damage from a stroke also are biased to detect strokes in the left lateral, perisylvian area. Only two items on that scale, visual field cuts and ataxia, are directly related to functions affected by posterior circulation strokes.

Degenerative cortical diseases including dementias most often affect anterior brain regions (e.g., frontal lobes, anterior temporal lobes). Recall from Chapter 2 the principle of C-shaped development and degeneration: The frontal regions at the tips of the C shape are the last to develop and the first to degenerate. Situated posteriorly, the occipital lobes are less likely to be affected by degenerative diseases, but are not completely protected. **Posterior cortical atrophy** is a degenerative condition that primarily affects the occipital lobes and posterior temporal lobes. Most cases are atypical presentations of Alzheimer disease, although some have the pathophysiology of other dementias such as Lewy bodies, corticobasal syndrome, or prion disease (Borruat, 2013; Crutch et al., 2012). The onset of posterior cortical atrophy is around 50 to 65 years old, over 10 years earlier than typical forms of Alzheimer disease (AD). Visuospatial and visuoperceptual deficits are common, with relatively spared memory, language, and executive functions. The degenerative process begins slowly, often with several years between the initial symptoms and a diagnosis of dementia (Borruat, 2013). Functional impairments affect not only object identification, reading, and driving, but also walking, especially on uneven ground or stairs (Borruat, 2013). People with posterior cortical atrophy also complain of difficulties localizing objects, problems navigating in their environment due to deficits in gauging depth or distance, and spatio-motor problems like challenges with putting keys into locks or using remote controls and other tools (Yerstein, 2021).

Deficits and disorders associated with posterior damage are often outside of the speech-language pathologist's scope of practice, but they are important to recognize and understand. Much of our communication and cognitive processing relies on visual input and processing. Disruptions to the visual system thus can impact communication and cognition. Communication assessments commonly include picture description and reading tasks. If a patient cannot adequately process the visual stimulus, that must be taken into consideration so that the resulting incorrect response is not misdiagnosed as a communication problem.

Visual Pathways

Damage to the visual system can affect communication in a variety of ways. **Visual field cuts** impact reading and writing and can impact conversations if extralinguistic cues such as gestures and facial expression are not perceived correctly. In most cases, people are aware of visual field cuts and can compensate by moving their head or eyes to see the things that fall in their blind spots.

The visual system follows the principle of contralateral sensorimotor control, but with an added twist. Instead of the right eye being connected to the left occipital lobe, images from *the right visual field of each eye* are sent to the left occipital lobe. This means that what you see in the right side of space with your left eye and the right side of space with your right eye all end up in the left occipital lobe and vice versa: the images in the left side of space seen by your left eye and your right eye are transmitted to the right occipital lobe (Figures 9–2 and 9–3).

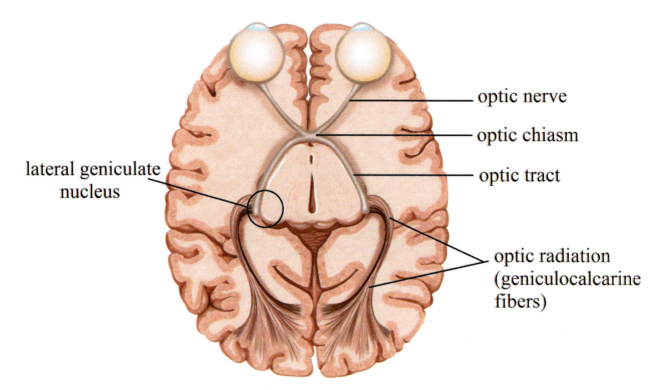

Figure 9–2. A. & B. Visual pathway from retinas to occipital lobe. From *Clinical Neuroscience for Communication Disorders: Neuroanatomy and Neurophysiology* (p. 112) by Blake, M. L. and Hoepner, J. K. Copyright © 2023 Plural Publishing, Inc. All rights reserved.

When light waves hit your eye, they are refracted by the lens on the anterior eyeball so that the right and left sides are reversed, and the image is inverted. The image that is processed by the **retina** on the posterior eyeball is thus upside-down and backward. As axons from retinal neurons exit from the eye and extend posteriorly toward the thalamus, half of the axons from each eye cross over in a structure called the **optic chiasm**. These axons that cross over are carrying images from the left side of space perceived by the left eye and the right side of space perceived by the right eye. After this crossover, all the signals in the left visual pathway represent the right side of space perceived by each eye, and all the signals in the right visual pathway represent the left side of space perceived by each eye.

The neurons in the visual pathway synapse in the **lateral geniculate nucleus** of the thalamus. Axons of thalamic neurons form the **optic radiations** or **geniculocalcarine fibers** as they extend posteriorly to the region surrounding the calcarine sulcus on the medial occipital lobes. About half of these fibers, those carrying signals representing the upper visual field, extend anteriorly to swing around the lateral ventricle in the temporal lobe before extending posteriorly and synapsing inferior to the calcarine sulcus. These fibers are called **Meyer's loop**. The remaining half extend directly to the occipital lobe and synapse superior to the

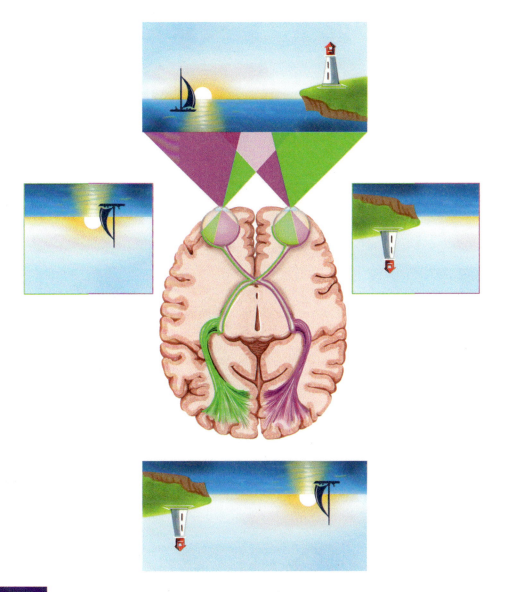

Figure 9–3. Reversal and inversion of visual image along the visual pathway. From *Clinical Neuroscience for Communication Disorders: Neuroanatomy and Neurophysiology* (p. 112) by Blake, M. L. and Hoepner, J. K. Copyright © 2023 Plural Publishing, Inc. All rights reserved.

calcarine sulcus. Because of this arrangement, the top half of the visual fields are represented inferior to the calcarine sulcus and the lower visual field is represented on the superior aspect of the sulcus (Figure 9–4).

After signals are processed in the primary visual cortex, there are connections to more anterior regions of the occipital lobes and pathways to the temporal and parietal lobes (Figure 9–5). The ventral pathway extends to the inferior temporal lobe. It is called the **"what" pathway** because visual images are integrated with language and memory so that images can be recognized, remembered, and meaning is attached. This pathway allows for vision for perception

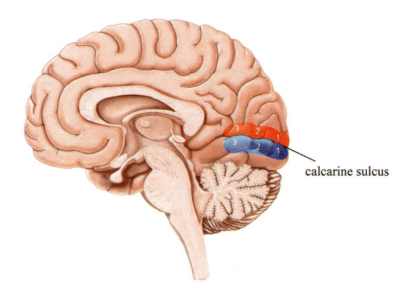

Figure 9–4. Regions of visual field represented in medial occipital regions. From *Clinical Neuroscience for Communication Disorders: Neuroanatomy and Neurophysiology* (p. 110) by Blake, M. L. and Hoepner, J. K. Copyright © 2023 Plural Publishing, Inc. All rights reserved.

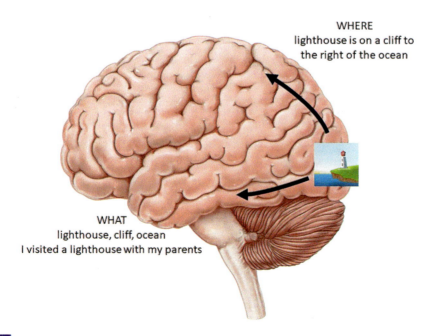

Figure 9–5. Dorsal and ventral visual pathways.

(Trojano & Conson, 2008). The dorsal pathway extends to the superior parietal lobes. This is called the **"where" pathway**. Visual images are integrated into the broader context so that items can be localized within a visual scene. The dorsal pathway has been described as vision for action (Trojano & Conson, 2008) such as map reading and navigation in one's environment.

Visual Field Cuts

Damage to the occipital lobe that interrupts the geniculocalcarine fibers results in a homonymous visual field cut, meaning that vision is lost in the same portion of the visual field of both eyes. A lesion that cuts the entire pathway in one hemisphere will result in a contralateral **homonymous hemianopsia**. A smaller lesion that interrupts a portion of the pathway will result in a contralateral **homonymous quadrantanopsia**. Illustrations of visual field cuts to different areas of the visual pathways are shown in Figure 9–6.

Unilateral damage to the primary visual cortex in the occipital pole will result in a homonymous hemianopsia with central sparing. This means that the person can see the central portion of the visual field of each eye, but the remainder of the contralateral visual field will be lost. The reason for the central sparing is uncertain but may be due to overlapping blood supply or duplicate representations of central vision in the occipital lobes.

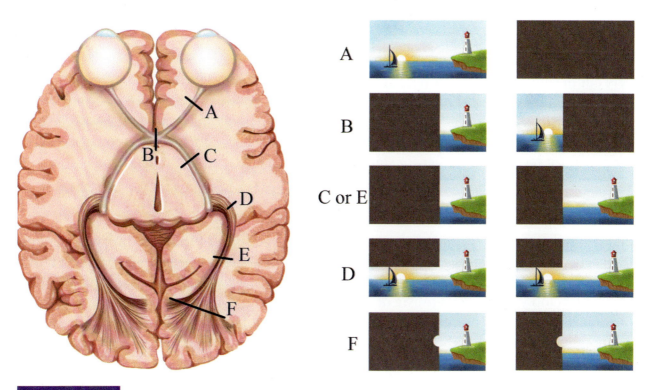

Figure 9–6. Visual field cuts. From *Clinical Neuroscience for Communication Disorders: Neuroanatomy and Neurophysiology* (p. 115) by Blake, M. L. and Hoepner, J. K. Copyright © 2023 Plural Publishing, Inc. All rights reserved.

> **Box 9–1 Breaking Down the Terminology**
>
> -opia or -opsia = related to vision
>
> Anopia or anopsia = loss of vision
>
> Homonymous = same side; refers to the same side of the visual field of each eye. All lesions to the visual pathways or structures posterior to the optic chiasm will result in homonymous visual field cuts.
>
> Heteronymous = opposite sides; refers to the opposite sides of the visual field of each eye (e.g., right visual field of the right eye and left visual field of the left eye).
>
> Hemi- = referring to half
>
> Quadrant- = referring to one quarter
>
> A homonymous heminanopsia means loss of half of the visual field, and the same half in both eyes, such as loss of the right visual field seen by the right eye and the left eye.
>
> A homonymous quadrantanopsia means loss of one quarter of the visual field, the same quadrant in both eyes, such as the loss of the lower left quadrant seen by the right eye and the left eye.

Anywhere from 30 to 50% of people with posterior circulation strokes will have a visual field cut of some form. Health-related quality of life is related to the extent of the visual field cut, with poorer quality of life reported by people with complete hemianopsia compared to those with quadrantanopsia (Cárdenas Belaunzarán et al., 2021). At least 15% of people with visual field cuts experience spontaneous improvement within the first-year post-stroke. The prognosis for recovery is higher for smaller visual field cuts.

Visual Processing Disorders

Bilateral damage to the primary visual cortex results in **cortical blindness**. Because the eyes themselves are intact and signals are processed in the thalamus, a person with cortical blindness can distinguish between light and dark although they cannot perceive images. Some people develop **visual anosognosia** or **Anton's syndrome**, which is cortical blindness without awareness of that blindness. Essentially, these individuals are blind, but they are not aware that they are blind. This is accompanied by confabulations in which they may describe what they "see" or how they navigate around their environment.

Damage affecting the dorsal "where" pathway in the superior occipital and parietal lobes interferes with localization and navigation. Cortical degeneration of Alzheimer disease can spread to the parietal lobe and disrupt visuospatial processing. Visuoconstruction and visuospatial processing also can be affected. These are described in more detail later in the section on Cognitive Disorders.

> ### Box 9–2 Prosopagnosia
>
> Candace was a 60-year-old female who experienced a left hemisphere (LH) intracranial hemorrhage in the inferior occipitotemporal region. This resulted in mild fluent aphasia, anomia, and prosopagnosia. While most cases of prosopagnosia are either associated with bilateral inferior occipitotemporal lobes or unilateral right damage, Candace's damage was constrained to the LH. In early rehabilitation, she was disoriented and confused, as she did not recognize the environment or rehabilitation staff. She frequently wandered and got lost within the facility, as her path finding was also impaired. Eventually, she attended outpatient sessions with her husband who she recognized from his voice and mannerisms. He claimed that she would not recognize him from across the street unless he spoke. She was very guarded at the outset of each outpatient visit and it took a few minutes for her to recognize her regular SLP. Candace learned to use voice, mannerisms, and other extralinguistic communication to recognize others.

Damage to the ventral "what" pathway can result in **visual agnosias**, in which a person can correctly perceive an item or image but is unable to recognize it or name it. Shown an item such as a brick, a person with visual agnosia could describe the color and texture and could generate ideas for what it might be used for, such as a weight to hold large papers or a small step to help reach the top cabinet, but would not be able to link it to the name "brick" and may not state its primary function as a building material. **Prosopagnosia** is a specific form of visual agnosia related to faces. People with prosopagnosia can perceive faces, can tell if two faces are the same or different, and can differentiate features such as distinguishing brown from green eyes and full from thin lips, but faces do not hold meaning for them. They cannot recognize familiar faces of famous people, friends or family members. Some cannot recognize their own face. To compensate, they recognize people by voices, hair styles, or another differentiating feature. Prosopagnosia can be congenital, but also can be the result of damage to the inferior temporal lobe, more often in the right hemisphere (RH).

Assessment and Treatment of Visual Disorders

Visual field cuts and visual processing disorders are outside of the scope of practice of speech-language pathologists. Assessment and treatment are best conducted by neuro-ophthalmologists. However, it is important for SLPs to recognize these disorders/deficits and how they may impact communication. SLPs may also suggest compensatory strategies that might facilitate communication and cognition.

If a person is aware of their visual field cut, they may spontaneously compensate for it by moving their head and eyes in order to see the entire visual field. Compensatory strategies for unilateral neglect, such as a red line or the person's own arm as an anchor to mark the right or left edge of a page or book, could be used (refer to Chapter 8).

Speech Disorders

Speech disorders are rare following damage to the posterior hemispheres because the sensorimotor regions and pathways are located more anteriorly. Dysarthrias due to posterior circulation strokes are caused by interruption of corticobulbar tracts and damage to other brainstem structures and the cerebellum. These are covered in Chapter 11.

Language Disorders

Language disorders associated with posterior hemispheric damage include alexia and agraphia. These are covered in Chapter 7. While visual attention deficits are typically associated with damage to the parietal (especially right parietal) lobes, slower visual attention processing can occur after posterior circulation strokes and this reduction in processing speed can affect reading ability (Petersen et al., 2016).

Cognitive Disorders

Visuospatial abilities including visuospatial perception, visuospatial construction (also called visuoconstruction), and spatial cognition can all be affected after posterior damage. The RH has commonly been reported to be more involved in visuospatial processing. However, the posterior left hemisphere (LH) also plays a role, and visuospatial deficits can be seen after damage to either hemisphere. Some evidence suggests that the LH is better for object recognition (Kato et al., 2012) and categorical distinctions, such as if an object is above, below, or to the left or right of another object (Slotnick et al., 2001; Trojano & Conson, 2008). The RH is better at spatial relationships (Kato et al., 2012) and making decisions about precise coordinates, such as if an object is more than one inch away from another (Slotnick et al., 2001; Trojano & Conson, 2008). The coordinate processes are important for localization and judging distances. Another hypothesis is that the LH is better for familiar items/tasks while the RH engages for novel tasks (Kalbfleisch & Gillmarten, 2013).

Visuoperception

Visuoperception involves localizing and discriminating items/images, judging distances, orientation, and dimensions. Impairments include distortions of colors or images, difficulty with reading, writing, and distance judgment.

Face processing, including recognition and interpretation of facial expression, is a critical component of communication. The fusiform gyrus (also known as the lateral occipitotemporal gyrus, located on the inferior surface of the temporal lobe), the occipital face area, and the posterior superior temporal sulcus are all part of the face network (Barton et al., 2021). Damage to these regions, particularly in the RH, can result in acquired prosopagnosia.

> **Box 9–3 Novelty Is in the Brain of the Beholder**
>
> Novelty differs from person to person. A mechanic can quickly recognize and differentiate engine components. Dermatologists can identify a variety of types of skin lesions. Art enthusiasts can recognize the work of different artists and identify the influences on new artists based on stylistic characteristics. Given these differences, it shouldn't be surprising that research fails to consistently report clear RH versus LH differences related to novelty in visuoperception tasks, because any one task may be considered familiar to some people but novel to others, resulting in use of different hemispheres across people.

Visuoconstruction

Visuoconstruction abilities include drawing, building, and some aspects of writing. Processes involved in accurate and efficient visuoconstruction include not only motor and construction but also visuoperception, attention, and decision making. The copying/drawing network thus includes not only superior parietal, supramarginal and angular gyri, but also the middle-occipital gyrus, superior temporal gyrus, and frontal lobes (Biesbroek et al., 2014).

The label **constructional apraxia** has been used to describe difficulties in putting elements in the correct relationship to each other. This can appear as disorganized drawings (Figure 9–7) or difficulty putting building blocks together correctly to form a specific design. Both the left and right hemispheres contribute to visuoconstruction, so lesions on either side of the brain can cause impairments (e.g., Carson et al., 2019). Damage to the LH often results in drawings that are simplified or distorted, and errors appear to be related to motor planning or lexical semantics. In contrast, drawings by people with damage to the RH often have omissions (refer back to descriptions of unilateral neglect in Chapter 8) and errors that reflect spatial deficits.

Copying and drawing by people with dementia, who often have bilateral posterior degeneration, have gross distortions and perseverations as well as simplifications. In some forms of dementia such as Alzheimer disease, drawing is more impaired than copying. This is thought to be due to the need for semantic memory for drawing (e.g., you have to think about a clock and how it looks before being able to draw it). In Lewy body dementias, copying and drawing often are impaired to similar extents and they show deficits in discrimination of both size and form, identifying overlapping figures, and visual counting. Across types of dementia, complex figure copying tasks can be sensitive to the progression of the disease (Trojano & Conson, 2008).

Spatial Cognition

Spatial cognition involves more complex processes than visuoperception, including recognizing shapes or geometric patterns, mental rotation, and maze learning. Deficits in spatial cognition can affect picture description or recognition and daily activities such as organizing a closet or selecting an appropriate sized storage container for leftover food.

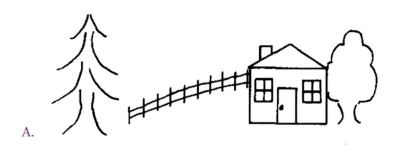

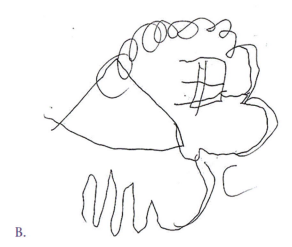

Figure 9–7. A. Scene copy prompt. Reprinted from Brain and Cognition, Vol. 4, Ogden, Anterior-posterior interhemispheric differences in the loci of lesions producing visual hemineglect, Page 59, Copyright (1985), with permission from Elsevier. B. Scene copying from an individual with constructional apraxia.

Assessment and Treatment of Cognitive Disorders

As with the visual field cuts, assessment and treatment of posterior-lesion cognitive disorders generally falls outside of the scope of practice of SLP. The exception is disorders that impact communication, such as alexia, agraphia, and difficulty interpreting emotional facial expressions (extralinguistic apragmatism). These are all discussed in Chapters 7 and 8.

Posterior Damage Syndromes

There are several syndromes associated with damage to the occipital lobe and adjoining parietal and temporal lobes. These are relatively rare but highlight the functions of this region. The syndromes can occur in isolation or in combination with other deficits. For example, posterior cortical atrophy can cause visuospatial and visuoperceptual deficits along with Gerstmann and Balint syndromes (Crutch et al., 2012).

Gerstmann syndrome involves acalculia (difficulty with simple math calculations), agraphia, left-right disorientation, and finger agnosia (refer back to Chapter 7). Remember that agnosias are deficits in recognition. Finger agnosia is the inability to name fingers (e.g., ring finger, index finger, pinky). This syndrome is typically caused by damage to the language-dominant (most often left) inferior posterior parietal lobe, often involving the angular gyrus.

The triad of deficits that make up **Balint syndrome** are **simultagnosia, oculomotor apraxia**, and **optic ataxia**. All three of these represent a disconnection between vision and motor control. Simultagnosia is the inability to process more than one item at a time. In a visual scene like the Cookie Theft picture (refer back to Figure 7–8), the individual will be able to see the child, the stool, and the cupboard as isolated elements. Each is processed individually and not as a group from which you infer that the child is on the stool to reach into the cupboard. It has been described as though "the visual world becomes unglued" (Beh et al., 2014, p. 8). It is thought to be due to a very restricted window of visual attention, one that encompasses only one item at a time. Oculomotor apraxia is difficulty in purposefully shifting eye gaze. Optic ataxia is reduced coordination of the visual and motor systems that primarily affects visually guided, goal-directed movements (Beh et al., 2014). Patients have difficulty reaching toward objects in their visual field. If their phone was sitting on a table in front of them, they would not be able to use their vision to reach over and pick it up. However, if the phone rang, then they could use the auditory signal to guide their reach. Balint syndrome is caused by bilateral damage to occipital and parietal lobes.

Swallowing Disorders

Like dysarthrias, dysphagia rarely occurs with damage to the posterior hemispheres due to the absence of motor regions or pathways. Posterior circulation strokes that cause dysphagia due to damage to the brainstem or cerebellum are covered in Chapter 11.

Summary

The visual pathways carry signals from the eyes to the occipital lobes. The left visual field of each eye is represented in the right occipital lobe and vice versa. Damage to the visual pathways result in visual field cuts, in which a portion of the visual field essentially disappears. Damage to cortical regions of the occipital, parietal, and temporal lobes interrupts processing of visual stimuli causing visuoperceptual and visuoconstruction deficits or difficulties recognizing and localizing items. Speech and language deficits are uncommon after posterior lesions, with the exception of reading and writing.

Key Concepts

- While visual and visual processing deficits are typically outside the scope of practice of SLPs, they can impact communication and performance on speech-language evaluations.
- Visual field cuts restrict what a person can see. Most people are aware of these impairments and can spontaneously compensate for them.
- Visual processing deficits impact how people interpret or understand visual images or inputs.
- Posterior cortical lesions rarely affect speech or swallowing.

References

Aroor, S., Singh, R., & Goldstein, L. B. (2017). BE-FAST (Balance, Eyes, Face, Arm, Speech, Time): Reducing the proportion of strokes missed using the FAST mnemonic. *Stroke, 48*(2), 479–481.

Barton, J. J. S., Davies-Thompson, J., & Corrow, S. L. (2021). Prosopagnosia and disorders of face processing. *Handbook of Clinical Neurology, 178*, 175–193.

Beh, S. C., Muthusamy, B., Calabresi, P., Hart, J., Zee, D., Patel, V., & Frohman, E. (2015). Hiding in plain sight: A closer look at posterior cortical atrophy. *Practical Neurology, 15*(1), 5–13.

Biesbroek, J. M., van Zandvoort, M. J. E., Kuijf, H. J., Weaver, N. A., Kappelle, L. J., Vos, P. C., . . . Postma, A. (2014). The anatomy of visuospatial construction revealed by lesion-symptom mapping. *Neuropsychologia, 62*(1), 68–76.

Borruat, F. X. (2013). Posterior cortical atrophy: Review of the recent literature. *Current Neurology and Neuroscience Reports, 13*(406), 1–8.

Cárdenas Belaunzarán, J., Cano Nigenda, V., Barboza, M. A., González Olhovich, I., & Arauz, A. (2021). Prognostic factors for long-term recovery of homonymous visual field defects after posterior circulation ischemic stroke. *Journal of Stroke and Cerebrovascular Diseases, 30*(8), 1–6.

Carson, L., Filipowicz, A., Anderson, B., & Danckert, J. (2019). Representational drawing following brain injury. *Neuropsychologia, 133*.

Crutch, S. J., Lehmann, M., Schott, J. M., Rabinovici, G. D., Rossor, M. N., & Fox, N. C. (2012). Posterior cortical atrophy. *Lancet Neurology, 11*, 170–178.

Handelsmann, H., Herzog, L., Kulcsar, Z., Luft, A. R., & Wegener, S. (2021). Predictors for affected stroke territory and outcome of acute stroke treatments are different for posterior versus anterior circulation stroke. *Scientific Reports, 11*(1).

Kalbfleisch, M. L., & Gillmarten, C. (2013). Left brain vs. right brain: Findings on visual spatial capacities and the functional neurology of giftedness. *Roeper Review, 35*(4), 265–275.

Kato, H., Seki, M., Shindo, J., Yamazaki, T., Sato, Y., Utsumi, H., & Nagata, K. (2012). The relationship between visuospatial ability and cognitive function in patients with right-hemisphere infarction. *Journal of the Neurological Sciences, 322*(1–2), 129–131. https://doi.org/10.1016/j.jns.2012.07.020

Ogden, J. A. (1985). Anterior-posterior interhemispheric differences in the loci of lesions producing visual hemineglect. *Brain and Cognition, 4*(1), 59–75. https://doi.org/10.1016/0278-2626(85)90054-5

Petersen, A., Vangkilde, S., Fabricius, C., Iversen, H. K., Delfi, T. S., & Starrfelt, R. (2016). Visual attention in posterior stroke and relations to alexia. *Neuropsychologia, 92*, 79–89. https://doi.org/10.1016/J.NEUROPSYCHOLOGIA.2016.02.029

Slotnick, S. D., Moo, L. R., Tesoro, M. A., & Hart, J. (2001). Hemispheric asymmetry in categorical versus coordinate visuospatial processing revealed by temporary cortical deactivation. *Journal of Cognitive Neuroscience, 13*(8), 1088–1096.

Trojano, L., & Conson, M. (2008). Visuospatial and visuoconstructive deficits. *Handbook of clinical neurology* (3rd ed., pp. 373–391). Elsevier Inc.

Yerstein, O., Parand, L., Liang, L.-J., Isaac, A., & Mendez, M. F. (2021). Benson's disease or posterior cortical atrophy, revisited. *Journal of Alzheimer's Disease, 82*(2), 493–502. https://doi.org/10.3233/JAD-210368

10
SUBCORTICAL STRUCTURES

Chapter Overview

Basal Ganglia
   Disorders and Diseases of the Basal Ganglia
      Parkinson Disease
      Huntington Disease
      Corticobasal Syndrome
   Speech Disorders
   Language Disorders
   Cognitive Disorders
      Executive Function and Awareness
      Memory and Attention
      Social Cognition
   Swallowing Disorders
Thalamus
   Functions of the Thalamus
      Sensorimotor Functions
      Cognition and Emotion
      Cortical Arousal
   Disorders and Diseases of the Thalamus
   Speech Disorders
   Language Disorders
   Cognitive Disorders
   Swallowing Disorders
Summary
Key Concepts
References
Other Resources

This chapter covers two major subcortical structures: the basal ganglia and the thalamus. These structures are extensively connected with the motor and somatosensory systems which makes them critically important for sensorimotor control of speech production and swallowing. They also are integral components of language, emotion, and cognitive networks. Due to these connections, damage to any of these structures has the potential to impact not only speech and swallowing, but also broader aspects of communication.

Basal Ganglia

The basal ganglia consist of a set of bilateral structures: caudate nucleus, putamen, globus pallidus (external and internal segments), subthalamic nucleus, and substantia nigra (Figures 10–1 and 10–2). The caudate and putamen together are called the striatum (Latin: *stripes*), while the putamen and the dual segments of the globus pallidus are called the lenticular nucleus (Latin: *lens shaped*). There are multiple circuits (sometimes called loops) that connect areas of the cortex through the basal ganglia. Connections within the basal ganglia tend to be unilateral (e.g., left basal ganglia structures create separate networks from the right basal ganglia). Three important basal ganglia circuits are the motor loop, the cognitive-associative loop, and the limbic loop (Birba et al., 2017).

The motor loop has connections to pre- and primary motor cortical areas as well as cortical sensory areas (Figure 10–3). These provide input to the striatum (caudate and putamen). The internal segment of the globus pallidus (GPi) is the primary output site, with connections to the thalamus and to areas of the motor cortex.

The cognitive-associative loop originates in the dorsolateral prefrontal and lateral orbitofrontal cortices and connects through the caudate and the thalamus (Figure 10–4). This loop is involved in cognition and executive functioning. A recent model of language processing (Jacquemot & Bachoud-Lévi, 2021) proposes that the striatum is a critical piece of a verbal executive network. It regulates verbal attention and verbal working memory that impact all levels of language: phonology, morphology, syntax, and lexical-semantics. These striatal functions are important for complex language processing requiring controlled (nonautomatic) processing.

The limbic loop involves the medial orbitofrontal region and amygdala with connections through the ventral striatum and mediodorsal thalamus that connect back to the frontal lobe (Figure 10–5). This loop is involved in emotions, motivation, and reward-based learning.

A variety of neurotransmitters are present within the basal ganglia circuits. Dopamine (DA) modulates signals within the basal ganglia circuits. Because it can cause either excitatory or inhibitory signals depending on the receptors on the postsynaptic neurons, it can increase or decrease the potential for movement execution. Acetylcholine (ACh) can counteract or balance out the function of DA. Glutamate has an excitatory role and GABA, as always,

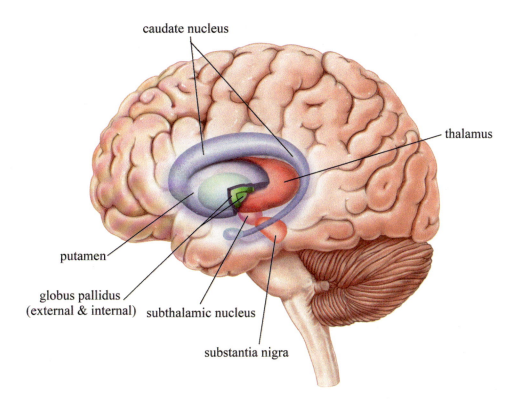

Figure 10–1. Basal ganglia structures in situ. From *Clinical Neuroscience for Communication Disorders: Neuroanatomy and Neurophysiology* (p. 27) by Blake, M. L. and Hoepner, J. K. Copyright © 2023 Plural Publishing, Inc. All rights reserved.

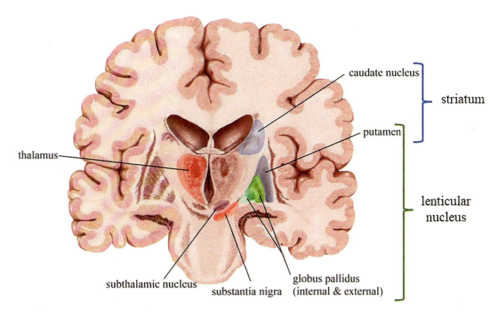

Figure 10–2. Coronal slice of basal ganglia structures. Adapted from *Clinical Neuroscience for Communication Disorders: Neuroanatomy and Neurophysiology* (p. 27) by Blake, M. L. and Hoepner, J. K. Copyright © 2023 Plural Publishing, Inc. All rights reserved.

> **Box 10–1 Terminology**
>
> Basal ganglia: basal = near the base of the brain; ganglion = collection of cell bodies. In anatomical terminology, typically *nucleus* is used to describe a group of cell bodies in the CNS and *ganglion* is used for PNS structures. The basal ganglia are an exception to this rule.
>
> Striatum = caudate + putamen. These two structures have a striped appearance due to connecting gray matter segments.
>
> Lenticular or lentiform nucleus = putamen + globus pallidus (both internal & external). Lenticular/lentiform refers to the lens shape of these structures from a lateral view.

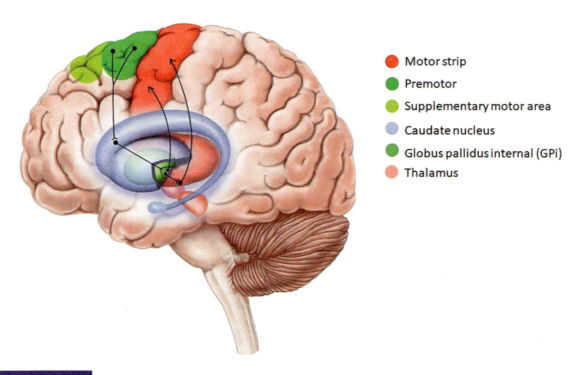

Figure 10–3. Motor loop.

plays an inhibitory role. The combination of excitatory and inhibitory neurotransmitters and signals is best understood in terms of the motor functions. A balance of excitatory and inhibitory signals is critical for smooth, efficient motor function. Too much excitation leads to excessive unwanted or unintended movements, while too much inhibition causes reduction in movement initiation or range of motion (Figures 10–6 and 10–7).

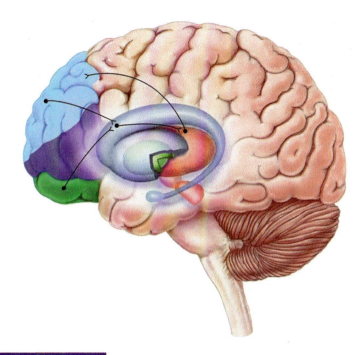

Figure 10–4. Cognitive-associative loop

- Dorsolateral prefrontal cortex
- Lateral orbitofrontal prefrontal cortex
- Medial orbitofrontal prefrontal cortex
- Caudate nucleus
- Thalamus

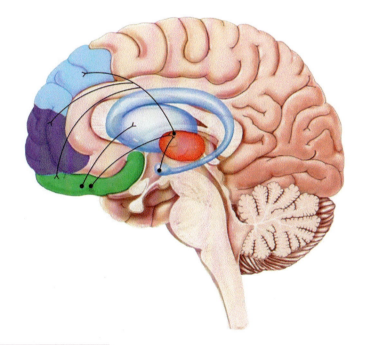

Figure 10–5. Limbic loop.

- Dorsolateral prefrontal cortex
- Lateral orbitofrontal prefrontal cortex
- Medial orbitofrontal prefrontal cortex
- Ventral striatum
- Mediodorsal thalamus

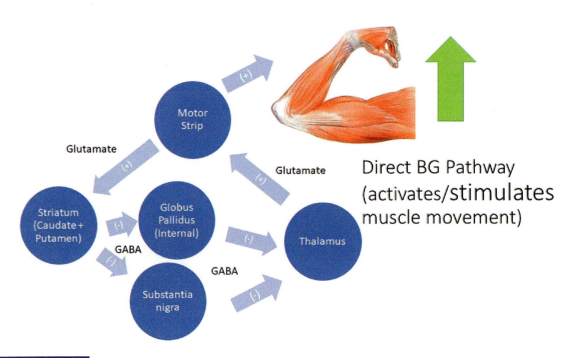

Figure 10–6. Direct, excitatory basal ganglia pathway.

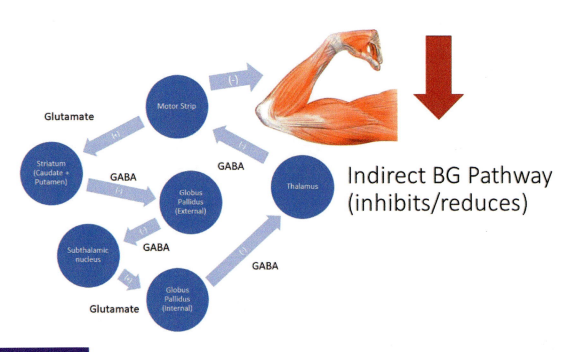

Figure 10–7. Indirect, inhibitory basal ganglia pathway.

Disorders and Diseases of the Basal Ganglia

The basal ganglia can be damaged by degenerative diseases such as Parkinson disease (PD), progressive supranuclear palsy, multiple systems atrophy, corticobasal syndrome (CBS), and some dementias. Strokes, hypoxia, traumatic brain injuries, infections, and exposure to some drugs also can impact these structures. Dystonias, or involuntary muscle contractions, can affect speech and swallowing and are typically attributed to damage or dysfunction of the basal ganglia, although the cause of the dysfunction is not always evident. Several prominent or familiar diseases are described in more detail here due to their known impact on communication and swallowing.

Dementias can occur in some basal ganglia diseases such as Huntington and Parkinson. These often are called subcortical dementias because of the location of the primary degeneration. Most dementias, however, involve both cortical and subcortical regions either because of the extensive connections between structures/regions, or because of spreading degeneration that occurs with the disease processes. Recall the concept of **diaschisis**, whereby damage can happen to remote cortical structures that become disconnected from their inputs. In this book the dementias are discussed in relation to the primary site of degeneration. Frontotemporal dementia is covered in Chapter 6, even though it also affects the basal ganglia. Similarly, progressive supranuclear palsy is covered in Chapter 11 because the primary degeneration is in the brainstem.

Parkinson Disease

Parkinson disease (PD) is a result of degeneration of dopaminergic neurons in the substantia nigra. In the vast majority of cases, the cause is idiopathic, meaning that the cause is unknown. However, there are some forms that are hereditary. Risk factors include exposure to environmental chemicals such as pesticides, melanoma, high milk and dairy consumption, and TBI. Parkinsonism is an umbrella term that encompasses a variety of disorders that share some motor signs with PD, but may have a different (or unknown) etiology or additional signs and symptoms that are not part of the classic PD diagnosis.

Degeneration of dopaminergic neurons in the substantia nigra is a key diagnostic feature of PD (refer back to Figure 3–12). The degeneration begins unilaterally but extends bilaterally with disease progression. Loss of these neurons reduces the connection between the midbrain and the striatum through the nigrostriatal pathways. As noted previously, dopamine is a critical neurotransmitter in the basal ganglia circuits. It can create either excitatory or inhibitory signals, depending on the type of postsynaptic receptors. This dual role explains the presence of both too much and too little movement in the presenting signs and symptoms.

PD also causes proteins in the brain (specifically, alpha-synuclein) to clump. The resulting abnormal protein structures are called Lewy bodies. They interrupt the functions of neurons, resulting in a variety of cognitive deficits and often lead to Lewy body dementia.

> ### Box 10–2 Muhammad Ali
>
> Muhammed Ali, one of the greatest boxers in history, developed Parkinsonian signs and symptoms such as a resting tremor, hypophonia, and micrographia. There is some controversy over whether his disease was early-onset idiopathic PD or Parkinsonism caused by repeated brain injury. Brain injury, especially repeated injury, is a known risk factor for degenerative neurologic diseases such as PD and Alzheimer. New evidence from medical records released with permission from Ali's family suggests that the symptoms developed prior to Ali's retirement, and followed the typical pattern of idiopathic PD (Okun et al., 2022). It may never be known to what extent boxing contributed to the onset or progression, but it is likely that boxing was not the sole cause of the disease.

Finally, there is loss of non-dopaminergic cells in a variety of areas, including brainstem nuclei, the olfactory bulb, and the hypothalamus. This impacts many different neurotransmitter systems and is thought to cause the non-motor symptoms.

The motor signs and symptoms are characterized by both too much and too little movement. Excessive, unwanted movement is seen in resting tremor, most obvious in the hands. When a person with PD has their arms/hands resting, a 3 to 5 Hz tremor can affect one or both hands. This is often called a "pill rolling tremor," as the fingers and thumb rub together as if the person were rolling a bead or pill between them. Because this is a resting tremor, when they engage their hands in activity, the tremor disappears. Alternatively, some individuals demonstrate a hand-flapping resting tremor, where the hand rotates back and forth at the wrist in the motion of opening a door knob.

Reduction of movement can be seen across multiple muscle groups and systems. Many people with PD have reduced facial expression. The term "masked facies" is used because the limited facial movement makes it look like they're wearing a mask. Reduced range of motion affects the articulators; the lips and tongue do not move as much as needed, resulting in reduced articulatory precision. Speech is often faster than normal and can increase in speed the longer someone talks. This can seem counterintuitive at first, but actually is a logical consequence of reduced movement. If the articulators do not move as far, they can move between positions faster. The increasing speed over time is a phenomenon called **festination**. The range of motion decreases over time, resulting in faster, smaller movements. In lay terms, this is often described as mumbling. The vocal folds also do not adduct as tightly as needed, resulting in a breathy voice and reduced loudness (hypophonia). Gait also is affected. Reduced range of motion leads to a shuffling gait. With festination, the shuffling steps become smaller and smaller, and faster and faster over time. When asked to turn around, a "pedestal turn" is seen: the person takes many very small steps in order to make a 180-degree turn, as if they are standing on a small pedestal and have to carefully turn to avoid falling off.

> **Box 10-3 Michael J. Fox – "Shaky Dad"**
>
> Depending upon your generation, you may have first come to know of Michael J. Fox as the witty Alex P. Keaton on the TV series "Family Ties," Marty McFly in the "Back to the Future" movie trilogy, or Mike Flaherty in "Spin City." Regardless, you likely know of his PD diagnosis and foundation. During filming of the TV series "Spin City," Michael would often stand behind objects to hide the resting tremor present in his hands. After receiving a diagnosis of early-onset PD, Michael began receiving a fairly typical treatment regimen with a drug called levodopa, which has a side effect of paroxysmal dyskinesias such as erratic, writhing movements of the face, arms, legs, and trunk. This led to the nickname used by his children: Shaky Dad. These dyskinesias commonly occur a few to several years after levodopa treatments. These symptoms typically occur either at the peak of the levodopa dose or at the beginning and end of the dose.

Huntington Disease

Huntington disease is an inherited disease related to a mutation of the huntingtin gene. Children of a parent with the huntingtin mutation have a 50/50 chance of inheriting the disease. Subsequently, individuals with HD are often familiar with the consequences and progression of the disease in family members. There currently is no cure. The disease causes degeneration of neurons in the striatum, primarily inhibitory neurons and circuits (refer back to Figure 3–13), upsetting the balance between excitatory and inhibitory signals, resulting in excessive, unwanted movement. HD results in choreiform (dance-like) unwanted movements. These can be small or large movements affecting muscle groups. They can affect the limbs, neck, facial muscles, and articulators. The movements are present while the person is awake, but disappear during sleep. Difficulty sustaining movements such as sticking out one's tongue or holding an arm out straight are common. Both speech and swallowing impairments are present in HD. Speech is characterized by inconsistent timing and imprecise articulation. All phases of the swallow are impaired due to the movement inconsistencies.

While the motor symptoms are most easily recognized and typically are the focus of the disease, families may be more concerned about the behavioral and mental changes (Eddy et al., 2016). Cognitive deficits impact executive functions, attention, planning, inhibition, and cognitive flexibility. Visuospatial processing also is affected resulting in poor visual working memory and spatial manipulation (Coppen et al., 2018). People with HD develop difficulties recognizing emotions conveyed through both prosody and facial expression (Henley et al., 2012). Mental and behavioral changes include irritability, apathy, anxiety, and depression (Eddy et al. 2016).

Corticobasal Syndrome

Corticobasal syndrome (CBS, also known as corticobasal degeneration or corticobasal ganglionic degeneration) is a disease characterized by loss of neurons in the cortex and basal ganglia. The cause is unknown, although many individuals have accumulations of tau protein in the brain which interrupt neuronal functions. As with other diseases of the basal ganglia, motor, cognitive, and language disorders occur. While the specific signs/symptoms differ across individuals depending on the regions affected, there are some commonalities (Refer back to Box 1–2 in Chapter 1 for case description).

Motor symptoms begin unilaterally and become bilateral as the disease progresses. These include muscle stiffness and clumsy or uncoordinated movements; apraxia, or difficulties producing purposeful movements due to motor programming deficits; postural or action tremor; bradykinesia (slowness of movements); ataxic gait; and dystonia.

Aphasia and apraxia of speech may occur, along with dysarthria and dysphagia. In some cases, primary progressive aphasia or primary progressive apraxia of speech may be early signs of the disease. Cognitive abilities such as attention, memory, executive functions, and inhibition are commonly affected, and some people may develop behavioral affective issues including apathy and irritability.

Speech Disorders

Hypokinetic dysarthria is associated with PD and is characterized by too little movement and reduced range of motion. Articulatory precision is reduced as the lips, tongue, and other articulators do not make the full excursion to hit the articulatory targets. For example, when producing velar sounds /k/ and /g/, the posterior tongue may not be retracted and elevated enough to touch the velar contact point. It is important to note that the "hypo" in hypokinetic refers to a reduction in the extent or range of motion, not to the speed of movement. In fact, oftentimes hypokinetic dysarthria is characterized by an increased rate of speech. Both of these contribute to reduced intelligibility. A weak, breathy voice accompanies the reduced articulatory precision due to reduced adduction of the vocal folds (Table 10–1).

Hyperkinetic dysarthria can be caused by HD or dyskinesias. The unwanted movements of the facial muscles and articulatory muscle groups disrupt speech production. These can affect articulatory precision, resonance, and/or voicing. The patterns depend upon the muscle groups impacted and the form of the movements. For example, dystonic sustained or repetitive (myoclonus) muscle contractions can impact individual components of speech (respiration, phonation, articulation, etc.) depending on the structures involved, while choreiform movements associated with HD unpredictably interrupt multiple components (Table 10–2).

One specific form of hyperkinetic dysarthria is **spasmodic dysphonia**. Adductor spasmodic dysphonia is characterized by strong adduction (closure) of the vocal folds when someone begins to speak. Speech production is very effortful as the person must use additional, in some cases excessive, respiratory support to push the air through the tightly adducted vocal folds to create vibration/voicing. The resulting voicing is typically described as strained and strangled. Abductor spasmodic dysphonia is the unpredictable abduction (opening) of the

Table 10-1. Speech and Resonance Characteristics of Hypokinetic Dysarthria

Vocal Characteristic	Hypokinetic Dysarthria
Respiration	Generally fine
Phonation	Breathy voice, monotone
Articulation	Reduced articulatory precision
Resonance	Hypernasality possible
Prosody	Reduced
Other	Fast rate of speech

Table 10-2. Speech and Resonance Characteristics of Hyperkinetic Dysarthria

Vocal Characteristic	Hyperkinetic Dysarthria		
	Huntington Disease	Adductor Spasmodic Dysphonia	Velopharyngeal Myoclonus
Respiration	Irregular	Increased effort needed	OK
Phonation	Irregular	Consistent strained-strangled vocal quality	OK
Articulation	Irregular	OK	OK
Resonance	Irregular	OK	Rhythmic changes associated with velar pulsation
Prosody	Irregular	Affected by effort	OK
Other		Slow rate of speech due to laryngeal effort	

vocal folds during speech production. This results in inconsistent breathiness and voicelessness. Spasmodic dysphonia and other dystonias are assumed to be related to basal ganglia functioning but, in many cases, there are no clear neurological or physiological changes that can be localized.

Apraxia of speech is not generally associated with diseases of the basal ganglia. However, it can occur in CBS when the neurons in the frontal motor programming regions are affected.

Language Disorders

Language disorders typically are subtle, or at least are not part of the more striking signs and symptoms of basal ganglia diseases. Some studies have suggested that action language and syntax are predominantly affected in HD and PD (Birba et al., 2017). Interruption of the cognitive-associative loop and the verbal executive network can cause difficulty at all levels of language (phonetics, phonology, morphology, syntax, and lexical semantics) due to problems with selection, monitoring, and inhibition of language processes (Jacquemot & Bachoud-Lévi, 2021). Characteristics of non-fluent aphasia occur with CBS, primarily anomia and reduced fluency of language production.

Pragmatics is affected due to the reduced use and comprehension of extralinguistic cues such as facial expression, gestures, and body language, as well as changes to prosody (a paralinguistic cue). Specifically for HD, the unpredictable, unwanted movements can interrupt or prevent natural gestures, body language, and facial expressions. Reduced facial expression in PD is related to the masked facies. Because these underlying problems are motoric, the resulting disruptions to communication are not considered extralinguistic apragmatism (see Chapter 8). However, receptive emotional aprosodia can occur with damage to the caudate nucleus (Sheppard et al., 2021). Differential diagnosis of sensorimotor deficits versus apragmatism requires careful attention to presentation of the deficits: are they related specifically to emotion, or are they present more consistently across a variety of situations? Deficits in social cognition described below also contribute to pragmatic communication challenges.

Cognitive Disorders

Executive Function and Awareness

Approximately 15 to 20% of individuals with PD exhibit executive function deficits due to the loss of dopamine in the dorsolateral prefrontal cortex. Difficulties with reward-related

---

Box 10–4 Is It Aphasia?

Language researchers can use slightly different definitions of "aphasia." While all agree that it is an acquired disorder of language that affects both comprehension and production, some use a purist definition that restricts the use of "aphasia" to discrete/focal lesions of the left hemisphere. They may use the phrase "aphasic characteristics" or "language deficits similar to aphasia" to differentiate the disorders associated with damage to structures outside the perisylvian left hemisphere. Others are more relaxed and will use "aphasia" to describe language disorders that fit the characteristics of stroke-related aphasia, regardless of the location of the lesion. An example is the label "thalamic aphasia."

learning and decision making based on values are present due to interruption of reward pathways through the ventral striatum (O'Callaghan et al., 2014). People with PD generally have good awareness of their cognitive abilities, although this changes when the disease impacts executive functioning. Interestingly, some may be less aware of dyskinesias caused by treatment (e.g., levodopa-induced dyskinesias) than are caregivers. It is possible that caregivers are more aware because they are more bothered by the movements than are the patients themselves (Chavoix & Insausti, 2017).

Cognitive decline is a core aspect of HD. Beginning with disinhibition and reduced executive functioning, the deficits develop into dementia with the progression of the disease. Awareness of deficits can be reduced in HD. Many people with HD underestimate the extent of their movement disorder as well as cognitive and affective changes. However, they usually are aware of depression and irritability (Chavoix & Insausti, 2017).

Memory and Attention

Attentional deficits occur in HD due to degeneration of the striatum. These co-occur with declines in executive function, planning, and cognitive flexibility. Memory and attention deficits in HD also impact visuospatial processing (Coppen et al., 2018).

Social Cognition

Both cognitive and affective theory of mind (ToM) can be affected by diseases of the basal ganglia. Cognitive ToM can be affected by PD, while affective ToM is typically spared until later stages of the disease (Poletti et al., 2012). In contrast, affective ToM is more commonly affected in HD. Deficits in recognition and processing of emotions can be an early sign of the disease (Henley et al., 2012). The resulting challenges to social cognition are due to both visuospatial deficits that impact recognition of facial expressions and affective ToM deficits that limit one's ability to understand others' emotional states. Alexithymia also may occur. This is a reduction in the ability to interpret and describe one's own emotional experiences (Eddy et al., 2016).

Swallowing Disorders

Oropharyngeal dysphagia in PD is common, occurring in at least 50% and up to 80% of individuals, although it is not commonly one of the primary complaints (Kalf et al., 2012; Suttrup & Warnecke, 2016). It is due to the reduction of dopaminergic neurons in the basal ganglia as well as the developing presence of Lewy bodies in the brainstem that interrupts the medullary swallowing center. The dysphagia often results in longer times needed for eating, reduced desire to eat, and difficulties selecting foods that they want to eat that they also can safely swallow. Lingual pumping results in difficulty with timing and initiation of tongue base retraction. As a result, food and liquids sometimes spill posteriorly, entering the pharynx before the person is ready. Coughing and choking are common symptoms. All of these decrease a person's quality of life. Since mealtimes are commonly a source of socialization, this too can be affected as patients may not feel comfortable eating with others (Leow et al., 2010).

The unwanted movements of HD can interrupt all phases of swallowing (Heemskerk & Roos, 2011). Dysphagia in this population is very common, and aspiration pneumonia is a leading cause of death for people with HD. Many patients and their caregivers express a fear of choking (Kalkers et al., 2022). In the oral preparatory phase, these result in impulsive or rapid food consumption, inadequate chewing prior to swallowing, and inappropriate rate and amount of food taken in and transferred posteriorly. In the oral phase, there may be residue, either short or delayed oral transit times, incoordination of the swallow, and repetitive swallows. Coughing and choking can occur in the pharyngeal phase, as can aspiration, changes to the timing and extent of laryngeal elevation and descent, and difficulty stopping breathing during the swallow.

Thalamus

The thalamus is a paired, egg-shaped structure found deep within each hemisphere (Figure 10–8). It is medial to the lenticular nucleus and forms the lateral walls of the third ven-

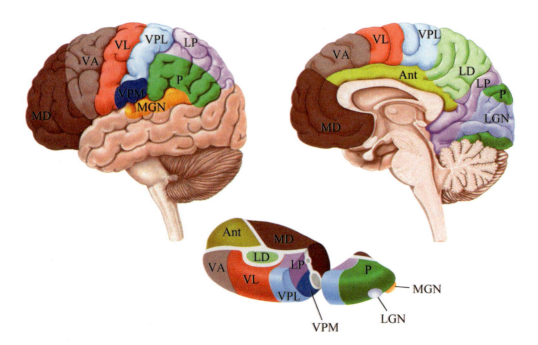

Figure 10–8. Thalamic nuclei and their cortical connections. MD=mediodorsal, Ant=anterior nuclear complex; LD=lateral dorsal; LP=lateral posterior; VL=ventral lateral; VA=ventral anterior; VPL=ventroposterolateral; VPM=ventroposteromedial; P=pulvinar; MGN=medial geniculate nucleus; LGN=lateral geniculate nucleus. From *Clinical Neuroscience for Communication Disorders: Neuroanatomy and Neurophysiology* (p. 85) by Blake, M. L. and Hoepner, J. K. Copyright © 2023 Plural Publishing, Inc. All rights reserved.

Table 10–3. Connections and Functions of Thalamic Nuclear Groups

Thalamic Nuclear Complex	Dom Primary Functions ains	Connections (Inputs & Outputs)
Mediodorsal (MD)	mood, emotion, cognition, personality	hippocampus, cortical association areas, prefrontal, orbitofrontal, limbic, hippocampus, hypothalamus
Anterior (Ant)	memory, emotion, executive function	hippocampus, frontal lobes, cingulate gyrus
Lateral Dorsal (LD) and Lateral Posterior (LP)	complex sensory integration	cortical association areas
Ventral Lateral (VL), Ventral Anterior (VA)	motor integration	primary motor, basal ganglia, cerebellum
Ventroposterolateral (VPL), Ventroposteromedial (VPM)	sensory relay	afferent spinal somatosensory neurons
Pulvinar (P)	language, vision	superior colliculus, angular, supramarginal gyri
Medial Geniculate Nucleus (MGN)	auditory	inferior colliculus, brainstem nuclei along auditory pathway
Lateral Geniculate Nucleus (LGN)	vision	optic nerve (CN II)

Source: Clinical Neuroscience for Communication Disorders: Neuroanatomy and Neurophysiology (p. 85) by Blake, M. L. and Hoepner, J. K. Copyright © 2023 Plural Publishing, Inc. All rights reserved.

tricle. The thalamus is made up of over 120 distinct nuclei; it receives inputs from nearly all areas of the cortex as well as ascending connections extending from the spinal cord and brainstem. As such, it has the capacity to influence nearly all CNS functions (Table 10–3).

Functions of the Thalamus

Sensorimotor Functions

The thalamus is most well-known for its role as a sensory gatekeeper. All sensory pathways coming into the brain have a synapse in the thalamus except for olfaction. This means all somatosensory (touch, pain, temperature), visual, auditory, and taste signals are relayed to their respective cortical areas through the thalamus. The signals can be enhanced or dampened as they pass through the thalamus. Beyond this gatekeeping, sensory signals from different modalities (e.g., touch and vision) are integrated in the thalamus before being sent to sensory association areas in the parietal lobes.

Motor integration occurs in ventral regions of the thalamus. Circuits connecting the motor cortex with the basal ganglia pass through the thalamus. Direct circuits result in excitatory signals sent from the thalamus to the motor cortex, while indirect circuits inhibit motor cortex functions.

Cognition and Emotion

The anterior and mediodorsal regions of the thalamus have connections to the frontal lobes, hippocampus, and the limbic system. These connections impact executive functions, memory, mood, emotions, and personality. Additional connections to the hypothalamus provide an avenue to influence the regulatory systems, and to integrate visceral information with emotion and cognition. These connections help to explain why your physical state impacts your cognition. For example, when you feel ill, it is often hard to concentrate or to critically or logically think through situations. These connections also facilitate the link between mood, memories, and sensory stimuli.

The pulvinar, the posterior segment of the thalamus, provides connections between visual and language areas. As such, it is important for visual components of language, namely reading and writing. These connections can influence communication including both basic language and expression of emotion and mood.

Cortical Arousal

The reticular formation of the brainstem is extensively connected to the thalamus and together they are responsible for cortical arousal.

Disorders and Diseases of the Thalamus

While the entire thalamus can be affected by infections or anoxia, most lesions are due to stroke (Hegde et al., 2011). Blood supply to the thalamus is complex and can differ from person to person. This makes it difficult to make predictions about the deficits that might occur from vascular lesions. For example, a stroke in a thalamic branch of the middle cerebral artery (MCA) may affect different thalamic nuclei in different people due to small differences in the exact placement of MCA branches and blood supply by MCA versus other cerebral arteries. Because of this, the resulting speech, language, and cognitive deficits can only be roughly characterized (Klostermann et al., 2013).

Degenerative diseases such as progressive supranuclear palsy (Halliday et al., 2005), and dementias including Lewy body and Alzheimer can affect thalamic neurons in motor and limbic sections, respectively.

Speech Disorders

Dysarthria has been reported in some cases of thalamic damage. Descriptions are fairly vague, mentioning hypophonia and deficits of articulation (de Witte et al., 2011) or parkinsonian-like dysarthria characteristics (Ackermann et al., 1993). Changes in prosody are uncommon. Apraxia of speech is not typically reported after thalamic lesions (de Witte et al., 2011). Due to the role of the thalamus in the basal ganglia circuits, it is not surprising that thalamic damage could impact speech production and that the deficits would overlap with those characteristics of Parkinson disease. The location of the damage likely plays a large role in whether or not dysarthria is present.

Language Disorders

There are several models of thalamic language function (Klostermann et al., 2013). Most suggest that the thalamus monitors language output, potentially aiding in integration of semantics and syntax, or triggering motor production.

Thalamic aphasia can result from thalamic lesions, especially those that affect the left anterior or ventrolateral regions. There are a variety of characteristics associated with thalamic aphasia because, as described earlier, most lesions affect multiple thalamic nuclei and often involve other subcortical regions along with the thalamus. Common characteristics of thalamic aphasia include comprehension deficits, anomia, and various types of paraphasias. Most deficits are mild. Some individuals have markedly reduced initiation of spontaneous speech, even mutism. Syntax and non-propositional speech are typically spared, and language production remains fluent.

Paralinguistic and extralinguistic components of apragmatism, in the form of receptive emotional aprosodia or reduced comprehension of emotional cues, can occur after damage to the thalamus (Sheppard et al., 2021).

Cognitive Disorders

Thalamic damage can cause a range of cognitive deficits, especially when the mediodorsal nucleus is affected. Many of the deficits are similar to those seen after prefrontal lobe damage such as executive function and attention deficits that impact selection and monitoring of responses, planning, impulsivity and decision making. Memory deficits most commonly affect verbal memory after left thalamic lesions and visual memory after right thalamic lesions. Visuospatial perception and integration can be impacted, in part due to connections between the thalamus and the frontal eye fields which "guide decisions about how to sample a complex scene" (Mitchell et al., 2014, p. 15342), but also due to difficulties with associative learning in which relationships between different items must be learned (Mitchell, 2015).

Visuospatial neglect can occur after strokes in either the right or left thalamus (de Witte et al., 2011; Karussis et al., 2000). Behavioral and mood disorders also have been reported, including depression, mania, personality disorders, behavioral changes, and apathy (de Witte et al., 2011).

Swallowing Disorders

Dysphagia can occur after lesions to the thalamus, but there is little information regarding how swallowing is affected. Logically, lesions that extend beyond the thalamus into either the internal capsule or the midbrain are more likely to result in dysphagia than lesions that are restricted to the thalamus. Individuals with hemorrhagic thalamic strokes who are older, have larger lesions, or have language or cognitive deficits also have a higher risk of dysphagia (Maeshima et al., 2014).

Summary

The basal ganglia and thalamus have extensive connections throughout the brain. Their primary roles in sensorimotor processing make them important components of speech and swallowing. They also influence language and cognition, so in addition to dysarthria and dysphagia, damage to these subcortical structures are likely to cause aphasia, apragmatism (typically paralinguistic or extralinguistic), executive dysfunction, and deficits in attention and memory.

Key Concepts

- The basal ganglia have a primary role in the motor system, and damage can cause a variety of motor disorders.
- Parkinson and Huntington diseases both affect the basal ganglia, but because of the complexity of the motor system, they have some opposite effects.
- Diseases affecting the basal ganglia impact speech and swallowing but also impact language and cognition due to loops/circuits connecting the basal ganglia to cortical areas.
- Hypokinetic dysarthria is characterized by not enough movement.
- Hyperkinetic dysarthria is characterized by excessive, unwanted movements.
- Damage to the thalamus can impact speech, language, cognition, and swallowing.

References

Ackermann, H., Ziegler, W., & Petersen, D. (1993). Dysarthria in bilateral thalamic infarction: A case study. *Journal of Neurology, 240*, 357–362.

Birba, A., García-Cordero, I., Kozono, G., Legaz, A., Ibáñez, A., Sedeño, L., & García, A. M. (2017). Losing ground: Frontostriatal atrophy disrupts language embodiment in Parkinson's and Huntington's disease. *Neuroscience and Biobehavioral Reviews, 80*, 673–687. https://doi.org/10.1016/J.NEUBIOREV.2017.07.011

Chavoix, C., & Insausti, R. (2017). Self-awareness and the medial temporal lobe in neurodegenerative diseases. *Neuroscience and Biobehavioral Reviews, 78,* 1–12. https://doi.org/10.1016/J.NEUBIOREV.2017.04.015

Coppen, E. M., van der Grond, J., Hart, E. P., Lakke, E. A. J. F., & Roos, R. A. C. (2018). The visual cortex and visual cognition in Huntington's disease: An overview of current literature. *Behavioural Brain Research, 351,* 63–74. https://doi.org/10.1016/J.BBR.2018.05.019

de Witte, L., Brouns, R., Kavadias, D., Engelborghs, S., de Deyn, P. P., & Mariën, P. (2011). Cognitive, affective and behavioural disturbances following vascular thalamic lesions: A review. *Cortex, 47*(3), 273–319. https://doi.org/10.1016/j.cortex.2010.09.002

Eddy, C. M., Parkinson, E. G., & Rickards, H. E. (2016). Changes in mental state and behaviour in Huntington's disease. *The Lancet Psychiatry, 3*(11), 1079–1086. https://doi.org/10.1016/S2215-0366(16)30144-4

Halliday, G. M., Macdonald, V., & Henderson, J. M. (2005). A comparison of degeneration in motor thalamus and cortex between progressive supranuclear palsy and Parkinson's disease. *Brain, 128,* 2272–2280. https://doi.org/10.1093/brain/awh596

Heemskerk, A.-W., & Roos, R. A. C. (2011). Dysphagia in Huntington's disease: A review. *Dysphagia, 26,* 62–66. https://doi.org/10.1007/s00455-010-9302-4

Hegde, A. N., Mohan, S., Lath, N., & Tchoyoson Lim, C. C. (2011). Differential diagnosis for bilateral abnormalities of the basal ganglia and thalamus. *Radiographics, 31,* 5–30. https://doi.org/10.1148/rg.311105041

Henley, S. M. D., Novak, M. J. U., Frost, C., King, J., Tabrizi, S. J., & Warren, J. D. (2012). Emotion recognition in Huntington's disease: A systematic review. *Neuroscience and Biobehavioral Reviews, 36*(1), 237–253. https://doi.org/10.1016/J.NEUBIOREV.2011.06.002

Jacquemot, C., & Bachoud-Lévi, A. C. (2021). Striatum and language processing: Where do we stand? *Cognition, 213.* Advance online publication. https://doi.org/10.1016/J.COGNITION.2021.104785

Kalf, J. G., de Swart, B. J. M., Bloem, B. R., & Munneke, M. (2012). Prevalence of oropharyngeal dysphagia in Parkinson's disease: A meta-analysis. *Parkinsonism and Related Disorders, 18*(4), 311–315. https://doi.org/10.1016/J.PARKRELDIS.2011.11.006

Kalkers, K., Schols, J. M. G. A., van Zwet, E. W., & Roos, R. A. C. (2022). Dysphagia, fear of choking and preventative measures in patients with Huntington's disease: The perspectives of patients and caregivers in long-term care. *Journal of Nutrition Health Aging, 26*(4), 332–338. https://doi.org/10.1007/s12603-022-1743-6

Karussis, D., Leker, R. R., & Abramsky, O. (2000). Cognitive dysfunction following thalamic stroke: A study of 16 cases and review of the literature. *Journal of the Neurological Sciences, 172*(1), 25–29. https://doi.org/10.1016/S0022-510X(99)00267-1

Klostermann, F., Krugel, L. K., Ehlen, F., Saalmann, Y. B., & Hebb, A. O. (2013). Functional roles of the thalamus for language capacities. *Frontiers in Systems Neuroscience, 7,* 1–8. https://doi.org/10.3389/fnsys.2013.00032

Leow, L. P., Huckabee, M.-L., Anderson, T., & Beckert, L. (2010). The impact of dysphagia on quality of life in ageing and Parkinson's disease as measured by the Swallowing Quality of Life (SWAL-QOL) Questionnaire. *Dysphagia, 25,* 216–220. https://doi.org/10.1007/s00455-009-9245-9

Maeshima, S., Osawa, A., Yamane, F., Ishihara, S., & Tanahashi, N. (2014). Dysphagia following acute thalamic haemorrhage: Clinical correlates and outcomes. *European Neurology, 71*(3–4), 165–172. https://doi.org/10.1159/000355477

Mitchell, A. S. (2015). The mediodorsal thalamus as a higher order thalamic relay nucleus important for learning and decision-making. *Neuroscience and Biobehavioral Reviews, 54,* 76–88. https://doi.org/10.1016/j.neubiorev.2015.03.001

Mitchell, A. S., Sherman, X. S. M., Sommer, M. A., Mair, R. G., Vertes, R. P., & Chudasama, Y. (2014).

Symposium advances in understanding mechanisms of thalamic relays in cognition and behavior. *The Journal of Neuroscience, 34*(46), 15340–15346. https://doi.org/10.1523/JNEUROSCI.3289-14.2014

O'Callaghan, C., Bertoux, M., & Hornberger, M. (2014). Beyond and below the cortex: the contribution of striatal dysfunction to cognition and behaviour in neurodegeneration. *Journal of Neurology, Neurosurgery & Psychiatry, 85*, 371–378. https://doi.org/10.1136/jnnp-2012-304558

Okun, M. S., Mayberg, H. S., & DeLong, M. R. (2022) Muhammad Ali and young-onset idiopathic Parkinson disease–The missing evidence. *JAMA Neurology, E1–2.* https://jamanetwork.com/journals/jamaneurology/fullarticle/2797272

Poletti, M., Enrici, I., & Adenzato, M. (2012). Cognitive and affective Theory of Mind in neurodegenerative diseases: Neuropsychological, neuroanatomical and neurochemical levels. *Neuroscience and Biobehavioral Reviews, 36*(9), 2147–2164. https://doi.org/10.1016/J.NEUBIOREV.2012.07.004

Sheppard, S. M., Meier, E. L., Zezinka Durfee, A., Walker, A., Shea, J., & Hillis, A. E. (2021). Characterizing subtypes and neural correlates of receptive aprosodia in acute right hemisphere stroke. *Cortex, 141*, 36–54. https://doi.org/10.1016/J.CORTEX.2021.04.003

Suttrup, I., & Warnecke, T. (2016). Dysphagia in Parkinson's disease. *Dysphagia, 31*, 24–32. https://doi.org/10.1007/s00455-015-9671-9

Other Resources

PD https://www.nia.nih.gov/health/parkinsons-disease
HD https://hdsa.org/

11

BRAINSTEM, CRANIAL NERVES, AND CEREBELLUM

Chapter Overview

Overview
Brainstem
   Cranial Nerves
   Disorders and Diseases of the Brainstem
   Speech Disorders
   Language Disorders
   Cognitive Disorders
   Swallowing Disorders
Cerebellum
   Disorders and Diseases of the Cerebellum
   Speech Disorders
   Language Disorders
   Cognitive Disorders
   Swallowing Disorders
Summary
Key Concepts
References

Overview

The brainstem and cerebellum are located inferior to the posterior cerebrum, and receive blood supply through the vertebrobasilar system. The brainstem serves multiple functions in speech and swallowing. Most important are the cranial nerves that carry motor signals to muscles necessary for speech and swallowing and sensory signals from structures in the head and neck. For swallowing, the brainstem houses the central pattern generator that controls the involuntary sequential and rhythmic movements in the pharyngeal and esophageal phases of swallowing. The brainstem's role in language and cognition are less obvious, and are related primarily to reticular formation and reticular activating system functions for activation of the cortex.

The cerebellum is attached to the dorsal surface of the brainstem. Its primary role is in the sensorimotor system, but it also affects language and cognitive processing. Connections between the cerebrum and the cerebellum travel through the brainstem.

This chapter covers the speech, language, cognitive, and swallowing disorders caused by damage to the brainstem and cerebellum. Assessment and treatment for these disorders are covered in Chapters 12 and 13 because the principles for addressing dysarthria, dysphagia, and cognitive deficits are similar regardless of the location of lesion that causes them.

Brainstem

The brainstem is made up of three segments: **midbrain**, **pons**, and **medulla oblongata** (Figure 11–1). The midbrain is the most superior; when dissected out, the thalami appear to

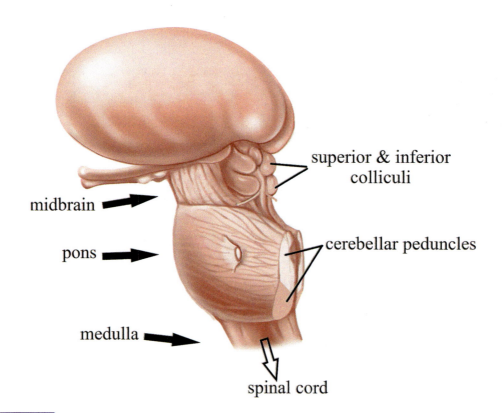

Figure 11–1. Lateral view of the brainstem. From *Clinical Neuroscience for Communication Disorders: Neuroanatomy and Neurophysiology* (p. 85) by Blake, M. L. and Hoepner, J. K. Copyright © 2023 Plural Publishing, Inc. All rights reserved.

grow out of the top of the midbrain. On the dorsal surface of the midbrain are the superior and inferior colliculi, which are connected to the visual and auditory systems, respectively. The pons are readily recognizable by the anterior bulge and the posterolateral cerebellar peduncles which are masses of fibers that extend into and out of the cerebellum. The medulla oblongata extends from the base of the pons to the point at which the structure becomes the spinal cord. This name change occurs at the cervicomedullary junction where the structure leaves the cranium through the foramen magnum, the large hole in the base of the skull.

Throughout the brainstem are white matter tracts. Many are axons that are extending from the brain down to the spinal cord, or ascending from the spinal cord up to the brain. Others are running to or from the cerebellum. Amidst the white matter tracts are nuclei, or groups of cell bodies with a similar function. Many of these are cranial nerve nuclei (refer back to Figure 2–19), both cell bodies of lower motor neurons (LMNs) with their axons extending out through the cranial nerves, or cell bodies of neurons that receive signals from sensory neurons and then send signals up to the brain .

The reticular formation is a relatively large nucleus that extends from the midbrain down through the upper medulla. It has widespread impacts on sensory, motor, cognitive, and emotional processes in the cortex (Figure 11–2). It can modify pain signals from the body and influence motor and cognitive connections between the cerebellum and cortex. Cognition, including memory and decision making, are impacted by connections to the frontal and temporal lobes including the dopaminergic pathways that trigger the reward system. Arousal, sleep patterns, and even stress responses are affected by reticular formation projections to the brain. Arousal is a generalized state of responsiveness, controlled by several interconnected areas in the upper brainstem and thalamus. A variety of neurotransmitter systems also are involved. The redundancy created by the distributed control means that permanent disorders of arousal are fairly rare.

Cranial Nerves

Recall from Chapter 2 that there are 12 pairs of cranial nerves that innervate structures in the head and neck. Most have both sensory and motor functions, although some like olfactory and optic nerves are sensory only, and others like the hypoglossal nerve have only motor functions. The motor components of cranial nerves are made up of LMNs that receive signals from upper motor neurons (UMNs). The six cranial nerves with direct involvement in speech and swallowing will be discussed here.

CN V is the **trigeminal nerve.** It exits the brainstem from the pons and immediately divides into three branches (hence the name trigeminal; Latin: *three twins*). The most superior branch, the ophthalmic, carries somatosensory (pain, touch, and temperature) signals from the upper part of the face and head, including the eyes and scalp. The maxillary branch similarly carries somatosensory signals, but from the mid-face including the upper lips, nose, and mucous membranes of the mouth. The third branch, the mandibular, carries somatosensory information from the lower face and lower jaw including the mouth and the tongue. Additionally, it contains motor nerves that innervate the muscles of mastication—those that are used for chewing.

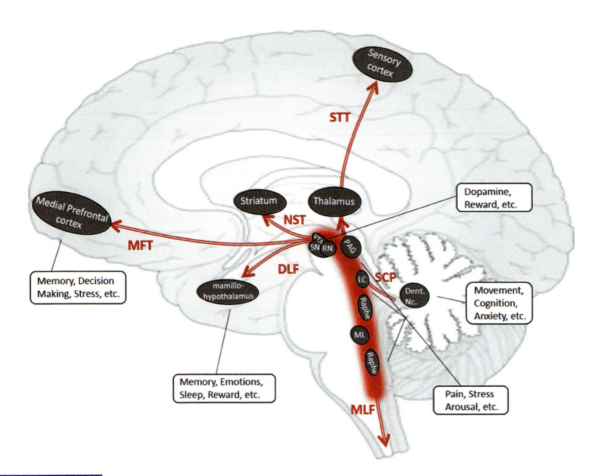

Figure 11–2. Reticular formation connections. From Zhang Y, Vakhtin AA, Jennings JS, Massaband P, Wintermark M, Craig PL, et al. (2020) Diffusion tensor tractography of brainstem fibers and its application in pain. *PLoS ONE 15*(2): e0213952. https://doi.org/10.1371/journal.pone.0213952. This is an open access article, free of all copyright, and may be freely reproduced, distributed, transmitted, modified, built upon, or otherwise used by anyone for any lawful purpose. The work is made available under the Creative Commons CC0 public domain dedication.

CN VII, the **facial nerve**, innervates the muscles of facial expression. These include all the muscles that create smiles, frowns, and raised eyebrows to create surprised or quizzical looks. Muscles for lip retraction and rounding that create some vowel sounds such as those to make siren sounds (wee-ooo-wee-ooo) are also innervated by the facial nerve. In addition to muscles, motor branches innervate salivary glands that release saliva to moisten and help break down food in preparation for swallowing. The sensory component of the facial nerve carries taste information from the anterior portion of the tongue. Adequate taste perception is important for stimulating appetite.

CN IX is the **glossopharyngeal nerve**. The motor component aids swallowing in three ways. First, it innervates the stylopharyngeus muscle that elevates and dilates the pharynx so a food

Box 11-1 Case 11-1. Denise

Denise was a 35-year-old female who woke up one morning to severe pain in her right ear. That was her only symptom for approximately 24 hours. The next day, she noticed a mild weakness on the right side of her face. Concerned with the progressing weakness, she went to her local emergency department. She was diagnosed with Bell palsy and started on a course of prednisone. By the following day, she had complete paralysis of that side of the face. Her facial droop made it difficult to smile and she frequently lost a bit of liquid out of the corner of her mouth when drinking. She lost her sense of taste and developed drooling. She had so much difficulty closing her right eye that she had to cover it with gauze and tape it shut when she slept. Resolution of the pain in her ear and jaw along with the other symptoms didn't begin until several days after the onset. Denise continues to have mild facial asymmetry that is evident when she smiles (Figure 11-3).

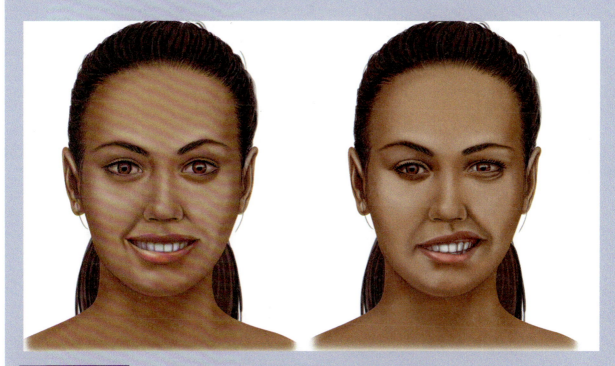

Figure 11-3. Bell palsy unilateral facial weakness.

bolus can easily move through the region. Second, it innervates posterior salivary glands. Third, the sensory component of CN IX carries pain, touch, and temperature signals from the pharyngeal region and taste information from the posterior one third of the tongue and pharynx.

CN X is the **vagus nerve** (Latin: *wanderer*). This is the most complex and wide-ranging cranial nerve, with branches to various internal organs throughout the abdomen. The first three branches are the only ones with a direct effect on speech and swallowing. The **pharyngeal branch** innervates the velum (soft palate). Elevation of this structure closes off the nasal cavity from the pharynx and is necessary for producing non-nasal speech sounds (all phonemes except m, n, and ng), and during swallowing to prevent food and liquid from getting into the nasal cavity. The **superior laryngeal nerve** has two branches. The internal branch carries somatosensory information from the larynx above the vocal folds. The external branch innervates the cricothyroid muscle which lengthens and tenses the vocal folds to change vocal pitch. The **recurrent laryngeal nerve** innervates all of the intrinsic muscles of the larynx. These are the muscles that adduct (close) and abduct (open) and tense the vocal folds. Vocal fold adduction is required for voicing as well as protection of the airway during swallowing.

CN XI, **spinal accessory**, innervates the trapezius and sternocleidomastoid muscles in the neck that are used to move the head and can contribute to non-verbal communication such as nodding and shaking your head or shrugging your shoulders. Some branches of the spinal accessory nerve blend with branches of the vagus nerve, and so have an impact on pharyngeal and laryngeal function.

CN XII is the **hypoglossal nerve** that innervates nearly all of the muscles of the tongue (the only exception is the palatoglossus). Extrinsic muscles create large, positional movements of the tongue, retracting or protruding both for articulation of speech sounds but also to move food in and out of the chewing surface of the teeth and then to push the bolus posteriorly to the pharynx to be swallowed. The intrinsic muscles change the shape of the tongue, elongating or flattening it to create various vowel and consonant sounds. It might help you to remember the phrase "movers and shapers" referring to extrinsic and intrinsic muscles, respectively.

The **pharyngeal plexus** is a network of branches from the vagus and glossopharyngeal nerves. These blended nerves innervate pharyngeal, velar, and laryngeal muscles and are critical for controlling swallowing.

Disorders and Diseases of the Brainstem

Brainstem function can be affected by strokes, tumors, and degenerative diseases. Given the small size of the brainstem (approximately the length and diameter of your thumb), even small strokes or tumors can have devastating effects. Strokes occur from blood clots in the vertebrobasilar arteries and their branches.

Tumors can develop in the brainstem as in other areas of the CNS. While brainstem gliomas are relatively common in children, adult-onset brainstem gliomas are rare. When they occur they most often are in the pons, but can extend into the medulla or midbrain (Reyes-Botero et al., 2012). Signs and symptoms depend on the location and which structures are impacted. The most common include headache, spasticity and weakness, dysarthria, dysphagia, and difficulties with eye movements. A characteristic sign of brainstem tumors are "crossed deficits" with weakness of the face contralateral to weakness in the body (Hu et al., 2016).

Brainstem nuclei are implicated in several degenerative diseases such as Alzheimer, progressive supranuclear palsy (PSP), and Parkinson disease (PD). PD is perhaps the most understood, as the substantia nigra nuclei (discussed in Chapter 10) are located in the midbrain. Sleep disorders, specifically REM sleep behavior disorder, are common in PD and have been linked to changes in brainstem nuclei. Other nuclei that are part of cholinergic and

Box 11–2 Case 11–2. Don

Don was a 62-year-old man who experienced an ischemic stroke in the medial medulla. He experienced right-sided (contralateral) hemiplegia sparing the face, right-sided (contralateral) loss of touch and body position sense, and left-sided (ipsilateral) hypoglossal paralysis. This caused his tongue to deviate to the left when protruded (Figure 11–4) and resulted in severe oral phase dysphagia. Initially, there was only slight deviation of the tongue and almost no tongue movement, even on the unaffected side. He received a percutaneous endogastric tube (PEG-tube) for non-oral nutrition. He was seen intermittently for follow-up evaluations. Approximately three months later, he began to regain movement in the left side of his tongue. He resumed swallowing therapy and was eventually able to resume an oral diet, which was supplemented by non-oral feedings. He continued to experience dense hemiparesis on his right side.

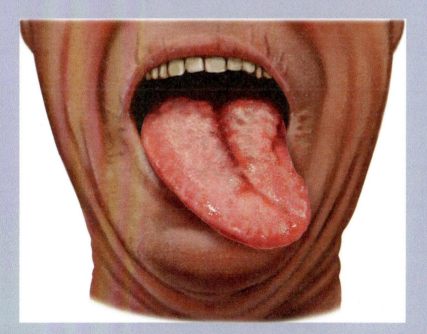

Figure 11–4. Ipsilateral tongue deviation associated with medial medullary syndrome. Adapted from *Clinical Neuroscience for Communication Disorders: Neuroanatomy and Neurophysiology* (p. 291) by Blake, M. L. and Hoepner, J. K. Copyright © 2023 Plural Publishing, Inc. All rights reserved.

serotonergic pathways also may degenerate in dementias, contributing to cognitive changes and mood disorders such as depression (Grinberg et al., 2011).

Progressive supranuclear palsy (PSP) is a tau-opathy that predominantly affects the superior brainstem, basal ganglia, and frontal lobes. The name reflects that it is a degenerative disease that affects brainstem regions superior to the cranial nerve nuclei (hence *supranuclear*). This disease is rare, affecting only about 7 people per 100,000 worldwide (Swallow et al., 2022). Despite its rarity, it is important to speech-language pathologists because it affects speech, cognition, and swallowing. The degeneration affects multiple neurotransmitter systems including dopamine and GABA in the brainstem and basal ganglia as well as acetylcholine and serotonin in the frontal cortex. The resulting signs and symptoms impact motor and cognitive systems, especially gait and balance. Postural rigidity and retrocolic (head tilted back) posture are common, leading to falls and stiffness in the early stages. A characteristic sign is vertical gaze palsy, in which there is difficulty in moving the eyes upward. When present, this is a strong confirmative sign for PSP; however, it often occurs late in the disease if at all. This particular sign is due to degeneration of regions of the substantia nigra that have connections to the superior colliculus.

Cranial nerve damage results in ipsilateral sensory and motor deficits. Motor deficits are characterized by weakness and flaccid muscle tone. Damage to the UMNs in the brainstem prior to where they cross over and synapse in cranial nerve motor nuclei will cause contralateral motor deficits.

Speech Disorders

Damage to cranial nerves with motor functions will cause ipsilateral flaccid weakness. For those cranial nerves involved in speech production, this will present as flaccid dysarthria and the specific characteristics will be related to the function of the affected CN (Table 11–1). Over time, fasciculations will appear as individual muscle fibers spontaneously contract, and the affected muscle(s) will atrophy.

Damage to the facial nerve will result in ipsilateral weakness of the face. Weakness of the lips will impact production of labial consonants, vowels dependent upon lip shape, and pressure consonants like /p/ and /b/ that require a tight lip seal to create the burst of air. Damage to UMNs that synapse with facial nerve LMNs causes spastic weakness of the contralateral lower face. The impact on speech production will be similar to LMN damage.

Characteristics of flaccid dysarthria related to the vagus nerve will depend upon which branch(es) are affected. Damage to the pharyngeal branch will result in hypernasality, especially with pressure consonants because the velum will not be able to completely seal off the nasopharynx. Damage to the superior laryngeal nerve will reduce the ability to change pitch due to weakness of the cricothyroid muscle. Recurrent laryngeal nerve damage will result in ipsilateral vocal fold paresis or paralysis. Voicing will be hoarse and breathy because the vocal folds will not achieve adduction. Over time, the affected vocal fold will atrophy. The resulting difference in the thickness of the two vocal folds will cause **diplophonia** or voicing

Table 11–1. Consequences of Lower Motor Neuron (Cranial Nerve) Damage. All Weakness Will Be Ipsilateral to the Lesion

	General Findings	Speech	Swallowing
Trigeminal	Ipsilateral flaccid weakness of muscles of mastication; reduced sensation of the face	Minimal effect	Reduced chewing force on affected side
Facial	Ipsilateral flaccid weakness of the entire half of the face	Air escapes with plosive consonants; slight distortion of vowels dependent upon lip shape	Pocketing of food on weak side; drooling from weak side
Vagus	Ipsilateral flaccid weakness; may be restricted to a single branch depending on location of the lesion Pharyngeal: weakness of velum and pharyngeal muscles Superior laryngeal nerve: weakness of ipsilateral cricothyroid muscle; reduced somatosensation from larynx above the vocal folds Recurrent laryngeal nerve: paralysis of ipsilateral vocal fold	Pharyngeal branch: hypernasality Superior laryngeal nerve: reduced pitch variation Recurrent laryngeal nerve: weak, breathy, hoarse voice, diplophonia develops over time	Pharyngeal branch: nasal regurgitation Slowed movement of bolus, pooling in the valleculae and pyriform sinuses on the affected side Superior laryngeal nerve: reduced cough reflex due to reduced sensitivity of laryngeal tissues Recurrent laryngeal nerve: increased risk of penetration & aspiration due to inadequate vocal fold adduction

continues

Table 11-1. *continued*			
	General Findings	**Speech**	**Swallowing**
Hypoglossal	Unilateral weakness of the tongue	Slight imprecision of articulation, more pronounced for velars than other consonants	Difficulties moving food onto chewing surface of teeth on affected side; difficulty clearing food that is pocketed in cheek on the affected side.
Pharyngeal Plexus	Reduced velopharyngeal closure/seal, reduced pharyngeal constriction, reduced laryngeal adduction (ipsilateral to lesion)	Hypernasality, breathiness	Reduced pharyngeal clearance (ipsilateral to lesion), pooling in pyriform sinuses due to reduced cricopharyngeal opening (ipsilateral to lesion), risk of aspiration

with two pitches as the two vocal folds vibrate at different frequencies. UMN damage will affect all branches. Voice quality will be harsh, often described as strained-strangled with hypernasality and reduced range and control of pitch.

Hypoglossal nerve damage will result in weakness of the ipsilateral tongue and over time fasciculations and atrophy will occur. Range of motion will be reduced. Articulation will be relatively good, as the tongue has more strength than needed for speech production. UMN damage will have similar consequences: weakness, but resulting in mild dysarthria at best.

Damage to trigeminal, glossopharyngeal, and spinal accessory nerves rarely cause dysarthria because they each have a relatively small role in sensorimotor control for speech production.

A stroke or tumor also can affect the UMNs descending through the brainstem or the cranial nerve nuclei themselves (Table 11-2). Such damage would create spastic weakness. Whether the symptoms are ipsilateral or contralateral to the lesion depends on if the damage is located before (contralateral) or after (ipsilateral) UMN axons decussate.

PSP, because it affects multiple regions of the CNS, often causes a mixed dysarthria that can have characteristics of hyperkinetic, hypokinetic, spastic, and even ataxic dysarthria. The specific presentation can change over time with increasing degeneration of different areas of the brain.

	General Findings	Speech	Swallowing
Trigeminal	Spastic weakness of muscles of mastication; reduced facial sensation	Minimal effect	Reduced chewing force on affected side
Facial	Spastic weakness of the contralateral lower face; upper face movement (e.g., raising eyebrows) is intact	Air escapes with plosive consonants; slight distortion of vowels dependent upon lip shape	Pocketing of food on weak side; drooling from weak side
Vagus	All branches will be affected similarly. Spastic weakness of velar, pharyngeal, and laryngeal muscles.	Slow speech production; mild hypernasality; strained-strangled vocal quality due to laryngeal muscle spasticity	Nasal regurgitation; pharyngeal dysphagia with slowed movement of bolus; potential for pooling in pyriform sinuses and valleculae with risk of aspiration
Hypoglossal	Spastic weakness of the tongue	Slight imprecision of articulation, more pronounced for velars than other consonants	Difficulties moving food onto chewing surface of teeth on affected side; difficulty clearing food that is pocketed in cheek on the affected side.
Pharyngeal Plexus	Reduced velopharyngeal closure/seal, reduced pharyngeal constriction, reduced laryngeal adduction	Hypernasality, breathiness	Nasal regurgitation, reduced pharyngeal pressures resulting in Reduced pharyngeal clearance, pooling in pyriform sinuses due to reduced cricopharyngeal opening, risk of aspiration

Table 11–2. Consequences of Upper Motor Neuron Damage. All Effects Will Be Unilateral and Typically Contralateral* to the Lesion

*If UMN damage occurs after the fibers cross over in the brainstem, the signs/symptoms will be ipsilateral.

Language Disorders

Language disorders are not expected with damage to the brainstem. Cortico-cerebellar connections that support language may be affected, but diagnoses of aphasia or apragmatism are rare. If they do occur, traditional methods of assessment and treatment (covered in Chapters 7 and 8) could be used.

Cognitive Disorders

Cognitive disorders are typically not directly related to brainstem damage. However, damage to the reticular formation can affect cortical arousal and attention processes. Disorders of consciousness include **coma, unresponsive wakefulness syndrome (vegetative state)**, and **minimally conscious state** that are defined by the level of wakefulness and awareness (Goldfine & Schiff, 2011). In a coma, the person is not awake and is not responsive to any stimulation. In unresponsive wakefulness syndrome, patients have periods of wakefulness where they open their eyes and have some reflexive, generalized movements. In this state, their responses are not purposeful; they may show movements (blinking or gross hand or leg movement) that appear to correspond with stimulation or commands, but the correspondence is reflexive or coincidental. Patients in minimally conscious states have longer periods of wakefulness and have some purposeful responses, such as following people with their eyes, responding to simple commands such as opening their eyes or mouth, or squeezing someone's hand. They may respond to simple yes/no questions or commands although the responses are inconsistent and not always accurate.

In PSP, anywhere from 30 to 80% of patients show changes in cognition, with increasing incidence as the disease progresses. Cognitive deficits include slowed thinking; executive dysfunction; and poor initiation, planning, and abstract thinking. Such deficits affect their ability to make medical decisions (Gerstenecker et al., 2019). Patients may be aware of some of their deficits, but may not be able to inhibit perseverative or inappropriate movements. They tend to be apathetic about their disease and deficits so while they can report awareness, they do not seem to care.

Swallowing Disorders

Swallowing disorders associated with cranial nerve damage can be characterized by phases of swallowing (Refer back to Table 11–1). Oral preparatory phase function is affected by damage to trigeminal (motor or sensory—reduced mastication strength; reduced oral sensation), facial (motor or sensory—pocketing and drooling), and hypoglossal (motor—reduced bolus formation/cohesion). Oral phase function is primarily affected by damage to the hypoglossal nerve (motor—reduced tongue base retraction). Pharyngeal phase function can be affected by damage to the pharyngeal plexus (motor—pharyngeal constriction, reduced hyolaryngeal excursion) and vagus nerve (motor—reduced velopharyngeal closure, reduced pharyngeal constriction, and reduced laryngeal closure; sensory—reduced pharyngeal and laryngeal sensation). Esophageal function can be affected by upstream factors, such as reduced pharyngeal constriction leading to poor opening of the cricopharyngeus.

Dysphagia often occurs later in the progression of PSP but early relative to Parkinson disease. Oral preparatory impairments include poor bolus control and reduced mastication (Clark et al., 2020). Oral phase impairments include reduced bolus propulsion and oral clearance. Pharyngeal impairments include delayed swallow onset, impaired velar function, and pharyngeal residue. Esophageal dysfunction includes reduced cricopharyngeal opening and esophageal dysmotility. It is typically associated with aspiration.

Assessment and treatment of dysphagia are covered in Chapter 13.

Cerebellum

The cerebellum plays a critical role in sensorimotor functions including motor learning, error correction, balance and equilibrium, and coordination of complex sequential movements. It also has extensive connections with cortical structures involved in cognition and language.

Motorically, damage to the cerebellum results in several characteristic motor signs: **decomposition of movement**, **hypotonia**, **ataxia**, **astasia-abasia** (difficulty standing and walking), and **intention tremor** (also called cerebellar tremor). Decomposition of movement is just what it sounds like. Movements that require multiple joints or muscle groups are no longer performed smoothly, but in small segments sequentially. For example, when picking up a spoon off of a table, there is a smooth coordination of flexion/extension at the shoulder, elbow, wrist, and finger joints. Cerebellar damage can result in a segmented series of movements first at the shoulder then the elbow, followed by the wrist and then the fingers.

Hypotonia, or reduced muscle tone can be seen in the limbs, along with reduced damping or stopping of a reflexive movement. The latter is often referred to as pendular reflexes because instead of a rapid jerking movement that quickly stops, the initial movement is followed by a continuing to-and-fro motion.

Box 11-3 Pendular Reflexes

When your patellar tendon reflex is tested, a doctor lightly taps the tendon extending from your patella (kneecap) to your lower leg. This creates a reflexive extension of your knee joint. In normal reflexes, there is a quick extension of the leg and then it returns to its original position. The rapidity of the quelling or damping of the movement is due in part to descending cerebellar signals. In cerebellar damage this damping effect is decreased or lost. In this case, after the initial extension of your leg, it would continue to swing out and back like a pendulum on a clock, each time with a little shorter excursion until it finally stopped. The action is a bit like a playground swing, swinging less and less until it stops.

Ataxia, or uncoordinated movements, involve both inaccurate movements, called **dysmetria**, and **dysdiadochokinesis**, which is difficulty with alternating movements. Dysmetria includes both hypermetria, or overshoot and hypometria, or undershoot. One typical screening task is the finger-to-nose task. The physician will ask the patient to touch their nose and then her finger, then back to nose. She will move her finger each time so the movement has to change direction after each touch of the nose. Hypermetria happens when the person reaches too far and overshoots the target. Hypometria is when the patient does not reach far enough to touch the physician's finger.

Astasia and abasia affect walking and standing, respectively. Astasia is difficulty walking due to loss of precise coordination of multiple joints and muscle groups. Essentially, the muscles and joints of the limbs and trunk do not work together for a common goal. Abasia is difficulty standing or sitting upright against the force of gravity. We rarely think about the effect of gravity on our daily lives, but when we're sitting or standing, our trunk and leg muscles must have a constant level of contraction to counteract the force of gravity which would pull us down to the ground. The loss of the cerebellar contribution to this muscle contraction makes it difficult to maintain an upright posture.

Intention tremors appear only once an action is started and typically increase the closer one gets to the target. This is in contrast to the resting tremor of Parkinson disease, in which the tremor is apparent at rest and ceases once movement starts.

Deficits in language, cognition, and affect related to cerebellar damage started appearing in research papers in the 1950s (Schmahmann, 2001). Today, the consensus is that the cerebellum modulates, but does not generate, communication and cognitive functions. In other words, it does not generate words, syntactic constructions, or plans to achieve goals, but rather regulates and modifies the timing, sequencing, adaptation, and automatization of language and cognitive skills. There are several theories of how the cerebellum carries out these functions. One is dysmetria of thought, which extends the motor timing function to the timing and selection of cognitive and language processes (Schmahmann, 2001). Disruption of the timing of selecting, integrating, and producing responses results in difficulties with language

Box 11-4 Resting Versus Intention Tremors

Imagine two patients, one with PD and one with cerebellar damage, each sitting at the doctor's office and asked to sign their name on a medical form. The person with PD and a resting tremor would show pill-rolling hand tremors as they sat quietly. Once they started to move their arm to pick up the pen, the tremors would cease, and they could sign their name. The person with cerebellar intention tremor would show no tremors while sitting quietly. The tremors would begin when they lifted their arm, and the tremors would increase in amplitude the closer their hand came to the pen. They may have significant difficulty producing a legible signature due to the intention tremor.

comprehension and production. A second theory is that cerebellar damage causes difficulty with forming internal models, such as identifying and integrating features of a stimulus and the context in which it occurs and adjusting interpretations and responses based on feedback (Stoodley, 2012). Other models suggest that language and cognitive deficits are caused by cerebellar diaschisis. In this model, the loss of excitatory cerebello-cerebral signals alters the blood flow to cortical regions responsible for language and cognitive functions. Finally, there may be direct influences of the cerebellum on cortical regions of the frontal and parietal lobes through feedforward (cortico-ponto-cerebellar) and feedback (cerebello-thalamo-cortical) pathways (de Smet et al., 2007; Paquier & Mariën, 2005).

Disorders and Diseases of the Cerebellum

There are a variety of causes of cerebellar lesions or dysfunction. Strokes can occur due to interruption of the vertebrobasilar blood flow. There are also several hereditary degenerative diseases of the cerebellum.

Friedreich ataxia has onset in childhood with unsteady gait that expands to ataxia of the upper limbs and dysarthria, followed by cognitive decline (Refer to Box 5–4 in Chapter 5). Most people do not survive past middle age.

Spinocerebellar ataxia (SCA) is a degenerative genetic disease that affects the cerebellum and associated structures. There are over 40 different types depending on the specific gene mutation. The presentations always include ataxia with other symptoms varying according to other structures affected. These can include oculomotor disorders, parkinsonism, peripheral neuropathy, dysautonomia, cognitive impairment, sleep disturbances, and chronic pain.

Non-hereditary diseases and disorders that affect the cerebellum include traumatic brain injury, multiple sclerosis, and multiple system atrophy. The cerebellum can be affected by systemic disorders (e.g., alcoholism, celiac disease, heatstroke, hypothyroidism, and deficiencies of thiamin or vitamin E) and some toxins (e.g., carbon monoxide and some heavy metals).

Speech Disorders

Due to the role of the cerebellum in coordination of complex and sequential movements, damage often results in **ataxic dysarthria**. This type of dysarthria is characterized by inconsistent or irregular productions across the speech components, including articulatory breakdowns, irregular production of sequential movement rates, variations in loudness, and altered prosody (Table 11–3). The prosody often is described as "excess and equal stress" or "scanning speech" as each syllable is produced with the same amount of stress (i.e., duration and loudness) instead of a combination of strong and weak syllables.

In addition to problems with coordination within systems, coordination across multiple muscle groups is interrupted. For example, voicing and articulation are not synced as they should be. This leads to voicing of unvoiced consonants or devoicing of voiced consonants.

Table 11–3. Speech and Resonance Characteristics of Ataxic Dysarthria

Vocal Characteristic	Ataxic Dysarthria
Respiration	Variation in loudness
Phonation	Variation in loudness, monopitch, harsh vocal quality
Articulation	Irregular articulatory breakdowns, distorted vowels, prolonged phonemes
Resonance	Irregular hypo/hypernasality
Prosody	Excess and equal stress
Other	"Drunken" sounding speech; complaints of stumbling over sounds or words

Essentially, /p/ can sound like /b/ and vice versa. Coordination of velar movement also is affected, so there can be intermittent hyper- or hyponasality.

Language Disorders

In 2014, a group of researchers developed a consensus paper to summarize the prevailing understanding about the cerebellum's role in language (Mariën et al., 2014). They concluded that cerebellar damage affects various levels of language. A summary of these and other findings are provided in Table 11–4.

There is no standard agreement on the use of the label "aphasia" for the language deficits associated with cerebellar damage. This is in part due to the heterogeneity of presentation: not every person with cerebellar damage presents with the same pattern of language deficits. It also may reflect the reluctance of some people to use the term aphasia when there is not observable damage to the left perisylvian area (refer to Box 10–4). The cerebellum has been proposed as a component of a network for emotional prosody (Grandjean, 2021). As such, damage could cause emotional aprosodia.

Cognitive Disorders

Cerebellar damage can affect a variety of cognitive functions including attention, memory, visuospatial processing, and executive function. Whether they are present or not depends on the location of damage, both in terms of the functional area(s) and the hemi-

Table 11–4. Cerebellar Effects on Speech, Language, and Cognition

Language Domain	Potential Deficits or Disorders
Speech and Language Perception	Phonetic timing; segregation of auditory signal; binding cross-modal stimuli
Verbal Fluency	Sequencing
Syntax	Inconsistent and limited evidence of disruptions but may cause expressive or receptive agrammatism
Language Production	Anomia and paraphasias (semantic or phonemic)
Reading	Incoordination of eye movements, attention disruption, as well as phonological and semantic processing deficits can impact reading ability
Writing	Spatial dysgraphia; central agraphia
Higher Level Language	Word association, figurative language, semantic absurdities
Pragmatics	Impulsive, inappropriate behaviors with inappropriate overfamiliarity
Verbal Working Memory	Articulatory control processes such as phonological recoding and storage

sphere affected. Due to contralateral connections between the cerebellum and cerebrum, language processing is affected most often after right cerebellar damage, while visuospatial deficits are most commonly associated with left cerebellar damage. Impairments in working memory, executive function, and emotional processing are seen with bilateral damage (Stoodley, 2012).

After studying groups of patients with cerebellar lesions, Schmahmann and Sherman described a common collection of symptoms and called it Cerebellar Cognitive Affective Syndrome (Schmahmann, 2001). This syndrome includes executive function deficits such as planning, reasoning, working memory, verbal fluency, and set shifting; spatial cognition, visuospatial disorganization, and visuospatial memory; and linguistic changes including aprosodia, agrammatism, and anomia. These are accompanied by personality changes such as flat affect, disinhibition, and inappropriate behaviors. Other deficits include changes to both implicit and procedural learning, and visuospatial deficits in mental rotation, orientation, and navigation. In terms of pragmatics and social cognition, identification and interpretation of facial and prosodic cues can be affected, and some people show reduced empathy after cerebellar lesions.

Swallowing Disorders

Given the complex sensorimotor processes involved in swallowing, it is not surprising that cerebellar damage can cause dysphagia. Similar to thalamic lesions, however, there are few studies examining specific characteristics of cerebellar dysphagia. Disruption of coordination of the sequencing and timing of oral, lingual, pharyngeal, and/or esophageal musculature can result in oropharyngeal and/or esophageal dysphagia. Individuals with cerebellar lesions due to diseases that affect multiple neural structures, such as multiple systems atrophy (MSA) or forms of SCA that involve multiple structures, are more likely to have dysphagia than those with damage restricted to the cerebellum (Rangarathnam et al., 2014). In one study of people with SCA the most common symptom was coughing and choking, both on food/liquid and on saliva (Vogel et al., 2015).

Summary

The brainstem and cerebellum have extensive connections with the cerebral hemispheres and also sensory and motor projection tracts that connect the brain with the body. Impairments can be caused by direct damage to those structures or to the pathways to and from cerebral structures. Damage due to tumor, disease, stroke, or other brain injuries can have widespread impacts on communication, cognition, and swallowing.

Key Concepts

- The 12 pairs of cranial nerves each have a specific area of innervation; damage will lead to sensory impairments and/or weakness of that specific area.
- Six pairs of cranial nerves innervate structures with core functions for speech and swallowing.
- Flaccid dysarthria is caused by damage to cranial nerve lower motor neurons. Spastic dysarthria results from brainstem damage to upper motor neurons that synapse onto LMNs.
- Language and cognitive disorders are rare after brainstem lesions.
- Swallowing can be impaired with damage to any of the cranial nerves that innervate oral, pharyngeal, or laryngeal structures.
- Cerebellar lesions can cause ataxic dysarthria.
- Disruptions in timing and coordination of movements due to cerebellar damage can affect any phase of swallowing.
- Damage to the cerebellum can affect various aspects of language and cognition.

References

Clark, H. M., Stierwalt, J. A., Tosakulwong, N., Botha, H., Ali, F., Whitwell, J. L., & Josephs, K. A. (2020). Dysphagia in progressive supranuclear palsy. *Dysphagia, 35*, 667–676.

de Smet, H. J., Baillieux, H., de Deyn, P. P., Mariën, P., & Paquier, P. (2007). The cerebellum and language: The story so far. *Folia Phoniatrica et Logopaedica, 59*(4), 165–170. https://doi.org/10.1159/000102927

Gerstenecker, A., Grimsley, L., Otruba, B., Cowden, L., Marson, D. C., Gerstenecker, K. T., . . . Roberson, E. D. (2019). Medical decision-making in progressive supranuclear palsy: A comparison to other neurodegenerative disorders. *Parkinsonism & Related Disorders, 61*, 77–81.

Goldfine, A. M. & Schiff, N. D. (2011). Consciousness: Its neurobiology and the major classes of impairment. *Neurologic Clinics, 29*(4), 723–737. https://doi.org/10.1016/j.ncl.2011.08.001

Grandjean, D. (2021). Brain networks of emotional prosody processing. *Emotion Review, 13*(1), 34–43.

Grinberg, L., Rueb, U., & Heinsen, H. (2011). Brainstem: Neglected locus in neurodegenerative diseases. *Frontiers in Neurology, 2*. https://www.frontiersin.org/articles/10.3389/fneur.2011.00042

Hu, J., Western, S., & Kesari, S. (2016). Brainstem glioma in adults. *Frontiers in Oncology, 6*. https://doi.org/10.3389/fonc.2016.00180

Mariën, P., Ackermann, H., Adamaszek, M., Barwood, C. H. S., Beaton, A., Desmond, J. . . . Ziegler, W. (2014). Consensus paper: Language and the cerebellum: An ongoing enigma. *Cerebellum, 13*(3), 386–410. https://doi.org/10.1007/s12311-013-0540-5

Paquier, P. F., & Mariën, P. (2005). A synthesis of the role of the cerebellum in cognition. *Aphasiology, 19*(1), 3–19. https://doi.org/10.1080/02687030444000615

Rangarathnam, B., Kamarunas, E., & McCullough, G. H. (2014). Role of cerebellum in deglutition and deglutition disorders. *Cerebellum, 13*(6), 767–776. https://doi.org/10.1007/s12311-014-0584-1

Reyes-Botero, G., Mokhtari, K., Martin-Duverneuil, N., Delattre, J.-Y., & Laigle-Donadey, F. (2012). Adult brainstem gliomas. *The Oncologist, 17*(3), 388–397. https://doi.org/10.1634/theoncologist.2011-0335

Schmahmann, J. D. (2001). The cerebellar cognitive affective syndrome: Clinical correlations of the dysmetria of thought hypothesis. *International Review of Psychiatry, 13*(4), 313–322. https://doi.org/10.1080/09540260120082164

Stoodley, C. J. (2012). The cerebellum and cognition: Evidence from functional imaging studies. *Cerebellum, 11*(2), 352–365. https://doi.org/10.1007/s12311-011-0260-7

Swallow, D. M. A., Zheng, C. S., & Counsell, C. E. (2022). Systematic review of prevalence studies of progressive supranuclear palsy and corticobasal syndrome. *Movement Disorders Clinical Practice, 9*(5), 604–613. https://doi.org/10.1002/mdc3.13489

Vogel, A. P., Fendel, L., Brubacher, K. P., Chan, V., & Maule, R. (2015). Dysphagia in spinocerebellar ataxia and multiple system atrophy-cerebellar. *Speech, Language and Hearing, 18*(1), 39–43. https://doi.org/10.1179/2050572814Y.0000000047

12
ASSESSMENT AND TREATMENT OF COGNITIVE DISORDERS

> **Chapter Overview**
>
> Assessment of Cognitive Disorders
>   Approaches to Assessment
>   Test Batteries and Participation-Level Assessments
>   Attention
>   Executive Function and Awareness
>   Memory
>   Social Cognition
>   Goal Attainment Scales
> Treatment of Cognitive Disorders
>   Approaches to Treatment
>   Metacognitive Strategy Training
>   Generalized Attention
>   Executive Function and Anosognosia
>   Memory
>   Social Cognition
> Summary
> Key Concepts
> References

Assessment of Cognitive Disorders

As described in Chapters 6, 7, and 8, cognitive disorders of attention, memory, executive function, and social cognition can occur after damage to the perisylvian region of either hemisphere or to the frontal lobes. The specific presentation of the disorders often differs based on location and extent of lesions, especially in consideration of the co-occurring communication strengths and weaknesses. Despite these differences, most assessment and treatment tools and approaches can be used regardless of the location of the brain damage, and then the results should be interpreted within the broader context of the whole person and all of the strengths and weaknesses they present. This is particularly important when cognitive disorders are suspected to co-occur with aphasia, as most of these assessments and treatments are language-based. This chapter covers the four primary domains of cognition (attention, memory, executive function, social cognition) used throughout the book. Pragmatic aspects of communication, such as discourse comprehension and production, are covered in Chapter 8.

This is not designed to be a comprehensive review of assessments or treatments, but rather to provide basic guidance for approaching assessment and treatment. Additionally, understanding how cognitive domains are assessed can increase understanding of those domains and how they function in daily life.

Approaches to Assessment

Cognition underlies all aspects of communication, and both influences and is influenced by a variety of personal and environmental factors. Think about how your ability to study and perform well on an exam is affected by your mood, emotions, and confidence level; how tired, hungry, or healthy you are; or whether the room is hot, cold, noisy, or too quiet. A thorough assessment will involve examination not only of the body structures and functions (e.g., attention, memory, executive function), but also activity- and participation-level functions (refer back to the WHO-ICF model in Figures 5–1 and 5–2). The assessment should include consideration of personal and environmental factors and how they either facilitate or impede success.

SLPs need a strong knowledge of cognitive domains and how they interact with and influence communication; the best, most reliable and valid ways of assessing them; and how to administer, interpret, and report the results. Providing education about cognitive abilities and deficits and communicating the assessment results to clients and family members or caregivers also are important skills. General principles for cognitive assessment based on work by MacDonald and Shumway (2022) are provided in Table 12–1.

The Contextualized Hypothesis Testing Assessment model (Ylvisaker & Gioia, 1998) is one way to conduct a thorough assessment while determining strengths and weaknesses. The assessment activity and context should parallel a real-life activity for the individual (e.g., work-like tasks, school-homework tasks, etc.). Like real-life contexts, demands should fluctuate up and down to determine the effects and necessary adjustments. There are four principles of this model: (1) Assessment does not happen just once or in just one context. The process of assessment should continue as long as there are changes in the patient's abilities or environments. (2) Assessments should be done within realistic, functional contexts. Assessing attention in a quiet room may have little relevance to the patient's ability to attend to an activity in other spaces. (3) Assessments should involve a variety of people

Table 12–1. Evidence-Based Principles for Cognitive-Communication Assessment

Principle	Description
SLP Assessment Knowledge	SLPs should have or seek out knowledge and skills for selecting, administering, and interpreting an appropriate screening or assessment tool based on the client's profile and stage of recovery
Timing	Assessment should begin as early as possible in recovery from acquired brain injury
Comprehensive	Assessments should be comprehensive, including communication, cognition, physical influences (e.g., hearing, vision, motor speech), emotional influences, and control factors (e.g., awareness, self-regulation)
Individualized	Assessments should be developed in consideration of personal, physical, and health factors; severity of cognitive-communication deficits and stage of recovery; and communication contexts and goals
Collaborative Goal Setting	Goals are developed in collaboration with client, family, and other relevant people
Co-occurring or Comorbid Factors	Co-occurring conditions are identified through case history and medical record review, and considered in the assessment and diagnostic process. These can include fatigue, sleep challenges, depression, pain, anxiety, etc.
Assessment Measure Selection	Selection of assessments involves consideration of: • Sensitivity and scope to identify cognitive-communication disorders • Ability to characterize components contributing to communication performance • Ability for results to generalize to functional settings • Ability to inform treatment planning
Assessment Measures: Standardized	Measures should be selected based on reliability, validity, and sensitivity and specificity for identifying cognitive-communication disorders; and administered in line with standardization procedures; additional informal or observational assessment may be needed to create a full picture of the individual's abilities

continues

Table 12–1. *continued*

Principle	Description
Assessment Measures: Contextual (Activity & Participation; Individual & Close Other)	In recognition of the limitations of standardized impairment-level assessments especially for subtle deficits, contextualized assessment of communication should be used including interviews, checklists, activity-level assessments, patient-reported outcome measures, observations, and evaluation of environmental demands that impact communication
Assessment Measures: Communication	SLPS should prioritize communication given that we have specialized knowledge and training regarding communication, and because communication is an essential human ability
Collaborative Contextualized Hypothesis Testing	Assessment should involve collaboration with other medical and rehabilitation professionals and should be designed to identify strengths, weaknesses, and factors that facilitate or impede communication and full social participation
Communication Partners	Examine the resources and skills that potential communication partners bring and their willingness and ability to learn and provide additional supports as needed
Environmental Demands	Consider the situations, contexts, and environments where individuals live and communicate, and the demands that influence success
Assessment Interpretation or Formulation	Interpretation of assessment results should occur in relation to the individual and family's goals and preferences; encompass impairment, activity and participation levels; and consider environmental barriers and facilitators
Communication of Assessment Findings	Comprehensive assessment findings should be clearly communicated both in written and verbal form to all relevant stakeholders (e.g., individual, family, medical team)
Telepractice	Telepractice should be considered as an option for assessment to increase accessibility

Note: Based on MacDonald & Shumway, 2022.

in various contexts. Collaborative assessments are informative—for example, how do the patient's memory deficits affect their ability to learn the steps to transfer from a wheelchair to a bed?—and provide more realistic assessments of the patient's ability to be independent and successful in real life than standardized testing. (4) Assessments should be conducted using a hypothesis testing format to determine internal and external factors that interact with deficits. This allows you to determine the extent to which hunger or fatigue impacts a patient's ability to focus on a treatment task, or how much their dislike of a fellow patient impacts their success in a conversational exchange.

Test Batteries and Participation-Level Assessments

Often SLPs will begin an assessment with a test battery that covers a variety of domains (Table 12–2). This will provide an overall picture of the patient's relative strengths and weaknesses. This can be followed by more targeted and more sensitive evaluation of specific areas. For example, if a patient performs poorly on attentional tasks in the test battery, the clinician may decide to administer a specific test of attention to determine what type(s) of attention are impaired.

Attention

There are a variety of tests and tasks used to assess general attention (Table 12–3). Tests for unilateral neglect are covered in Chapter 8. Attention tests typically include a series of

Table 12–2. Select Cognitive Test Batteries

Test/Authors	Domains	Notes
Cognitive Linguistic Quick Test-Plus (CLQT+; Helm-Estabrooks, 2017)	Attention, memory, language, visuospatial skills, executive function	Can be used with people with aphasia Ages 18–89 Spanish & English versions
Burns Brief Inventory of Communication and Cognition (Burns, 1997)	Language (comprehension, production, reading, writing), visuospatial skills, prosody, abstract language, orientation, memory, visual perception, auditory & visual attention	Separate inventories for right hemisphere, left hemisphere, and complex neuropathology Ages 18–80

continues

Test/Authors	Domains	Notes
Repeatable Battery for the Assessment of Neuropsychological Status Update (RBANS Update; Randolph, 2012)	Memory (immediate & delayed), visuospatial and visuoconstruction skills, language, attention	Can be used as screening tool or full assessment Spanish & English versions Ages 12 and up
Scales of Cognitive & Communicative Ability for Neurorehabilitation (SCCAN; Milman & Holland, 2012)	Language (comprehension, production, reading, writing), orientation, memory, attention, problem solving	Can be used with people with aphasia Ages 18–90
Scales of Cognitive Ability for Traumatic Brain Injury (SCATBI; Adamovich & Henderson, 1992)	Perception, orientation, organization, recall, reasoning	Appropriate for mild as well as more severe deficits Adolescent to adult
Sydney Psychosocial Reintegration Scale – 2 (SPRS-2; Tate, 2011)	Assesses amount of change related to brain injury in 3 areas: work and leisure activities; interpersonal relationships; and living skills	Clinician-guided questionnaire; can also be completed by a close informant (e.g., family member, close friend)

visual or auditory stimuli (shapes, images, tones, or words) that the patient must respond to. Increased complexity can involve presenting two or more different tones, for example, with the instruction that the patient only respond to one of them, and ignore the other. Or could include background noise—white noise, garbled speech, or intelligible speech—that must be ignored in order to respond to the target stimulus. Functional tasks, those that are more similar to everyday activities, include finding targets on a map, menu, or phone book, or listening for lottery numbers in a string of digits.

A thorough assessment involves going beyond the standardized tests and examining a variety of types of attention (focused, sustained, alternating, etc.) with different types of materials: both interesting and boring, and a range of complexity from easy to challenging. Questionnaires or structured conversations with other rehabilitation professionals (occupational or physical therapists) and with family members who spend sufficient time with the person can shed light on what situations are most challenging for focusing or sustaining attention.

Table 12–3. Select Assessments of Attention

Test/Authors	Areas Included	Notes
Brief Test of Attention (Schretlen et al., 1996)	Auditory divided attention	Patient hears a series of digits and/or letters and has to count how many times one target letter/digit occurs
Paced Auditory Serial Addition Task (PASAT; Gronwall, 1977)	Auditory divided and sustained attention	Patient is given a series of digits; they must add each consecutive pair (e.g., given: 1-5-6-8, the person would respond 6 [1+5], 11 [5+6], 14 [6+8])
Ruff Selective Attention Test (Ruff, 1992)	Visual selective and sustained attention	Visual search (identify target numbers amidst letters or other numbers) and cancellation
Symbol Digit Modalities Test (Smith, 1973)	Visual divided attention	Digits are paired with a meaningless symbol, then a series of symbols is shown and the patient has to write down the digit that matches each symbol. Accuracy and speed are recorded.
Sustained Attention to Response Task (SART; Robertson et al., 1997)	Visual sustained attention, working memory, inhibitory control	Computerized go/no-go task; series of numbers are presented, and patient is instructed to respond to some but withhold responding to others
Test of Everyday Attention (TEA; Robertson et al., 1994)	Visual selective and sustained attention; attention switching Auditory working memory	Map reading, phonebook search tasks for visual attention; listening for lottery numbers and counting high- and low-pitched tones to determine movement of an elevator for auditory attention

Source: Adapted from *The Right Hemisphere and Disorders of Cognition and Communication: Theory and Clinical Practice* (p. 117) by Blake, M. L. Copyright © 2018 Plural Publishing, Inc. All rights reserved

Executive Function and Awareness

Tests of executive function have varying levels of **ecological validity** (how well results generalize to everyday abilities), and while they target executive functions, they always involve multiple domains (Table 12–4). For example, nearly all are language-based, require focused or sustained attention, and many have memory demands.

Assessment of awareness typically involves asking a person about their abilities, either generally (what has changed since your stroke/brain injury/diagnosis?) or specifically (are

Box 12-1 Testing Attention

One example of an attentional assessment task is the elevator task from the Test of Everyday Attention (Robertson et al., 1994). There are four variations of the task.

- Elevator counting: In this test of sustained attention, patients/clients are asked to pretend they are in an elevator whose door-indicator is not functioning. They have to figure out which floor the elevator is on by counting a series of tape-presented tones as a measure of sustained attention.
- Elevator counting with distraction: Patients/clients have to count the low tones in the pretend elevator while ignoring the high tones as a test of auditory selective attention.
- Visual elevator: Subjects have to count up and down as they follow a series of visually presented "doors" in the elevator (reversal task) as a measure of attentional switching.
- Auditory elevator with reversal: The same as the visual elevator subtest except that it is presented at fixed speed on tape.

Table 12-4. Select Measures of Executive Function

Test/Authors	Areas Included	Notes
Behavioural Assessment of Dysexecutive Syndrome (BADS; Wilson et al., 1996)	planning, prioritization, problem solving, cognitive flexibility, inhibitory control	Six tasks including planning a path through a zoo, planning a path to find a lost key, sorting cards based on rules (color or number of each color in a row), temporal judgments of how long activities take
Behavior Rating Inventory of Executive Functions (BRIEF; Gioia et al., 2000)	inhibitory control, cognitive shifting, emotional control, working memory, planning, organization, self-monitoring	Adult and child versions. Child version includes teacher- and parent-report scales
Dysexecutive Questionnaire (DEX; Burgess et al., 1996; Wilson et al., 1996)	intentionality, inhibition, executive memory, affect	Self-report measure of how executive dysfunction affects everyday activities often used in conjunction with the BADS

Table 12–4. continued

Test/Authors	Areas Included	Notes
Frontal Systems Behavior Scale (FrSBe) Grace & Malloy, 2001)	intentionality, disinhibition, apathy	Rating scale; forms for self and family; Allows comparisons between pre- and post-injury Adults 18–95 Data for various clinical groups including dementias, TBI, stroke, Huntington and Parkinson
Functional Assessment of Verbal Reasoning and Executive Strategies (FAVRES; MacDonald, 2005)	executive function, verbal reasoning, complex comprehension	Functional tasks include planning schedules and selecting a gift within specific parameters; writing a letter to request a response to a problem; Assesses identifying facts, weighing their importance, generating alternatives, predicting consequences, and generating rationales for answer choices
Student Version – Functional Assessment of Verbal Reasoning and Executive Strategies (S-FAVRES; MacDonald, 2013)	executive function, verbal reasoning, complex comprehension	Functional tasks include planning schedules and selecting a gift within specific parameters; writing a letter to request a response to a problem; Assesses identifying facts, weighing their importance, generating alternatives, predicting consequences, and generating rationales for answer choices. Designed for adolescents 12–19 years
Hayling Sentence Completion Test (Burgess & Shallice 1997)	response inhibition, fluid ability	Sentence competition tasks; one set requires completion with an expected word, the other with a word that does not fit Adults 18–80

continues

Table 12–4. *continued*		
Test/Authors	Areas Included	Notes
Multiple Errands Test (Shallice & Burgess, 1991) MET-Simplified (Alderman et al., 2003) MET-Home (Burns et al., 2019) MET-Hospital Version (Knight, Alderman & Burgess, 2002) VMET (Rand et al., 2009)	planning, strategy allocation	Patients/clients given tasks or errands to be completed. Scores based on efficiency, following rules, accuracy of interpretation, success Several versions available: • MET-SV simplified • MET-Home, for use in a client's home • VMET for virtual administration; • MET-HV hospital version; simplified from original
Naturalistic Action Test (Schwarz et al., 2002)	executive function & strategy allocation	Evaluates accuracy and types of errors made during everyday tasks. Can be used for TBI, dementia, and stroke
Trail Making Test (Reitan, 1958)	mental flexibility, visual scanning, attention	Part A: Task involves connecting numbers 1–25 that are distributed across a page Part B: Task involves alternately connecting numbers and letters (e.g., A-1-B-2 . . .) distributed across a page can be used for TBI and stroke

Source: Adapted from *The Right Hemisphere and Disorders of Cognition and Communication: Theory and Clinical Practice* (pp. 161–162) by Blake, M. L. Copyright © 2018 Plural Publishing, Inc. All rights reserved

you having difficulty controlling your emotions?) (Table 12–5). Awareness of cognition (and pragmatics) in acute stages is particularly challenging to assess because often the patient has not had the opportunity to experience the effects of their brain injury/disease, and thus may not recognize the presence of a deficit. For example, the first few days in the hospital after a brain injury or stroke, a patient is faced with a large number of people coming and going, various tests, and visitors. Everything is provided for them, and they may have few everyday decisions other than perhaps what they want to eat. In this situation, a patient may state that

Box 12–2 The Paradox of Assessing and Intervening for Executive Dysfunction in the Clinic

By definition, executive functions are non-routine, novel, goal-directed behaviors. In contrast, standardized assessments have strict instructions, little relevance to the person's life, and are conducted in quiet, controlled settings. It is very difficult to accurately create an authentic task and environment that is representative of what an individual needs to do in their everyday life.

Shortcomings of assessments that purport to measure executive functions:

- They are administered within environments that lack visual, auditory, and related factors that make everyday contexts more challenging.
- They isolate a specific task, which reduces task complexity and interference from outside factors or other tasks.
- They fail to incorporate emotions, internal states (pain, fatigue, internal thought patterns), and stressors.
- They fail to address stress and time pressure present in novel tasks.

Shortcomings of interventions in clinic contexts:

- They take place in a constrained environment (e.g., prototypical white walled clinic room with a table, chairs, and a garbage can).
- They use contrived tasks instead of the real activities that the individual needs to perform during everyday tasks at work, home, school, and in the community.
- They lack the people, relationship factors, visual and auditory demands, task complexity, distractions, authentic time constraints and stress, emotions, unpredictability and variability of authentic contexts.

Fortunately, we can find out specifically what the individual needs to do and where, modify environments to be more representative of real-life environments, add people and task demands, recreate disruptions and inconsistencies, and create a sense of time pressure. This is a good opportunity to use contextual hypothesis testing as an authentic assessment (Keegan et al., 2023; Ylvisaker & Gioia, 1998) and metacognitive strategy instruction for intervention (Byrnes, 1996; Lawson & Rice, 1989; Ylvisaker et al., 2008).

they have no memory problems (no one can remember the names of all the doctors, nurses, and technicians who come in), and there are no changes to their planning/organization or problem solving. A week later, asked to plan when to tell their family to visit based on their rehab schedule, they may recognize that planning and problem solving are more difficult than they were previously.

Table 12–5. Select Measures of Awareness of Cognition and/or Pragmatics

Test/Authors	Domains	Notes
Awareness Questionnaire (AQ; Sherer, 2004)	Cognition, emotion, pragmatics, hemiparesis, neglect; functional implications of deficits	
Head Injury Behavior Scale (HIBS; Godfrey et al., 2003)	Emotion, pragmatics; functional implications of deficits	
Patient Competency Rating Scale (PCRS; Prigatano & Klonoff, 1998)	Cognition, emotion, pragmatics; Functional implications of deficits	Designed for acute care settings
Patient Competency Rating Scale-NeuroRehab (PCRS-NR; Borgaro & Prigatano, 2003)	Cognition, emotion, pragmatics; Functional implications of deficits	Adapted for rehabilitation settings
Self-Awareness of Deficit Interview (SADI; Fleming et al., 1996)	Cognition, emotion, pragmatics; Functional implications of deficits; Compliance with treatment recommendations	
Visual-Analogue Test for Anosognosia for Language (VATA-L; Cocchini et al., 2010)	Aphasia; Functional implications of deficits	

Source: Adapted from *The Right Hemisphere and Disorders of Cognition and Communication: Theory and Clinical Practice* (p. 184) by Blake, M. L. Copyright © 2018 Plural Publishing, Inc. All rights reserved

As described in Chapter 4, awareness is both implicit and explicit. The questionnaires and rating scales all assess explicit awareness: tell me what you notice is wrong, or different. A good assessment will involve observing the individual to see if they implicitly change their behaviors, or if they have emotional responses to challenges even if they verbally report not having any changes or challenges. A person with memory deficits may ask if they can write things down (sometimes accompanied by a comment about how they don't have memory problems, but they used to write lists prior to their brain injury); people with brain injury who do not report any executive function deficits may show visible frustration, anger, or anxiety when given a task that is challenging. These are indicators of implicit awareness.

Memory

Assessment of memory may be the most intuitive of the cognitive domains, perhaps because we all have taken many tests throughout school that assess what we remember and learned from class, a book, a movie, etc. Tests can include visual or auditory tasks, and can include verbal (language) or visual (symbols, images) stimuli (Table 12–6). Most assess short term memory. Some ask patients to guess how well they will do on the test, which adds a metamemory component.

Social Cognition

Assessment of social cognition has its own challenges, given that it is nearly impossible to re-create a naturalistic social interaction in a standardized setting. Many assessments focus on specific components of social cognition, such as identification or interpretation of emotional

Table 12–6. Select Assessments of Memory

Test/Authors	Areas Included	Notes
Brief Assessment of Prospective Memory (BAPM; Man et al., 2011)	Prospective memory	Shortened version of the Comprehensive Assessment of Prospective Memory (CAPM); Self-report of frequency of forgetting items/activities Ages 16–90
Cambridge Test of Prospective Memory (CAMPPROMPT; Emslie et al., 2005)	Prospective memory	Time and event-based tasks to assess whether people remember to do tasks within specified time intervals Designed for adults
Comprehensive Assessment of Prospective Memory (CAPM; Shum & Fleming, 2014)	Prospective memory	Self-report of frequency of forgetting items/activities, importance of memory lapses, reasons for remembering or forgetting
Contextual Memory Test-2 (CMT-2; Toglia, 2019)	Metamemory	Predictions of performance on immediate and delayed recall of objects in a scene; evaluation of use of strategies Ages 7–adulthood Online version available
Everyday Memory Questionnaire-Revised (Royle & Lincoln, 2008)	Metamemory	Questionnaire assessing frequency of forgetting daily activities Designed for adults

continues

Table 12–6. continued

Test/Authors	Areas Included	Notes
N-Back Tasks (Cohen et al., 1994)	Short-term and working memory	Series of stimuli (digits, letters, images, words) presented, clients must report the one that was N-back (e.g., 1 back, 2 back, 3 back . . .)
Oxford Cognitive Screen–Memory Subtests (Demeyere et al., 2015)	Orientation, episodic memory	Recall and recognition tasks Computerized (tablet) version available Designed for adults
Prospective and Retrospective Memory Questionnaire (PRMQ; Smith et al., 2000)	Prospective & retrospective memory	Self- and proxy-report Designed for research purposes; clinical validity not ensured Available in over 25 languages
Rivermead Behavioral Memory Test, 3rd Edition (RBMT-3; Wilson et al., 2017)	"Everyday memory"	Stories for recall of verbal information; multicultural pictures for face recognition; new skill learning Ages 16–89

Source: Adapted from *The Right Hemisphere and Disorders of Cognition and Communication: Theory and Clinical Practice* (pp. 199–200) by Blake, M. L. Copyright © 2018 Plural Publishing, Inc. All rights reserved

cues (Table 12–7). Clinicians should supplement standardized tests with informal assessment or observation of patients in communicative contexts.

Goal Attainment Scales

Goal attainment scales (GAS) are a tool for collaborative goal setting and evaluation. In this process, clients set and measure their own goals. This includes (1) self-selected goal targets, (2) self-assessed performance outcomes, and (3) review of concrete evidence to elicit self-confrontation. This increases their awareness and ownership of their goals, as well as motivating change. GAS have been shown to increase goal achievement (Hoepner et al., 2021; Malec, 1999; Turner-Stokes, 2009). Table 12–8 provides a generic framework for setting and measuring goals through GAS (Hoepner, 2023). The overarching goal and levels 1 to 5

Table 12-7. Select Measures of Social Cognition

Test/Authors	Areas Included	Notes
Levels of Emotional Awareness Scale (Lane et al., 1990)	Emotional awareness—body sensations, general emotions, specific emotions, combinations of emotions	Describe your feelings and those of characters in scenarios Adult and child versions
Reading the Mind in the Eyes Test (RMET; Baron-Cohen, 2001)	Recognition of emotions	Created for autism assessment Identify emotion conveyed by photos of people's eyes Available in over 30 languages Ages 16 to adult
The Awareness of Social Inference Test (McDonald et al., 2003)	Emotion identification, interpretation of sarcasm and white lies	Video scenarios of interactions; identify what was meant and how it made people feel. Ages 13–75
Self-Report Tools		
Balanced Emotional Empathy Scale (BEES; Mehrabian, 1996)	Emotional empathy	Self-report of ability to experience other people's feelings or emotions Designed for adults
Bermond-Vorst Alexithymia Questionnaire (Vorst & Bermond, 2001)	Emotional abilities and processes	Self-report questionnaire Ages 18 and up
Empathy Quotient (Baron-Cohen & Wheelwright, 2004)	Empathy	Self-report questionnaire; short version available Designed for adults
Faux-Pas Recognition Test (Gregory et al., 2002; Stone et al., 1998)	Recognition of appropriate and inappropriate social interactions	Scenarios of interactions; patient must decide if a social faux-pas occurred Adult & child versions available Available in over 15 languages

continues

Table 12–7. continued

Test/Authors	Areas Included	Notes
Interpersonal Reactivity Index (IRI; Davis, 1980)	Empathy, perspective-taking, personal distress, and fantasy	Self-report Designed for adults
Toronto Alexithymia Scale (Bagby et al., 1994)	Identifying and describing emotions and externally focused thinking	Self-report questionnaire Ages 16 to adult

Table 12–8. Self-Selected Goal Attainment Scale Framework

		Goal: This goal should be framed in the client/family's words or words they agree upon and understand.
+2	5	Dream a little—if you woke up tomorrow morning and everything was great, this is what it would look like (equidistant from better than expected)
+1	4	Better than expected—equal increment from expected outcome level
0	3	Expected outcome—equal increment above baseline
–1	2	Baseline—this is how you're performing at the outset
–2	1	Worsened—equidistant increment below baseline

Note: Reprinted with permission from SLACK Incorporated.

Source: Hoepner (2023). *Counseling and Motivational Interviewing in Speech-Language Pathology.*

are set by the client with the help of the clinician. Ideally, the goal and levels are written in the client's own words. Typically, the baseline level is established first, as this represents the client's current level of function. The end goal or ceiling criteria is set next, which is what the client ultimately hopes to accomplish. The clinician can work backward to establish the "expected" and "better than expected" levels, so that there are equal increments between criteria levels. Establishing equal intervals is critical for measuring outcomes (Turner-Stokes, 2009). Regression below baseline is established last, following the equal intervals from the already established levels. The regression level is present in case the client worsens from their initial status. Monitoring one's goals follows a consistent process. First, the client is asked to recall their goals, in their own words, at the outset of each session. Before the close of the session, have them rate their performance according to their own criteria. Ask questions to corroborate and validate their assessment (e.g., "What makes your performance a 3?" or

"Explain to me why you think it is a 1"). If the clinician believes that the rating is inaccurate, it can be helpful to jointly review the criteria for each level. Correction is not necessary, the clinician simply prompts self-correction by asking the client to review the criteria and explain their rating. This typically leads the client to adjust their ratings to match the criteria.

Treatment of Cognitive Disorders

The majority of the evidence supporting treatment for cognitive disorders comes from research on traumatic brain injury (TBI). As described in Chapter 14, TBI affects systems and networks throughout the brain, and often impacts attention, executive function, awareness, and memory. The treatments described below generally are appropriate for cognitive disorders associated with focal right hemisphere (RH) damage as well as TBI. Most of the treatments described here are based on the International Cognitive (INCOG) panel of experts who systematically examined existing evidence for cognitive treatments and developed recommendations based on that evidence.

Approaches to Treatment

Evidence suggests that the most effective treatments are individualized and personalized, created in partnership with the client to target the goal(s) that they want to achieve. The treatments should be contextualized, meaning that they are conducted in naturalistic settings and target activities or skills that will be useful in everyday situations and environments.

As described in Chapter 5, there are many components to consider when developing treatments, and often it is difficult to identify the **active ingredients**, or those components that make the most difference in a client's progress. Sheila MacDonald and Elyse Shumway reviewed existing treatment studies to identify the factors and components shown to be effective (Table 12–9). The list is long. The good news is that there are a lot of things an SLP can do to develop and implement effective treatments. The bad news is that there are a lot of things an SLP needs to consider in the process.

In the following sections we describe evidence-based treatment approaches for cognitive disorders. Each section also includes a table of recommended practices. These are based on reviews by an international group of cognitive rehabilitation experts; this group is called INCOG. Most of the available evidence is from people with moderate-to-severe TBI. However, the recommendations can be used as a starting point for considering treatment approaches for other populations such as MS, tumors, COVID-19 (long COVID), or RH stroke for which specific treatment evidence may not be available.

Metacognitive Strategy Training

Metacognitive strategy training (MST) is a system for breaking down tasks or problems into smaller steps to facilitate goal achievement. It is a powerful clinical tool for treating a variety

Table 12–9. Evidence-Based Principles for Cognitive-Communication Treatment

Principle	Description
SLP Treatment Access & Onset	Treatment by SLPs should be accessible to all individuals who could benefit from them and should be offered as soon as possible based on an individual's condition
Person-Centered	Treatments should be created with consideration of personal factors and preferences and should engage the individual as a partner
Individualized	Treatments should be individualized based on a person's goals, in consideration of pre-injury communication style and life demands; and current abilities, goals, life demands and roles. Factors that influence performance and available supports should inform the design of the treatment
Cognitive-Communication	Treatment should begin with verbal memory, executive function. and functional outcomes, progressing to higher-level skills (problem solving, reasoning) as appropriate
Context	Contextualized treatments are more effective than de-contextualized; they involve a variety of methods used in daily life contexts and naturalistic settings, selected to meet the individual's personal goals
Dosage & Intensity	Intensive treatment is more effective than less intensive
Community SLP	When leaving inpatient facilities, individuals should be referred to outpatient or community-based rehabilitation
Education	Information about consequences, strategies, and resources related to a person's brain injury should be provided in written and verbal form to individuals and their families/caregivers
Meaningful	Treatment should be meaningful for the individual and relevant for their environment and situation
Environmental Supports & Routines	Relevant supports such as calendars, white boards, signs, notebooks, etc. should be provided
Groups	Group interactions provide opportunities for social engagement, practicing strategies, and sharing experiences

Table 12–9. *continued*	
Principle	**Description**
Augmentative or Assistive Technology	Augmentative and Alternative Communication (AAC) should be used for individuals who could benefit from them
Telepractice	Telepractice should be explored as an option for making treatment more accessible
Cognitive Rehab for All Acquired Brain Injury	Cognitive and communication treatment is effective and should be provided to all individuals with brain injury
SLP Role in Cognitive Rehabilitation	SLPs should advocate for their role in cognitive rehabilitation and provide education about the contributions of SLPs to cognitive rehab research and practice
Technology	Various forms of technology should be explored to find the one(s) that are most appropriate for each individual, taking into consideration their strengths and weaknesses and the functional benefits of different technologies
Online Connection	Social media and virtual groups are options for social engagement
Long Term	Many brain injuries have long-term consequences and impacts; individuals and their families should be given education about the long-term nature of the injury, including the additional impact of aging and life transitions
Treatment Outcomes	Outcome measures that evaluate an individual's performance in real environments and situations (home, work, school, etc.) should be used to determine treatment decisions and discharge

Principles based on MacDonald & Shumway, 2022.

of cognitive deficits including attention and executive function as well as social cognition. MST is most likely to be effective when the patient has input into the goal and strategy so that they are relevant and important to the patient, which will increase their motivation and investment in the training.

Once a goal has been selected, the clinician should work with the client to generate or pick a strategy that the client is willing to try, believes will help, and is willing to use. The clinician provides education about exactly what the strategy is, when it should be used, how it should be used, and how it will benefit the patient. In development of the strategy, the clinician must determine whether the patient's cognitive abilities (strengths & weaknesses)

Table 12–10. Metacognitive Strategy Training (MST) Components	
MST Components	**Activities**
Pre-Task	Set goal and steps to achieve goal
	Create self-instructional phrases
	Collect all necessary items/tools
	[Optional: Client predicts how well they will perform]
Task Execution	Pace through steps
	Use self-instructional phrases
	Monitor performance and adjust as needed based on clinician feedback
Post-Task	Review the process
	Check success. If goal not met, identify source of failure
	Summarize process
	[Optional: Compare performance with prediction]

will support use of the strategy. It is especially important to consider the patient's level of awareness. If they are not aware of their need for the strategy or able to identify situations in which it is and is not needed, then MST may not be the most appropriate treatment.

The training can be split into pre-task, execution, and post-task phases as shown in Table 12–10. Throughout all of them, the client can use self-instructional phrases to keep them on task (e.g., "one step at a time", "focus on the task"), and monitor their progress and performance and adjust as needed if the steps are not moving them closer to achieving the goal.

Repeated practice is necessary for successful MST. In the acquisition phase, the client is learning about the strategy, when to use it, and how to use it. Massed practice—longer, focused sessions—are most effective. Errorless learning, where errors on the part of the client are minimized, also helps them to learn the strategy more effectively. Once the client is able to use the strategy well, practice continues until the strategy is mastered and they can use it routinely. During this mastery phase, the clinician fades the explicit cues and transitions the clients to self-cueing. In the generalization phase, practice extends to other situations, environments, and similar tasks. This includes practice in everyday contexts and environments. Examples of MST programs are shown in Figure 12–1.

Generalized Attention

INCOG recommendations for attention treatments (Bayley et al., 2023a) are summarized in Table 12–11. The strongest evidence supports the use of metacognitive strategy training. Such

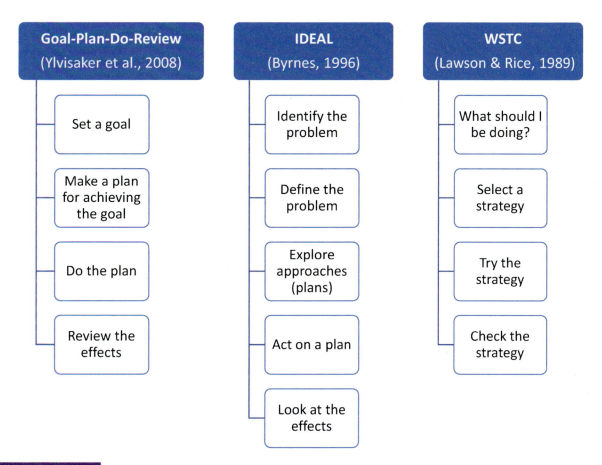

Figure 12–1. Metacognitive strategy training programs.

strategies should be constructed and practiced with tasks that are relevant and important for each patient to facilitate maximal benefit. Similarly, dual-task training can be effective for patients with divided attention deficits, but since the gains do not generalize broadly, the tasks practiced in therapy should be similar to those that the patient experiences in their daily life.

Environmental manipulation, or adjusting the environment to support success in the presence of attentional deficits, is useful for a variety of patients. This can include turning off a radio or TV when the person needs to focus on a task or a conversation, providing protected time when the person can focus on the task at hand without interruption, and providing all necessary tools for a task before they start. Such adjustments can, and often should, be used in conjunction with other treatments or training strategies. As the person's attention improves, adding those demands back into the context can help move toward more realistic demands. Thus the clinician begins to turn the TV back on, perhaps at a lower volume and gradually increasing it to match real-world demands.

In the inpatient or rehabilitation setting, SLPs should rely on the expertise of other rehab team members to provide assessment and treatment of mental health and sleep issues that may exacerbate attentional deficits.

Table 12–11. INCOG Recommendations for Attention Treatment

RECOMMENDED Practices	Notes
Metacognitive strategy training with functional everyday activities	Works well for mild-moderate attention deficits Strong evidence to support this recommendation
Training can be done in real-world contexts and settings	Generalization may not occur with decontextualized tasks
Dual task training	Gains are restricted to tasks similar to those used in training
Cognitive-behavior therapy for developing strategies to maximize attention	Works well for people with mild-mod TBI when anxiety and depression negatively impact attention
Contribution of sleep-wake disorders	Identification and treatment of sleep-wake disorders may have a positive impact on attention
Consideration and adjustment of environment and tasks	Modifying the environment and tasks can improve functional abilities in the presence of attentional deficits
NOT RECOMMENDED	**Notes**
Decontextualized computer-based tasks	Limited evidence that such tasks create improvement on everyday attention
Use of random auditory alerting tones during activities	Evidence is conflicting
Mindfulness-based meditation	Gains in attention have not been demonstrated

Executive Function and Anosognosia

The INCOG recommendations for treatment of deficits of executive function and awareness (Table 12–12) all specifically focus on patients with TBI (Jeffay et al., 2023). However, these should be appropriate for patients with similar cognitive deficits due to focal RH damage. Metacognitive strategy training again is recommended, and as with attentional deficits, it is important to develop the strategies on an individual basis to fit the needs and goals of each patient.

Direct corrective feedback is recommended for patients with anosognosia. This can take various forms. It can be verbal feedback from the clinician either during or after task completion. In a group setting, the feedback can come from other group members. For some

Table 12–12. INCOG Recommendations for Executive Function and Awareness Treatment

RECOMMENDED Practices	Notes
Metacognitive Strategy Training (MST)	For individuals with deficits in problem solving, planning, and organization with awareness of their need for a strategy and the ability to determine when the strategy should be used
	Focus strategies on patient-specific challenges and functional goals
	Most effective when individuals have awareness of their deficits and can identify contexts in which strategies should be employed
	MST can be provided via telerehabilation in cases where it is the most efficient or only option for providing treatment
Strategies for Self-Monitoring	For individuals with reduced self-awareness
Self-Awareness Training	Video feedback and other self-awareness training to increase identification and correction of errors
Strategies for Analyzing and Synthesizing Information	For individuals with reasoning impairments
Rhythmical/Music Therapy	For individuals with impairments in executive function
	Therapy should include: rhythmical training, structured cognitive-motor training, and assisted music playing related to the individual's interests
Virtual Reality	Can be used in addition to in-person therapy if technology is available.
Group Based Interventions	Useful with TBI resulting in deficits in executive function and problem solving
	Telerehabilitation is not recommended for group-based intervention because outcomes are not as good as in-person groups

patients, particularly those with anosognosia for unilateral neglect or apragmatism, a task or interaction can be video recorded and then discussed together.

Video modeling is an effective approach for addressing awareness of communication and behaviors (Hoepner & Olson, 2018; Hoepner et al., 2021). Communication partners video natural conversations in natural settings (e.g., talking about their day over coffee in the morning). The videos are reviewed in the presence of a clinician who guides discussions about communication strengths and challenges for both communication partners. Clients can develop increased awareness of their deficits and their partners can learn how their responses can either support or hinder the effectiveness of the communication exchange.

Memory

The most effective treatments for memory deficits are (a) compensatory strategies and (b) environmental supports, external aids, and reminders (Bayley et al., 2023b; Table 12–13). In teaching compensatory strategies, including metacognitive strategy training, practices that promote learning include: well-defined treatment goals that are relevant to the patient, breaking activities into small steps, using various stimuli and information when teaching strategies, including strategies that involve some effortful processing such as imagery or verbal elaboration, and minimizing errors during the acquisition phase of training. As noted above in relation to MST, training strategies requires a lot of time and opportunities for practice.

External aids and environmental supports take many forms. Low-tech options include notebooks, calendars, white boards, labels, and to-do lists. High-tech options include smartphones, digital assistants, or other computerized devices. It is important to engage the patient in the selection of external aids to find one that they are willing to learn and to use. The choice is not just what they like best, however. Other factors that must be considered and weighed by the clinician include the person's age, the severity and type of their memory impairment, strengths and weaknesses of other cognitive abilities (e.g., attention, executive function), and physical and sensory abilities. For example, if they want to use a smartphone, they'll need to have the physical dexterity to use the phone and the visual acuity to see the screen. A patient's history of use of devices—both prior to the brain injury and any devices/systems used in previous treatment—also should be reviewed. If a patient has extensive experience using a smartphone, then that might be an appropriate device. If they tried using notebooks and calendars in another rehab setting and were unwilling or unable to learn them, then those might not be the best options.

The INCOG group notes that there is no evidence that computerized memory training or games have a lasting effect on memory ability. These may be used by a clinician in conjunction with strategy training, but should never be the only method of treatment.

Social Cognition

Social cognition includes emotional recognition and processing, theory of mind (ToM), empathy, and social inferencing. There are few treatments for acquired deficits of social

Table 12–13. INCOG Recommendations for Memory Treatment	
RECOMMENDED Practices	**Notes**
Internal Compensatory Strategies	For individuals with mild–moderate memory impairments and/or preservation of some executive functions
	Can include instructional or metacognitive strategies
	Multiple strategies can be used and can be components of both individual and group therapy
External Aids, Environmental Supports and Reminders	For individuals with memory impairment, especially severe deficits
	High tech—smartphones, Siri
	Low tech—notebooks, calendars, whiteboards
	Caregivers/family must also be trained to use the supports
Selection of External Memory Aids Should Be Based on Personal Factors	Personal factors include: age, severity of memory impairment, pre-morbid use of memory devices, cognitive strengths and weaknesses, physical limitations
Key Instructional Practices Can Help Improve Learning	• Goals clearly defined • Use methods that break tasks into smaller steps • Provide time and opportunity for practice • Distributed practice should be used • Use variations in stimuli and information when teaching strategies • Use effortful processing strategies • Goals should be relevant to the client • Use errorless learning or other methods for reducing errors
Group-Based Interventions	Use with clients with mild-moderate memory deficits
NOT RECOMMENDED	**Notes**
Computer-Based Training	No evidence that such techniques result in lasting improvement of memory; should be used only when developed by a clinician to aid in strategy development with a plan for transfer to everyday tasks, and used in conjunction with evidence-based compensatory strategies

cognition; most have been developed for children on the autism spectrum. The recommendations made by INCOG (Table 12–14) combine both cognitive-communication and social cognition.

T-ScEmo is a multifaceted treatment for social cognition and emotional regulation (Westerhof-Evers et al., 2017). The treatment induced a focus on emotion perception, perspective taking and self-monitoring, and social behavior, including both awareness and inhibition of less desired behaviors and increasing positive social behaviors. Other programs have focused on self-regulation (Ownsworth et al., 2000), inferencing, and interpreting non-literal and non-verbal communication (Gabbatore et al., 2015).

There are a variety of tasks and approaches that have been effectively used in social cognition treatment including role-playing and video feedback. Group treatments may be especially useful for social cognition because the social interactions are more natural and often clients may feel more comfortable interacting with fellow clients than with clinicians. A combination of individual and group sessions provides practice in multiple social settings.

Table 12–14. INCOG Recommendations for Cognitive-Communication and Social Cognition Treatment

RECOMMENDED Practices	Notes
Recognize Communication Can Vary Depending on Internal and External Factors	External factors: communication partners, environment, communication demands Internal factors: priorities, fatigue, physical variables, sensory abilities, psychosocial factors, behavioral control, emotions
Evaluation and Treatment Should Be Culturally Responsive	Factors to consider include: pre-morbid characteristics, languages, literacy and language proficiency, cognitive abilities, communication style and cultural influences, gender identity
Clinicians and Medical Staff Should Complete Cultural Competence Training	Cultural backgrounds have important influences on a variety of communication behaviors
Individualized, Contextualized Treatment Should Be Grounded in Principles Of Rehabilitation	Refer back to principles of treatment in Table 12–9 and Chapter 5
Communication Partner Training	Partners' behavior and communication style has strong impacts on clients' communicative success

Table 12–14. *continued*

RECOMMENDED Practices	Notes
Communication Strategy & Metacognitive Awareness Training	Metacognitive strategies can be used to increase communication effectiveness and awareness
Reintegration to Daily Functions, Activities With Assistance in Adjusting	Gradual reintroduction into daily activities and social interactions
Communication-Coping Treatment	Strategies for coping with communication challenges include scripts, imagery, and rehearsal
Focus on Confidence, Self-Esteem and Identity Formation	Re-creating identities after brain injury support recovery and positive outcomes
Education for Individual and Family About Cognitive–Communication Disorders	interact-ABI-lity program is one resource: https://abi-communication-lab.sydney.edu.au/courses/interact-abi-lity
Practice Communication in Naturalistic, Real-World Settings	Goal attainment scaling recommended for measuring outcomes
Augmentative and Alternative Communication (AAC) Should Be Provided When Appropriate	Most appropriate for severe communication disorders; communication partners need to be trained in using AAC devices
Group therapy	Groups may be useful when social communication deficits are present
Telerehabilitation Can Be Used for Communication Partner Training (CPT)	Outcomes are similar for in-person and virtual CPT
Social Cognition Treatments Should Be Provided When Appropriate	In-person emotion perception, perspective-taking, theory of mind, and social behavioral treatments are recommended
NOT RECOMMENDED	**Notes**
Computerized Social Cognition Treatments	There is no evidence that gains generalize to everyday activities

Summary

Methods and tasks for assessing and treating cognitive disorders are generally appropriate for a variety of etiologies. Clinicians should use a person-centered approach to select and adapt materials for each client. Thorough, ecologically-valid assessments are driven by hypothesis testing, involve a variety of people, settings, and situations, and are designed to identify strengths as well as weaknesses. Treatments should be designed and implemented based on research evidence while being tailored to an individual's needs.

Key Concepts

- Cognitive deficits can occur after damage to various areas of the brain. The specific presentation differs depending on location.
- Assessment and treatment should consider the whole person, including body structure/function, activity and participation levels.
- Personal and environmental factors should be considered in both assessment and treatment decisions.
- Cultural factors should be taken into consideration for assessment and treatment, specifically for social cognition.
- Goal attainment scaling is a process for establishing client-driven goals and measuring progress toward goal achievement.
- Metacognitive strategy training is an effective and powerful approach for a variety of cognitive deficits.

References

Alderman, N., Burgess, P. W., Knight, C., & Henman, C. (2003). Ecological validity of a simplified version of the multiple errands shopping test. *Journal of the International Neuropsychological Society, 9*, 31–44.

Bagby, R. M., Parker, J. D., & Taylor, G. J. (1994). The twenty-item Toronto Alexithymia Scale—I. Item selection and cross-validation of the factor structure. *Journal of Psychosomatic Research, 38*(1), 23–32.

Baron-Cohen, S., & Wheelwright, S. (2004). The empathy quotient: An investigation of adults with Asperger syndrome or high functioning autism, and normal sex differences. *Journal of Autism and Developmental Disorders, 34*, 163–175.

Baron-Cohen, S., Wheelwright, S., Hill, J., Raste, Y., & Plumb, I. (2001). The "Reading the Mind in the Eyes" Test revised version: A study with normal adults, and adults with Asperger syndrome or high-functioning autism. *The Journal of Child Psychology and Psychiatry and Allied Disciplines, 42*(2), 241–251.

Bayley, M., Ponsford, J., Velikonja, D., Janzen, S., Harnett, A., & McIntyre, A. (2023a). INCOG 2.0 guidelines for cognitive rehabilitation following traumatic brain injury, part II: Attention and information processing speed. *Journal of Head Trauma Rehabilitation, 38*(1), 38–51.

Bayley, M., Ponsford, J., Velikonja, D., Janzen, S., Harnett, A., & Patsakos, E. (2023b). INCOG 2.0 guidelines for cognitive rehabilitation following traumatic brain injury, part V: Memory. *Journal of Head Trauma Rehabilitation, 38*(1), 83–102.

Blake, M. L. (2018). *The right hemisphere and disorders of cognition and communication: Theory and clinical practice.* Plural Publishing Inc.

Borgaro, S. R., & Prigatano, G. P. (2003). Modification of the Patient Competency Rating Scale for use on an acute neurorehabilitation unit: the PCRS-NR. *Brain Injury, 17*(10), 847–853.

Burgess, P. W., Alderman, N., Wilson, B. A., Evans, J. J., & Emslie, H. (1996). *The Dysexecutive Questionnaire.* Thames Valley Test Company.

Burgess, P. W., & Shallice, T. (1997). *The Hayling and Brixton Tests.* Pearson Assessment.

Burns, M. S. (1997). *Burns Brief Inventory of Communication and Cognition.* Psychological Corporation.

Burns, S. P., Dawson, D. R., Perea, J. D., Vas, A., Pickens, N. D., & Neville, M. (2019). Development, reliability, and validity of the Multiple Errands Test Home version (MET–Home) in adults with stroke. *American Journal of Occupational Therapy, 73*(3), 1–10. https://doi.org/10.5014/ajot.2019.027755

Byrnes, J. P. (1996). *Cognitive development and learning in instructional contexts.* Allyn & Bacon.

Cocchini, G., Gregg, N., Beschin, N., Dean, M., & Della Sala, S. (2010). Vata-L: Visual-Analogue Test Assessing Anosognosia for language impairment. *The Clinical Neuropsychologist, 24*(8), 1379–1399. http://doi.org/10.1080/13854046.2010.524167

Cohen, J. D., Forman, S. D., Braver, T. S., Casey, B. J., Servan-Schreiber, D., Noll, D. C. (1994). Activation of prefrontal cortex in a non-spatial working memory task with functional MRI. *Human Brain Mapping, 1*, 293–304. https://doi.org/10.1002/hbm.460010407

Davis, M. H. (1980). *Interpersonal Reactivity Index (IRI)* [Database record]. APA PsycTests. https://doi.org/10.1037/t01093-000

Demeyere, N., Riddoch, M. J., Slavkova, E. D., Bickerton, W.-L., & Humphreys, G. W. (2015). The Oxford Cognitive Screen (OCS): Validation of a stroke-specific short cognitive screening tool. *Psychological Assessment, 27*(3), 883–894. http://doi.org/10.1037/pas0000082

Emslie, H., Wilson, B. A., Evans, J. J., Foley, J., Shiel, A., Watson, P., . . . Groot, Y. (2005). *Cambridge Prospective Memory Test (CAMPROMPT).* Pearson Assessment.

Fleming, J. M., Strong, J., & Ashton, R. (1996). Self-awareness of deficits in adults with traumatic brain injury: How best to measure? *Brain Injury, 10*(1), 1–15.

Gabbatore, I., Sacco, K., Angeleri, R., Zettin, M., Bara, B. G., & Bosco, F. M. (2015). Cognitive pragmatic treatment: A rehabilitative program for traumatic brain injury individuals. *Journal of Head Trauma Rehabilitation, 30*(5), E14–E28.

Godfrey, H. P., Harnett, M. A., Knight, R. G., Marsh, N. V., Kesel, D. A., Partridge, F. M., & Heidi Robertson, R. (2003). Assessing distress in caregivers of people with a traumatic brain injury (TBI): A psychometric study of the Head Injury Behaviour Scale. *Brain Injury, 17*(5), 427–435.

Goia, G. A., Isquith, P. K., Guy, S. C., & Kenworthy, L. (2000). *Behavior rating inventory of executive function (BRIEF): Professional manual.* Psychological Assessment Resources.

Grace, J., & Malloy, P. F. (2001). *FrSBe Frontal System Behaviour Scale.* Psychological Assessment Resources.

Gregory, C., Lough, S., Stone, V., Erzinclioglu, S., Martin, L., Baron-Cohen, S., & Hodges, J. R. (2002). Theory of mind in patients with frontal variant frontotemporal dementia and Alzheimer's disease: Theoretical and practical implications. *Brain, 125*(4), 752–764. https://doi.org/10.1093/brain/awf079

Gronwall, D. M. (1977). Paced auditory serial-addition task: A measure of recovery from concussion. *Perceptual and Motor Skills, 44*(2), 367–373. http://doi.org/10.2466/pms.1977.44.2.367

Helm-Estabrooks, N. (2017). *Cognitive Linguistic Quick Test-Plus.* Psychological Corporation.

Hoepner, J. K. (2023). *Counseling and motivational interviewing in speech-language pathology*. Slack Inc.

Hoepner, J. K. & Olson, S. E. (2018). Joint video self-modeling as a conversational intervention for an individual with traumatic brain injury and his everyday partner: A pilot investigation. *Clinical Archives of Communication Disorders, 3*(1), 22–41.

Hoepner, J. K., Sievert, A., & Guenther, K. (2021). Joint video self-modeling for persons with traumatic brain injury and their partners: A case series. *American Journal of Speech-Language Pathology, 30*(2S), 863–882.

Jeffay, E., Ponsford, J., Harnett, A., Janzen, S., Patsakos, E., Douglas, J., & Green, R. (2023). INCOG 2.0 guidelines for cognitive rehabilitation following traumatic brain injury, part III: Executive functions. *The Journal of Head Trauma Rehabilitation, 38*(1), 52–64.

Keegan, L. C., Hoepner, J. K., Togher, L., & Kennedy, M. (2023). Clinically applicable sociolinguistic assessment for cognitive-communication disorders. *American Journal of Speech-Language Pathology, 32*(2S), 966–976. https://doi.org/10.1044/2022_AJSLP-22-00102

Knight, C., Alderman, N., & Burgess, P. W. (2002). Development of a simplified version of the Multiple Errands Test for use in hospital settings. *Neuropsychological Rehabilitation, 12*(3), 231–255.

Lane, R. D., Quinlan, D. M., Schwartz, G. E., Walker, P. A., & Zeitlin, S. B. (1990). The Levels of Emotional Awareness Scale: A cognitive-developmental measure of emotion. *Journal of Personality Assessment, 55*(1–2), 124–134.

Lawson, M. J., & Rice, D. N. (1989). Effects of training in use of executive strategies on a verbal memory problem resulting from closed head injury. *Journal of Clinical and Experimental Neuropsychology, 11*(6), 842–54. http://doi.org/10.1080/01688638908400939

MacDonald, S. (2005). *Functional Assessment of Verbal Reasoning and Executive Strategies*. CCD Publishers.

MacDonald, S. (2013). *Student Version–Functional Assessment of Verbal Reasoning and Executive Strategies*. CCD Publishers.

MacDonald, S., & Shumway, E. (2022). Optimizing our evidence map for cognitive–communication interventions: How it can guide us to better outcomes for adults living with acquired brain injury. *International Journal of Language and Communication Disorders*. Advance Online Publication. https://doi.org/10.1111/1460-6984.12817

Malec, J. F. (1999). Goal attainment scaling in rehabilitation. *Neuropsychological Rehabilitation, 9*(3–4), 253–275.

Man, D. W. K., Fleming, J., Hohaus, L., & Shum, D. (2011). Development of the Brief Assessment of Prospective Memory (BAPM) for use with traumatic brain injury populations. *Neuropsychological Rehabilitation, 21*(6), 884–898. http://doi.org/10.1080/09602011.2011.627270

McDonald, S., Flanagan, S., Rollins, J., & Kinch, J. (2003). TASIT: A new clinical tool for assessing social perception after traumatic brain injury. *The Journal of Head Trauma Rehabilitation, 18*(3), 219–238.

Mehrabian, A. (1996). *Manual for the Balanced Emotional Empathy Scale (BEES)*. Available from Albert Mehrabian, University of New South Wales.

Milman, L. H., & Holland, A. L. (2012). *SCCAN: Scales of Cognitive and Communicative Ability for Neurorehabilitation*. Pro-Ed.

Ownsworth, T. L., McFarland, K., & Mc Young, R. (2000). Self-awareness and psychosocial functioning following acquired brain injury: An evaluation of a group support programme. *Neuropsychological Rehabilitation, 10*(5), 465–484.

Prigatano, G. P., & Klonoff, P. S. (1998). A clinician's rating scale for evaluating impaired self-awareness and denial of disability after brain injury. *The Clinical Neuropsychologist, 12*(1), 56–67.

Rand, D., Rukan, S., Weiss, P. L., & Katz, N. (2009a). Validation of the Virtual MET as an assessment tool for executive functions. *Neuropsychological Rehabilitation, 19*(4), 583–602.

Randolph, C. (2012). *Repeatable Battery for the Assessment of Neuropsychological Status Update (RBANS Update)*. The Psychological Corporation.

Reitan, R. M. (1958). Validity of the Trail Making test as an indicator of organic brain damage. *Perceptual and Motor Skills, 8*, 271–276.

Robertson, I. H., Manly, T., Andrade, J., Baddeley, B. T., & Yiend, J. (1997). Oops!: Performance correlates of everyday attentional failures in traumatic brain injured and normal subjects. *Neuropsychologia, 35*(6), 747–758.

Robertson, I. H., Ward, T., Ridgeway, V., & Nimmo-Smith, I. (1994). *Test of Everyday Attention*. Pearson Assessment.

Ross-Swain, D. (1996). *RIPA-2: Ross Information Processing Assessment*. Pro-Ed.

Royle, J., & Lincoln, N. B. (2008). The Everyday Memory Questionnaire-revised: Development of a 13-item scale. *Disability and Rehabilitation, 30*(2), 114–121. http://doi.org/10.1080/09638280701223876

Ruff, R. M., Niemann, H., Allen, C. C., Farrow, C. E., & Wylie, T. (1992). The Ruff 2 and 7 selective attention test: A neuropsychological application. *Perceptual and Motor Skills, 75*(3_suppl), 1311–1319.

Schretlen, D., Bobholz, J. H., & Brandt, J. (1996). Development and psychometric properties of the brief test of attention. *The Clinical Neuropsychologist, 10*(1), 80–89.

Schwartz, M. F., Buxbaum, L. J., Ferraro, M., Veramonti, T., & Segal, M. (2002). *Naturalistic Action Test*. Pearson Assessment.

Shallice, T. & Burgess, P. W. (1991). Deficits in strategy application following frontal lobe damage in man. *Brain, 114*, 727–741.

Sherer, M. (2004). *The Awareness Questionnaire*. The Center for Outcome Measurement in Brain Injury.

Shum, D., & Fleming, J. (2014). *Comprehensive Assessment of Prospective Memory: Clinical assessment and user manual*. Griffith Health Institute.

Smith, A. (1973). *Symbol Digit Modalities Test*. Western Psychological Services.

Smith, G., Del Sala, S., Logie, R. H., & Maylor, E. A. (2000). Prospective and retrospective memory in normal ageing and dementia: A questionnaire study. *Memory, 8*(5), 311–321. https://www.ed.ac.uk/ppls/psychology/research/facilities/philosophy-and-psychology-library/psychological-tests/prmq&sa=D&source=docs&ust=1680957714425924&usg=AOvVaw22RaCfJGCpU09-c5cFdo64

Tate, R. L. (2011). *Manual for the Sydney Psychosocial Reintegration Scale version 2 (SPRS-2)*. Rehabilitation Studies Unit, University of Sydney.

Toglia, J. (2019). *Contextual Memory Test 2* (CMT-2). https://cmt.multicontext.net

Turner-Stokes, L. (2009). Goal attainment scaling (GAS) in rehabilitation: A practical guide. *Clinical Rehabilitation, 23*(4), 362–370.

Vorst, H. C., & Bermond, B. (2001). Validity and reliability of the Bermond–Vorst alexithymia questionnaire. *Personality and Individual Differences, 30*(3), 413–434.

Westerhof-Evers, H. J., Neumann, D., Visser-Keizer, A. C., Fasotti, L., Schönherr, M. C., Vink, M., & Spikman, J. M. (2017). Effectiveness of a treatment for impairments in social cognition and emotion regulation (T-ScEmo) after traumatic brain injury: A randomized controlled trial. *Journal of Head Trauma Rehabilitation, 32*(5), 296–307.

Wilson, B. A., Cockburn, J., & Halligan, P. W. (1987). *Behavioural Inattention Test*. Pearson Assessment.

Wilson, B. A., Emslie, H., Evans, J. J., Alderman, N. & Burgess, P. W. (1996) *Behavioural Assessment of the Dysexecutive Syndrome (BADS)*. Pearson.

Wilson, B. A., Greenfield, E., Claire, L., Baddeley, A., Cockburn, J., Watson, P., . . . Nannery, R. (2017). *Rivermead Behavioural Memory Test – 3rd Edition (RBMT-3)*. Pearson Assessment.

Ylvisaker, M., & Gioia, G. A. (1998). Cognitive assessment. In *Traumatic brain injury rehabilitation: Children and adolescents* (pp. 159–179).

Ylvisaker, M., Szekeres, S. F., & Feeney, T. J. (2008). Communication disorders associated with traumatic brain injury. In R. Chapey (Ed.), *Language intervention strategies in aphasia and related neurogenic communication disorders* (5th ed., pp. 879–962). Lippincott Williams & Wilkins.

13

ASSESSMENT AND TREATMENT OF DYSARTHRIA AND DYSPHAGIA

Chapter Overview

Assessment of Dysarthria and Dysphagia
   Dysarthria
      Perceptual Assessment
      Motor Assessment (Strength and Tone)
      Instrumental and Acoustic Assessment
   Dysphagia
      Dysfunction by Phases of Swallowing
      Dysfunction by Underlying Disease Processes
   Cranial Nerve Exam
   Oral Mechanism Exam
   Intervention for Dysarthria
   Intervention for Dysphagia
Summary
Key Concepts
References

Assessment of Dysarthria and Dysphagia

Assessment for both dysarthrias and dysphagia begins with a cranial nerve examination and an oral mechanism exam (OME) to assess the integrity of the cranial nerves, muscles, and structures involved in speech production and swallowing. For dysarthria, assessment also involves speech production and intelligibility, addressed through perceptual and acoustic measures. For dysphagia, a clinical swallowing examination (CSE) includes a cranial nerve exam,

OME, and food trials. An instrumental assessment such as modified barium swallow (MBS)/ video fluoroscopic swallowing study (VFSS) or fiberoptic endoscopic examination of swallowing (FEES) may be used for a more specific or definitive diagnosis.

A brief cognitive screening (formal or informal) provides information about alertness, attention, memory, impulsivity, and decision making which are important for safety, especially with dysphagia in which eating or drinking too quickly, or the wrong thickness or texture, can have serious consequences.

To round out the areas of the WHO-ICF, an interview should be conducted to gather information about the onset and course of the speech/swallowing difficulty, and to determine how the changes are affecting the person's ability to eat safely, communicate, or participate in daily activities. For people with an unfamiliar accent or dialect, the SLP may want to inquire about what speech characteristics are new and which may be typical of the person's pre-morbid speech patterns.

When dysphagia is present, the interview should include a discussion of typical food preferences, allergies, and/or cultural norms. Cultural and personal preferences can be used to identify foods that represent different textures and viscosities. Likewise, identifying any food allergies is crucial. It is also critical to elicit the client and family's decisions on dietary modifications and if relevant, non-oral feeding options to ensure that quality of life is addressed.

Dysarthria

Dysarthria can affect respiratory, phonatory, resonatory, articulatory, and/or prosody functions (Duffy, 2019) (often abbreviated as RPRAP). Subtypes of dysarthria (Unilateral Upper Motor Neuron [UUMN], spastic, flaccid, ataxic, hyperkinetic, hypokinetic, and mixed) were covered in previous chapters. As a reminder, they are differentiated by patterns of impaired strength, coordination, and timing. Spastic dysarthria is caused by damage to both the pyramidal and extrapyramidal motor systems, resulting in weakness and increased tone, which disrupts all subsystems (RPRAP). Speech is characteristically strained or strangled with imprecise articulatory placement resulting in less intelligible speech. UUMN dysarthria is similar to spastic dysarthria but more mild, typically caused by unilateral cortical stroke. Flaccid dysarthria also causes weakness but with reduced or absent tone. Typically, etiology is related to damage to lower motor neurons (LMNs) including cranial nerves (specifically VII, IX, X, XII). Consonant production is often markedly impaired. Ataxic dysarthria is typically caused by damage to the cerebellum or cerebellar inputs/outputs. Ataxia is characterized by irregular breakdowns in articulation, slurring of speech, breakdowns in prosody and stress, and highly variable pitch and loudness. Hyperkinetic dysarthria is caused by damage to basal ganglia control circuits. Individuals with Huntington disease and Tourette syndrome both may exhibit uncontrolled variations in loudness, dysphonia, extended pauses and overall slow rate of speech, along with irregular breakdowns in articulation. Hypokinetic dysarthria is marked by monotone, soft and breathy phonation, and variable speaking rate with quick bursts of imprecise speech (mumbling and festinating speech). Hypokinetic damage leads to high velocity and low amplitude movements that account for the hallmark soft, rapid, and imprecise speech of individuals with Parkinson disease (PD).

Perceptual Assessment

Perceptual assessment is a key element of dysarthria assessment. Through a series of speech tasks (counting, reciting, repeating, reading aloud, etc.), clinicians evaluate the quality and characteristics of respiration, phonation, resonance, articulation, and prosody (Table 13–1). Specific tasks are described in later sections on the cranial nerve and oral mechanism examinations.

Motor Assessment (Strength and Tone)

Strength is most commonly tested through the Medical Research Council Manual Muscle Testing scale (0–5) (Medical Research Council, 1976). While strength testing is somewhat subjective, following this scale provides operationalized and more objective information (Table 13–2). Range of motion is typically estimated, although oral goniometers (which measure angles of opening and closure/joint position) can be used to specify range of motion when necessary. Tone can be measured by palpating the muscle or by moving a joint through its typical range of motion to determine any resistance during passive stretch (extension) and return to rest position (flexion). Eliciting stretch reflexes is another way to determine if there is spasticity (increased tone and hyperreflexivity) or flaccidity (decreased or absent tone and hyperreflexivity). While some oral motor reflexes are easier to elicit, such as the jaw jerk reflex, intraoral reflexes are difficult to directly elicit. Instrumental assessments of tone are emerging (Dietsch et al., 2014; Table 13–3), although since they were initially developed for large muscles they may not be sensitive enough for the small muscles in the oral structures. Specific tasks for assessing motor function are described in later sections on the cranial nerve and oral mechanism examinations.

Instrumental and Acoustic Assessment

Rusz et al. (2021) provide comprehensive guidelines for recording and analyzing speech samples for dysarthria associated with movement disorders. The recording environment should be at minimum a quiet room, although a soundproof booth is ideal. An omnidirectional, head-mounted microphone is recommended, with the microphone close to the cheek.

1. **Vocal tasks:** Tasks include a sustained vowel /a/ as long and steadily as possible on one breath. Sequential movement rates (SMRs) and alternating movement rates (AMRs) on one breath with at least 12 repetitions, reading a passage at a comfortable pitch and loudness (the Rainbow Passage is recommended for English speakers) and eliciting a monologue of a self-selected topic of a duration of 60 to 90 seconds or picture description as an alternative.

Table 13–1. RPRAP Assessment

RPRAP Domain	Impairments	Perceptual Expectations	Perceptual Assessments	Perceptual Judgments	Stimulability Tasks
Respiration	1. Muscle weakness 2. Increased or decreased tone 3. Incoordination	1. Reduced loudness 2. Monoloudness 3. Short phrases 4. Sudden forced inhalation 5. Speaking on inadequate air	1. Loudness level 2. Count from 1–20 on one breath 3. Produce /ah/ from soft to loud 4. Observe conversational speech	1. Inspiration: expiration pattern (1–2 sec. inspirations: 6–12 sec. expirations) 2. Speech timing (start of expiration?) 3. Pauses to communicate or only for breathing 4. Running out of air 5. Length of breath groups	1. Ask client to take a bigger breath and start talking at beginning of expiration

13 ASSESSMENT AND TREATMENT OF DYSARTHRIA AND DYSPHAGIA 311

RPRAP Domain	Impairments	Perceptual Expectations	Perceptual Assessments	Perceptual Judgments	Stimulability Tasks
Phonation	1. Laryngeal muscle weakness 2. Increased or decreased tone 3. Incoordination	1. Breathy 2. Hoarse 3. Monopitch 4. Reduced loudness 5. Low pitch 6. Strained 7. Strangled 8. Dysphonic 9. Harsh 10. Inappropriate pitch 11. Tremors 12. Voicing errors	1. Spontaneous cough 2. Sustained /ah/ 3. Sing high and low notes 4. Oral reading 5. Conversation	1. Too loud or too soft 2. Maintaining appropriate loudness 3. Softer at the end of utterances? 4. Shout loudness 5. Fatigue with prolonged talking?	1. Ask client to speak louder 2. Ask client to speak softer 3. Ask client to match your pitch

continues

Table 13–1. *continued*

RPRAP Domain	Impairments	Perceptual Expectations	Perceptual Assessments	Perceptual Judgments	Stimulability Tasks
Resonance	1. Velopharyngeal weakness 2. Increased tone	1. Hypernasality 2. Nasal emission	1. Prolonged /i/ while occluding nose and releasing 2. Read nasal and non-nasal sentences 3. Place mirror under nose to check for fog with emission 4. Use flashlight to examine movement of soft palate	1. Sound hypernasal? 2. Audible air escaping through nose 3. Is speech less hypernasal on non-nasal sounds?	1. Ask client to open mouth wide during speech 2. Ask client to repeat nasal and non-nasal words to achieve contrast
Articulation	1. Weakness 2. Incoordination 3. Decreased range of motion 4. Increased tone 5. Unpredictable movements	1. Imprecise consonant production 2. Irregular breakdowns 3. Distorted vowels	1. Check oral motor movements for non-speech tasks 2. Diadochokinesis 3. Repeat words and phrases 4. Conversation	1. Are specific sounds misarticulated? 2. Are AMRs slow? 3. Irregular rhythm of AMRs 4. Intelligibility levels	1. Ask client to produce specific consonants 2. Have client try over-articulating sounds

13 ASSESSMENT AND TREATMENT OF DYSARTHRIA AND DYSPHAGIA

RPRAP Domain	Impairments	Perceptual Expectations	Perceptual Assessments	Perceptual Judgments	Stimulability Tasks
Prosody	1. Increased or decreased tone in larynx 2. Decreased range of motion 3. Unpredictable movements 4. Weakness and incoordination of tongue and lips	1. Reduced stress 2. Slow rate 3. Poor intonation differentiation	1. Examine syllable stress across words and phrases 2. Contrastive stress comparisons	1. Intonation 2. Changes in pitch during speech 3. Differences between declarative and interrogative sentence patterns 4. Repeat sentence with different meanings 5. Assess rate (normal is 130–220 wpm, 3–5 syllables per sec, and 12–20 syllables per breath group) 6. Observe articulation to pause time ratio 7. Observe rhythm in conversation	1. Ask client to speak slowly 2. Ask client to try pauses 3. Practice repeating contrastive stress 4. Ask client to imitate intonation patterns

NOTE: AMR = Alternating Movement Rate.

Table 13–2. Medical Research Council (MRC) Scale

Degree of Movement	Muscle Function	Movement Grade or Score (MRC)	
No Movement Observed	No contractions are palpable	0	Zero
	Tendon activation can be palpated but no visible movement of joint	1	Trace
Range of Motion	Partial range of motion	2−	Poor−
	Full range of motion	2	Poor
	Partial range of motion without gravity	2+	Poor+
Strength Against Resistance	Gradual return to rest position from test position	3−	Fair−
	Holds test position without return to rest position (no added pressure)	3	Fair
	Holds test position to slight pressure	3+	Fair+
	Holds test position for slight to moderate pressure	4−	Good−
	Holds test position to moderate pressure	4	Good
	Holds test position for moderate to strong pressure	4+	Good+
	Holds test position to strong pressure	5	Normal

2. **Acoustic analyses:** Praat, Wavesurfer, and the commercial acoustic analysis programs such as TF32 and Computerized Speech Lab are commonly used. The Dysarthria Analyzer program is freely available and provides automated acoustic analyses of dysarthric speech (Czech Technical University in Prague, available at http://dysan.cz/).

3. **Acoustic measures:** Rusz et al. (2021) recommend 14 specific measures. Their paper provides normative expectations for each of the measures. These include: loudness (reading passage), fundamental frequency (reading and sustained vowel), frequency perturbation (jitter), amplitude perturbation (shimmer), noise (HNR), oral diadochokinesis (SMRs), voice onset time, articulatory rate and pause characteristics, and pause duration. See Table 1, pp. 809 to 810 from Rusz et al. (2021) for details.

Table 13–3. Instrumental Assessments for Muscle Tone

Tool	Motor Function/Measurement	Notes
OroSTIFF (Epic Medical Concepts & Innovations; Mission, Kansas)	Rigidity and hypokinesia	Reliable for use with Parkinson disease
Myotonometer (Neurogenic Technologies, Inc; Missoula, Montana)	Tissue compliance: depresses tissue at incrementally increasing magnitudes and measuring return to rest	Not sensitive to small movements such as those produced in the tongue, cheeks, and jaw
Myoton (Müomeetria; Tallinn, Estonia)	Tissue compliance: depresses tissue and measuring return to rest	Discrepancies between measurement of tone at rest versus during active contraction

4. Outside of the acoustic assessment, Rusz et al. (2021) also emphasize the importance of speech measures, such as the Sentence Intelligibility Test (Yorkston & Beukelman, 1981), Communicative Effectiveness Index (Lomas et al., 1989), and/or the Voice Handicap Index 10 (Rosen et al., 2004) as well as perceptual voice measures such as the Consensus Auditory-Perceptual Evaluation of Voice (CAPE-V; Behlau, 2003).

Dysphagia

Dysphagia is an impairment to oral, pharyngeal, and esophageal swallowing function that alters intake and safety, along with quality of life. Similar to dysarthria, it can include sensory impairments, weakness, incoordination, altered timing, difficulty coordinating swallow with breathing cycles, and is often affected by concomitant cognitive impairments. Dysphagia impairments are often described by swallowing phases but can also be described in conjunction with underlying disease processes. Table 13–4 provides an overview of dysphagia assessments.

Dysfunction by Phases of Swallowing

Oral preparatory phase impairments affect the process of bringing food or drink into one's mouth, retrieving it from the utensil, cup, or straw and forming a bolus. Liquid boluses are formed by grouping the liquid into a cohesive collection between the tongue and the palate.

> ### Box 13–1
> ### Case 13–1. Joe
>
> Joe was a 65-year-old male who experienced a large, right middle cerebral artery (MCA) stroke two days ago. Physically, Joe was limited to moderate assistance of two for basic mobility. Speech was marked by mild-moderate unilateral upper motor neuron (UUMN) dysarthria. Joe neglects things on his left side and has poor cognitive and physical endurance. During the evaluation he was very distractible and became overwhelmed by too much visual and auditory stimulation. Joe required setup and constant support during meals to ensure safe and adequate oral intake. Poor cognitive and physical endurance, impaired attention, and sensory issues were primary contributors to oral intake. He demonstrated left lateral pocketing, which he clears with maximal verbal and tactile cueing. Swallow onset was delayed anywhere from 2 to 10 seconds given the attention and alertness impairments. Joe's voice was occasionally wet and gurgly with thin liquids. He demonstrated frequent coughing with densely textured solids. He especially had trouble with less cohesive textures, like ground meats.
>
> Given this background on stroke and this case description, answer the following questions:
>
> 1. Identify systems affected by this stroke, and any anatomical correlates.
>   (Hint: what key structures fall within the right MCA distribution?)
>   a. What accounts for his UUMN dysarthria?
>   b. What accounts for his left neglect?
>   c. What accounts for his limited endurance and attention impairments?
>   d. What accounts for his eating and swallowing difficulties?
> 2. Identify disorders that would typically be addressed by a speech-language pathologist.
>   (Hint: think speech, language, cognitive, and swallowing subsystems)
> 3. Identify disorders that would typically be addressed by a related profession and include the names of those disciplines. (refer back to Table 1–1)

Solid foods require mastication (chewing) and mixing with saliva as a part of the process of forming a cohesive bolus. Impairments to muscles of mastication and coordination of those movements can lead to loss of bolus control. Impairments to oral-facial structures (e.g., lips, cheeks, tongue) can lead to problems with retrieval and formation of a cohesive bolus. Incohesive boluses may break and spill anteriorly (out of the mouth), laterally (between the teeth and cheeks), or posteriorly (prior to readiness for onset of the pharyngeal swallowing response).

Oral phase impairments primarily relate to bolus transport. The intrinsic muscles of the tongue shape the dorsal surface of the tongue to cup or hold the bolus in place, while the

Table 13–4. Dysphagia Assessment Approaches

Domains	Recommended Practices	Description
Personal Factors	Interview	Addresses client and/or family's report on history and progression of the swallowing impairments. Question food preferences, allergies, and cultural or religious restrictions. Address quality of life (e.g., SWAL-QOL; McHorney et al., 2002).
Body Structures and Body Functions	Cognitive screening	Non-standardized observations of orientation, attention, alertness, and decision making.
Body Structures and Body Functions	Oral mechanism examination (speech & swallowing structures, strength, mobility, and sensory function)	Examines integrity of anatomical structures, strength and mobility of muscular structures, and sensation of the swallowing mechanism.
Body Structures and Body Functions	Clinical swallowing examination	Clinical assessment of food trials, observation of clinical signs and symptoms.
Body Structures and Body Functions	Instrumental assessment (modified barium swallow study and/or flexible endoscopic evaluation of swallowing)	Direct examination of anatomical structures and swallow physiology through radiographic or video examination.

extrinsic muscles of the tongue are responsible for anterior to posterior bolus propulsion. Impaired strength may lead to poor oral clearance (e.g., residuals remain in the mouth, on the surface of the tongue, oral sulci, or palate), while impaired coordination may lead to spillage of the bolus anteriorly, laterally, or posteriorly. Again, posterior loss of the bolus prior to the onset of the pharyngeal swallowing response puts the individual at risk for aspiration.

The transition between the oral and pharyngeal phase includes tongue base retraction and contact with the posterior pharyngeal wall. At this same time, the hyolaryngeal complex moves anteriorly and superiorly, eliciting onset of the pharyngeal swallow. **Pharyngeal phase impairments** are complex, relating to timing of onset of the pharyngeal swallowing response, closure of the velopharyngeal port, contraction of the pharyngeal muscles, movement of the epiglottis, and adduction (closure) of the larynx. As the tongue passes posteriorly through the faucial arches during oral transport, a multi-component pharyngeal swallowing response is evoked. This includes closure of the velopharyngeal port through muscles in the velum and pharyngeal wall. Along with an oral seal, closure of the velopharyngeal port prevents food and liquid from being forced out of the nose and creates positive pressure to drive the bolus downward, toward the esophagus. Simultaneously, the hyolaryngeal complex elevates, inverting the epiglottis to deflect food and liquid away from the larynx. Likewise, the pharyngeal constrictors contract in sequence to propel the food through the pharynx and into the esophagus. The bolus passes through the pharynx, through a combination of pushing (constrictor muscles narrow the space and push the bolus down) and pulling (lowering of air pressure below the constriction that pulls the bolus down). For example, as the superior pharyngeal constrictor contracts, the middle constrictor relaxes, causing a drop in pressure in the mid pharynx, which draws the bolus toward that space. Next, the middle pharyngeal constrictor contracts, squeezing the bolus toward the inferior constrictor, which relaxes, creating more space and dropping pressure in the inferior pharynx, relaxing the cricopharyngeus and opening the upper esophageal sphincter (UES) and drawing the bolus toward that space and into the upper esophagus. Alterations to strength, timing, and physiology of this mechanism can lead to poor pharyngeal clearance, reduced efficiency, and residuals (leftover food or liquid that remains in the pharynx) that place the person at risk for aspiration.

The esophageal phase begins as the tail end of the bolus passes through the UES. As the bolus enters the esophagus, an autonomic, peristaltic wave moves the bolus toward the stomach. Alterations to esophageal motility can alter this stripping wave, causing the bolus to move to and fro, upward toward the pharynx.

Dysfunction by Underlying Disease Processes

Numerous disease processes result in dysphagia. What follows is a summary of some of the common consequences you may encounter.

- Parkinson disease can result in lingual pumping, problems with initiation of oral phase transfer and onset of the pharyngeal swallow. Discoordination of swallow and respiration timing can result in pharyngeal impairments.
- Huntington disease can result in irregular movements and difficulty timing oral and pharyngeal swallows. Discoordination of the swallow can lead to loss of bolus control and risk for aspiration.
- Unilateral cortical strokes can result in unilateral oral and pharyngeal weakness, coordination, and timing issues, all of which can affect oral and pharyngeal clearance and safety. Both right and left hemisphere strokes may result in global attention impairments, fatigue, and unilateral sensory impairments.
- Brainstem strokes can result in severe impairments to oral pharyngeal functions. This can result in incoordination, timing issues, and weakness to complete paresis of oral and pharyngeal structures. Sensory functions may be impaired as well, although sensation is typically good in lateral medullary strokes.

- Dementias result in sensory-awareness impairments which are often exacerbated by cognitive function. This can result in insufficient intake, impulsivity, and fluctuating attention to the eating process. Biomechanical changes are also present early in the disease process.
- Traumatic brain injuries can result in a variety of motor and sensory impairments, often exacerbated by cognitive impairments as well. Because most traumatic brain injuries include both diffuse and discrete areas of damage, impairments are different for each individual.
- Amyotrophic lateral sclerosis can result in severe impairments to oral pharyngeal function, as well as decreased respiratory drive to protect the airway and lungs. Early interventions focus on energy conservation and minimizing risks for aspiration. There is some recent evidence that proactive strengthening therapy is useful, as long as fatigue is avoided (Donohue & Coyle, 2020; Plowman et al., 2016; Robison et al., 2018). Often non-oral feeding options are a part of the eventual treatment management plan, including supplementation initially to full non-oral feeding as the disease progresses.

Cranial Nerve Exam

A full cranial nerve exam assesses the integrity of all 12 pairs of cranial nerves. SLPs typically conduct an abbreviated version, focusing on those involved in speech production and swallowing. You will need a flashlight, tongue depressor, cotton balls or swab, and gloves.

CN V Trigeminal: innervates muscles of mastication (chewing) and sensation to the face.

- Observe the jaw at rest to examine for symmetry.
- Have the client open/close jaw, open against pressure, close against pressure, resist opening & closing, move jaw to right and left with and without resistance.
- Place a finger at the temporomandibular joint to feel for crepitus or popping at the joint and ask if there is pain.
- Use a tongue depressor or swab to touch various portions of the maxillary and mandibular gums. Have the client raise their hand when they feel it. Afterward, ask them if it feels the same on both sides. Do the same for the inner surface of the cheeks on each side; same for sensation of the tongue surface.
- Have the person close their eyes, use a cotton ball to touch various portions of the lower face (jawline, cheeks) and forehead.
- Have them raise their hand on the corresponding side and tell you where or point to where on the face. Ask them if it feels the same on both sides and on the forehead versus the lower face.

CN VII Facial: innervates muscles of facial expression and taste to the anterior two thirds of the tongue.

- Observe the face at rest for symmetry.

- Have the client smile, retract lips, purse lips, close lips and blow up cheeks, maintain lip seal when cheeks are pressed.
- Examine forehead motility by having the person raise their eyebrows and wrinkle/furrow their forehead.
- Repeat with pressure on the eyebrows to gauge strength and provide resistance to wrinkling forehead by spreading a thumb and index finger from above eyebrows to "hairline."
- Taste is rarely assessed directly.

CN IX glossopharyngeal: co-innervates the soft palate and taste to the posterior one third of the tongue.

- Shine flashlight on velum to examine symmetry at rest.
- Have the client say "uh, uh, uh" to examine elevation of the velum.
- Use a tongue depressor or swab to check sensation of the faucial pillars and the velum. Ask the client if it feels the same on both sides.
- Using the tongue depressor, check for a gag reflex.
- Again, taste is rarely assessed directly.

CN X vagus: innervates soft palate and larynx providing both motor and sensory inputs.

- Have the client sustain "ah."
- Ask the client to create nasal and non-nasal sounds (e.g., ma-ma-ma) to depress and elevate the soft palate
- Ask the client to glide pitch from low to high to lengthen and tense vocal folds
- Ask the client to cough or glottal coup; clear throat to assess rapid adduction and abduction of vocal folds
- An s/z ratio can be used to gauge laryngeal valving/closure.
- Have the person sustain an /s/ sound as long as they can x3 and a /z/ sound as long as they can x3. Calculate the average duration of /s/ and /z/.
- Laryngeal sensation is typically addressed instrumentally (not clinically), if at all (sensory testing through an air puff with FEES to examine laryngeal adductor response).

CN XI spinal accessory: innervates accessory muscles of the neck.

- Observe the neck at rest for symmetry.
- Have the client shrug their shoulders with and without resistance.

- Have the client turn their head over their left and right shoulders with and without resistance.

CN XII hypoglossal: innervates all but one of the tongue muscles.

- Using a flashlight, observe the tongue at rest by having the client open their mouth and letting the tongue drop to the floor of the mouth. That ensures that there is no muscle activation. If you observe it when it is sticking out, typically there is some activation and movement, some people have a difficult time keeping it at rest/preventing movement.
- Have the client stick out tongue, elevate and depress tongue tip (against palate and lower teeth, try to touch nose and chin), wiggle tongue from side to side, maintain position against pressure, produce alveolar and velar consonants.
- Have the client protrude the tongue against pressure (tongue depressor), push against the left and right cheek to resistance, to the left and right corners of the mouth with protrusion against resistance (tongue depressor).

Oral Mechanism Exam

The oral mechanism examination (OME; also called an oral motor exam) includes each of the cranial nerve observations discussed in the previous section, including symmetry at rest, motor, and sensory functions. In addition, the exam includes diadochokinesis (DDK), which is composed of alternating motion rates (AMRs) and sequential motion rates (SMRs). AMRs include repetition of a single syllable at a maximum rate (e.g., puh, puh, puh . . .), while SMRs include repetition of a sequence of syllables at maximum rate (e.g., puh, tuh, kuh . . .). Additional measures include laryngeal palpation to gauge hyolaryngeal excursion; counting from 1 to 20 to gauge articulatory agility, coordination, rate/timing, and respiratory endurance; breath holds to gauge laryngeal closure; and other speech tasks.

Intervention for Dysarthria

As with any speech or language treatment, the overall goal for dysarthria treatments is to improve efficiency and effectiveness of communication. Depending on the characteristics of the dysarthria, this may involve increasing respiratory support, loudness, and articulatory precision, and/or improving resonance and prosodic characteristics of speech production. Table 13–5 has examples of some common treatments for dysarthria.

Behavioral treatments for dysarthria are those that focus on the behaviors people use to produce speech: breath support, speed and precision of articulation, etc. In general, these are effective at improving intelligibility (Finch et al., 2020; Gandhi et al., 2020; Muñoz-Vigueras, 2021; Whillans et al., 2022). The most well-studied and most effective treatment for dysarthria is the Lee Silverman Voice Treatment (LSVT) LOUD program. This was initially designed

Box 13–2
Case 13–2. Mildred

Mildred is an 83-year-old woman with Parkinson disease. Her face is marked by rigidity and lack of expression (masked faces). Muscle rigidity is present in facial structures and evident upon palpation of the masseter and buccal muscles. Postural instability and gait rigidity is also present. Mildred demonstrates extended oral processing with textured solids. Lingual pumping is evident in direct observation during meals and was documented through radiographic via the modified barium swallow (MBS). Oral diadochokinesis is marked by a clear, festinating pattern of decline. The same pattern is evident in her gait, which is marked by shuffling and short quick steps when changing direction, starting, or preparing to change direction. Speech is hypophonic (soft) and marked by imprecise articulation of sounds (mumbling pattern). She is able to raise her volume intensity and overarticulate when cued but does not sustain that volume nor clear articulation. She demonstrates a wet and gurgly voice with thin liquids. Mildred expresses her dislike of thickened liquids clearly. She reports that there is nothing wrong with her swallow, she's doing fine. She has had two recent episodes of extended upper respiratory infections, but no documented pneumonias. Lingual pumping, extended oral processing, premature pooling of liquids and chewable solids, and consistent laryngeal penetration before pharyngeal swallow onset was observed on the MBS. Instances of trace aspiration before onset of the pharyngeal swallow were evident twice with thin liquids. Oral and pharyngeal clearance is fine with no evidence of oral-pharyngeal residuals. Cognition appeared to be relatively intact, although processing was slow. A pattern of slow rise time but gradual improvement is noted (i.e., starting out interactions with slower responses and extended processing but becoming quicker to respond and sharper as the interaction goes on).

Given this background on Parkinson disease and this case description, answer the following questions:

1. Identify systems affected by Parkinson disease, and any anatomical correlates.
    a. What accounts for her eating and swallowing difficulties?
    b. What accounts for her speech difficulties?
    c. What accounts for her cognitive difficulties?
2. Identify disorders that would typically be addressed by a speech-language pathologist. (Hint: think speech, language, cognitive, and swallowing subsystems)
3. Identify disorders that would typically be addressed by a related profession and include the names of those disciplines. (refer back to Table 1–1)

Table 13–5. Examples of Common Treatments for Dysarthria

Domains	Outcomes	Description
Respiration & Phonation	Increased respiratory support Increased maximum phonation time Increased vocal loudness	Laryngeal/respiratory strength training (e.g., EMST trainers) LSVT LOUD
Articulation	Increased articulatory precision Improved vowel differentiation Slower rate	LSVT LOUD Behavioral: repetition, drills External pacing (pacing boards, metronomes, delayed auditory feedback) Alphabet boards
Resonance	Reduced hypernasality	LSVT LOUD Palatal lift CPAP
Prosody	Natural prosody	Behavioral: imitation and repetition

NOTE: EMST = expiratory muscle strength trainers; LSVT = Lee Silverman Voice Treatment; CPAP = continuous positive airway pressure.

for hypokinetic dysarthria associated with PD, but benefits have been reported for a variety of other types of dysarthria (https://www.lsvtglobal.com; Finch et al., 2020; Gandhi et al., 2020). LSVT LOUD is an intensive treatment that focuses on vocal loudness and re-calibrating sensory perception of vocal loudness. This latter component is critical because many people with PD perceive their loudness as adequate although others around them perceive it as too soft. The increased respiratory support, postural adjustments, and large speech movements result in improvements not only in volume but also hypernasality, vowel differentiation, articulatory precision, and speech intelligibility. Expiratory muscle strength trainers (EMST) can also be used to improve respiratory strength for speech and swallowing (Schindler et al., 2021; Silverman et al., 2006).

Other behavioral treatments include external pacing strategies to reduce speech rate. These can involve using a metronome or a visual cue (e.g., serial presentation of words or underlining words during reading), or an alphabet board in which the speaker touches the first letter of each word as they produce it. The alphabet board has the added benefit of providing the listener with the first letter of the word, which can in turn improve their perception. When speech rate is decreased, the person with dysarthria has more time to move their articulators, but the listener also has more time to process the speech signal. Singing treatments (e.g., ParkinSong [Tamplin et al., 2019, 2020]) address all speech systems (respiration, phonation, articulation, resonance, and prosody) and have the added benefit of social interaction.

Prosthetics are used primarily for hypernasality, in which a palatal lift is designed to support the soft palate and compensate for reduced strength and range of motion and in turn decrease hypernasality. Continuous positive airway pressure (CPAP) can be used to improve soft palate tone and reduce hypernasality. **Alternative and augmentative communication (AAC)** devices can be used for people with severe dysarthria, and can be used in combination with behavioral or prosthetic treatments to increase communication effectiveness.

Intervention for Dysphagia

A broad range of interventions exist for addressing swallowing disorders and related impairments. The overall goals are to improve safety, ensure adequate intake, and quality of life through modified diets, environmental modifications, strengthening, and compensatory techniques. While it is not within the scope of this textbook to address all of them, Table 13–6 provides an overview of the basic intervention approaches and treatment domains.

Table 13–6. Intervention Approaches for Dysphagia

Domains	Recommended Practices	Description
Motor	Strengthening/skills training	• Oral/pharyngeal motor strengthening exercises (e.g., Masako maneuver, Mendelsohn maneuver, falsetto, Shaker exercises, tongue movement to resistance, etc.) • Laryngeal/respiratory strength training (e.g., EMST trainers) • Iowa Oral Performance Instrument strengthening (IOPI) • Possibly neuromuscular electrical stimulation (NMES) if not contraindicated/where evidence applies
	Compensatory/skills training	• Postural maneuvers (e.g., chin tuck, head turn, tuck and turn, head tilt, head back)

Table 13–6. *continued*

Domains	Recommended Practices	Description
		• Compensatory maneuvers (e.g., supraglottic swallow, super supraglottic swallow) • Diet modifications (can include texture modifications or liquid viscosity modifications/thickened liquids)
Sensory	Compensatory/skills training	• Finger sweeps for residuals • Increasing awareness • Postural maneuvers • Liquid rinse to clear residuals • Sensory stimulation (thermal tactile taste stimulation)
Cognition	Sensory and awareness supports, environmental modifications	• Monitoring and supporting alertness and attention to eating • Reducing environmental distractions and demands
Quality of Life	Address personal preferences and empower choice	• Identify preferred and pleasurable foods • Address the social factors related to eating (e.g., dining with family and friends) • Monitor client satisfaction: SWAL-CARE (McHorney et al., 2002)

Summary

Evaluation of motor and sensory systems is at the core of assessment of dysarthria and dysphagia. Cognition also should be evaluated to determine the potential impact of cognition on speech and swallowing. This also will inform what kinds of treatments and compensatory strategies might be most appropriate and effective. Treatments for dysarthria focus on improving intelligibility through strengthening and sensory (kinesthetic) placement training. Dysphagia interventions foster safe and adequate oral intake through diet modifications, strengthening, sensory interventions, and compensatory techniques. Ensuring eating and psychosocial quality of life is also an important consideration.

Key Concepts

- Addressing the integrity of sensorimotor systems through the OME/cranial nerve exam is important for both dysarthria and dysphagia.
- The MRC provides a standard method for rating strength.
- The CSE is a systematic method for clinical observations of swallowing functions.
- The RPRAP is a systematic method for making perceptual observations regarding speech production/dysarthria.
- Acoustic assessment provides objective data regarding respiration, resonance, articulation, and phonation as a part of a full dysarthria assessment.
- Instrumental assessments such as the MBS/VFSS and FEES can directly identify impairments to oral, pharyngeal, and upper esophageal functions.
- Cognitive status can influence carryover of intervention techniques for both dysarthria and dysphagia. Further, it can affect swallowing safety, so assessing and intervening for cognitive impairments is crucial.
- Dysarthria interventions are designed to improve speech intelligibility.
- Dysphagia interventions are designed to support quality of life and to ensure safe and adequate intake to meet nutritional needs.

References

Behlau, M. (2003). Consensus auditory-perceptual evaluation of voice (CAPE-V). *ASHA, 9,* 187–189.

Dietsch, A. M., Solomon, N. P., Sharkey, L. A., Duffy, J. R., Strand, E. A., & Clark, H. M. (2014). Perceptual and instrumental assessments of orofacial muscle tone in dysarthric and normal speakers. *Journal of Rehabilitation Research & Development, 51*(7).

Donohue, C., & Coyle, J. L. (2020). The safety, tolerability, and impact of respiratory–swallow coordination training and expiratory muscle strength training on pulmonary, cough, and swallow function surrogates in amyotrophic lateral sclerosis. *Perspectives of the ASHA Special Interest Groups, 5*(6), 1603–1615.

Duffy, J. R. (2019). *Motor speech disorders: Substrates, differential diagnosis, and management, 4th Edition.* Elsevier Health Sciences.

Finch, E., Rumbach, A. F., & Park, S. (2020). Speech pathology management of non-progressive dysarthria: A systematic review of the literature. *Disability and Rehabilitation, 42*(3), 296–306. https://doi.org/10.1080/09638288.2018.1497714

Gandhi, P., Tobin, S., Vongphakdi, M., Copley, A., &; Watter, K. (2020). A scoping review of interventions for adults with dysarthria following traumatic brain injury. *Brain Injury, 34*(4), 466–479. https://doi.org/10.1080/02699052.2020.1725844

Lomas, J., Pickard, L., Bester, S., Elbard, H., Finlayson, A., & Zoghaib, C. (1989). The communicative effectiveness index: Development and psychometric evaluation of a functional communication measure for adult aphasia. *Journal of Speech and Hearing Disorders, 54*(1), 113–124.

McHorney, C. A., Robbins, J., Lomax, K., Rosenbek, J. C., Chignell, K., Kramer, A. E., & Earl Bricker, D. (2002). The SWAL–QOL and SWAL–CARE outcomes tool for oropharyngeal dysphagia in adults: III. Documentation of reliability and validity. *Dysphagia, 17,* 97–114.

Medical Research Council. (1976). *Aids to examination of the peripheral nervous system.* Memorandum no. 45. Her Majesty's Stationary Office.

Muñoz-Vigueras, N., Prados-Román, E., Valenza, M. C., Granados-Santiago, M., Cabrera-Martos, I., Rodríguez-Torres, J., & Torres-Sánchez, I. (2021). Speech and language therapy treatment on hypokinetic dysarthria in Parkinson disease: Systematic review and meta-analysis. *Clinical Rehabilitation, 35*(5), 639–655. https://doi.org/10.1177/0269215520976267

Plowman, E. K., Watts, S. A., Tabor, L., Robison, R., Gaziano, J., Domer, A. S., . . . Gooch, C. (2016). Impact of expiratory strength training in amyotrophic lateral sclerosis. *Muscle & Nerve, 54*(1), 48–53.

Robison, R., Tabor-Gray, L. C., Wymer, J. P., & Plowman, E. K. (2018). Combined respiratory training in an individual with C9orf72 amyotrophic lateral sclerosis. *Annals of Clinical and Translational Neurology, 5*(9), 1134–1138.

Rosen, C. A., Lee, A. S., Osborne, J., Zullo, T., & Murry, T. (2004). Development and validation of the voice handicap index-10. *The Laryngoscope, 114*(9), 1549–1556.

Rusz, J., Tykalova, T., Ramig, L. O., & Tripoliti, E. (2021). Guidelines for speech recording and acoustic analyses in dysarthrias of movement disorders. *Movement Disorders, 36*(4), 803–814.

Schindler, A., Pizzorni, N., Cereda, E., Cosentino, G., Avenali, M., Montomoli, C., . . . Alfonsi, E. (2021). Consensus on the treatment of dysphagia in Parkinson's disease. *Journal of the Neurological Sciences, 430,* 120008.

Silverman, E. P., Sapienza, C. M., Saleem, A., Carmichael, C., Davenport, P. W., Hoffman-Ruddy, B., & Okun, M. S. (2006). Tutorial on maximum inspiratory and expiratory mouth pressures in individuals with idiopathic Parkinson disease (IPD) and the preliminary results of an expiratory muscle strength training program. *NeuroRehabilitation, 21*(1), 71–79.

Tamplin, J., Morris, M. E., Marigliani, C., Baker, F. A., Noffs, G., & Vogel, A. P. (2020). ParkinSong: Outcomes of a 12-month controlled trial of therapeutic singing groups in Parkinson's disease. *Journal of Parkinson's Disease, 10*(3), 1217–1230. https://doi.org/10.3233/JPD-191838. PMID: 32538865.

Tamplin, J., Morris, M. E., Marigliani, C., Baker, F. A., & Vogel, A. P. (2019). ParkinSong: A controlled trial of singing-based therapy for Parkinson's disease. *Neurorehabil Neural Repair, 33*(6), 453–463. https://doi.org/10.1177/1545968319847948.

Whillans, C., Lawrie, M., Cardell, E. A., Kelly, C., & Wenke, R. (2022). A systematic review of group intervention for acquired dysarthria in adults. *Disability and Rehabilitation, 44*(13), 3002–3018. https://doi.org/10.1080/09638288.2020.1859629

Yorkston, K. M. & Beukelman, D. R. (1981). Communication efficiency of dysarthric speakers as measured by sentence intelligibility and speaking rate. *Journal of Speech and Hearing Disorders, 46,* 296–301.

14
DIFFUSE BRAIN DAMAGE

Chapter Overview

Diffuse Etiologies
    Traumatic Brain Injuries
        Assessment
        Intervention
    Alzheimer Dementia
        Assessment
        Intervention
    Multiple Sclerosis
    Prion Diseases
    Metastatic Tumors
Speech Disorders
Language Disorders
    Social Communication
Cognitive Disorders
Swallowing Disorders
Summary
Key Concepts
References
Resources

Diffuse Etiologies

By this point, you should have a solid understanding of the functions of various parts of the brain and what happens when there is damage to those areas. For instance, a left hemisphere (LH) stroke will typically cause aphasia, whereas a right hemisphere (RH) stroke will often cause apragmatism, and damage to the prefrontal cortices will result in executive dysfunction. For the most part, we have described those syndromes in the context of fairly discrete areas of damage (e.g., a stroke confined to a specific blood supply distribution). Diffuse etiologies, as the name suggests, are not as isolated nor discrete. Traumatic brain injuries, shower emboli, multiple sclerosis, some metastatic tumors, and some dementias result in damage scattered throughout the brain. Figure 14–1 compares and contrasts diffuse versus focal lesions. While we discuss discrete and diffuse etiologies as if they are mutually exclusive, there are situations when both discrete and diffuse lesions coexist.

Traumatic Brain Injuries

As discussed in Chapter 3, TBIs are usually characterized by both focal and diffuse damage. The net result is **coup** and **contre-coup** lesions caused by linear damage (refer back to Figures 3–8 and 3–9). Diffuse damage, often referred to as **diffuse axonal injury (DAI**; sometimes called traumatic axonal injury) is a result of trauma to axons caused by movement of the brain. Figure 14–2 depicts DAI. As noted by the circles around the individual lesions, they are small but many are scattered throughout the brain. Each of the imaging slices depicted in Figure 14–2 represents only lesions present in that slice, so you can extrapolate how many would exist across levels. In the acute phase, each small lesion is surrounded by swelling (similar to the penumbra that surrounds a vascular lesion caused by stroke). The numerous small "penumbras" add up to produce diffuse swelling and increase **intracranial pressure (ICP)**. ICP compresses brain tissue and can cause herniation of brain matter through fractures, surgical burr holes or bone flaps, and foramen/foramina. If damage is unilateral, it can cause a **midline shift,** where the opposite hemisphere is compressed lateral to midline. **Herniation** of the temporal lobe is referred to as uncal herniation, whereas herniation of the brainstem is known as tonsillar herniation. Both can result in additional brain damage. Figure 3–7 in Chapter 3 illustrates midline shift and herniation due to tumors. The same consequences can occur with TBI and ICP.

TBI results in a wide range of impairments, depending on severity and concentration of diffuse and focal lesions. Phases of recovery are used to discuss the nature of impairments associated with TBI. The Ranchos Los Amigos Levels of Cognitive Functioning (Ranchos LOCF; Hagan & Durnam, 1987) scale divides recovery into three periods, early phase (levels I–III), middle phase (IV–VI), and late phase (VII–X).

Early phase deficits are characterized by disorders of consciousness and coma emergence. **Level I** can best be characterized as a TV or movie coma, where the person is unresponsive to any stimuli and in a *persistent vegetative state*. **Level II** is marked by *generalized response* to external stimuli, meaning that physical and behavioral responses such as becoming restless or moving limbs are not directly related to the stimulus (e.g., pinching the big toe doesn't result in pulling away the big toe but rather a restless and *non-purposeful response*). **Level III** is characterized by a *localized* or *purposeful response* and marks initial emergence from a coma. A localized response would include pulling the foot away when the big toe is pinched. Individuals may be wakeful for short periods of time and have limited interactions with people within the environment.

Middle phase impairments are characterized by disorientation, impaired memory, and agitation. **Level IV** is a key transitional phase from coma emergence toward a *confused* and

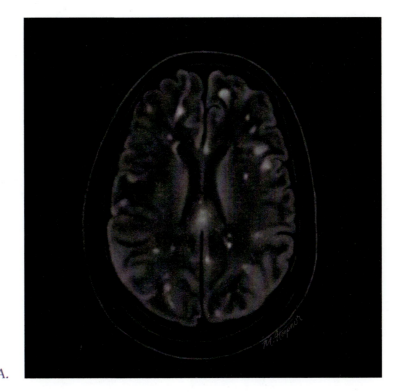

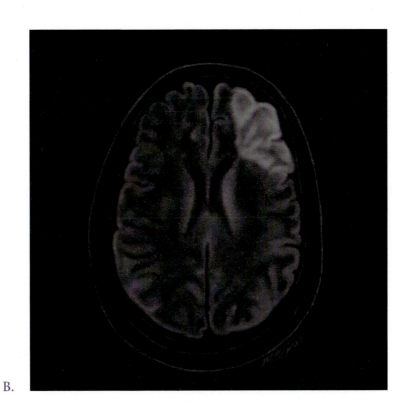

Figure 14–1. A. & B. Diffuse versus focal lesions.

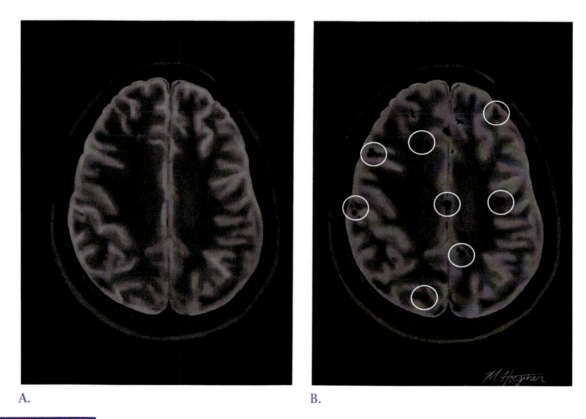

Figure 14–2. A. & B. **Diffuse axonal injury.**

agitated state. Individuals at level IV are disoriented to time and situation, possibly person and place. They are in a state of **posttraumatic amnesia (PTA)**. PTA includes both retrograde amnesia (loss of a period of memories prior to the injury) and anterograde amnesia (loss of ability to form new memories after the injury). As they begin to become oriented and recognize their state of confusion, they become restless and agitated. This agitation is often referred to as agitation without a purpose or direction. When we attempt to restrain or firmly redirect individuals (often due to a concern about their safety and/or our own), that agitation gains a purpose, which escalates the agitation and upset. Interventions for level IV are designed to orient and reduce agitation. **Level V** is characterized by a *confused, inappropriate*, and *non-agitated* state. The individual remains disoriented to time and situation. Their behaviors include inaccurate or unrelated responses, as well as inappropriate behaviors or communication expressions (e.g., expletives or confabulations). They can follow simple directions but memory, attention, and new learning is impaired. **Level VI** is marked by *confused* and *appropriate* responses. The person is emerging from PTA, becoming more consistently oriented to person, place, time, and situation. The individual engages in purposeful, goal-directed behaviors with some support. They begin to follow through with routine and relearned behaviors but new learning difficulties persist.

Late phase status ranges from automatic and appropriate to at or near baseline. **Level VII** is marked by *appropriate* but *automatic* responses. The individual's behaviors are automatic, with robot-like physical movement characteristics. They can complete routine tasks appropriately and do well in familiar settings. While they are likely to initiate social interactions, their awareness and judgment is still impaired. Some new learning is possible. **Level VIII** is characterized by *purposeful* and *appropriate* responses. The individual is consistently fully oriented and interacts appropriately with the environment. Executive functions and other social communication remains impaired. **Levels IX–X** are characterized by deficits in higher-order cognition and social communication. Impairments such as executive dysfunction, social communication and social cognition difficulties, memory (particularly new learning and working memory), and attention impairments are common. This affects interpersonal relationships, return to the community, school, and workplace settings.

Assessment

The Ranchos LOCF is used across phases of recovery to monitor status and predict upcoming needs. Assessments in the early and middle phases of recovery are at a more basic level than assessments in the late phase. A summary of early and middle phase recovery are included in Table 14–1. Late phase assessments are addressed in respective chapters about RH, LH, prefrontal, and cognitive functions.

Table 14–1. Assessments for Early and Middle Phases of Recovery From Traumatic Brain Injury

Test/Authors	Domains	Notes
Early Phase		
Western Neuro Sensory Stimulation Profile (WNSSP; Ansel & Keenan, 1989)	Level of consciousness	Conducted and rated by multiple members of the multidisciplinary team, preferably at different times of the day. Seeking best responses.
JFK Coma Recovery Scale – Revised (JFK CRS-R; Giacino & Kalmar, 2006)	Level of consciousness	Conducted and rated by multiple members of the multidisciplinary team, preferably at different times of the day. Seeking best responses.

continues

Test/Authors	Domains	Notes
Middle Phase		
Agitated Behavior Scale (ABS; Corrigan, 1989)	Agitation	Rated by multiple members of the multidisciplinary team at different times of the day and in different contexts/environments.
Westmead PTA Scale (WPTAS; Shores, 1995)	Post-traumatic amnesia	Assesses retrograde and anterograde amnesia to address PTA.
Galveston Orientation and Amnesia Test (GOAT; Levin et al., 1979)	Orientation	Questions address orientation to person (self and others), place, time, and situation.
Orientation Log (O-Log; Novack, 2000)	Orientation	Questions address orientation to person (self and others), place, time, and situation.
Confusion Assessment Protocol (CAP; Sherer et al., 2005)	Agitation, sleep, orientation	Addresses agitation and sleep disturbance, as well as orientation.

Box 14–1
Case 14–1. Early Phase Case: Kyle

Kyle was a 19-year-old male involved in a motor vehicle crash. He was driving home from a band concert at his local university when he was struck by an intoxicated driver who ran a red light. He was a freshman at that university studying music and elementary education. He was mostly taking general education courses at that point but hoped to teach music someday. At this point, Kyle could already play six instruments (percussion, piano, guitar, trumpet, trombone, baritone).

Medical records: Kyle had a severe TBI evidenced by bilateral temporal contusions (R>L), probable diffuse axonal injury (prolonged coma), initial midline shift, and brainstem compression. He had a percutaneous endogastric tube (PEG) and tracheostomy tube (for mechanical ventilation) for the initial 36 days of his hospitalization. After that he continued to use the PEG tube for nutritional intake and his tracheostomy remained in place although he was no longer ventilated. He used a continuous positive airway pressure device (C-PAP) inconsistently overnight. By one week post injury, he was an early Ranchos level III. He demonstrated inconsistent, localized responses to stimuli, depending on the time of day. Family reported several instances of very direct responses to stimuli and verbalizations. The SLP has observed a strong swallow following thermal tactile stimulation and tiny volumes of ice, sherbet, or honey thick liquids.

Some ongoing challenges: Kyle had periods of wakefulness, paired with periods of restlessness and sleep. He had many friends who visited frequently but they were unsure of how to interact. It was common for a group of his friends to hold conversations in his presence, with a clear sense of feeling uncomfortable and anxious in his presence. He also had several family members, immediate and extended family, who also struggled to know how to interact in his presence. At times his room was full of people and nursing staff had to shoo them away. His parents and younger brother (age 16) were completely distraught and struggled to manage their emotional response. They were pleased with the progress he made but remained devastated by how far he still had to recover. Family had many pertinent questions about what was to come and what will be. His physicians wouldn't and couldn't offer a straightforward prognosis.

Box 14–2
Case 14–2. Middle Phase Case: Ruth

Ruth was a 59-year-old widowed female who had worked in the hospital cafeteria for 30+ years doing everything from delivering food trays to patient rooms to working the cash register to making food in the kitchen. She was well-known and well-liked by most everyone in the hospital facility. Ruth fell down two flights of stairs as she was leaving work after her shift, sustaining bifrontal subdural hematomas, rib fractures, left scapular fracture, and a left temporal skull fracture. She was admitted to the hospital where she works and did not require surgical intervention but was intubated and sedated for 48 hours. Following extubation, she was intermittently alert and intermittently oriented most consistent with a level V–VI on the Ranchos LOCF ranging from confused/inappropriate to confused/appropriate. When she was fatigued, she became restless and agitated. She had little initiation, a stark contrast to the tremendously motivated employee she had been. By one week post injury, she was in rehabilitation with the multidisciplinary team, including occupational therapy, physical therapy, speech-language pathology, chaplaincy, social work, nursing. She was emerging from PTA but continued poor delayed recall, necessitating external memory devices and reminders. There were notable fluctuations in her performance, including how appropriate her interactions and problem-solving were, depending on her level of fatigue.

In Ruth's mind, it seemed odd that things sometimes made sense but were confusing at times. She knew that she was in the hospital and that she fell but wasn't always sure

continues

why she needed to stay at the hospital. It was confusing that she could work for an hour some days, while other times she was exhausted and overwhelmed after 10–15 minutes. It was strange to see colleagues in their work clothes when she was not. She wanted to help them, but she wasn't allowed to do so. Ruth felt like she didn't really have a say in her own rehabilitation. If they would just let her go home, she thought she would be fine.

Box 14–3
Case 14–3. Late Phase Case: Cam

Cam is a 26-year-old male who sustained a TBI in a motocross bike accident while in a competition. The accident was witnessed by numerous spectators, including Cam's parents. Prior to the accident, Cam was an A/B student who had planned to pursue a career in physical therapy. He had already been certified as a nursing assistant (CNA) prior to his accident. After his acute rehabilitation, he enrolled in a pre-physical therapy program in college. Early in his first semester he withdrew from the program, as he was not able to complete coursework successfully. Given his challenges with returning to school, he entered the workforce, first as a CNA and later in numerous vocational roles. As a CNA, he was effective in caring for residents but had substantial difficulty getting along with his colleagues. In a matter of 3 years, he had been hired and quit (often by just walking off the job) over 26 times. In the clinic room, Cam is engaging and kind, reserved and focused; on the job, he becomes rattled and confrontational. He admitted that he does not want to get to know his co-workers or be their friends. He is usually cordial with his supervisors but does not engage with co-workers. His two main goals are to find stable employment (and a career) and to find friends (including dating and finding a romantic partner). Since his accident, his only regular social partners are his father, grandmother, and his dog. He reports having no friends. His executive dysfunction and impairments in social communication and social cognition are his primary challenges. While he is very aware of these outside of the moment and in reflection, he has difficulty altering his behaviors in the moment. He also reports some mild difficulties with memory but compensates well through external memory aids.

Intervention

Interventions in the early and middle phases of recovery are quite different from many of the interventions during the late phase. A summary of early and middle phase interventions are found in Table 14–2. Late phase interventions are addressed in respective chapters on RH, LH, prefrontal, and cognitive interventions.

Table 14–2. Interventions for Early and Middle Phases of Recovery From Traumatic Brain Injury

Phases	Recommended Practices	Description
Early Phase	Monitoring and regulating level of stimulation	It is not possible to stimulate a person with a TBI out of a coma, however; sensory deprivation and overstimulation are both possible—these both slow recovery. The purpose is to attempt to moderate stimulation levels.
	Initial food trials and thermal tactile taste stimulation	Typically, individuals with TBI who experience prolonged coma have non-oral feeding through a percutaneous endogastric tube (PEG tube) or through a temporary nasogastric Corpak tube. Food trials are a form of diagnostic therapy.
	Oral hygiene and oral cleaning	Oral hygiene is crucial for oral and respiratory safety. It also contributes to normalization of taste and smell senses.
Middle Phase	Passive orientation (Bayley et al., 2023)	Providing contextualized orientation to person, place, time, and situation without quizzing for answers.
	Routines (Hoepner & Togher, 2022)	Establishing a daily schedule and routine to help with orientation and foster positive behaviors (reduce agitation).
	Memory book training (Sohlberg & Mateer, 1989)	Complements orientation and routine interventions. Fosters reflection and improved awareness of the situation, along with memory.
	Redirection and movement (Bayley et al., 2023)	In response to agitation, redirect the individual to another activity. Movement through space and to different environments typically reduces agitation as well.

Alzheimer Disease

Alzheimer disease (AD) is the most common dementia type and results in prototypical losses to memory and ability to care for oneself. AD is known as a global cortical dementia, meaning that if the person lives long enough, all cortical structures will eventually atrophy and become affected. While initial damage is characterized by atrophy in the anterior medial temporal lobe, hippocampus, hypothalamus, and posterior temporoparietal regions, atrophy becomes widespread (global) as the disease progresses (refer back to Figures 3–11 and 7–9). The initial atrophy in the hippocampus and anterior medial temporal lobe accounts for memory impairments, which are a hallmark of AD. Memory, particularly short-term and episodic memory, is impaired, while autobiographical and long-term retrospective memory remains intact. Impairments in short-term and working memory impair the ability to care for oneself and for higher level thinking, such as employment and instrumental activities of daily living (e.g., filling pill boxes for daily medications). Additionally, hypothalamic atrophy accounts for changes to temperature regulation, hunger-satiety, and other homeostatic mechanisms. This explains why, if you have ever been at a memory care facility, you have likely seen individuals with AD wrapped in blankets in the midst of even the warmest summer months. Failure to thrive is a common consequence of lateral hypothalamus atrophy. Less frequently, people experience medial hypothalamus atrophy, which results in overeating. Posterior temporoparietal atrophy is another area of initial changes with AD. Parietal atrophy results in impairments to orientation to space and movement, along with visuospatial construction and pathfinding impairments. Initially, individuals with AD get lost in unfamiliar environments but eventually they lose the ability to navigate familiar environments. Posterior temporal atrophy is associated with impairments to face recognition, reading comprehension, and changes to color recognition. As the disease progresses, nearly all of the cerebral cortex becomes atrophied and functions of the respective cortical areas become impaired. This includes a devastating loss to motor and sensory portions of the brain and to white matter networks that facilitate complex cognitive and language functions. Language tends to be relatively intact until the later stages of the disease when cortical atrophy is global.

Assessment

Assessments for AD are typically reflective of the primary temporoparietal areas of atrophy, acknowledging that atrophy becomes widespread. Assessments can help to determine current severity status and distinguish AD from other dementias. Staging is an important interprofessional tool for management and planning. Stages 1–2 are pre-dementia and rarely identified prospectively but often recognized retrospectively. Stage 3 is associated with mild cognitive impairment, while stage 4 is mild dementia, stage 5 is moderate, stage 6 is moderate-severe, and stage 7 is severe. For the purposes of this chapter, only assessments specific to AD are summarized (Table 14–3). Other assessments for memory, attention, and executive function are covered in Chapter 12.

Table 14–3. Assessments for Cognitive and Communication Disorders Associated With Alzheimer's Disease

Test/Authors	Domains	Description
Screening Tools		
Mini-Mental Status Exam (MMSE; Folstein et al., 1975; Folstein et al., 2010)	attention and calculation, memory, language, orientation	Screening for cognition and language.
Montreal Cognitive Assessment (MoCA; Nasreddine, 2004)	orientation, memory, visuospatial construction, attention, language, abstraction	Screening for cognition and language.
St. Louis University Mental Status (SLUMS; Tariq et al., 2006)	orientation, memory, attention, naming, digit span, and executive function	Screening for cognition and language.
Staging Assessments		
Global Deterioration Scale (GDS; Reisberg et al., 1982)	memory, concentration, orientation, language	Observational tool for caregivers and interprofessional team to examine dementia progression.
Clinical Dementia Rating (CDR; Morris, 1993)	memory, orientation, judgment, problem solving, community affairs, home and hobbies, and personal care	Clinician rating scale based on semi-structured interview with client and caregiver.
Mattis Dementia Rating Scale (MDRS; Vangel & Lichtenberg, 1995)	attention, initiation/perseveration, construction, conceptualization, and memory	Observational tool to examine dementia progression.
ABC Dementia Scale (ABC-DS; Mori et al., 2018)	daily activities, communication, memory, behaviors, care burden	Rating scale classifies individuals based on performance on activities of daily living, cognition, and behavioral & psychological symptoms.

continues

Table 14–3. *continued*		
Test/Authors	Domains	Description
Environmental Assessments		
Cohen-Mansfield Agitation Inventory (CMAI; Cohen-Mansfield, 1991)	physical & verbal expression of agitation	Observational tool.
Environment and Communication Assessment Toolkit (ECAT; Brush et al., 2012)	social and physical environmental barriers	Observational tool; addresses performance in public and private spaces.
Standardized Assessments		
Arizona Battery of Cognitive-Communication Disorders 2 (ABCD-2; Bayles & Tomoeda, 2005)	language and cognition	Assesses mental status, episodic memory, language expression, language comprehension, and visuospatial construction for individuals with MCI and mild to moderate dementia.
Functional Linguistic Communication Inventory 2 (FLCI-2; Bayles & Tomoeda, 2020)	functional language	Assesses functional language (greeting, naming, answering questions, writing, readings signs, reminiscing, etc.) for individuals with moderate to severe dementia.
Profiling Communication Ability in Dementia (P-CAD; Dooley et al., 2022)	cognitive–communication	Addresses 8 domains: attention, auditory comprehension, verbal expression, reading, writing, conversation, communication support, and functional communication.

Box 14–4
Case 14–4. Mild-Moderate/Stage 4–5: Mabel

Mabel was an 84-year-old woman who was living independently prior to a fall that led to admission in an orthopedic unit. When her family came to visit, they shared that she had been experiencing increasing struggles for quite some time. Her husband, Marv, had recently died and her family attributed some of her difficulties to that loss. Her adult children shared that she was still driving and still went grocery shopping on a weekly basis. Family was concerned whether she was getting the right things, as she had several new jars of peanut butter, multiple cans of beans and vegetables, and a stockpile of toiletries. Family reported that she was pretty "good" most days, but that they had increasing concerns about her during the night, which was when her falls occurred. At the time, she was oriented to self, roughly to place, but often disoriented to time. One daughter had been checking on her finances, which were becoming too difficult for her to handle. However, Mabel stated that she has no problem with her checking and bills. Family believed that she may need some help, but insisted that things had just been a little difficult since their father died 6 months prior. Nursing reported that she slept very little during the night, and that she spent most of that time wandering about in her room.

Box 14–5
Case 14–5. Moderate/Stage 5–6: Robert

Robert was a 69-year-old man who was living with his wife, Judy. The speech-language pathologist was asked to do a swallowing assessment, given a recent history of aspiration pneumonia. Robert was struggling to manage textured solids and thin liquids. He also required a great deal of support for self-feeding, which Judy reported was not as much trouble at home. He was likely struggling more than he did at home, but some problems were present at home as well. He recognized his wife consistently, but he was disoriented to place and time. Judy was clearly exhausted and admitted that she was overwhelmed with his care. She didn't feel like she could leave him at home. This was heightened by his fear of her leaving. He demanded her presence and assistance with a number of his "responsibilities" (i.e., workplace roles). He remained a partner in a family construction company with his two sons but hadn't truly played an active role for several years. Their two sons were busy with the business and were unable to provide much support to their parents. One son believed that his parents should move into an assisted living facility. Judy contended that moving wouldn't help, since Robert demanded her assistance and presence at all times. The other son feared his Dad was "dementing," just like Grandma had previously. That son believed that they needed to plan for the future. Both sons wanted to help.

Box 14–6
Case 14–6. Mod-Severe/Stage 6: William

William was a 78-year-old male who resided at a local nursing home. He frequently wandered around the facility searching for his wife, Betty. When she came, he acted as though she was always there. He often believed he was at work, doing maintenance on airplanes. He believed that the nurses were staff and that other residents were passengers. He was often found talking about planes while standing at the nurses' station. He frequently struggled to find the right words or lost his train of thought. Frustrated, he blew it off stating, "That's why I had to quit working." This often led to outbursts of anger and crying. Betty was unsure how much he remembered. At times he didn't appear to recognize her. Three years after his original diagnosis, she started visiting less frequently because she couldn't handle his outbursts. His daughter believed that he should still be at home, so he wouldn't be so frustrated. When his daughter visited, she went from staff office to office, searching for solutions. She frequently expressed dissatisfaction with her father's care.

Box 14–7
Case 14–7. Severe/Stage 6–7: Georgia

Georgia was an 88-year-old female who resided at a local skilled nursing facility. She required maximal assistance from staff for her personal cares. Despite attempts by staff to keep her well-kept and presentable, she appeared unkempt and had a flat affect. Staff was exhausted and frustrated by her behavioral outbursts during cares. When her sister and daughters came to visit, Georgia was often ambivalent and disinterested. Occasionally, she would engage in an interaction, saying a word or two. Family was frustrated and a bit unsure of how to interact with Georgia. It was common for her to stare blankly and not respond to their attempts to interact. Frustrated, they wondered if they should even bother coming at times.

Intervention

Many cognitive interventions have applications to a variety of disorders. Most of those covered in Chapter 12 are designed for people with acquired disorders that are expected to improve over time with recovery and rehabilitation. For progressive, degenerative diseases, the focus of intervention is to help maintain function and social interaction for as long as possible. Table 14–4 provides a summary of commonly used interventions for individuals with AD.

Table 14–4. Interventions for Cognitive and Communication Disorders Associated With Alzheimer's Disease

Domains	Recommended Practices	Description
Memory	Spaced retrieval training (SRT; Brush & Camp, 1998; Small & Cochrane, 2020)	Trains recall of information, compensatory strategies, or tasks over increasingly larger increments of time.
	Memory wallets (Bourgeois, 1990; 1992; 1993; 2019)	Small books designed to aid orientation but also stimulate conversation. 10–15 pages, including how to use, orientation information, reminders, and personal stories augmented with photos and captions.
	Structured external memory aid treatment (SEMAT; Lanzi et al., 2022)	Systematic instruction of three categories of EMAs (i.e., calendars, timers, and personal information) exploring different EMAs, using role plays and practice-based instruction, and practicing in their homes.
Visuospatial	Wayfinding and environmental supports	Personalizing resident's doors with "home" doors and photos.
Orientation	Validation therapy (Benjamin, 1995; Neal & Wright, 2003)	Affirms the individual's emotional state rather than correcting them. Redirects to a positive interaction or activity.
	Simulated presence (Bayles et al., 2005)	Uses technologies to reassure and redirect disoriented individuals to positive activities.
	Orientation boards and signage	Highly visible and accessible reminders of time and place including calendars and schedules.
Environment	Purposeful design (Borbasi et al., 2006)	More home-like/less institutional environments (bring in furniture, artwork), training staff and family, disguise exit doors with paintings.
Participation	Montessori approaches (Douglas et al., 2018; Douglas & Brush, 2022)	Encouraging participation in meaningful activity and empowering choices, within an adapted environment supportive of memory loss and sensory impairments.

Multiple Sclerosis

Multiple sclerosis (MS) is a disease of the myelin covering axons (oligodendroglia) in the central nervous system (CNS). Damage results in multiple areas of scarring (called sclerosis, plaques, or lesions). While lesions occur throughout the CNS, periventricular lesions (white matter lesions surrounding the ventricles) are the most recognizable feature on MRI scans (refer back to Figures 3–15 and 3–16). Depending upon the location and concentration of lesions, MS produces damage to vision, speech, language, swallowing, mobility, and activities of daily living (ADLs). Optic neuritis (inflammation of the optic nerve) is often one of the first symptoms, resulting in pain with eye movement, blurred vision, dim vision, or loss of color vision. MS typically results in a mixed dysarthria, as weakness and incoordination are both common impairments. Word finding difficulties (anomia) and problems with spelling are also common communication impairments. Assessments and interventions for the speech, language, and cognitive impairments associated with MS are selected based on the specific areas impacted; these are discussed in previous chapters.

Prion Diseases

Prion diseases, also known as **transmissible spongiform encephalopathies (TSEs)** are rare, progressive, and fatal neurodegenerative disorders. Prion diseases occur when normal prion proteins mutate due to transmissible pathogens and begin to clump in the brain. Prions are a crystalline protein, morphing from spear-shaped structures into cubic or star-shaped structures when they mutate. This causes damage to surrounding brain tissue, producing the hallmark sponge-like damage to brain tissue (Figure 14–3A & B). This damage causes memory impairment, hallucinations, confusion, difficulty speaking, personality changes, and difficulties with movement (often sporadic, ballistic movements, known to break limbs). Lesions are prominent in subcortical structures and the cortex. MRI scans typically reveal hyperintensity in the caudate nucleus and cortical ribboning (hyperintensity of cortical gyri) (Figure 14–4). Kuru and **Creutzfeld-Jakob disease (CJD)** are the most common variants among humans. Both have extended incubation periods of 5 to 15 years. Once the disease enters its active phase, progression is rapid and results in death within one year. About 10 to 15% of cases are inherited but most cases are idiopathic and spontaneous (Parchi et al., 1999; Schelzke et al., 2012). Although rare, prion diseases are important to consider because CJD is a form of bovine spongiform encephalopathy (BSE; commonly known as "mad cow disease") that mutated and crossed the species barrier to affect humans. There is concern that other TSEs may mutate in the future. This is one of the reasons that TSE diseases in deer species, such as chronic wasting disease, are being closely monitored. Further, because the initial incubation periods are quite extensive (up to 15–20 years), predicting an outbreak is difficult. Finally, changes to prion proteins are also evident in other degenerative diseases, such as AD—however, they are not pathogenic or transmissible. Due to the rapidly progressing nature

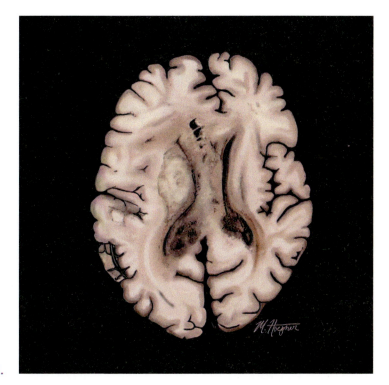

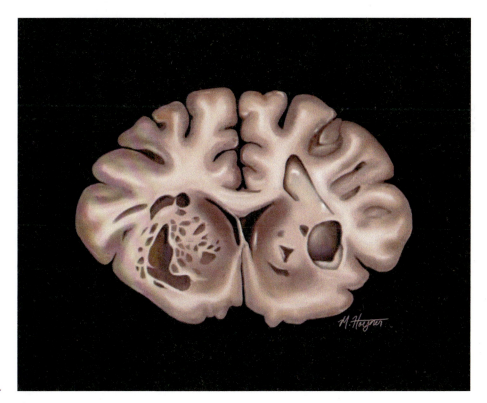

Figure 14-3. A. & B. Spongiform damage caused by prion disease.

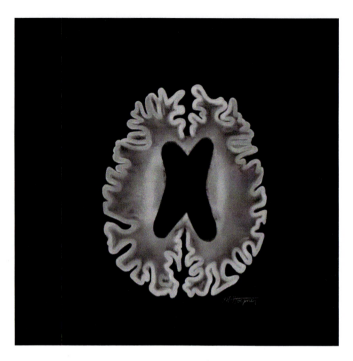

Figure 14-4. Cortical ribboning and subcortical atrophy on MRI.

of CJD and other TSEs, assessment and intervention focus on family education and needs, swallowing, and behavioral supports.

Metastatic Tumors

Metastatic tumors are malignant tumors that break away from the primary tumor, traveling through the blood and/or lymph systems to form tumors in other parts of the body or brain (Figure 14–5A & B). These metastases compress surrounding brain tissue. That compression leads to further inflammation and compression similar to the effects of the penumbra around vascular infarctions. While any cancerous tumor can metastasize to the brain, primary tumors from the lungs, breasts, colon, kidneys, and melanomas are most common. Metastases can result in one or multiple tumors in the brain, having a focal or diffuse effect on brain functions. Some metastases, like those from primary kidney tumors, have a propensity for bleeding, thus causing further cytotoxic damage to surrounding brain tissue. Pharmacological treatment of metastatic tumors often employs steroids, which can reduce inflammation but has the side effect of mind racing. Depending upon the nature and progression of metastatic tumors, assessment and intervention likely draw upon other cognition and communication assessments.

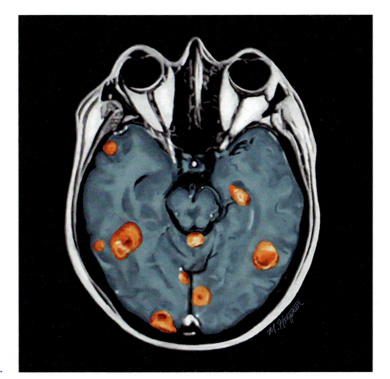

A.

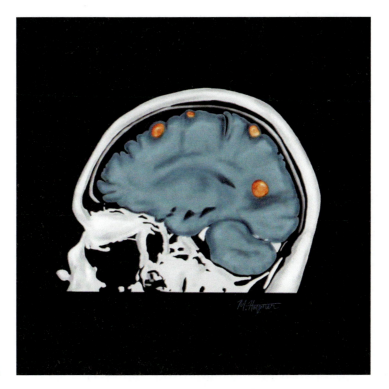

B.

Figure 14–5. A. & B. Metastatic tumors on gadolinium-enhanced MRI.

Table 14–5. Motor Speech Disorders by Structures Damaged	
Damaged Areas	Type of Motor Speech Disorder
Motor Strip	Unilateral Upper Motor Neuron (UUMN) or spastic dysarthria if bilateral
Corticospinal Tract	Unilateral Upper Motor Neuron (UUMN) or spastic dysarthria if bilateral
Cranial Nerve Nuclei	Lower Motor Neuron/flaccid dysarthria (voice, resonance, and articulatory changes)
Cerebellum	Ataxic dysarthria
Basal Ganglia	Hypokinetic or hyperkinetic
Pre-Motor/SMA	Apraxia of speech

Speech Disorders

Diffuse lesions have the potential to produce complex speech impairments. Because there is potential for damage to the motor strip, the corticobulbar tract, cranial nerves, premotor/supplementary motor regions, somatosensory cortices, basal ganglia, thalamus, brainstem, and cerebellum, mixed dysarthrias and apraxia of speech (AOS) are possible (Table 14–5). These less discrete speech disorders can be challenging to characterize, but some characteristics may be more prominent based on the areas of damage present. Assessments and interventions for AOS are in Chapter 7, and for dysarthrias in Chapter 13.

Language Disorders

Language is a distributed function, known to include contributions from the left and right cerebral hemispheres, basal ganglia, cerebellum, and thalamus. Since diffuse damage can affect any of these structures, a variety of language impairments are possible (Table 14–6). Assessments and interventions for language disorders can be found in Chapters 7 and 8.

Social Communication

As noted in other chapters, within the field of SLP "language" is often interpreted narrowly, excluding pragmatics and communication in social interactions. To ensure that these areas are captured, especially for people with TBI or other diffuse injuries that affect many areas of the brain, the terms **pragmatic communication** and **social communication** have been

Table 14–6. Language Impairments by Structures Damaged

Damaged Areas	Consequences
Left Anterior (Broca's Area)	Motor speech and language expression impairments, non-fluent aphasia
Left Posterior (Wernicke's Area)	Auditory comprehension impairments, fluent aphasia
Arcuate Fasciculus	Impaired repetition, conduction aphasia
Basal Ganglia	Altered phonetics, phonology, morphology, syntax and lexical semantic abilities
Thalamus	Comprehension impairments, anomia, paraphasias, possible reduced initiation or mutism
Cerebellum	Impairments in speech perception, verbal fluency sequencing, word association, figurative language, semantic absurdities; anomia, paraphasias, dysgraphia
Right Anterior	Apragmatism Expressive emotional aprosodia
Right Posterior	Apragmatism Receptive emotional aprosodia

used. While there are many definitions of social communication, essentially these refer to the use of communication skills (phonology, morphology, semantics, syntax), supported by requisite cognitive (attention, memory, executive function) and social cognitive (theory of mind, emotion processing) abilities that allow people to interact appropriately, efficiently, and effectively in social situations or interpersonal interactions.

Many models have been designed to map out the relationships and interactions between all of these components. Keegan and colleagues' (2023) SoCIAL model (Sociolinguistic Clinically Implementable and Applicable Lens; Figure 14–6) shows social communication as created by three aspects of cognition: cognitive communication, social cognition, and emotional cognition. Additionally, social communication occurs within, and is impacted by, contextual factors (this should remind you of apragmatism and communication in context) such as physical and neuropsychological abilities, the environment, the person's identity and sense of self, and the demands of the moment. Some of these factors may be relatively constant, such as someone's culture and dialect; others may change slowly (physical and cognitive abilities either improving or declining after injury), and yet others change in each communicative interaction, such as talking to a friend on campus versus your brother at home. All of this complexity and interconnectedness makes assessment and treatment of

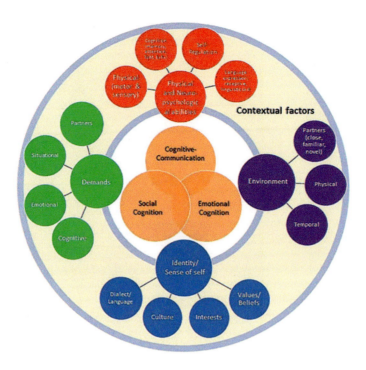

Figure 14–6. The Sociolinguistic Clinically Implementable and Applicable Lens (SoCIAL) model. Reproduced with Permission from ASHA Keegan, et al. (2023). Clinically Applicable Sociolinguistic Assessment for Cognitive-Communication Disorders. *American Journal of Speech-Language Pathology*. Vol 32.

cognitive and communication disorders terribly complicated and challenging but also vastly interesting.

Cognitive Disorders

Several cortical regions, as well as the basal ganglia, thalamus, and cerebellum are known to contribute to cognitive processes. Diffuse damage that includes any of these structures can produce corresponding impairments (Table 14–7). Assessments and interventions for cognitive disorders can be found in Chapter 12.

Swallowing Disorders

Similar to speech disorders caused by diffuse damage, damage may affect the motor strip, corticobulbar tract, cranial nerve nuclei, basal ganglia, thalamus, and cerebellum (Table 14–8). Cognitive impairments are likely to exacerbate those physiological impairments.

Table 14–7. Cognitive Disorders by Structures Damaged

Damaged Areas	Consequences
Dorsolateral Prefrontal Cortices	Executive dysfunction, attention impairments
Orbitomedial Prefrontal Cortices	Working memory impairments
Hippocampus	Short-term and long-term memory impairments
Amygdala	Emotional dysregulation
Anterior Cingulate Gyrus	Affects executive function, attention, memory, emotional processing, and motivation
Parietal	Attention impairments
Anterior Medial Temporal Lobe	Memory impairments
Insular Cortex	Apathy and reduced motivation
Thalamus	Global attention impairments
Reticular Formation	Rudimentary attention and awareness, orienting responses
Cerebellum	Motor learning

Table 14–8. Swallowing Disorders by Structures Damaged

Damaged Areas	Consequences
Motor Strip	Upper motor neuron (UMN) weakness contralateral to damage
Corticobulbar Tract	Upper motor neuron (UMN) weakness contralateral to damage
Cranial Nerve Nuclei	Impaired CN V could impair mastication and oral processing as well as oral sensation, CN VII could impair oral preparation, CN IX could compromise velopharyngeal closure and pharyngeal pressures, CN X could impair laryngeal sensation and closure increasing risk for aspiration, CN XII damage could affect oral processing
Cerebellum	Swallowing timing issues
Basal Ganglia	Swallowing coordination issues
Pre-Motor/SMA	Apraxia of swallow

Summary

Diffuse damage to the brain creates complex presentations that can include disorders of speech, language, cognition, and swallowing. Given that these processes are interconnected and can impact each other, the picture becomes even more complicated. Broad assessments are needed to identify strengths and weaknesses, and to determine which impairments are creating the biggest impact on behavior, communication, nutrition, and quality of life. Interventions designed for more focal damage may be appropriate, but if the diffuse damage is related to a degenerative disease process, then goals of intervention are typically for maintenance of function and quality of life rather than restoration or improvement of function.

Key Concepts

- Diffuse damage almost always affects speech, language, cognition, and swallowing.
- Patterns of deficits depend on the areas of the brain affected. Some diseases have characteristic patterns (e.g., Alzheimer), while others are more variable (TBI, MS, tumors).
- Assessment and treatment are challenging because of the multiple co-occurring deficits.
- Degenerative diseases add the extra challenge of changing profiles over time.

References

Ansell, B. J. & Keenan, J. E. (1989). The Western Neuro Sensory Stimulation Profile: A tool for assessing slow-to-recover head-injured patients. *Archives of Physical Medicine and Rehabilitation, 70(2),* 104–108.

Bayles, K. A., & Tomoeda, C. K. (2005). *ABCD-2: Arizona battery for cognitive communication disorders, Second edition.* Pro-Ed.

Bayles, K. A. & Tomoeda, C. K. (2020). *FLCI-2: Functional linguistic communication inventory. Second edition.* Pro-Ed.

Bayley, M., Ponsford, J., Velikonja, D., Janzen, S., Harnett, A., McIntyre, A., . . . Bayley, M. T. (2023). INCOG 2.0 Guidelines for cognitive rehabilitation following traumatic brain injury, part II: Attention and information processing speed. *Journal of Head Trauma Rehabilitation, 38(1),* 38–51.

Benjamin, B. J. (1995). Validation therapy: An intervention for disoriented patients with Alzheimer's disease. *Topics in Language Disorders, 15(2),* 66–74.

Borbasi, S., Jones, J., Lockwood, C., & Emden, C. (2006). Health professionals' perspectives of providing care to people with dementia in the acute setting: Toward better practice. *Geriatric Nursing, 27(5),* 300–308.

Bourgeois, M. S. (1990). Enhancing conversation skills in patients with Alzheimer's disease using a prosthetic memory aid. *Journal of Applied Behavior Analysis, 23(1),* 29–42.

Bourgeois, M. S. (1992). Evaluating memory wallets in conversations with persons with dementia. *Journal of Speech, Language, and Hearing Research, 35*(6), 1344–1357.

Bourgeois, M. S. (1993). Effects of memory aids on the dyadic conversations of individuals with dementia. *Journal of Applied Behavior Analysis, 26*(1), 77–87.

Bourgeois, M. S. (2019). Caregiving for persons with dementia: Evidence-based resources for SLPs. *Topics in Language Disorders, 39*(1), 89.

Brush, J., Calkins, M., Bruce, C., & Sanford, J. (2012). *Environment and Communication Assessment Toolkit for Dementia Care.* Health Professions Press. http://www.healthpropress.com

Brush, J. A. & Camp, C. J. (1998). *A therapy technique for improving memory: Spaced retrieval.* Menorah Park Center for the Aging.

Cohen-Mansfield, J. (1991). *Instruction manual for the Cohen-Mansfield agitation inventory (CMAI).* Research Institute of the Hebrew Home of Greater Washington.

Corrigan, J. D. (1989). Development of a scale for assessment of agitation following traumatic brain injury. *Journal of Clinical and Experimental Neuropsychology, 11*(2), 261–277.

Dooley, S., Hopper, T., & Walshe, M. (2022). *Profiling communication ability in dementia (P-CAD).* The O'Brien Press.

Douglas, N., Brush, J., & Bourgeois, M. (2018). Person-centered, skilled services using a Montessori approach for persons with dementia. *Seminars in Speech and Language, 39*(03), 223–230.

Douglas, N. F., & Brush, J. (2022). Person-centered memory care through Montessori for dementia and ageing: A quality improvement study. *Journal of Gerontological Nursing, 48*(8), 6–9.

Folstein, M. F., Folstein, S. E., & Fanjiang, G. (2010). *Mini-mental state examination: MMSE-2.* Psychological Assessment Resources.

Folstein, M. F., Folstein, S. E., & McHugh, P. R. (1975). "Mini-mental state." A practical method for grading the cognitive state of patients for the clinician. *Journal of Psychiatric Research, 12.* https://doi.org/10.1016/0022-3956(75)90026-6

Giacino, J., & Kalmar, K. (2006). *Coma Recovery Scale-Revised. Administration and scoring guidelines.* The Center for Outcome Measurement in Brain Injury. http://www.tbims.org/combi/crs

Hagen, C., & Durham, P. (1987). *Levels of cognitive functioning in rehabilitation of the head injured adult: Comprehensive physical management.* Professional Staff Association of Rancho Los Amigos Hospital.

Hoepner, J. K. & Togher, L. (2022). Living with cognitive communication disorders. In Papathanasiou & P. Coppens (Eds.), *Aphasia and related neurogenic communication disorders* (3rd ed.). Jones & Bartlett.

Keegan, L. C., Hoepner, J. K., Togher, L., & Kennedy, M. (2023). Clinically applicable sociolinguistic assessment for cognitive-communication disorders. *American Journal of Speech-Language Pathology, 32*(2S), 966–976. https://doi.org/10.1044/2022_AJSLP-22-00102

Lanzi, A. M., Wallace, S. E., Cohen, M. L., & Bourgeois, M. S. (2022). Structured external memory aid treatment (SEMAT) for older adults with mild cognitive impairment: long-term adherence and acceptability of treatment. *Aphasiology, 36*(2), 234–250.

Levin, H. S., O'Donnell, V. M., & Grossman, R. G. (1979). The Galveston orientation and amnesia test: A practical scale to assess cognition after head injury. *Journal of Nervous and Mental Disease, 167*(11), 675–684.

Mori, T., Kikuchi, T., Wada-Isoe, K., Umeda-Kameyama, Y., Kagimura, T., & Kojima, S. (2018). A novel dementia scale for Alzheimer's disease. *Journal of Alzheimer's Disease and Parkinsonism, 8*(2), 2–7.

Morris, J. C. (1993). The Clinical Dementia Rating (CDR): Current version and scoring rules. *Neurology, 43*(11), 2412–2414.

Nasreddine, Z. S., Chertkow, H., Phillips, N., Whitehead, V., Collin, I., & Cummings, J. L. (2004). The Montreal Cognitive Assessment (MoCA): A brief cognitive screening tool for detection of mild cognitive impairment. *Neurology, 62*(7), A132–A132.

Neal, M., Barton Wright, P., & Cochrane Dementia and Cognitive Improvement Group. (1996). Validation therapy for dementia. *Cochrane Database of Systematic Reviews, 2010*(1).

Novack, T. (2000). *The orientation log.* The Center for Outcome Measurement in Brain Injury. http://www.tbims.org/combi/olog

Parchi, P., Giese, A., Capellari, S., Brown, P., Schulz-Schaeffer, W., Windl, O., . . . & Kretzschmar, H. (1999). Classification of sporadic Creutzfeldt-Jakob disease based on molecular and phenotypic analysis of 300 subjects. *Annals of Neurology, 46*(2), 224–233.

Reisberg, B., Ferris, S. H., de Leon, M. J., and Crook, T. (1982). The global deterioration scale for assessment of primary degenerative dementia. *American Journal of Psychiatry, 139*, 1136–1139.

Schelzke, G., Kretzschmar, H. A., & Zerr, I. (2012). Clinical aspects of common genetic Creutzfeldt-Jakob disease. *European Journal of Epidemiology, 27*, 147–149.

Sherer, M., Nakase-Thompson, R., Yablon, S. A. & Gontkovsky, S. T. (2005). Multidimensional assessment of acute confusion after traumatic brain injury. *Archives of Physical Medicine and Rehabilitation, 86*, 896–904. https://doi.org/10.1016/j.apmr.2004.09.029

Shores, E. A. (1995). Further concurrent validity on the Westmead PTA Scale. *Applied Neuropsychology, 2*(3–4), 167–169. https://doi.org/10.1080/09084282.1995.9645356

Small, J. A. & Cochrane, D. (2020). Spaced retrieval and episodic memory training in Alzheimer's disease. *Clinical Interventions in Aging, 15*, 519–536.

Sohlberg, M. M., & Mateer, C. A. (1989). Training use of compensatory memory books: A three stage behavioral approach. *Journal of Clinical and Experimental Neuropsychology, 11*(6), 871–891.

Tariq, S. H., Tumosa, N., Chibnall, J. T., Perry III, M. H., & Morley, J. E. (2006). Comparison of the Saint Louis University mental status examination and the mini-mental state examination for detecting dementia and mild neurocognitive disorder—A pilot study. *The American Journal of Geriatric Psychiatry, 14*(11), 900–910.

Vangel, S. J. & Lichtenberg, P. A. (1995). Mattis Dementia Rating Scale: Clinical utility and relationship with demographic variables. *Clinical Neuropsychologist, 9*(3), 209–213. https://doi.org/10.1080/13854049508400481

Resources

Great overview of assessment domains and frameworks for dementia assessment:

Kipps, C. M., & Hodges, J. R. (2005). Cognitive assessment for clinicians. *Journal of Neurology and Neurosurgical Psychiatry, 76*(Suppl. I), i22–i30. https://doi.org/10.1136/jnnp.2004.059758

INDEX

A

Abasia, 267–268
ACT-R model for cognition, 9–10, **9**
Active ingredients, 100, 116, 291
Agrammatism, 83, 271, **271**
Agnosia
    Anosognosia (see also Impaired Self Awareness), **5**, 95, 137, **138**, **145**, 172, 176, 208–209, 212–213, 226, **286**, 296, 298, 303
    Finger agnosia, 162, 231
    Oral agnosia, 12, 175
    Simultagnosia, 231
    Prosopagnosia, 227, **227**, 228
    Visual agnosia, 227
    Visual anosognosia (see also Anton's syndrome), 226
Agrammatic, 157, **157**
    Telegrammatic, 157, **157**
    Telegraphic, 157, **157**, **171**
Agraphia, 84, 98, 160, 161–162, **161**, 230–231, **271**
Alexia, 84, 98, 160–162, **161**, 228, 230, 232
    Alexia without agraphia, 161
    Alexia with agraphia, 162, **161**
    Pure alexia, 160, **161**
Alexithymia, 247, **289–290**, 302, 305
Alternative and augmentative communication (AAC), 152, **152**, **166**, **293**, **301**, 324
Alzheimer disease (see dementia)
Amnesia, 93, 144, 332, **334**, 353
    Post-Traumatic Amnesia, 93, 144, 332, **334**,

Amyotrophic Lateral Sclerosis (ALS), **46**, 67, 76–77, 97, 131, 143, 319, 326–327
Angiograms, 71, 73, **73**
Anomia, **4**, **5**, 83, **85**, **153**, 160, 163, **174**, 184, 227, 246, 251, 271, **271**, 344, **349**
Anosognosia (see agnosia)
Anton's syndrome (see also visual anosognosia), 226
Anoxia, 45, 52–54, 250
Aphasia, 1, **5**, 12, **60–61**, 71, 79–80, 83–84, **85**, 86–87, 98, 111, 121, 125, 130, 133, 146, 149, **150–151**, 152–155, **153**, **154**, **156**, **157**, **158–159**, 157–158, 160, 162–163, **165–166**, **167**, 168, **168**, **169–171**, 171–173, **174**, 175–179, 183, 192, **194**, **227**, 244, 246, **246**, 251–252, 266, 270, 276, **279–280**, **286**, 305, 326, 329, **349**, 353
    Assessment of aphasia 163–168, **164**, **165–166**, **168**
    Conduction Aphasia, 160, 162, **149**, **174**
    Crossed Aphasia, 183
    Fluent Aphasia, 83, 153, 158, **158–159**, 172–173, 176
    Global Aphasia, 154, **154**, **165** **174**
    Intervention for aphasia, 168–171, **169–171**
    Mixed Transcortical Aphasia, 154, **155**, **174**
    Nonfluent Aphasia, 83–84, 86, 153, 155, **156**, **157**, 173, 246, **349**
    Primary Progressive Aphasia (see PPA)
    Transcortical mixed aphasia, 154, **155**
    Transcortical motor aphasia, **154**, **155**, 157, **174**
    Transcortical sensory aphasia, **154**, **155** 160

Apragmatism, 83–84, **85**, 86–87, 96, 98, 133, 183–184, 189, 192, **192**, 196–198, 201, 210, 213, 230, 246, 251–252, 266, 298, 329, 349, **349**
   Assessment of apragmatism, 189, 192–193, **193–196**
   Extralinguistic Apragmatism, 84, **192**, 197, 230, 246
   Intervention for apragmatism, 196–201, **197, 199, 200**
   Linguistic Apragmatism, 84, **85**, 184
   Paralinguistic Apragmatism, 84, 198
Apraxia, 1, **5**, 11–12, 80, 81–82, **81**, 86, 98, 132, 146, 148–149, **150–152**, 152, 157, 175–179, 183, 229, **230**, 231, 244–245, 251, 348, **348, 351**
   Apraxia of speech (AOS), 11–12, **81**, 81–82, 86, 98, 132, 146, 148–149, **150–151**, 152, 175–179, 183, 244–245, 251, 348, **348**
   Assessment of AOS, 149–152, **150–151**
   Intervention for AOS, 149–152, **151**
   Buccofacial/ oral-facial apraxia, 157
   Constructional apraxia, 229, **230**
   Oculomotor apraxia, 231
Aprosodia (see also apragmatism, paralinguistic), 84, 86, 188–189, **190**, 198, 213, 215–217, 246, 251, 254, 270–271, **349**
   Assessment of aprosodia, 193, **193–196**
   Intervention for aprosodia, 198
Arcuate fasciculus, 27, 148, 154, 157, 160, 177, **349**
Articulatory groping (see also apraxia of speech), 82, 149
Association tracts, 27
Astasia, 267–268
Astrocyte, 18, **20**, 54
Ataxia, 81, **107, 109**, 125–126, 220, 231, 267–269, 273, 308
   Friedreich ataxia, 107–109, 269
   Optic ataxia, **222**, 231, 308
   Spinocerebellar ataxia, 269
Attention, **4, 5**, 9–10, 21, 26, 42, **42**, 54, 62, 75, 85, 87–91, 96, 98, **117**, 134–137, **135**, 139, 142–143, 146, 171–172, **174**, 175, 176, **182**, 184, 201–206, **202, 208**, 212–213, 228, 229, 236, 243, 244, 247, 251, 252, 266, 270, **271**, 275–276, 291, 308, **316, 317**, 318–319, 325, 332, 333, 338, **339, 351**
   Alternating attention, 87, **88,**
   Assessment of attention, 205–206, **206**, 276, 279–281, **279–280, 281, 284, 339–340**
   Attentional Control, 75, 87, 90, **90**, 134, **137**, 201
   Attention networks
     Central executive network (CEN), 90, 134, 136, **137**
     Default mode network (DMN), 90–91, 134, **136–137**
     Dorsal attention network (DAN), 89, **89**, 90
     Ventral attention network (VAN), 89, **89**
     Salience network, 90–91, 134, **137**
   Divided attention, 87, **88**, 201, **281, 282**
   Intervention for attention disorders, 293, 294–295, **296,**
   Selective attention, 87, **88, 281, 282**
   Sustained Attention, 87, **88**, 89–90, 134, **139**, 201, 280–281, **281, 282**
   Unilateral neglect, 9, 137, **202**, 202–204, **204**, 209, 213, 227, 229, 279, 298
     Assessment of unilateral neglect, 206, **206**
     Intervention for unilateral neglect, 206–207
   Visual attention, 228, 229, **281**
Autonomic nervous system, 10, 16, 26, 97, 318

B

Balint syndrome, 231
Basal ganglia, 9–10, **11**, 29, 39, **41**, 60, **60**, 62, **62, 65, 81, 82, 92, 135**, 236, **237, 238, 240**, 241, 244–247, **249**, 250–253, 262, 308, 348, **348–349**, 350, **351**
Behavioral treatments, **301**, 321, 323
Benign tumor, 54
Biopsychosocial, 102, 105, 110–112, **111**, 123–124
Bradykinesia, 244
Brainstem, **11**, 12, 18, **19**, 27, **28**, 31–33, **31**, 35, 37, 39, **42**, 54, **62, 64**, 89, 176, 219–220,

228, 231, 241–242, 247, 249–250, **249**, 255–257, **256**, **258**, 260–262, 264, **265**, 266, 272–273, 318, 330, **334**, 348
Midbrain, 31, **31**, 39, 60, 82, 241, 252, 256–257, **256**, 260–261
Pons, **31**, 219, **256**, 257
Medulla, 31, **31**, 54, **61**, 247, 256–257, **256**, 260, **261**, 318
Broca's area, 23, **46**, **147**, 148, **153**, 155, 157, 163, **163**, **174**, 349

C

Cartesian dualism, 105, **107**
Central executive network (see attention networks)
Central nervous system (CNS), 13, 16, **16**, 18, 32, 36, 38, **41**, 42, **42**, 44, 48, 54, 58, **60**, 62, **69**, 75, 87, 98, **238**, 249, 260, 264, 344
Cerebellum, 9–10, **11**, 18, **19**, **28**, **31**, 35, **35**, 36–37, 39, **41**, **46**, 52, **60**, **64**, **81**, 82, **92**, **109**, **135**, 228, 231, **249**, 255–257, 267–273, 308, 348, **348**, **349**, 350, **351**
Cerebrum, 9, 18, **19**, **46**, 130, 255–256, 271
Circumlocution (see also aphasia), 160, 163
Cognitive reserve, 121, **122**
Cognitive-communication disorder, 96, **277**
Coherence, 186, **186**
Cohesion, 134, **136**, 140, 185–186, **195**, 217, 266
Coin Model, 122, **123**, 126
Coma (see disorders of consciousness)
Commissural tracts (see white matter)
Computed Tomography (CT or CAT scans), 4, 71, **72**
Concussion, 56, **57**, 59, 76–77, 303
Cortex, 10, 12, 18, 23, 26, 31–32, **36**, 37, **41**, 42, **42**, 44, 52, **60**, 63, **64**, 75, 90, **90**, **92**, **107**, 148–149, 172, 175, 178, **211**, 223, 225–226, 236, 244, 246, 249–250, 253–257, **258**, 262, 303, 338, 344, **351**
Cortical blindness (see also vision), 226
Corticobasal syndrome (CBS), 2, **5**, 152, 221, 241, 244

Coup and contre-coup lesion, 56–57, 330
Cranial nerves, 3, 32–33, **32**, 67, 97, 249, 255–260, 262, **263–264**, **265**, 266–267, 272, 307, 308–309, 344, **348**, 350, 351
Cranial nerve examination, 319–321
Cranial nerve nuclei, 32–33, **34**, 35, 257, 262, 264, 348, 350, **351**
Facial nerve, **32**, **34**, 258, 262
Glossopharyngeal nerve, **33**, **34**, 258, 260
Hypoglossal nerve, **33**, **34**, 257, 260, 264, 266
Optic nerve, **32**, **222**, 344
Pharyngeal plexus, 260
Spinal accessory nerve, 11, **34**, 260, 264, 320
Trigeminal nerve, **32**, **34**, 257, **263**, 264, **265**, 266, 319
Vagus nerve, **33**, **34**, 11, 260, 262, **263**, **265**, 266, 320
Pharyngeal branch, **33**, 260, 262, **263**, **265**
Superior laryngeal nerve, **33**, 260, 262, **263**
Recurrent laryngeal nerve, **33**, 260, 262, **263**

D

Decomposition of movement, 267
Default mode network (see attention networks)
Deep narratives, 118
Dementia, 12, 59, **60–62**, **69**, **69**, **70**, 71, 73, 93, **93**, 97, 120–122, 125–126, 129–130, 132, **131**, **132**, 134, 142–143, 146, 162–163, 172–173, 178–179, 183, 221, 229, 241, 247, 250, 262, **283–284**, 303, 305, 319, 330, 338, **339–340**, 352–354
Alzheimer disease, 12, **41**, 43, **46**, 59, 60, **69**, **69**, 125–126, 131, 172, **173**, 175, 215, 221, 226, 229, 233, **242**, 250, 261, 303, 338, **339**, 343, 350, 352–354
Assessment of dementia, 131, **132**, 338, **339–340**
Creutzfeldt-Jakob disease (CJD), **60**, 344
Fronto-temporal dementia (see also primary progressive aphasia), **61**, 130–132, **131**, 162, 241
Intervention for dementias, 131, 342, **342**
Vascular dementia, 59

Diaschisis, 52, 241, 269
Diffuse axonal injury (DAI), 1, **4**, 12, 57, 59, 146, 330, **332, 334**
Diplophonia, 262, **263**
Disorders of Consciousness, 266, 330
    Coma, **4**, 266, 330, **333–334, 337**, 353
    Minimally conscious state, 266
    Unresponsive wakefulness syndrome (vegetative state), 266, 330
DIVA model for speech 6–7, **7**
Dorsal stream (see language, prosody, or vision)
Dual stream model for language 7–9, **8**
Dysdiadochokinesis (see also ataxia), 268
Dyskinesias, **243**, 244, 247
Dysarthria, 1, **4**, 12, 80, 81–82, 81, **81**, 86, 98, **107**, 132, 146, **147**, 148–149, **148**, **150**, 175–176, 183, 213, 228, 231, 244, **245**, 251–252, 256, 260, 262, 264, 269, **270**, 272, 307–309, 314–315, **316**, 321, 323–327, **323**, 344, 348, **348**
    Ataxic dysarthria, 12, 81, **81**, 86, 148, 264, 269, **270**, 272, 308, **348**
    Flaccid Dysarthria, 81, **81**, 262, 272, 308, **348**
    Hyperkinetic dysarthria, **81**, 244, **245**, 252, 308
        Spasmodic dysphonia, 244–245
    Hypokinetic dysarthria, 81, 82, 244, **245**, 252, 308, 323, 327
    Spastic Dysarthria, 12, 81, **81**, 272, 308, **348**
    Unilateral upper motor neuron dysarthria (UUMN), 148, **148**, 183, 308, **316**, 348
Dysmetria (see also ataxia), 268
Dysphagia, 1, **4**, 80, 97–98, 142, **147**, 174–175, 183, 212, 217, 231, 244, 247–248, 252–254, 256, 260, **261**, 265, 267, 272–273, 307–308, 315, **317**, 318, 324, **324**, 325–327
Dystonia, 81, 241, 244–245

E

Echolalia, 157, 160
Ecological validity, 281, 302
Edema, 57
Electroencephalograms (EEG), 73
Empty speech (see also aphasia), 160

Evaluation, **94**, 112, **112**, 149, **165**, 178–179, 184, **194–195**, 214–216, 332, **261**, **278**, 279, **287**, **288**, **300**, 304, 315, **316–317**, 325–326
Executive Dysfunction (dysexecutive syndrome), 1, **5**, 85, 94, **107**, 130, 132, **133**, 137, **138, 141**, 143, 252, 266, **282, 285**, 305, 329, 333, **336, 351**
    Assessment of executive dysfunction, **117**, 131, **132, 194**, 279, 281–286, **282–284**, **285**, 338, **339**
    Intervention for executive dysfunction, 132, **133, 292**, 291–293, 296–298, **297**
Executive function, 9–10, 23, **24**, 62, 67, 75, 87, 93–94, **94**, 96, 98, **101**, **117**, 130–131, 134, **136**, 137, **137, 138–140**, 142, **146**, 171–172, 176–178, 187, **194**, 201, 207, **208**, 213, 221, 236, 243–244, 246–247, **249**, 250–251, 270–271, 275–276, **279**, 281, **282–284, 285**, 286, 291, **292**, 293, 296, **297**, 298, **299**, 303–304, 333, 338, **339**, 349, **351**
Excitotoxicity, 58
Experience-dependent neuroplasticity, 100, 126
Extralinguistics, **84**, 189, **193**

F

Facial nerve (see cranial nerves)
Festination, 242
Fissure, 18, 21, **21**, 23, 25–26, **27**, 39, **46**
    Sylvian fissure, 18, 21, **21**, 23, 25–26, **25**, 27, 39, **46**
Flaccidity, 81, 309
Frontal aslant tract, 29, **29**, 148
Functional MRI (fMRI), 13, 74, 177, 303
Functors, 157–158, **157**

G

Ganglion, **238**, 244
Geniculocalcarine fibers (see also optic radiations), 160, 222, **222, 225**
Gerstmann syndrome, 162, 231
Glossopharyngeal nerve (see cranial nerves)

Goal attainment scales, **114**, 288
Goal setting, **101**, 112, **112**, **114**, 125, **277**, 288
Gray matter, 18, **20**, 44, **238**
Gyrus, 8, 10, 18, **21**, 25, **25**, **46**, **60–61**, 64, **89**, 155, 160, 162, 172, **211**, 228–229, 231, **249**, **251**

H

Health condition, 102, **103**, **106**, 121
Hematoma, **4**, 50, **53**, **56**, 57, 71, **335**
   Epidural hematoma, 50, **53**
   Subdural hematoma, 50, **53**, **335**
Hemorrhagic stroke, 49–50, **52**, 252
   Intracerebral hemorrhage, 50–51, **53**
   Intracranial hemorrhage, 50, **227**
   Subarachnoid hemorrhage, 50, **53**
Herniation, 54, **55**, 330
Hippocampus, 10, 25, **41**, 60, 63, 87, **90**, **249**, 250, 338, **351**
Homonymous hemianopsia (see visual field cuts)
Homonymous quadrantanopsia (see visual field cuts)
Huntington Disease, **41**, 62, **65**, 107, 243, **245**, 252, 308, 318
Hypoglossal nerve (see cranial nerves)
Hypotonia, 267
Hypoxia, 52, 54, 241

I

IFSiP model for swallowing, 10–11, **11**
Impaired self-awareness (ISA); (see also anosognosia), 95, 142, 144, 304
Intersystemic reorganization, 152
Intracranial pressure, 51, 57, 59, 330
Ischemia, 49, 51, **51**, 73, **261**
   Embolic ischemic strokes, 49
   Ischemic penumbra, 49, **51**
   Thrombotic ischemic stroke, 49

J

Jargon, **85**, **159**, 172

L

Lateral geniculate nucleus, **34**, 222, **222**, 248, **248**, 249
Lenticular nucleus, 236, **237**, **238**, 248
   Lentiform nucleus, **238**
Life Participation Approach to Aphasia (LPAA), 168, 276

M

Magnetic Resonance Imaging (MRI) scan, **4**, 71, **72**, 74, 344, 346, **347**
Malignant tumors, 54, 118, 346
Mechanisms of action (see also RTSS), 87, 115–116, 118
Memory
   Assessment of memory, 279–280, **279**, **281**, **282**, 286–287, **287–288**
   Declarative Memory, 91, **208**
   Episodic Memory, 91–92, **92**, **208**, 338, **340**, 288
   Intervention for memory, **292**, 298, **299**, **337**, **339–340**, 343
   Long Term Memory, 92–93, **92**, **93**, 338, **351**
   Metamemory, 92, 95, **208**, **287**
   Nondeclarative Memory, 92
   Posttraumatic amnesia, 93, 332
   Prospective Memory, 91–93, **208**, **287**
   Semantic Memory, 8–9, 91–92, **92**, 143, 172, 176, 229
   Short Term Memory, **5**, 92–93, 287, **288**, 338, **351**
   Working Memory, 90, 92–93, **92**, **94**, **107**, **117**, 134–135, **136**, **137**, **140**, **165**, 171–172, **208**, 236, 243, 271, **271**, **281**, **282**, **288**, **333**, **335**, 338, **351**
Metacognition, 95
Metacognitive strategy training, **133**, 197, **197**, **285**, 291, **294**, **295**, **296**, **297**, 296, 298, **299**, **301**, 302
Metastatic tumors, 330, 346, **347**
Meyer's loop, 222
Microglia, 18, **20**
Midline shift, 54, 55, 330, **334**

Morphology, 54, 82, 83, 146, **147**, 176, 236, 246, 349,
Multiple Sclerosis, 43, 62, **66, 67, 69**, 97, 183, 269, 330, 344
Myelin, 18, 27, 59, 62, **66**, 344

N

Near-infrared spectroscopy (NIRS), 74
Neologism (also see aphasia and paraphasia), 83, 154
Neural plasticity, 100, **101**, 124
Neurogenesis, 100
Neuron, 18, **19, 20**, 27, 32–33, 36, 38, 40–45, 48–52, **51**, 58–60, **61**, 62, 67, 73, 75, 80–81, 98, 99, 100, 148, **163**, 212, 222, 236, 241, 243–245, 247, **249**, 250, 257, 272, 308

O

Oculomotor apraxia (see apraxia)
Oligodendrocytes, 18, 62
Optic ataxia (see ataxia)
Optic chiasm, 222, **222**, 226
Optic radiations (see also geniculocalcarine fibers), 160, 222, **222**, 225

P

Paralysis, **41**, 47, 259, 261, 262, 263, 276
Paraphasias (see also aphasia), 84, 154, **159**, 160, 163, **164**, 251, **271**, 349
  Phonemic paraphasias, 84, 154, 160, **164, 271**
  Semantic paraphasia, 84, **159**, 160, 163, **164, 271**, 349
  Pronoun confusion, **159, 164**, 185
Paresis, **47**, 80, 95, 137, 154, 201, 262, 318,
  Hemiparesis, 80, 102, 137, 201, 203, 209, 220, **261**, 286
Parkinson Disease, 10, **41**, 43, **46**, 60, 62, 65, 69, 97, 241, **242**, 251–252, 261, 267–269, 283, 309, 315, 318, **322**, 324
Patriarchal narratives, 118
Paucity of speech, 186

Peripheral nervous system (PNS), 16, **16**, 18, **238**
Perisylvian region, 21, **23**, 82, 133, 146, **147**, 154, 175–176, 212, 220, **246**, 270, 275
Pharyngeal plexus (see cranial nerves)
Phonology, 82–83, 146, **147**, 176, 236, 246, 349
  Phonological processing, 7–8, 82, **271**
Positron Emission Tomography (PET) scans, 73, **74**
Posterior cortical atrophy, **60**, 221, 231–232, 338
Posttraumatic amnesia (see memory)
Premotor, 36, 132, 146, 148, 152, 175, **238**, 348
Primary Progressive Aphasia (PPA), **60–61**, 130, 131, 162–163, **163**
  Assessment of PPA, 131–132, **131, 132**, 168, **168**, 175
  Intervention for PPA, 132
  Logopenic variant, **60**, 162–163, **163**
  Non-fluent variant, 162–163, **163**, 173
  Semantic dementia (also semantic variant), 162–163, **163, 168**
Prion diseases (transmissible spongiform encephalopathies), 221, 344
Projection tracts (see white matter)
Prosody, 9, 23, 25, 80, 82–86, **86**, 134, 148–149, **151, 157**, 158, 163, **164, 170, 182**, 184, 188, **192, 193–196**, 198, 243, **245**, 246, 251, 269–270, **270, 279**, 308–309, **313**, 323, 324,
  Emotional (affective) Prosody, 86, **86**, 134, 198
  Grammatical Prosody: 86, **86**, 184, 188
  Pragmatic Prosody, 86, **86**
  Prosody pathways/streams, dorsal and ventral, 189, **191**
Prosopagnosia (see agnosia)

R

Ranchos Los Amigos Levels of Cognitive Functioning scale, 330, 333, **335**
  Early phase, 330, **333, 334, 337**
  Middle phase, 330, 333, **333–335, 336, 337**
  Late phase, 330, 333, 326, **326**

Rehabilitation treatment specification system (RTSS), 100, 114–115, **115**, 123–124
   Treatment aims, 116, 118, 124
   Treatment target, **101**, 115–116, **117–118**, 118, 124

S

Salience network (see attention networks)
Schwann cells, 18, 54
Semantic, **4**, 8, 9, 61, 82–84, 91, **92**, 155, 158–160, 162–163, **164**, **168**, **170**, 172, 176, 188, 229, 236, 246, 251, 271, 349
   Semantic processing, 8, **271**
Somatic nervous system, 16
Social cognition, 2, 26, 95–96, 98, 129, 131, **132**, 134, 171, **185**, **196**, 201, 209–210, 212, 246–247, 271, 275–276, **278**, 287, **289**, 293, 293, 298, 300, **300–301**, 302, 333, **336**, 349, **350**
Social determinants of health, 71, 99, 118, **118**, 120, 123,
   Patient level factors, 120–121, 124, 276–277, 292
   Provider level factors, 120, 124
   System and policy level factors, 120, 122, 124,
Spastic, 12, 81, **81**, 148, 175, 260, 262, 264, **265**, 272, 308–309, **348**
Spasmodic dysphonia (see dysarthria), 244–245
Spinal accessory nerve (see cranial nerves)
Stereotypic words, 154
Striatum (see also basal ganglia), **61**, 236, **237**, **238**, 241, 243, 247, **258**
Stroke, also cerebrovascular accidents (CVAs), 3, 8, 11, 18, 43, **47**, 48, **49**, 50–52, **52**, 54, 59, 69, **69**, **70**, 71, 75–76, 80, 86, 93, 97, 120–122, 129, 134, 146, **146**, 148, **151**, 152–153, 162–163, **166**, 168, 171–173, **174**, 175, 182–183, **182**, 187, **192**, 201, 207, **208**, 209, 212, 220, 226, 228, 232, 241, 246, 250–252, 260, **261**, 264, 269, 272, 281, 283–284, **284**, 291, 308, **316**, 318, 329–330,

Sulcus, 18, **21**, 23, **24**, 25, 39, **46**, **64**, 89, 90, 175, **211**, 222–223, 228,
   Central sulcus, **21**, 24, **24**
Supplementary motor area (SMA), 132, 146, 148, 152, 157, 175, **238**, 348, **348**, **351**
Swallowing
   Oral phase, 97, 175, 248, **261**, 266–267, 316, 318
   Oral preparatory phase, 10, 96–97, 248, 266–267, 315
   Pharyngeal phase, 10, 97, 175, 212, 248, 256, 266–267, 272, 315–318
   Esophageal phase, 10, 97, 256, 267, 318
Synapse, 6, 18, 32, 33, 41, 222, 249, 262, 272
Syntax, 82–83, 146, **147**, 156, **157**, 158, **164**, 176, 236, 246, 251, **271**, 349

T

Thalamus, 9–10, 29, **30**, **31**, 33, 40, **42**, 55, 60, 82, 89, 222, 226, 236, **237–239**, 248–249, 250–252, 258, **258**, 348, **349**, 350, **351**
Theory of Mind (ToM): 25–26, 95–96, **132**, 133, **140**, **185**, 209, **211**, 212, 298, **301**, 349
   Affective ToM, 95–96, **211**, 247
   Cognitive ToM, 95–96, **211**, 247
Traumatic brain injury (TBI), **4**, 12, 37, 43, 56–59, **56**, **57**, **58**, **69**, **70**, 84, 121, 129, **130**, 134, 142, 146, 192, 269, **280**, 291, 330, **333**, **337**
Trigeminal nerve (see cranial nerves)

U

Unilateral neglect (see attention)
Unresponsive wakefulness syndrome (see disorders of consciousness)

V

Vagus nerve (see cranial nerves)
Vasogenic cytotoxicity, 51
Ventral stream (see language, prosody, or vision)
Verbosity, **184**, 186
   Verbose, 134, **138**

Visual system
  Anton's syndrome, 226
  Visual field cuts, 220, 221, 225–227, **225, 226**, 230–232
    Homonymous hemianopsia, 225
    Homonymous quadrantanopsia, 225
  Visual pathways, 222, **222**, **223**, 226
  Visual streams or pathways
    Dorsal "where" pathway, 26, **26**, 223, **224**, 225–226
    Ventral "what" pathway, 26, **26**, 223, **224**, 227

W

Wernicke's Area, 7, 25, **25**, **46**, **147**, **153**, **154**, 159, 160, **349**
White matter, 3, **4–5**, **17**, 18, **20**, 27, **28**, 32, 44, 59, 62, **66**, **67**, 71, 146, 152, 162, 257, 338, 344
  Association tracts, 27
  Commissural tracts, 27, **28**
  Projection tracts, 27, **28**, 29, 257, 272
World Health Organization - International Classification of Functioning, Disability, and Health (WHO-ICF), 102, **103**, **104**, **105**, **106**, 111, 124, 166, 276
  Activity limitations, **106**, **278**
  Body functions, **103**, **104**, **105**, **106**, 166, **168**, **317**
  Body structures, 102, **103**, **104**, **105**, **106**, **110**, 166, 168, 276, **317**
  Environmental factors, **103**, **104**, **106**, 276, 302
  Participation, **57**, 75, 102, **103**, **104**, **105**, **106**, **110**, 112, **113**, 124, 149, **151**, 166, 168, **169**, 183, **194–195**, 276, **278**, 279, 302, **343**
  Participation restrictions, **106**, 112
  Personal factors, 99, 102, **103**, **104**, **105**, **106**, **107**, 112, **117**, 121, 123–124, 149, **151**